Smile

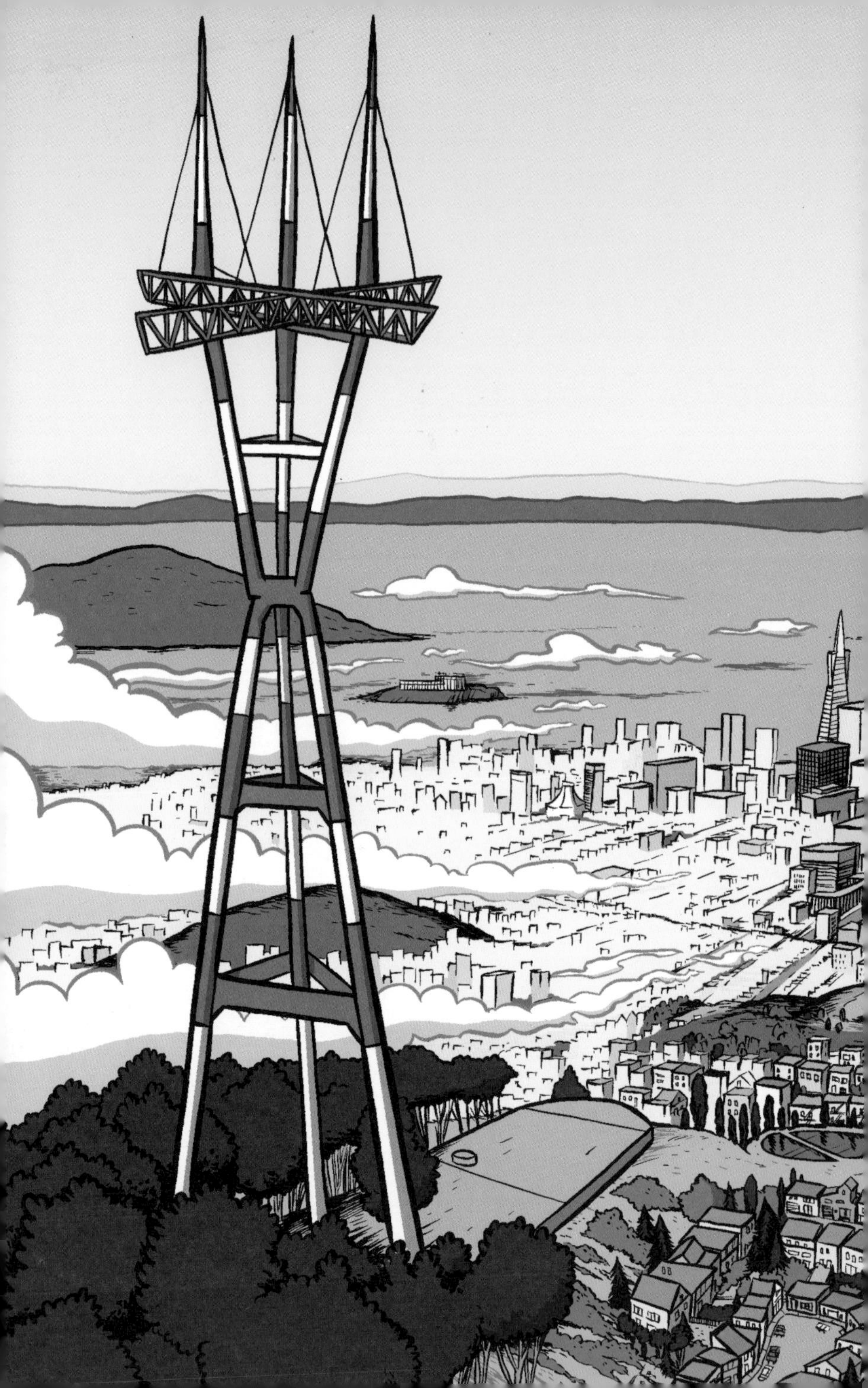

Smile

Raina Telgemeier
with color by Stephanie Yue

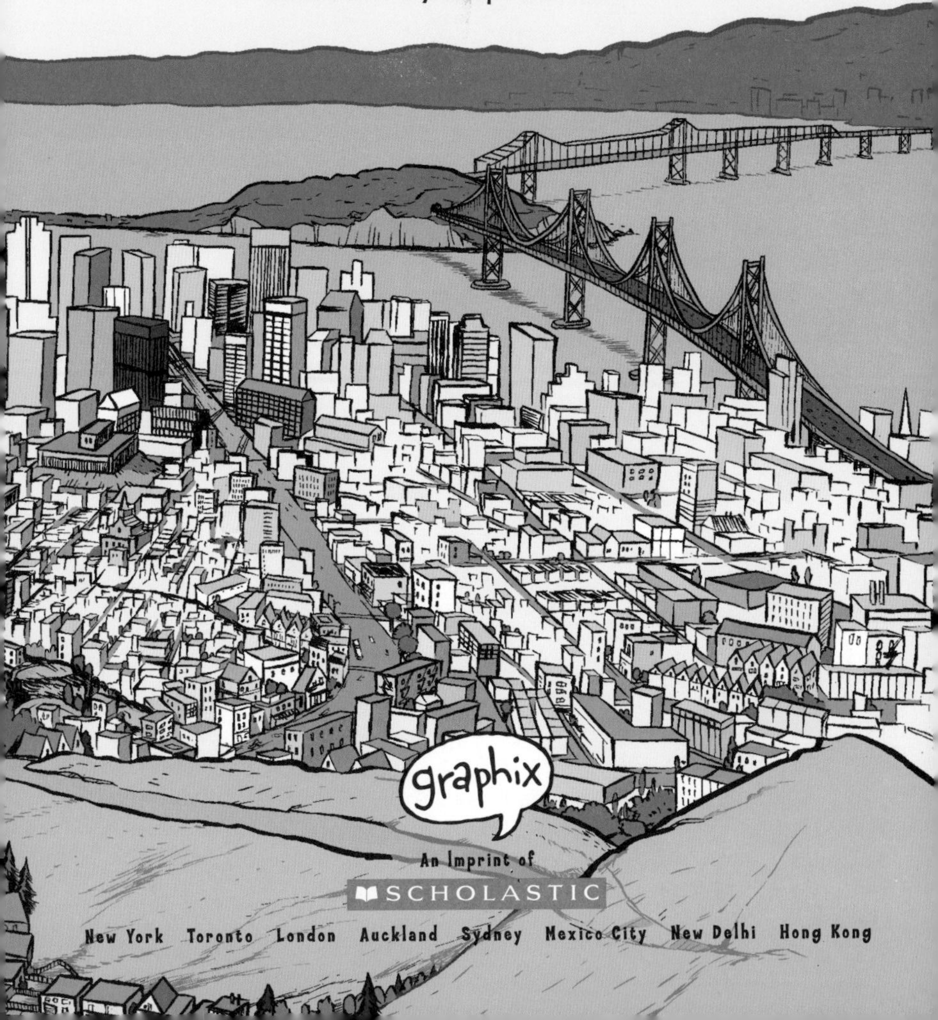

graphix
An Imprint of
SCHOLASTIC
New York Toronto London Auckland Sydney Mexico City New Delhi Hong Kong

All rights reserved. Published by Graphix, an imprint of Scholastic Inc., *Publishers since 1920.* SCHOLASTIC, GRAPHIX, and associated logos are trademarks and/or registered trademarks of Scholastic Inc. All other trademarks are the property of their respective owners and are used without permission.

This graphic novel is based on personal experiences, though some names have been changed, and certain characters, places, and incidents have been modified in service of the story.

Library of Congress Cataloging-in-Publication Data
Telgemeier, Raina.
Smile / Raina Telgemeier. – 1st ed.
p. cm.
ISBN: 978-0-545-13205-3 (hardcover)
ISBN: 978-1-338-74026-4 (paperback)
1. Youth–Dental care. 2. Girls–Dental care. 3. Self-esteem in adolescence.
4. Beauty, Personal. 5. Graphic novels. I. Title.
RK55.Y68.T45 2010
617.6'45–dc22
2008051782

7 6 5 4 3   21 22 23 24

First edition, February 2010
Edited by Cassandra Pelham
Book design by Phil Falco and John Green
Creative Director: David Saylor
Printed in China   62

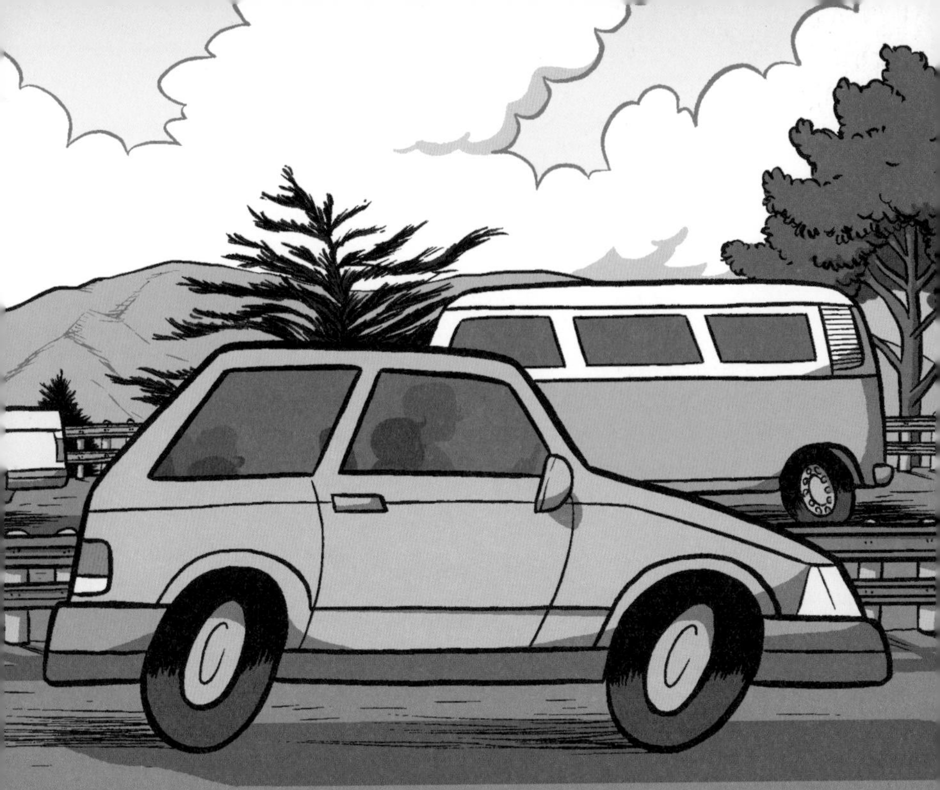

For Dave

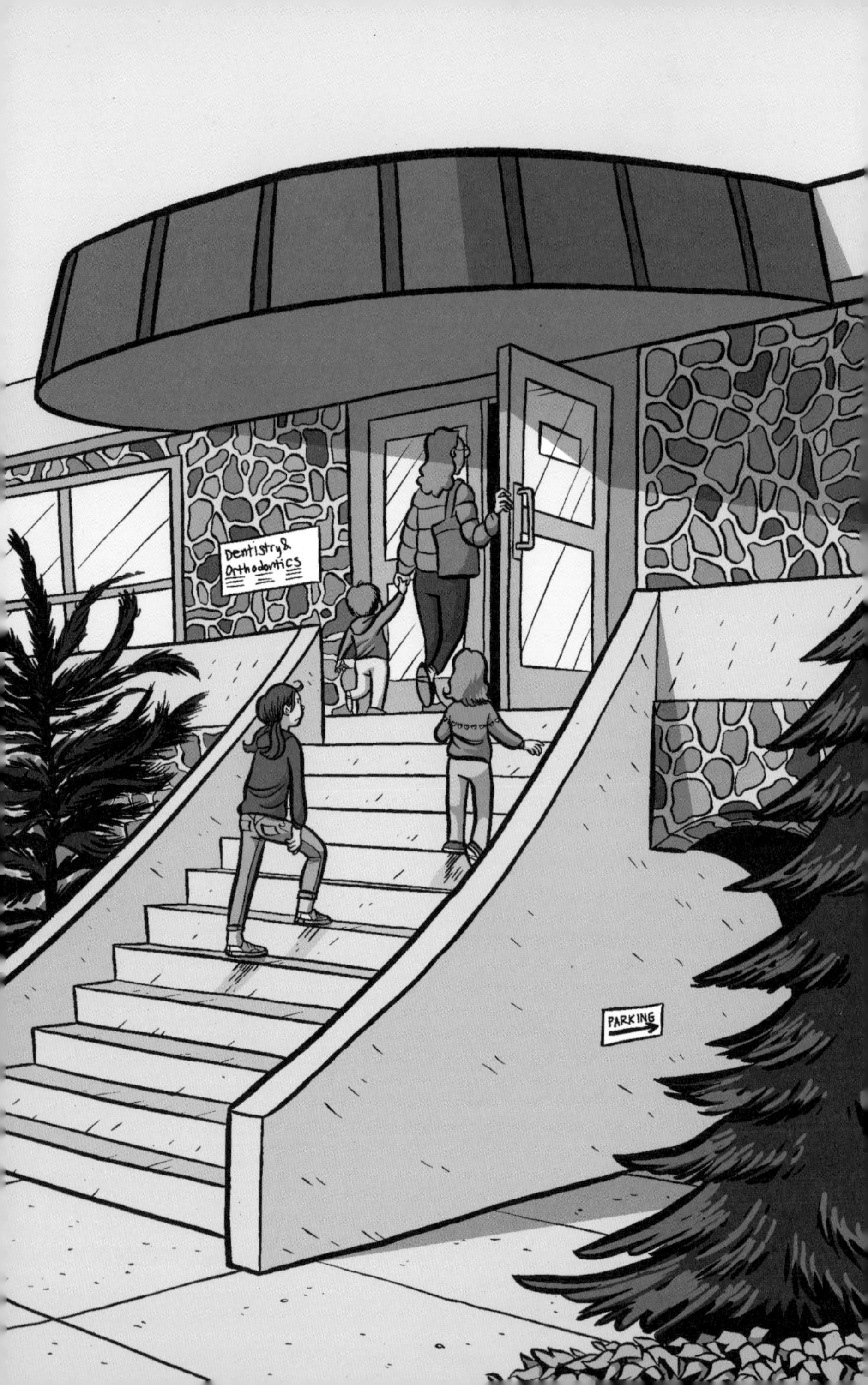
Dentistry &
Orthodontics
PARKING

CHAPTER ONE

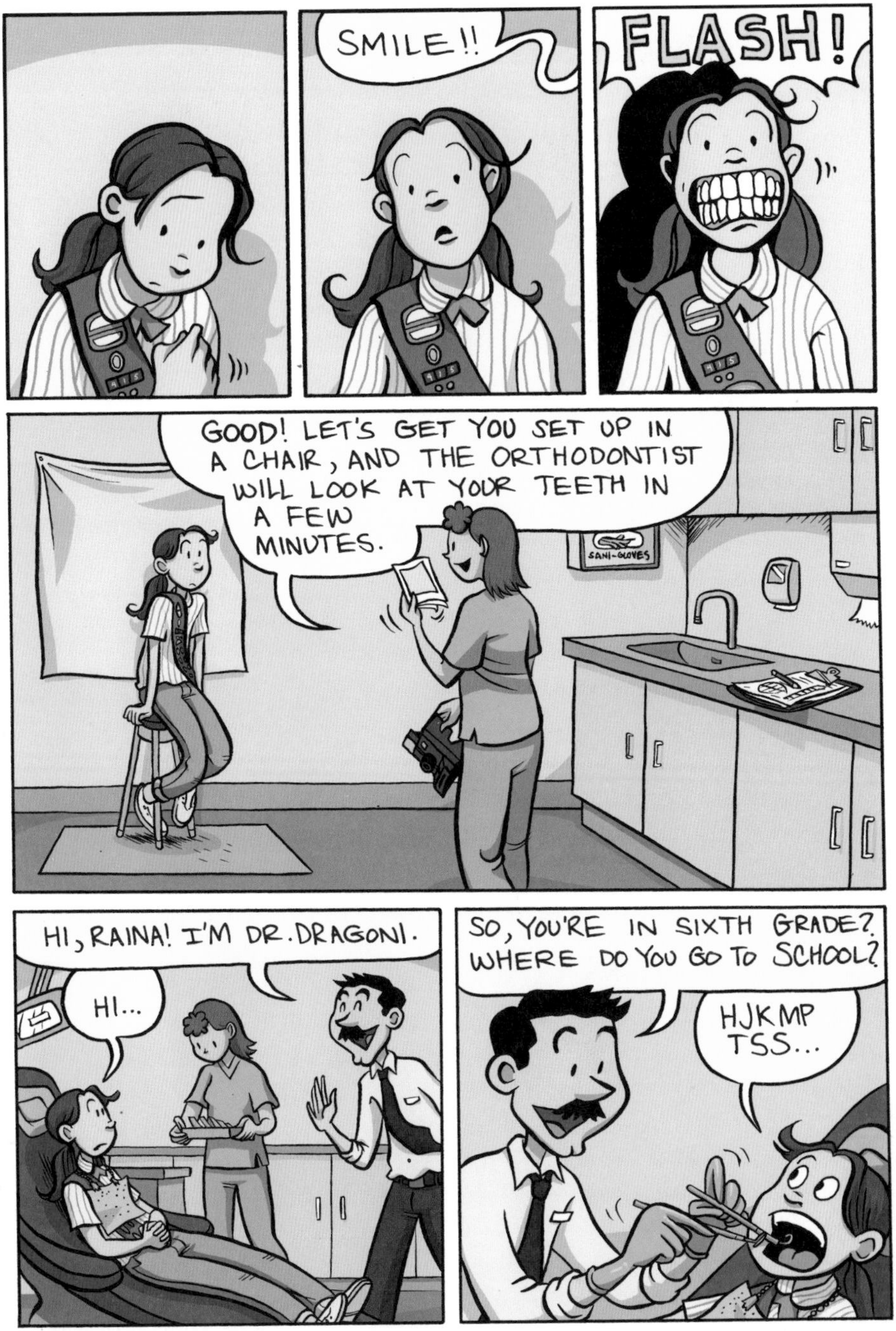

SMILE!!
FLASH!
GOOD! LET'S GET YOU SET UP IN A CHAIR, AND THE ORTHODONTIST WILL LOOK AT YOUR TEETH IN A FEW MINUTES.
SANI-GLOVES
HI, RAINA! I'M DR. DRAGONI.
HI...
SO, YOU'RE IN SIXTH GRADE? WHERE DO YOU GO TO SCHOOL?
HJKMP TSS...

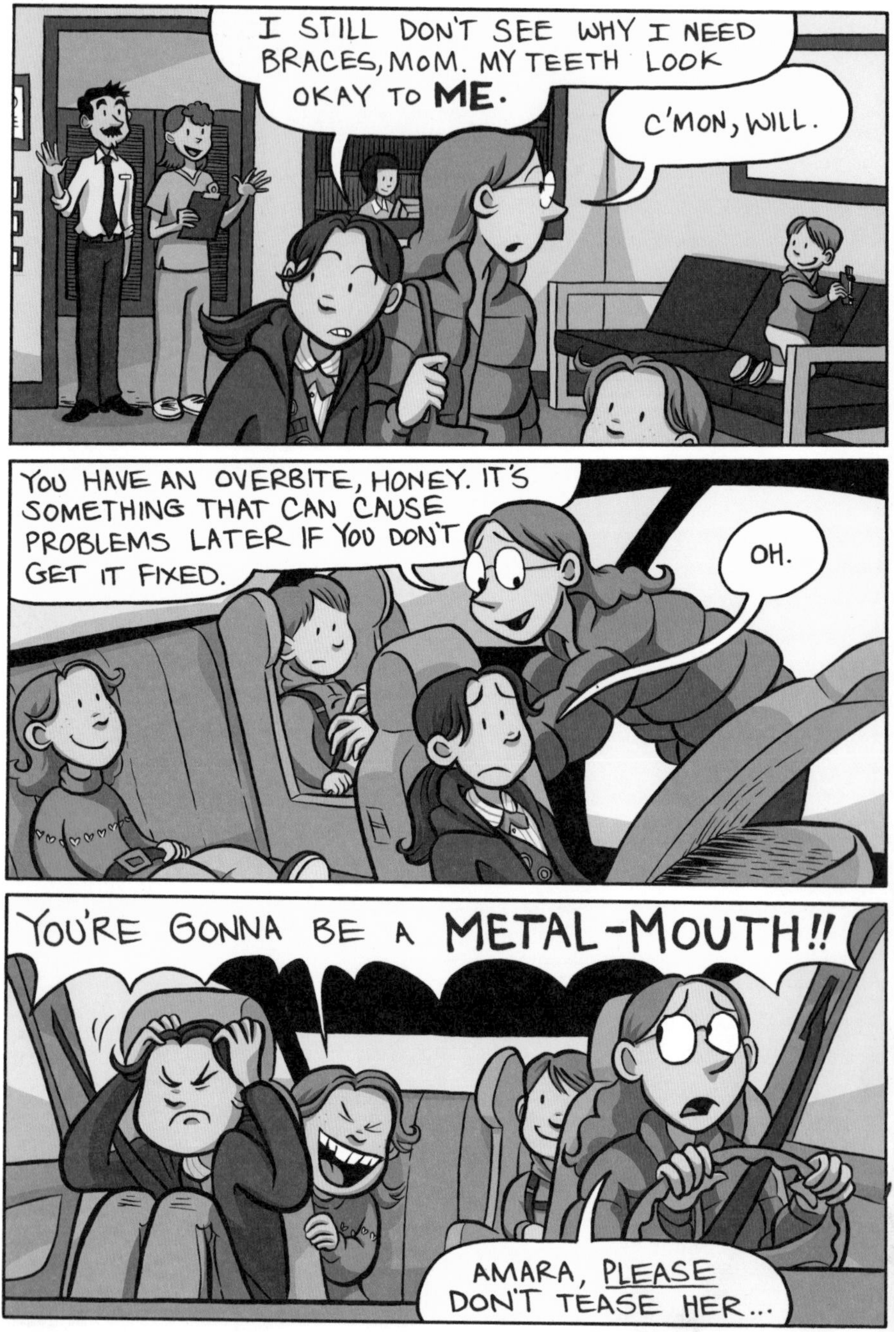
I STILL DON'T SEE WHY I NEED BRACES, MOM. MY TEETH LOOK OKAY TO **ME**.
C'MON, WILL.
YOU HAVE AN OVERBITE, HONEY. IT'S SOMETHING THAT CAN CAUSE PROBLEMS LATER IF YOU DON'T GET IT FIXED.
OH.
YOU'RE GONNA BE A METAL-MOUTH!!
AMARA, PLEASE DON'T TEASE HER...

3

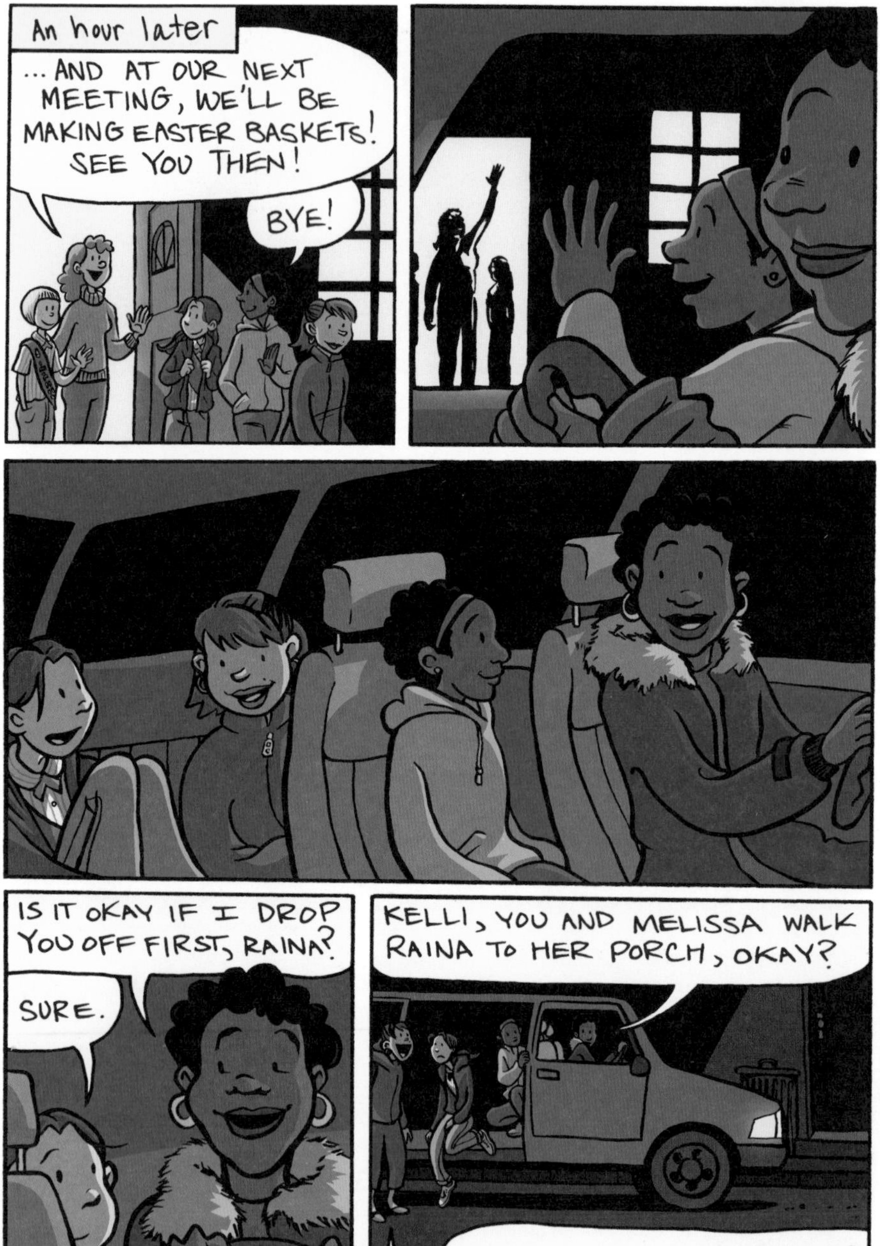
An hour later
...AND AT OUR NEXT MEETING, WE'LL BE MAKING EASTER BASKETS! SEE YOU THEN!
BYE!
IS IT OKAY IF I DROP YOU OFF FIRST, RAINA?
SURE.
KELLI, YOU AND MELISSA WALK RAINA TO HER PORCH, OKAY?
RACE YOU GUYS!!

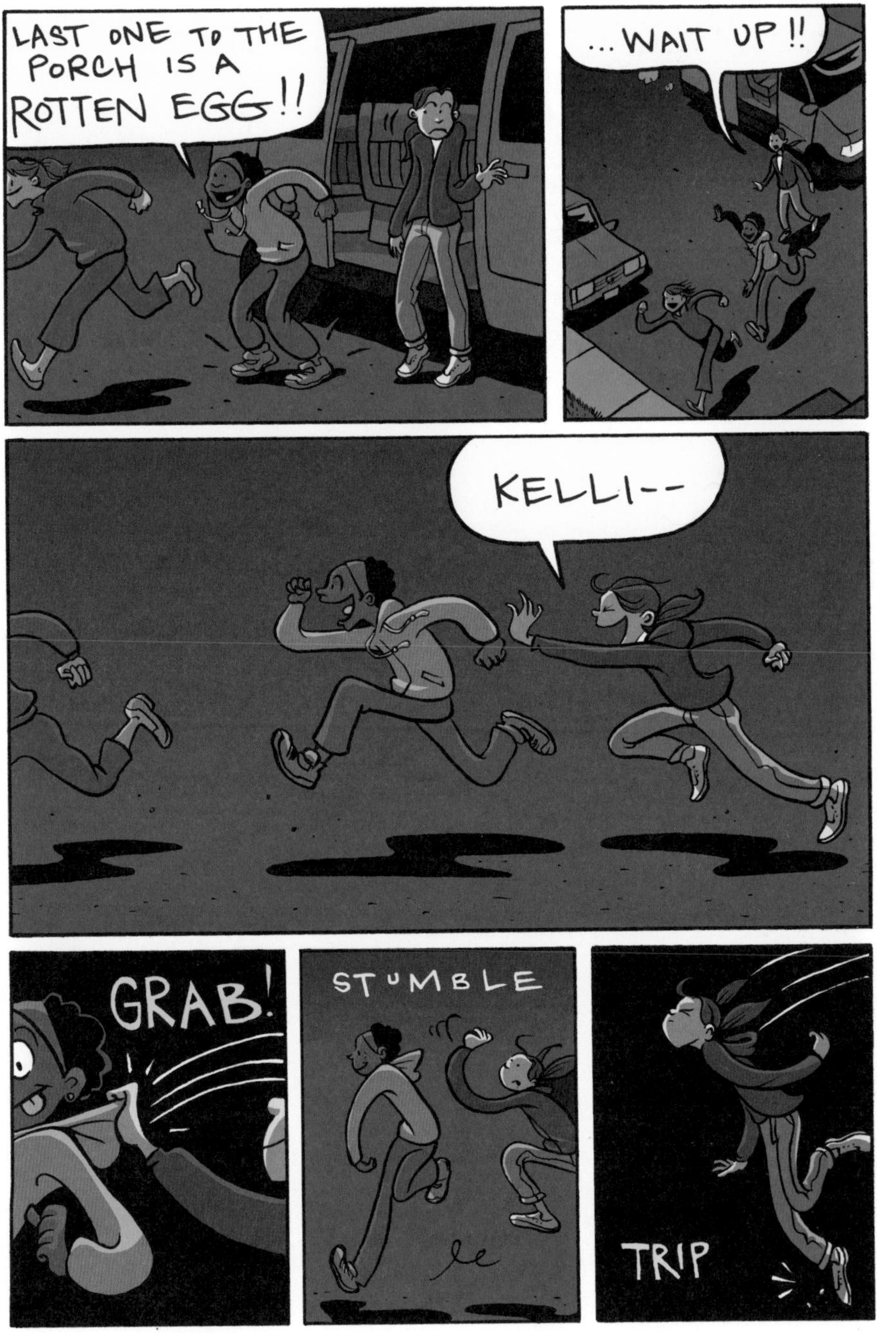
LAST ONE TO THE PORCH IS A ROTTEN EGG!!
...WAIT UP!!
KELLI--
GRAB!
STUMBLE
TRIP

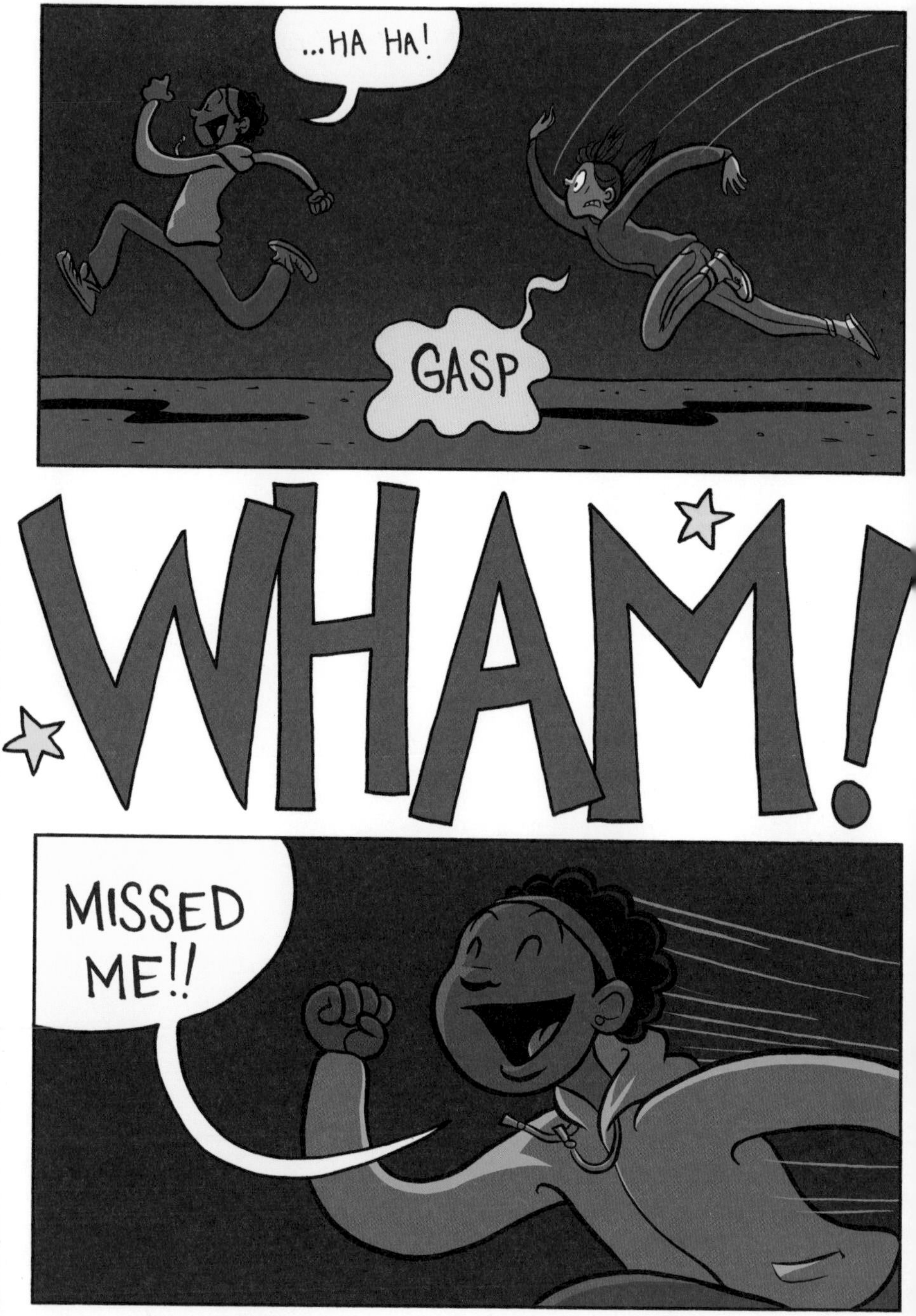
...HA HA!
GASP
WHAM!
MISSED ME!!

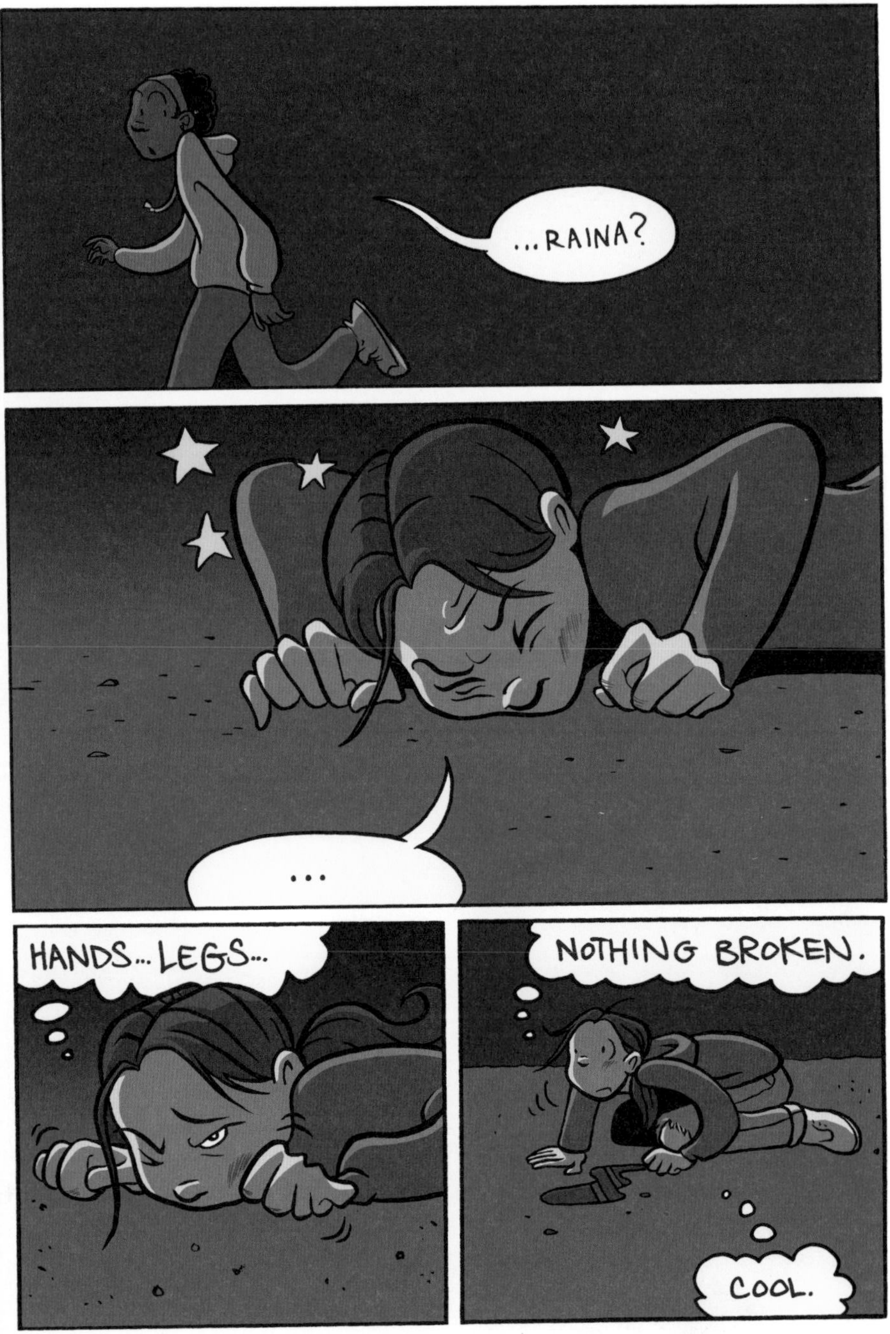
...RAINA?
...
HANDS... LEGS...
NOTHING BROKEN.
COOL.

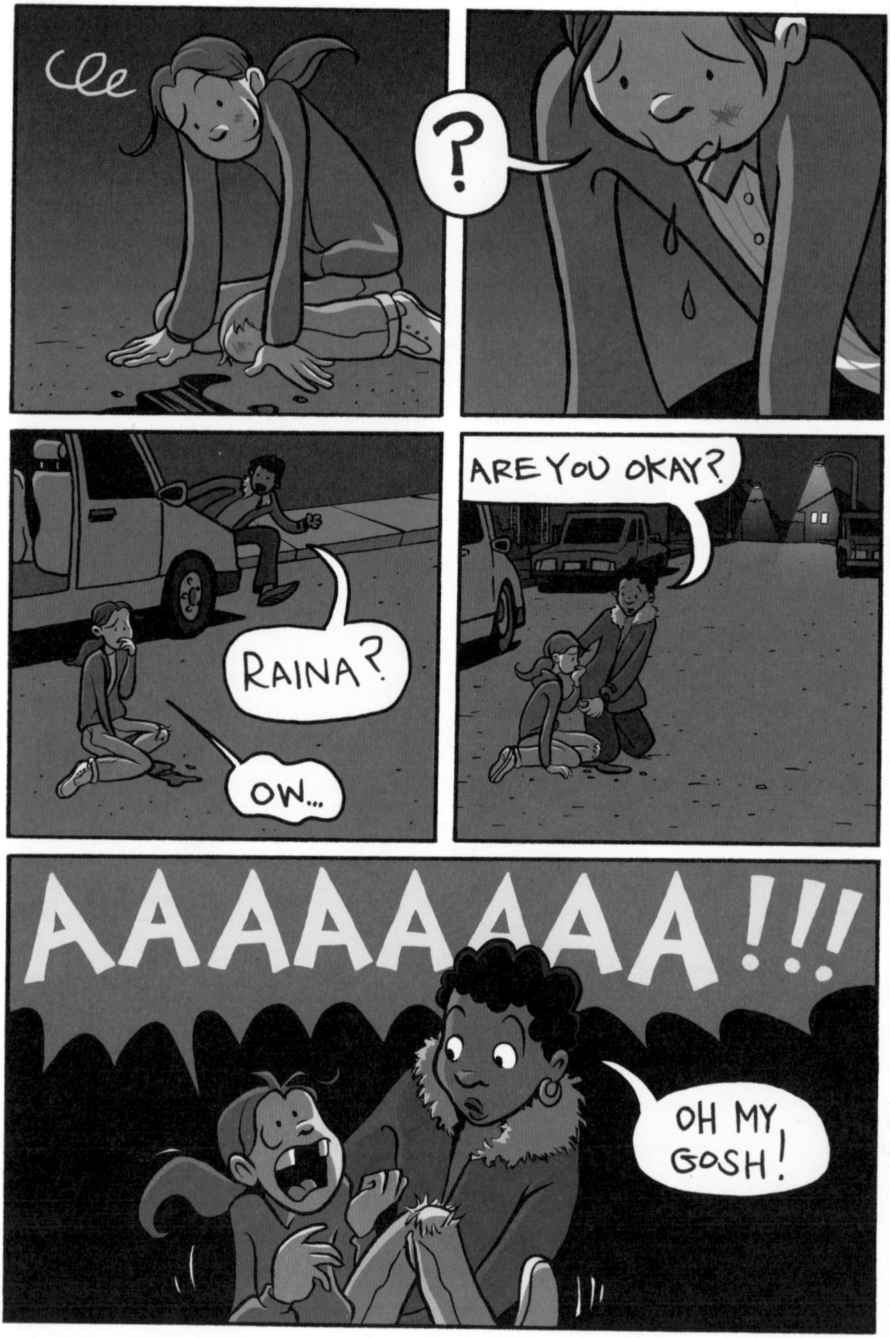

?
RAINA?
OW...
ARE YOU OKAY?
AAAAAAA!!!
OH MY GOSH!

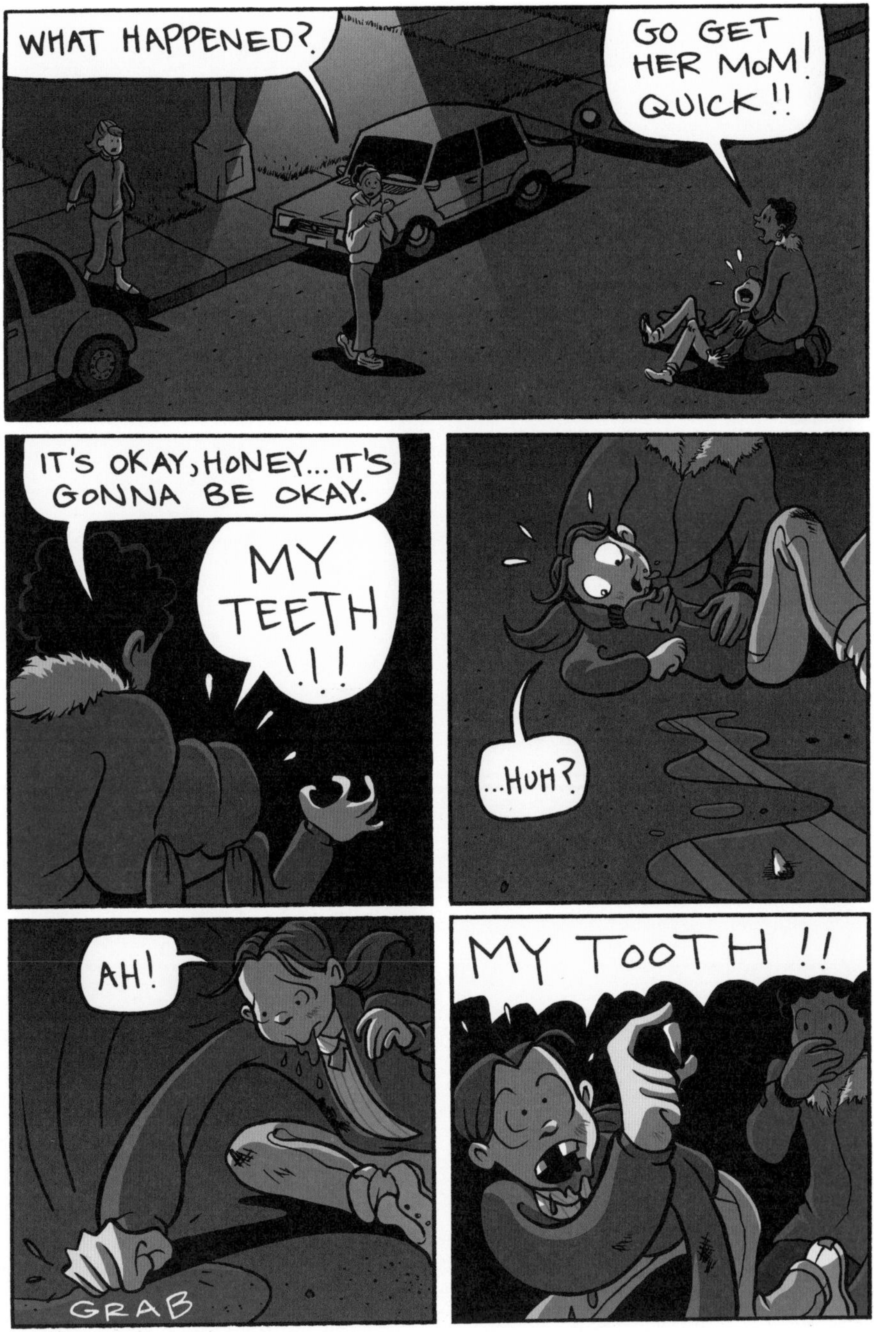
WHAT HAPPENED?
GO GET HER MOM! QUICK!!
IT'S OKAY, HONEY... IT'S GONNA BE OKAY.
MY TEETH !!!
...HUH?
AH!
GRAB
MY TOOTH !!

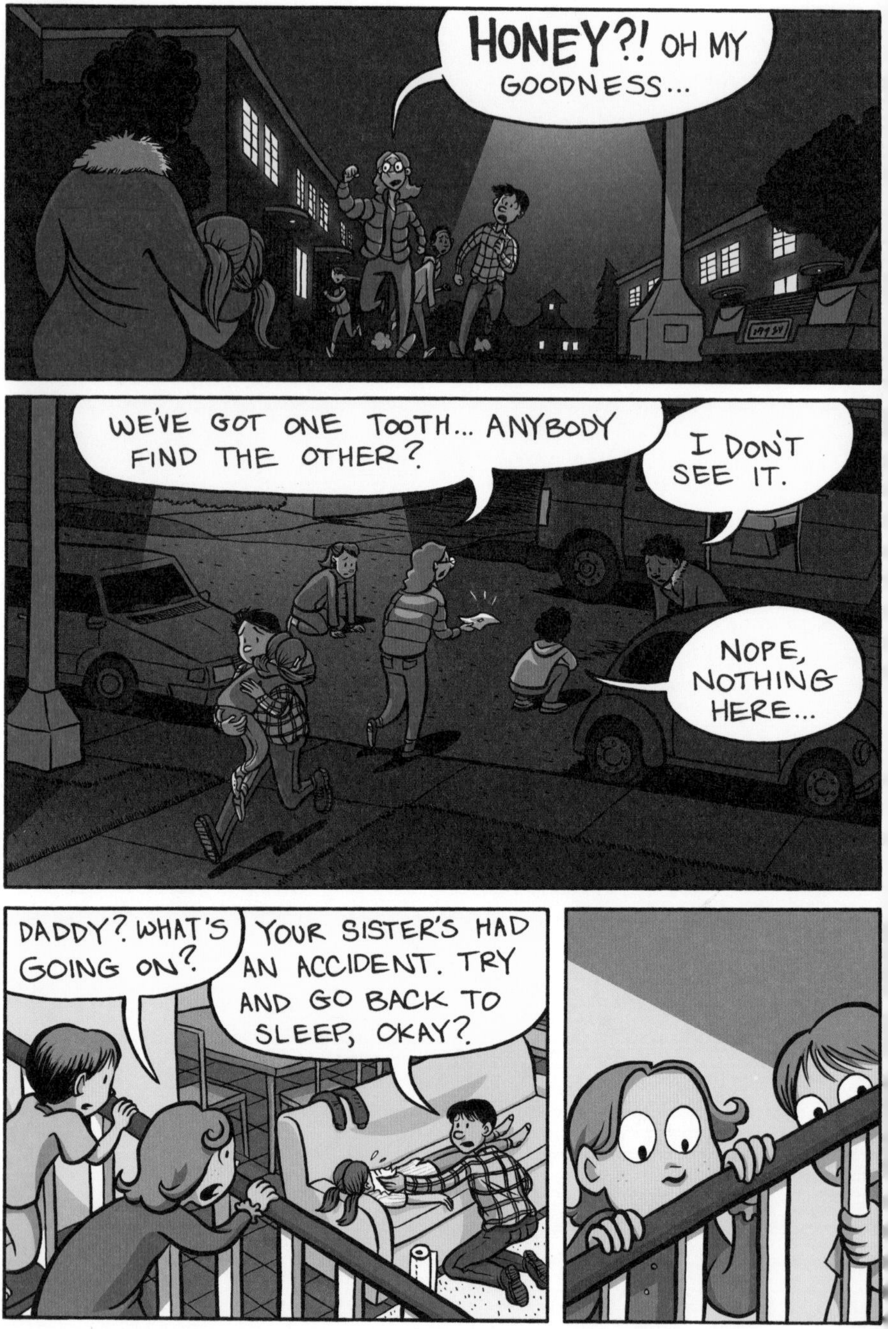
HONEY?! OH MY GOODNESS...
WE'VE GOT ONE TOOTH... ANYBODY FIND THE OTHER?
I DON'T SEE IT.
NOPE, NOTHING HERE...
DADDY? WHAT'S GOING ON?
YOUR SISTER'S HAD AN ACCIDENT. TRY AND GO BACK TO SLEEP, OKAY?

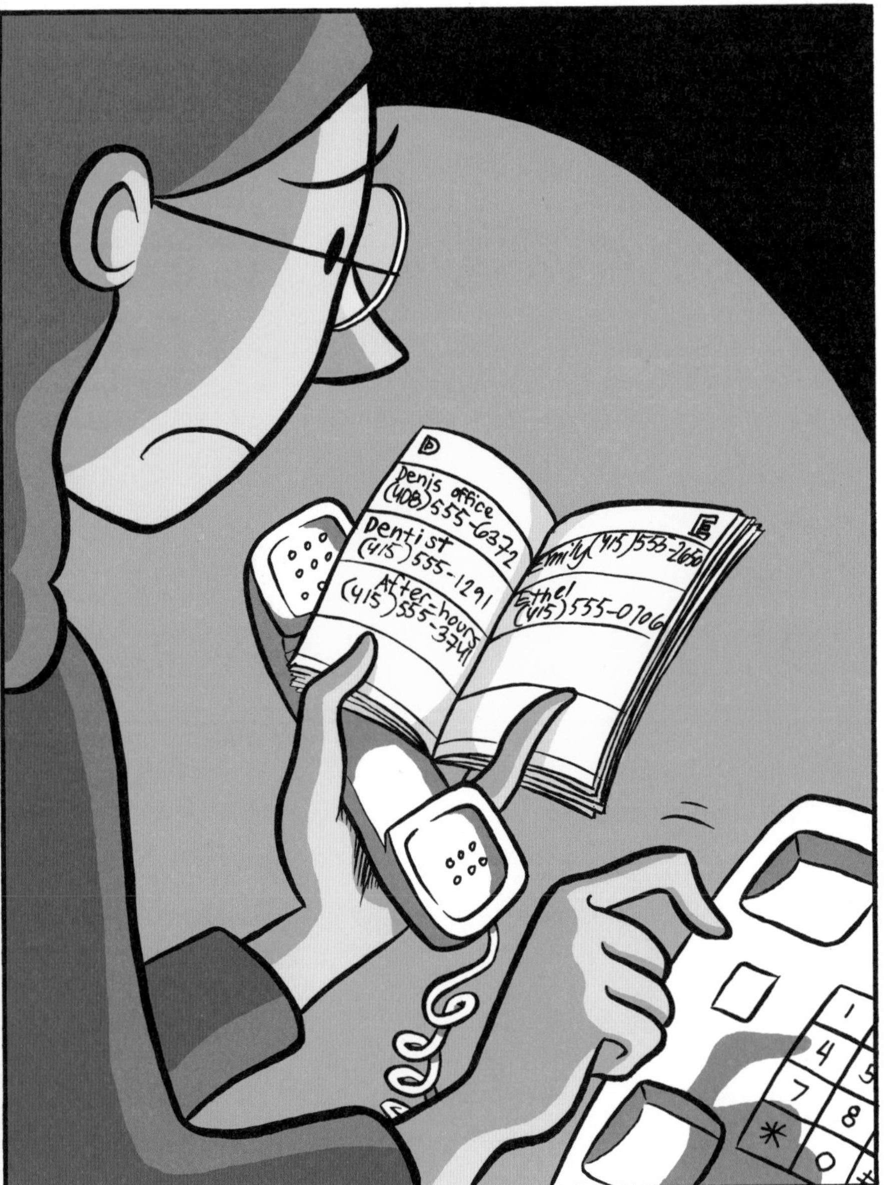
D
Denis office (408)555-6372
Dentist (415)555-1291
After-hours (415)555-3741
E
Emily (415)555-2650
Ethel (415)555-0706

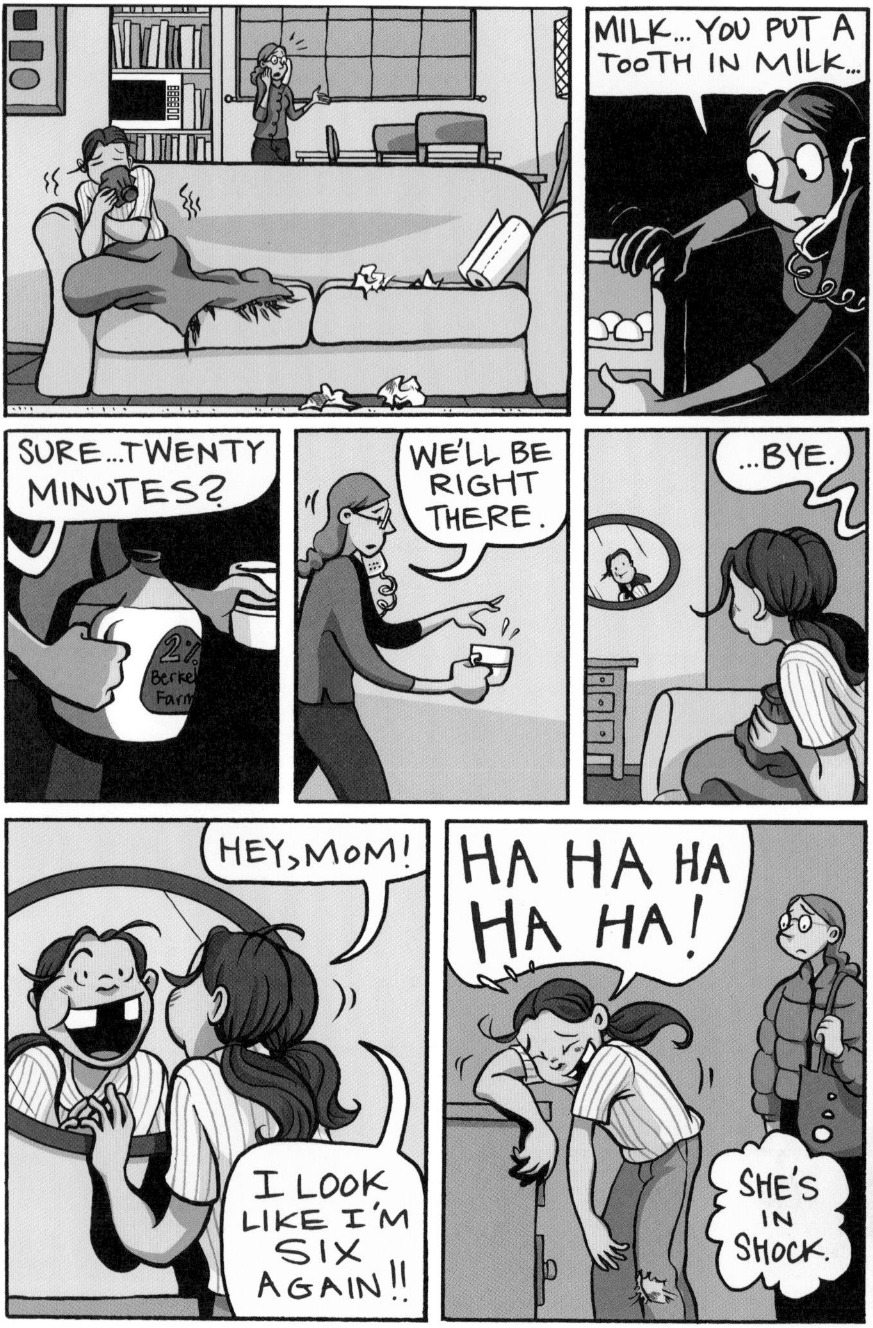
MILK... YOU PUT A TOOTH IN MILK...
SURE...TWENTY MINUTES?
2%
Berkel
Farm
WE'LL BE RIGHT THERE.
...BYE.
HEY, MOM!
I LOOK LIKE I'M SIX AGAIN!!
HA HA HA HA HA!
SHE'S IN SHOCK.

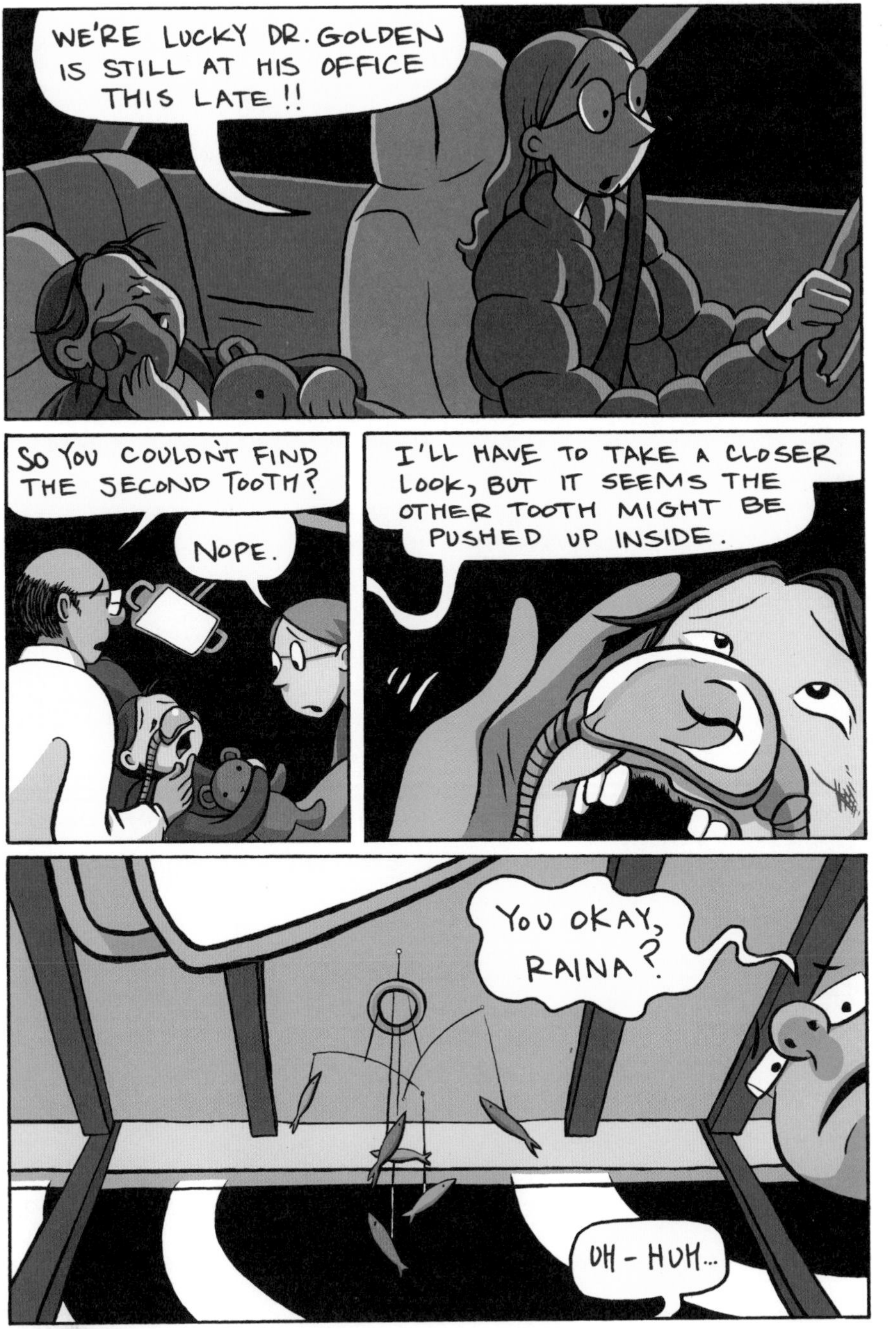
WE'RE LUCKY DR. GOLDEN IS STILL AT HIS OFFICE THIS LATE!!
SO YOU COULDN'T FIND THE SECOND TOOTH?
NOPE.
I'LL HAVE TO TAKE A CLOSER LOOK, BUT IT SEEMS THE OTHER TOOTH MIGHT BE PUSHED UP INSIDE.
YOU OKAY, RAINA?
UH-HUH...

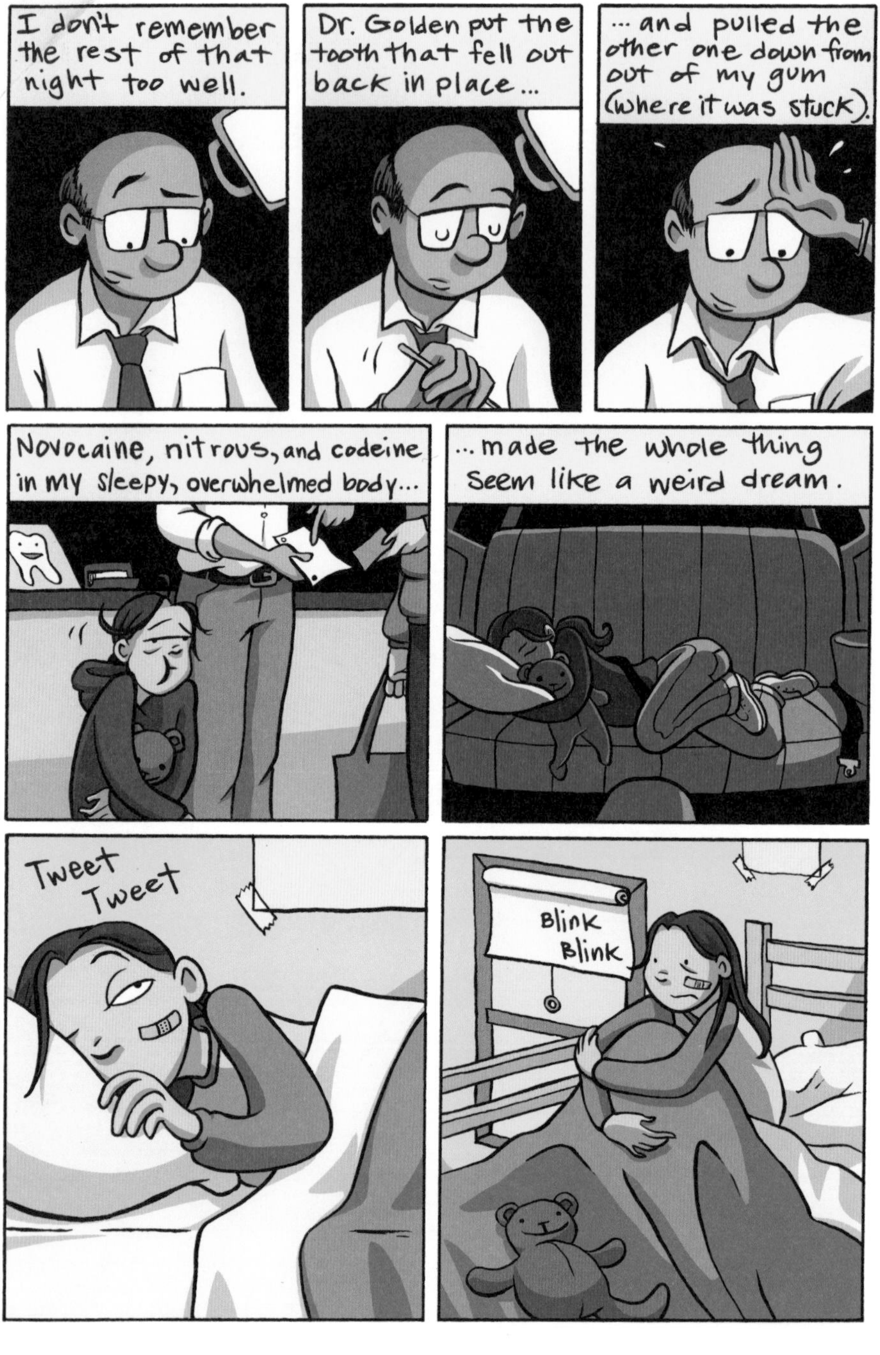
I don't remember the rest of that night too well.
Dr. Golden put the tooth that fell out back in place...
... and pulled the other one down from out of my gum (where it was stuck).
Novocaine, nitrous, and codeine in my sleepy, overwhelmed body...
... made the whole thing seem like a weird dream.
Tweet Tweet
Blink Blink

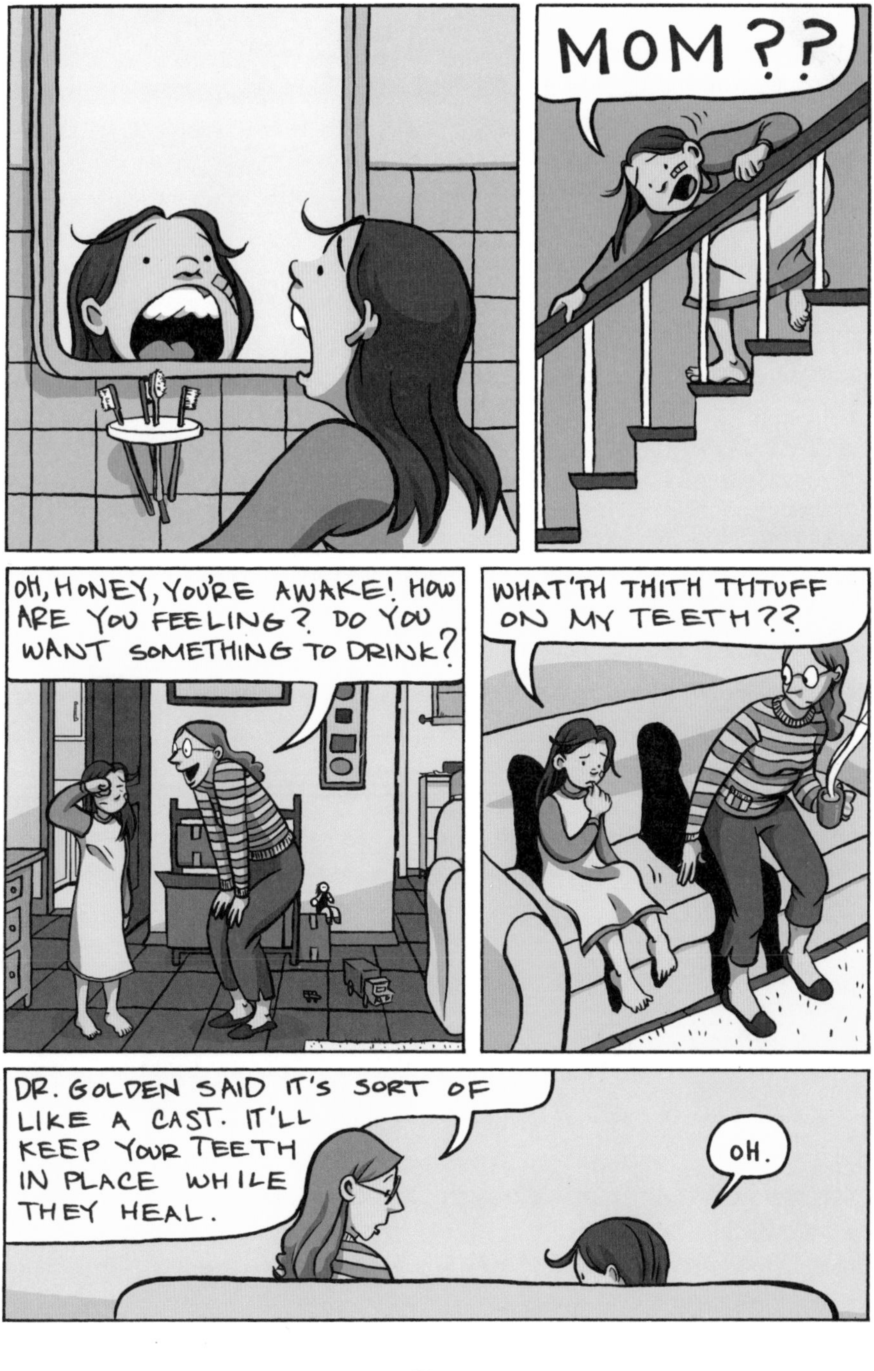
MOM??
OH, HONEY, YOU'RE AWAKE! HOW ARE YOU FEELING? DO YOU WANT SOMETHING TO DRINK?
WHAT'TH THITH THTUFF ON MY TEETH??
DR. GOLDEN SAID IT'S SORT OF LIKE A CAST. IT'LL KEEP YOUR TEETH IN PLACE WHILE THEY HEAL.
OH.

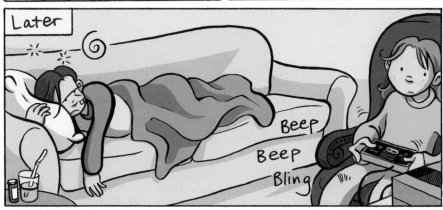

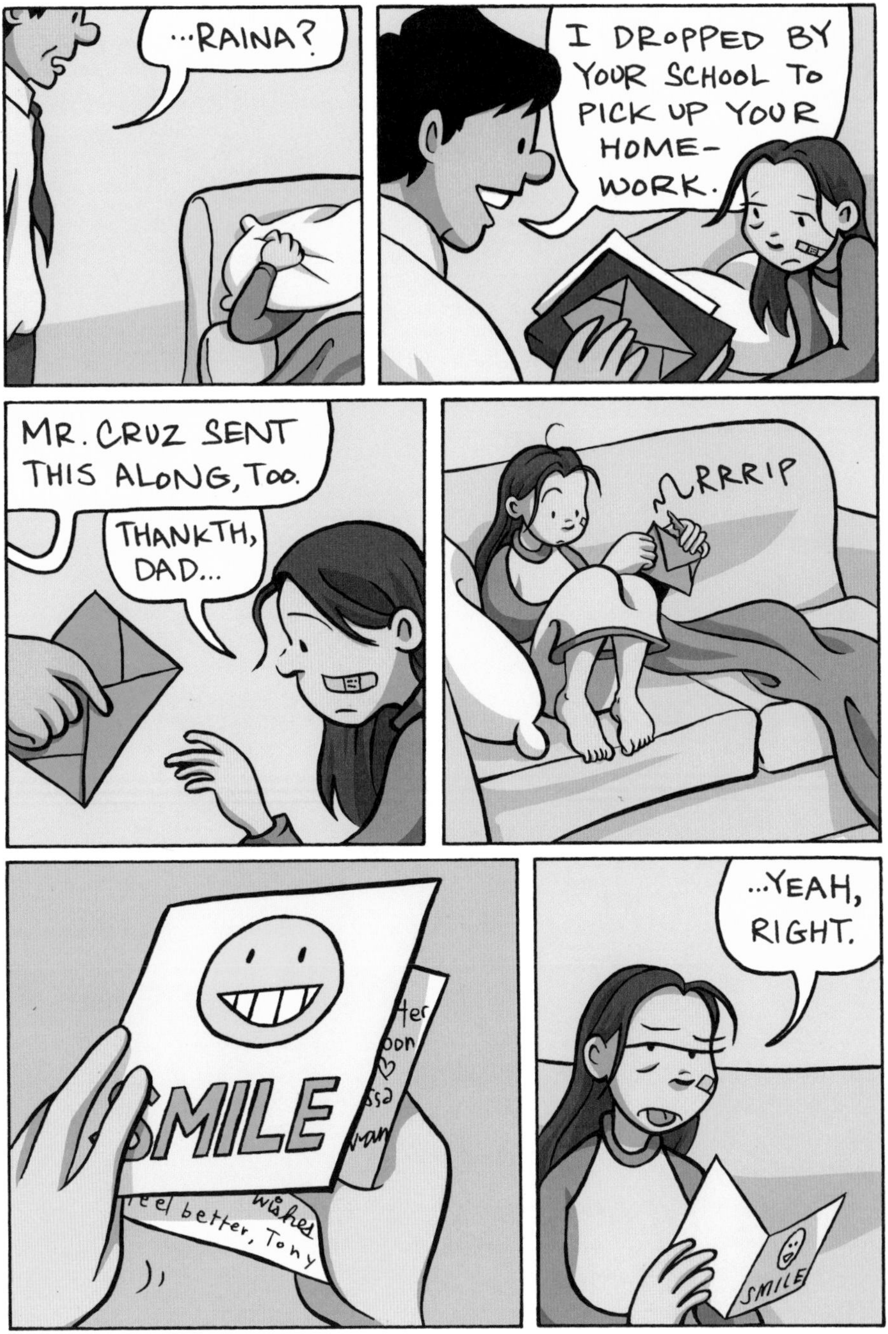
...RAINA?
I DROPPED BY YOUR SCHOOL TO PICK UP YOUR HOME-WORK.
MR. CRUZ SENT THIS ALONG, TOO.
THANKTH, DAD...
RRRIP
SMILE
wishes
better, Tony
...YEAH, RIGHT.
SMILE

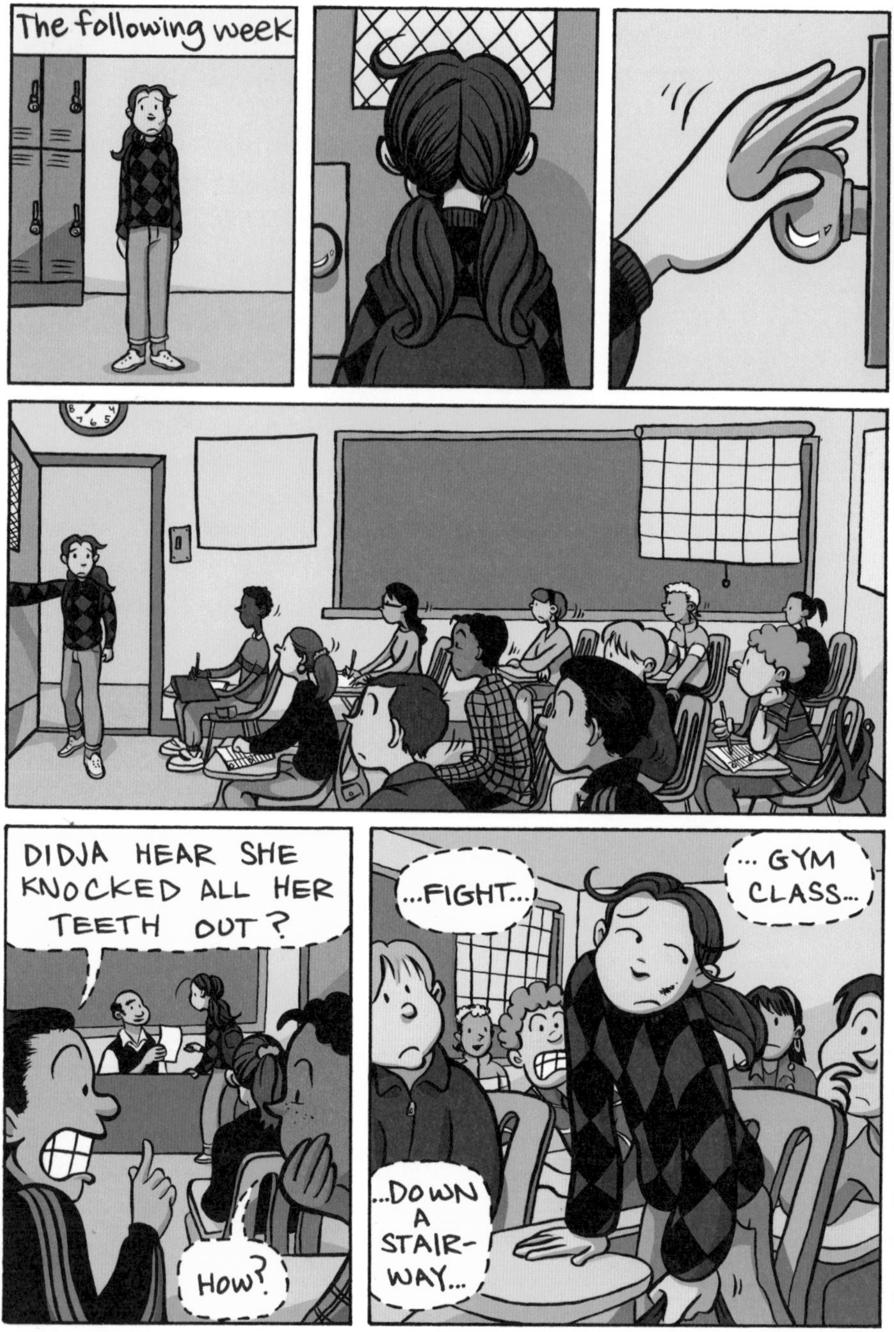
The following week
DIDJA HEAR SHE KNOCKED ALL HER TEETH OUT?
HOW?
...FIGHT...
... GYM CLASS...
...DOWN A STAIR-WAY...

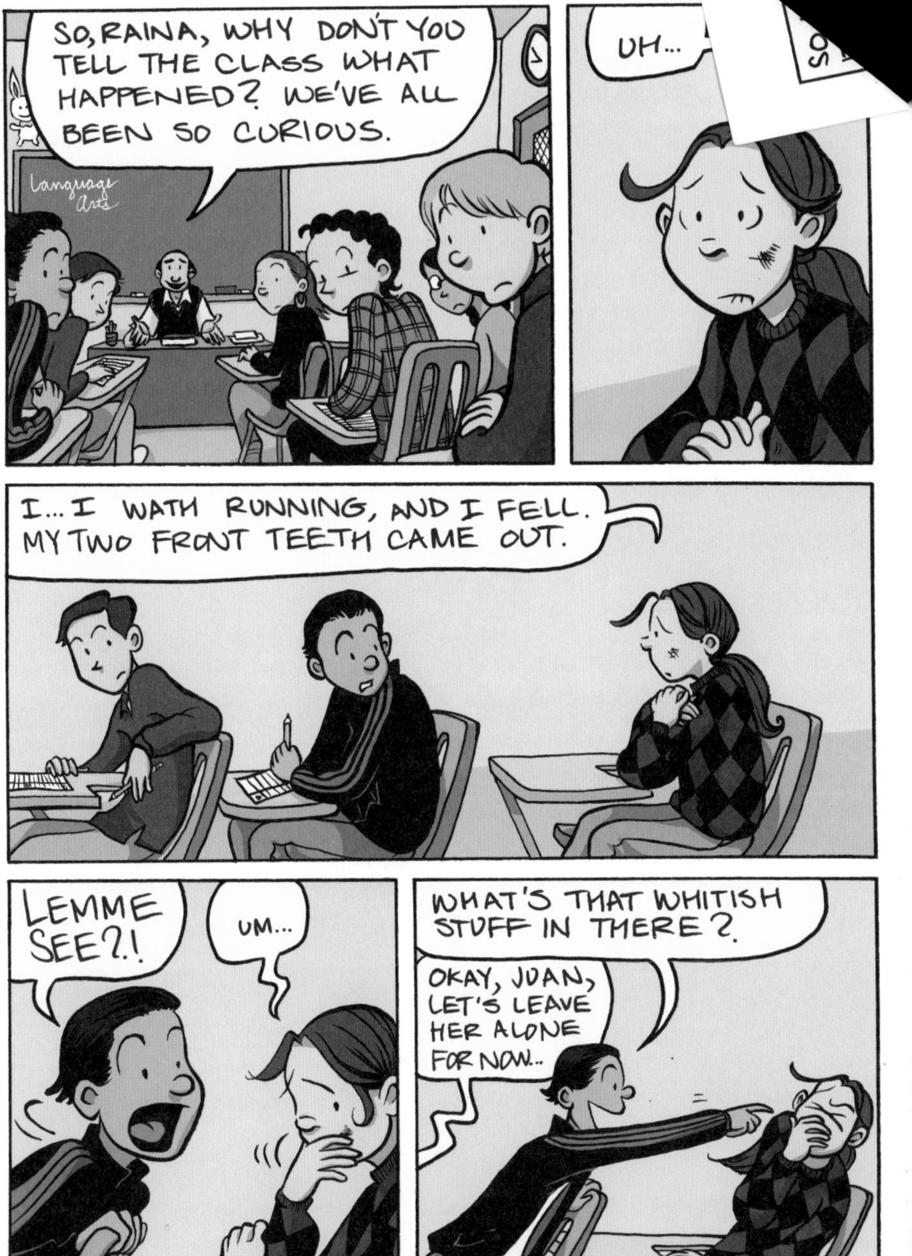
SO, RAINA, WHY DON'T YOU TELL THE CLASS WHAT HAPPENED? WE'VE ALL BEEN SO CURIOUS.
Language Arts
UH...
I... I WATH RUNNING, AND I FELL. MY TWO FRONT TEETH CAME OUT.
LEMME SEE?!
UM...
WHAT'S THAT WHITISH STUFF IN THERE?
OKAY, JUAN, LET'S LEAVE HER ALONE FOR NOW...

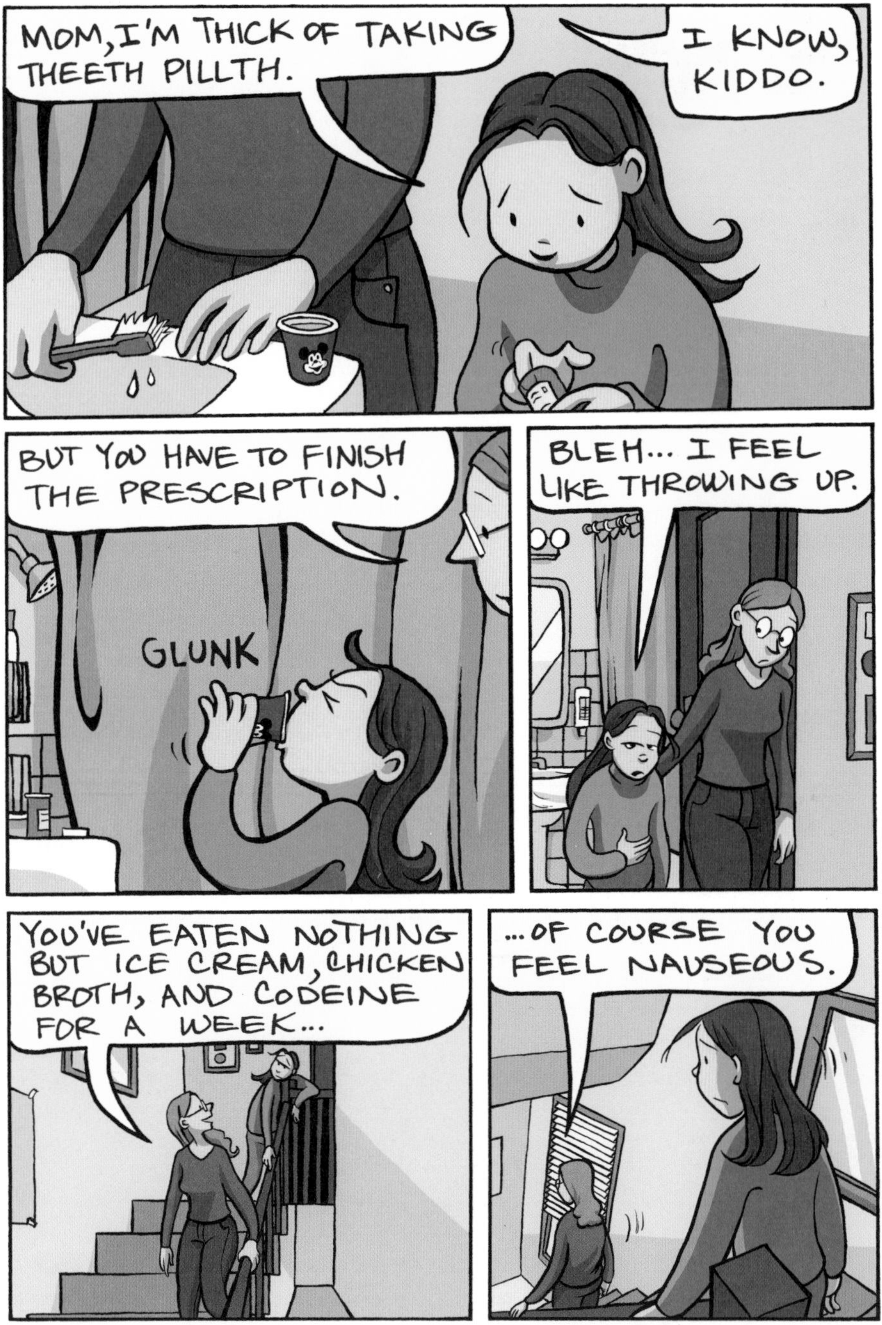
MOM, I'M THICK OF TAKING THEETH PILLTH.
I KNOW, KIDDO.
BUT YOU HAVE TO FINISH THE PRESCRIPTION.
GLUNK
BLEH... I FEEL LIKE THROWING UP.
YOU'VE EATEN NOTHING BUT ICE CREAM, CHICKEN BROTH, AND CODEINE FOR A WEEK...
...OF COURSE YOU FEEL NAUSEOUS.

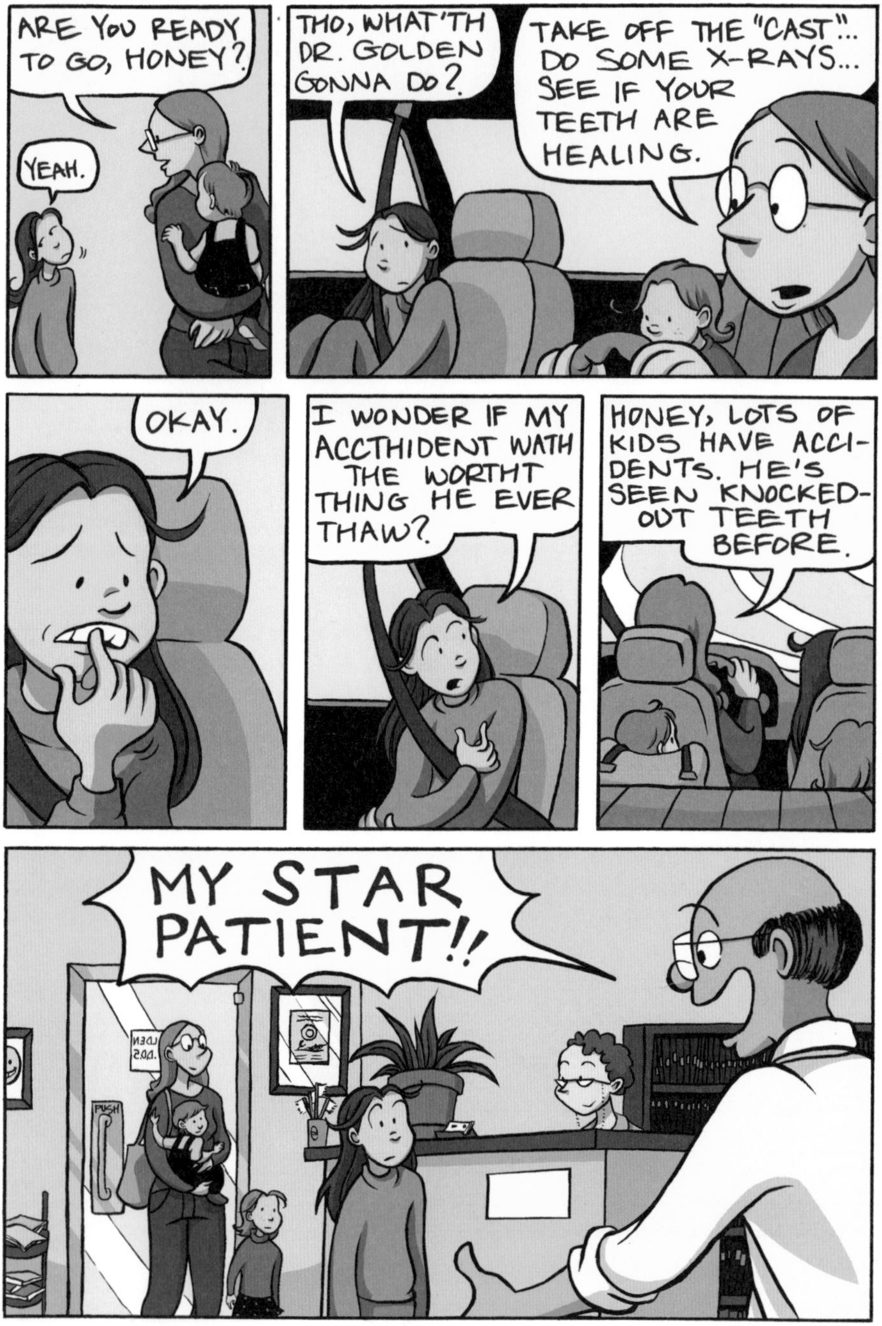
ARE YOU READY TO GO, HONEY?
YEAH.
THO, WHAT'TH DR. GOLDEN GONNA DO?
TAKE OFF THE "CAST"... DO SOME X-RAYS... SEE IF YOUR TEETH ARE HEALING.
OKAY.
I WONDER IF MY ACCTHIDENT WATH THE WORTHT THING HE EVER THAW?
HONEY, LOTS OF KIDS HAVE ACCIDENTS. HE'S SEEN KNOCKED-OUT TEETH BEFORE.
MY STAR PATIENT!!
PUSH

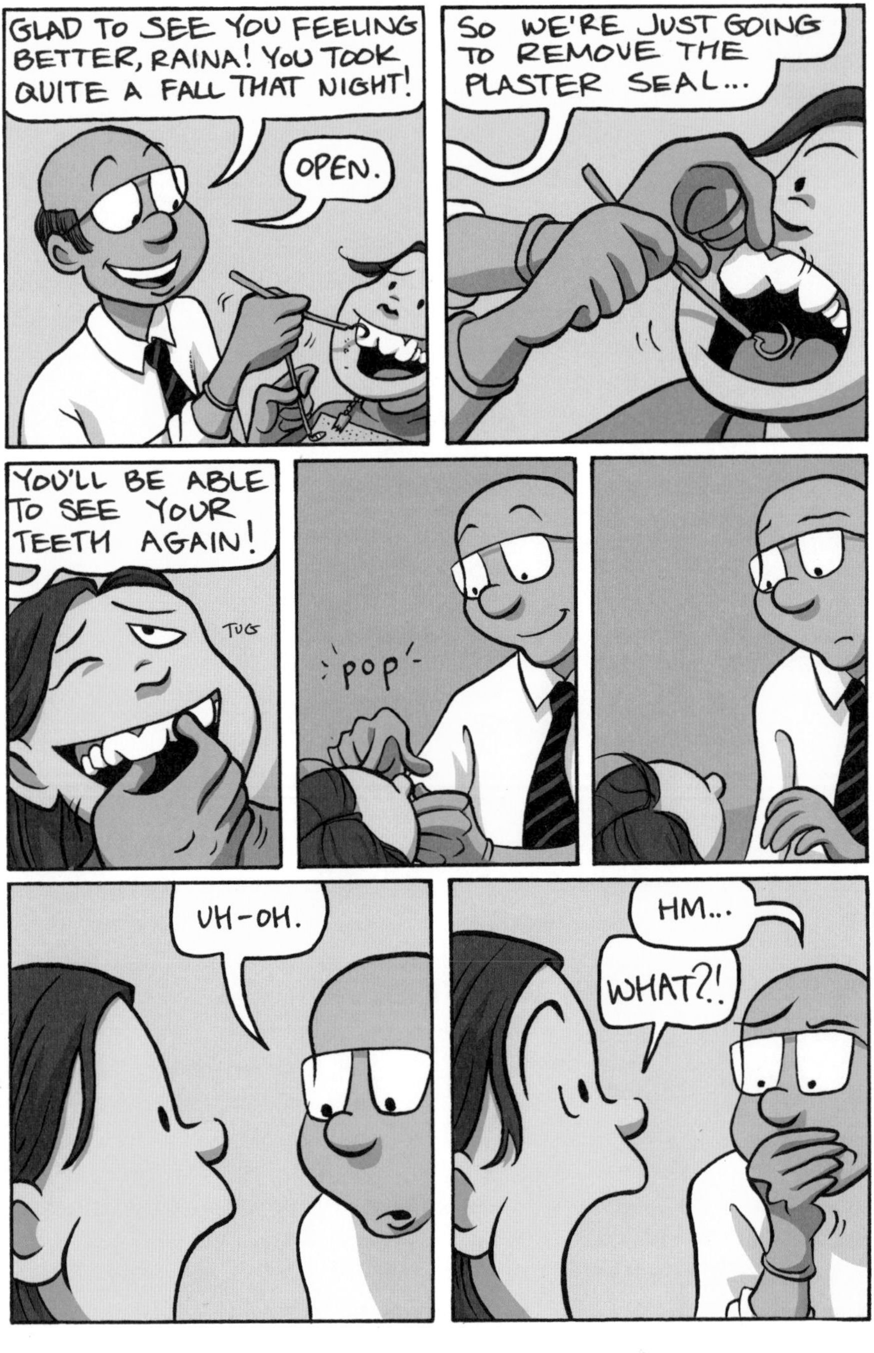
GLAD TO SEE YOU FEELING BETTER, RAINA! YOU TOOK QUITE A FALL THAT NIGHT!
OPEN.
SO WE'RE JUST GOING TO REMOVE THE PLASTER SEAL...
YOU'LL BE ABLE TO SEE YOUR TEETH AGAIN!
TUG
POP
UH-OH.
HM...
WHAT?!

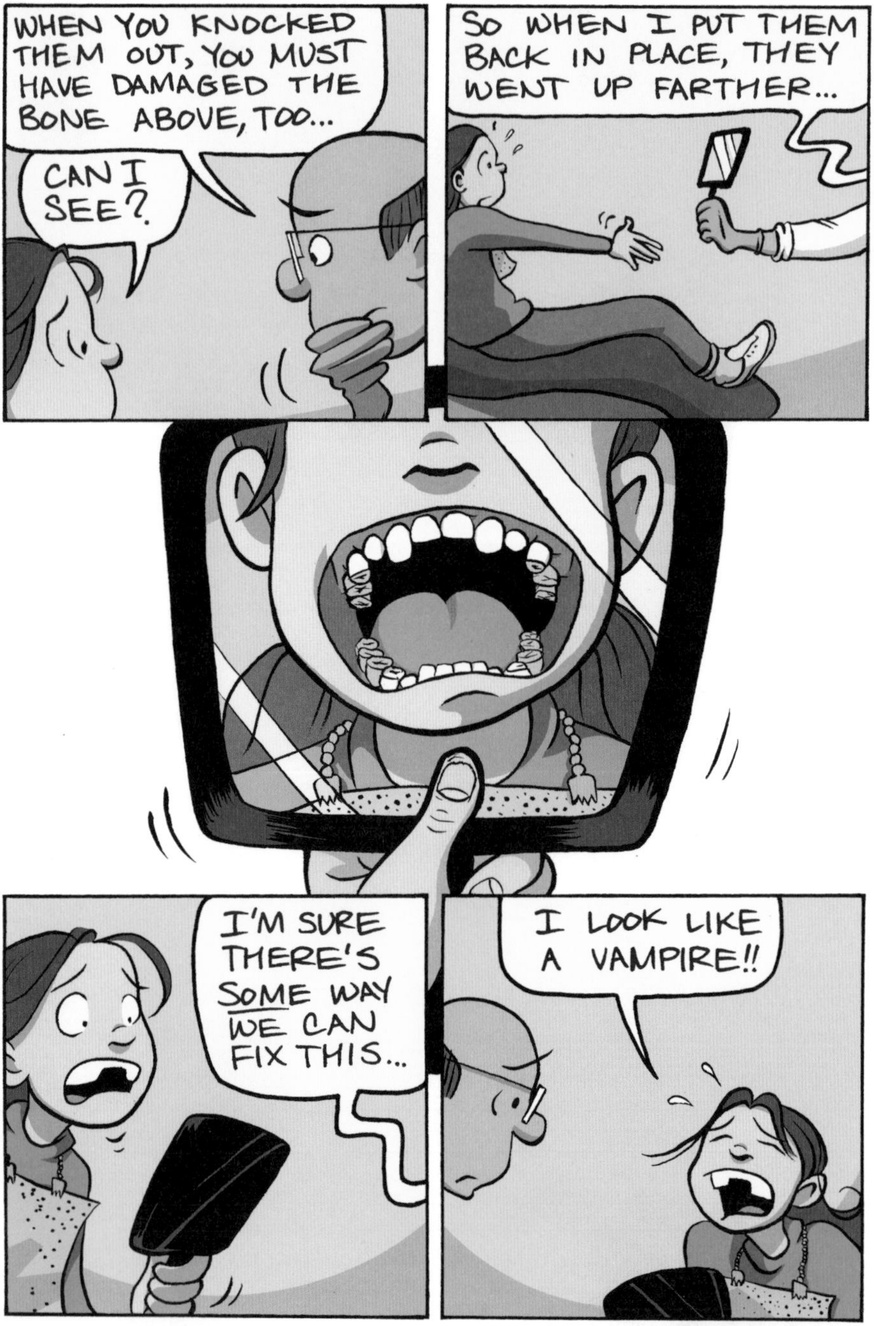
WHEN YOU KNOCKED THEM OUT, YOU MUST HAVE DAMAGED THE BONE ABOVE, TOO...
CAN I SEE?
SO WHEN I PUT THEM BACK IN PLACE, THEY WENT UP FARTHER...
I'M SURE THERE'S SOME WAY WE CAN FIX THIS...
I LOOK LIKE A VAMPIRE!!

LET'S LOOK AT YOUR X-RAYS...

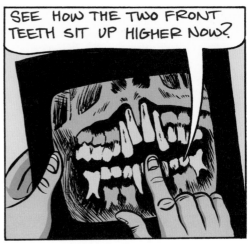

SEE HOW THE TWO FRONT TEETH SIT UP HIGHER NOW?

CAN YOU BRING HER FAMILY BACK HERE?

SURE.

...LOOKS LIKE THERE'S SOME NERVE DAMAGE TO THE FRONT FOUR...

LEMME SEE?

...TO AN ENDODONTIST FOR ROOT CANALS...

C'MON, SIS!

OKAY...

...TRY TO SAVE THOSE TEETH, SO SHE'S NOT WEARING DENTURES AT ELEVEN YEARS OLD...

HA HA HA!

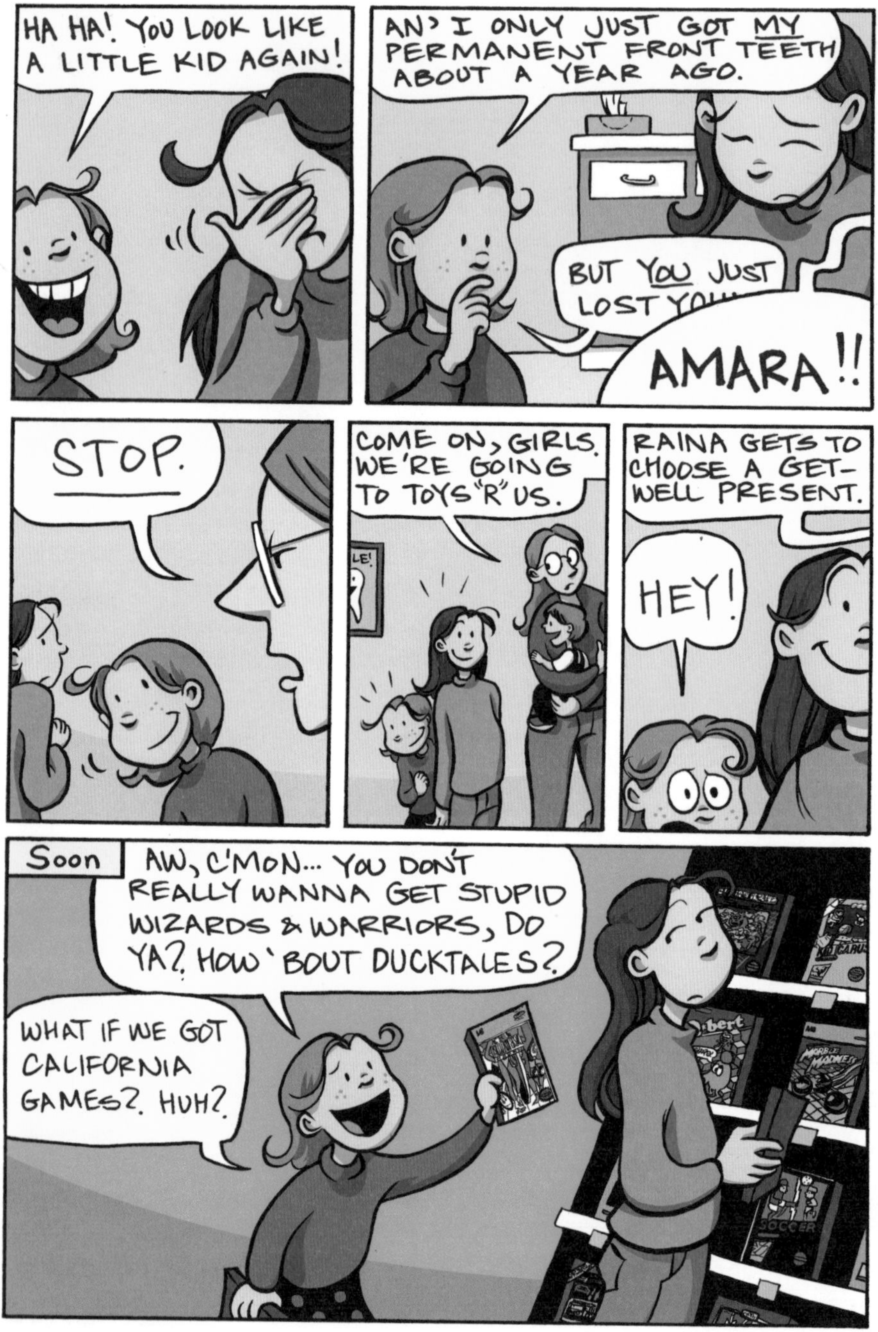
HA HA! YOU LOOK LIKE A LITTLE KID AGAIN!
AN' I ONLY JUST GOT MY PERMANENT FRONT TEETH ABOUT A YEAR AGO.
BUT YOU JUST LOST YOU
AMARA!!
STOP.
COME ON, GIRLS. WE'RE GOING TO TOYS "R" US.
RAINA GETS TO CHOOSE A GET-WELL PRESENT.
HEY!
Soon
AW, C'MON... YOU DON'T REALLY WANNA GET STUPID WIZARDS & WARRIORS, DO YA? HOW 'BOUT DUCKTALES?
WHAT IF WE GOT CALIFORNIA GAMES? HUH?

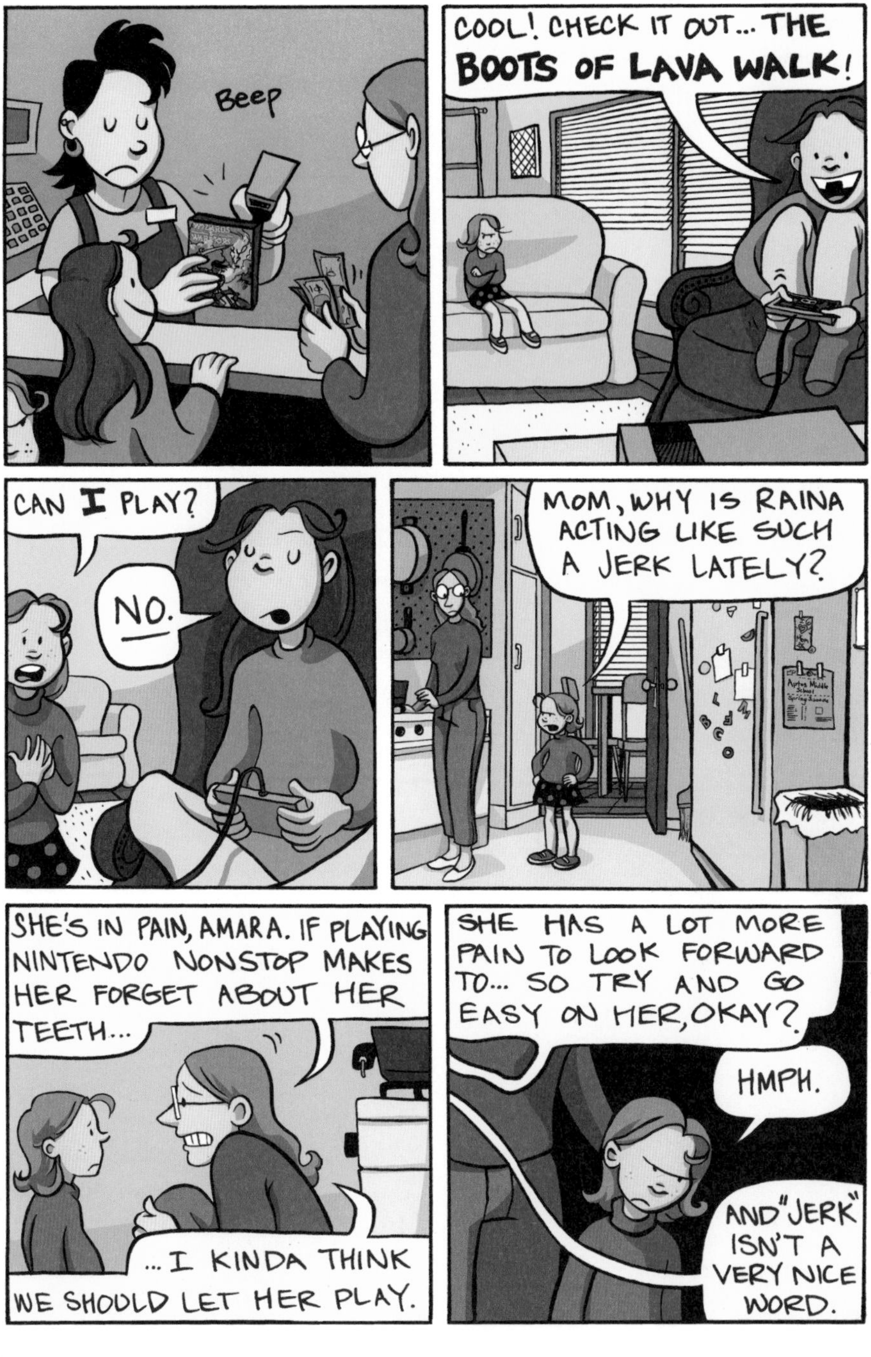
Beep
COOL! CHECK IT OUT... THE BOOTS OF LAVA WALK!
CAN I PLAY?
NO.
MOM, WHY IS RAINA ACTING LIKE SUCH A JERK LATELY?
SHE'S IN PAIN, AMARA. IF PLAYING NINTENDO NONSTOP MAKES HER FORGET ABOUT HER TEETH...
...I KINDA THINK WE SHOULD LET HER PLAY.
SHE HAS A LOT MORE PAIN TO LOOK FORWARD TO... SO TRY AND GO EASY ON HER, OKAY?
HMPH.
AND "JERK" ISN'T A VERY NICE WORD.

CHAPTER TWO

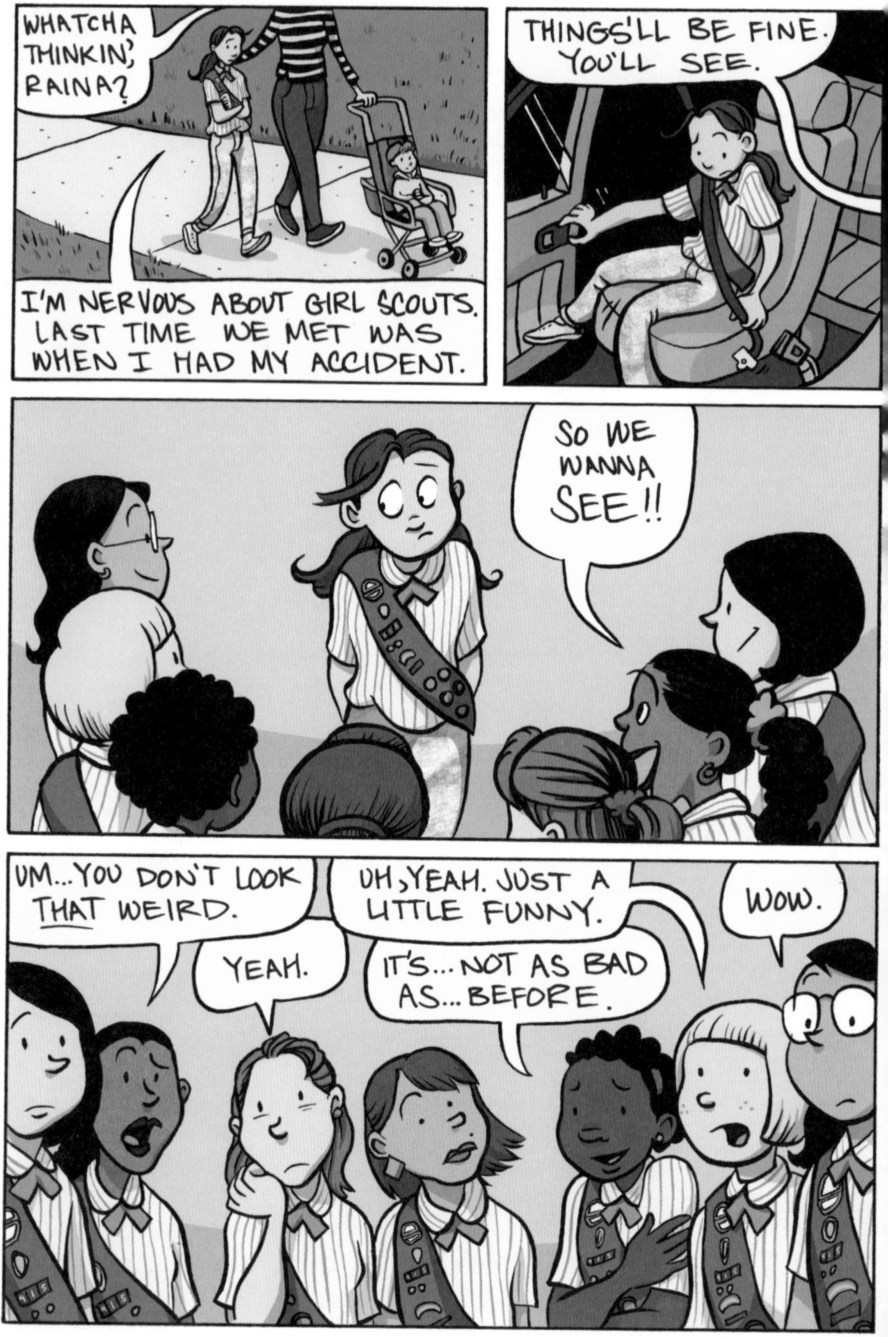
WHATCHA THINKIN', RAINA?
I'M NERVOUS ABOUT GIRL SCOUTS. LAST TIME WE MET WAS WHEN I HAD MY ACCIDENT.
THINGS'LL BE FINE. YOU'LL SEE.
SO WE WANNA SEE!!
UM... YOU DON'T LOOK THAT WEIRD.
YEAH.
UH, YEAH. JUST A LITTLE FUNNY.
IT'S... NOT AS BAD AS... BEFORE.
WOW.

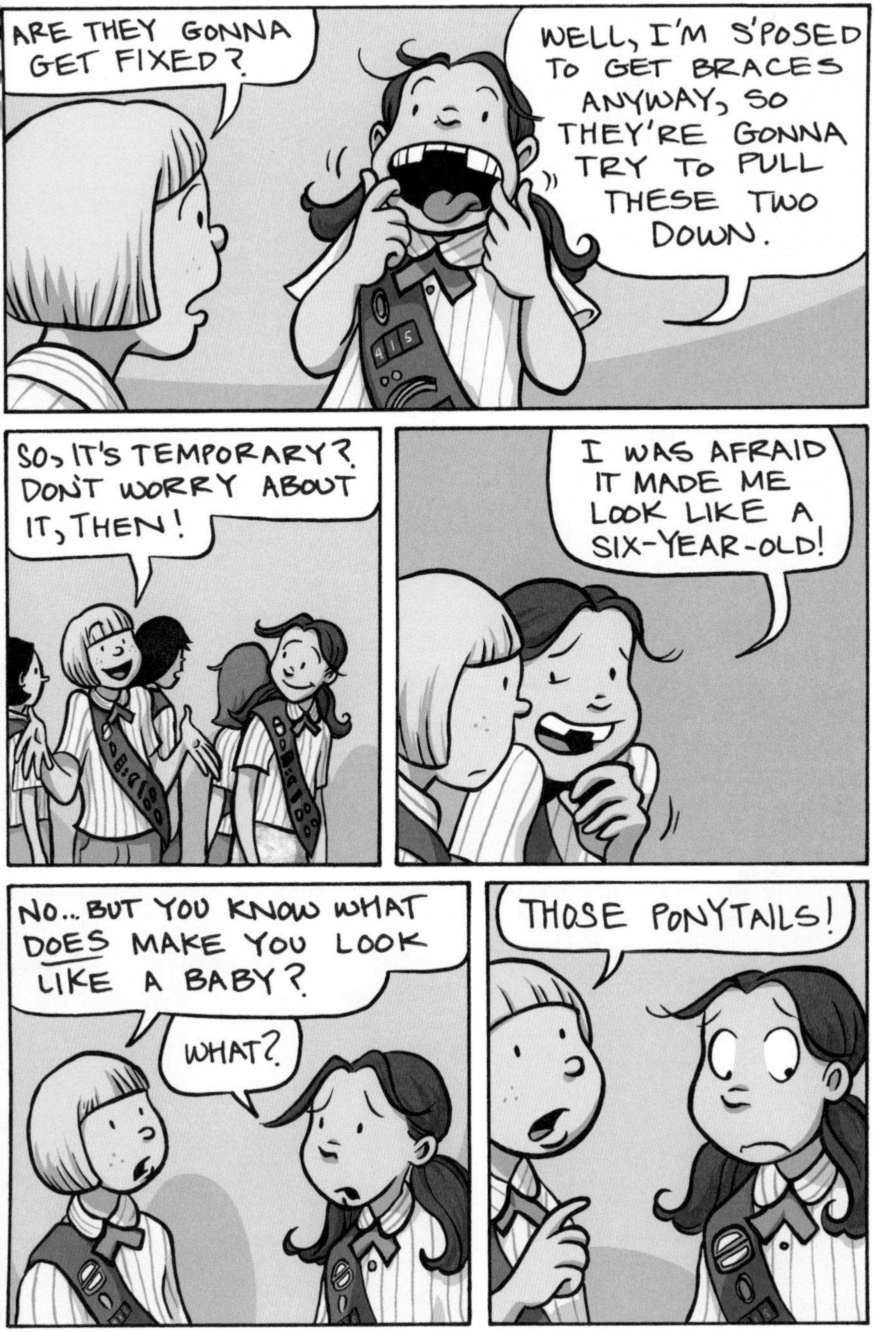
ARE THEY GONNA GET FIXED?
WELL, I'M S'POSED TO GET BRACES ANYWAY, SO THEY'RE GONNA TRY TO PULL THESE TWO DOWN.
SO, IT'S TEMPORARY? DON'T WORRY ABOUT IT, THEN!
I WAS AFRAID IT MADE ME LOOK LIKE A SIX-YEAR-OLD!
NO... BUT YOU KNOW WHAT DOES MAKE YOU LOOK LIKE A BABY?
WHAT?
THOSE PONYTAILS!

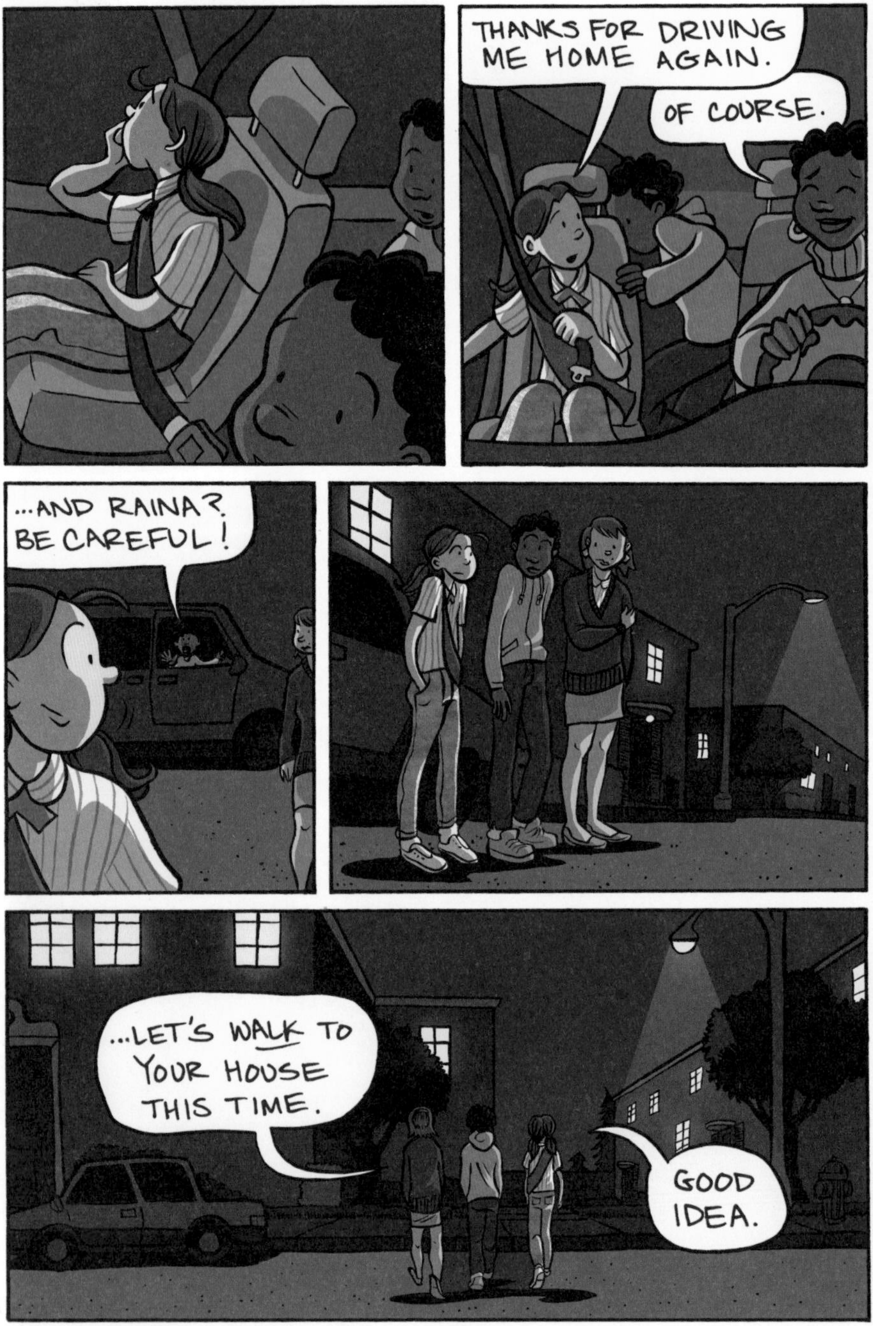
THANKS FOR DRIVING ME HOME AGAIN.
OF COURSE.
...AND RAINA? BE CAREFUL!
...LET'S WALK TO YOUR HOUSE THIS TIME.
GOOD IDEA.

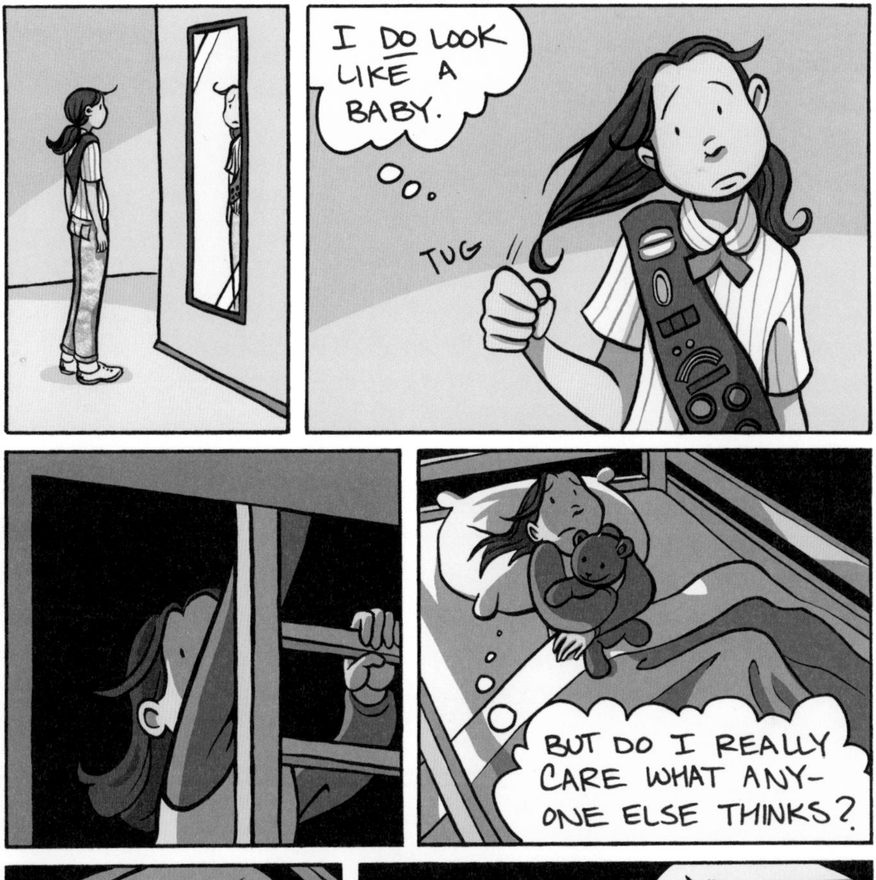
I DO LOOK LIKE A BABY.
TUG
BUT DO I REALLY CARE WHAT ANY-ONE ELSE THINKS?
...YES.

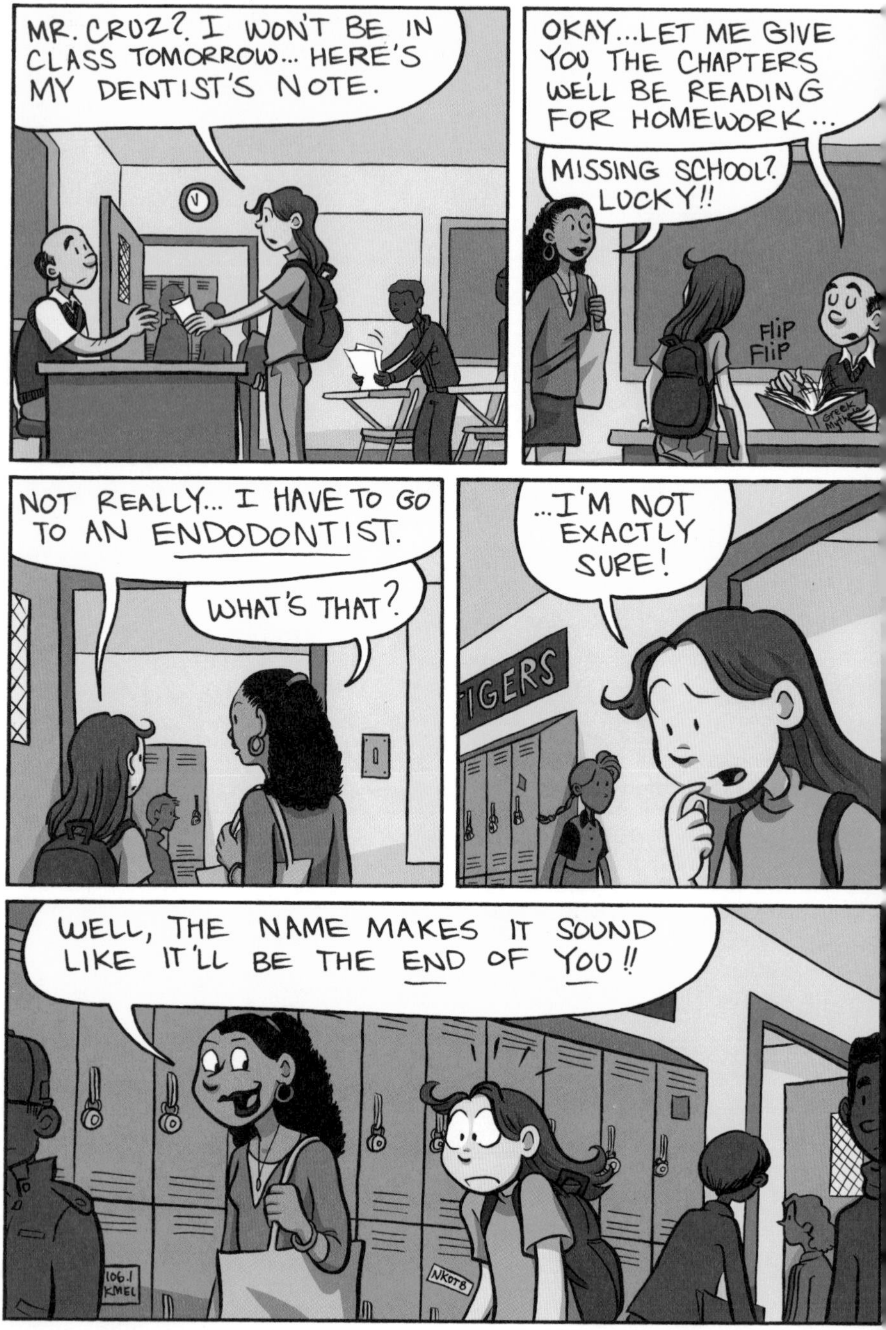
MR. CRUZ? I WON'T BE IN CLASS TOMORROW... HERE'S MY DENTIST'S NOTE.
OKAY...LET ME GIVE YOU THE CHAPTERS WE'LL BE READING FOR HOMEWORK...
MISSING SCHOOL? LUCKY!!
FLIP FLIP
GREEK MYTHS
NOT REALLY... I HAVE TO GO TO AN ENDODONTIST.
WHAT'S THAT?
...I'M NOT EXACTLY SURE!
TIGERS
WELL, THE NAME MAKES IT SOUND LIKE IT'LL BE THE END OF YOU!!
106.1 KMEL
NKOTB

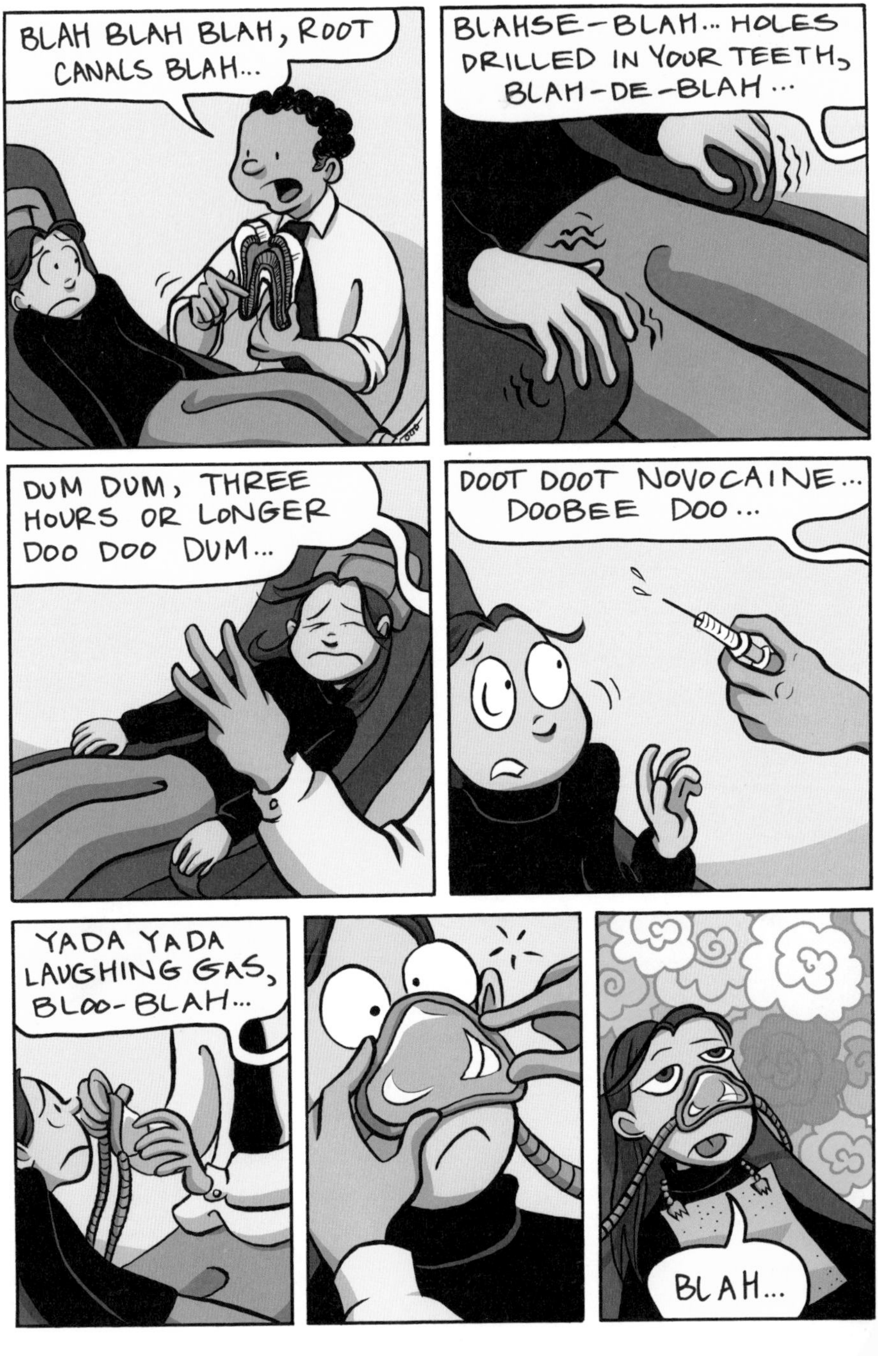
BLAH BLAH BLAH, ROOT CANALS BLAH...
BLAHSE-BLAH... HOLES DRILLED IN YOUR TEETH, BLAH-DE-BLAH...
DUM DUM, THREE HOURS OR LONGER DOO DOO DUM...
DOOT DOOT NOVOCAINE... DOOBEE DOO...
YADA YADA LAUGHING GAS, BLOO-BLAH...
BLAH...

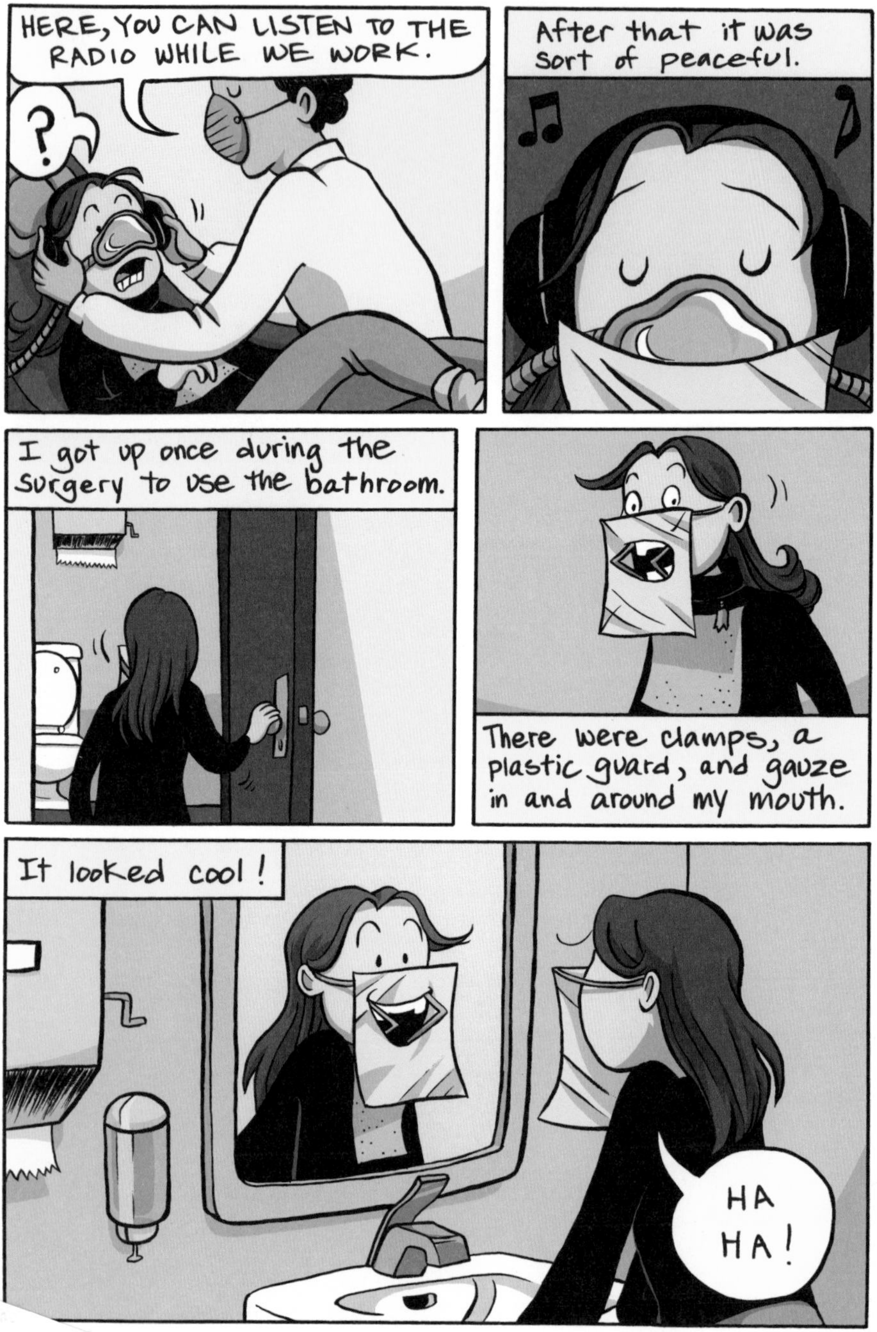
HERE, YOU CAN LISTEN TO THE RADIO WHILE WE WORK.
?
After that it was sort of peaceful.
I got up once during the surgery to use the bathroom.
There were clamps, a plastic guard, and gauze in and around my mouth.
It looked cool!
HA HA!

They had to give me several novocaine shots because they kept wearing off and things would start to hurt.

THERE WE GO.

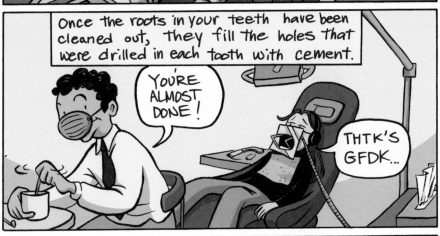

Once the roots in your teeth have been cleaned out, they fill the holes that were drilled in each tooth with cement.

YOU'RE ALMOST DONE!

THTK'S GFDK...

The cement is sealed with a red-hot metal tool...

...which I SMELLED as it accidentally touched the roof of my mouth before I felt it.

HISSSSS

OOOOO! SORRY!

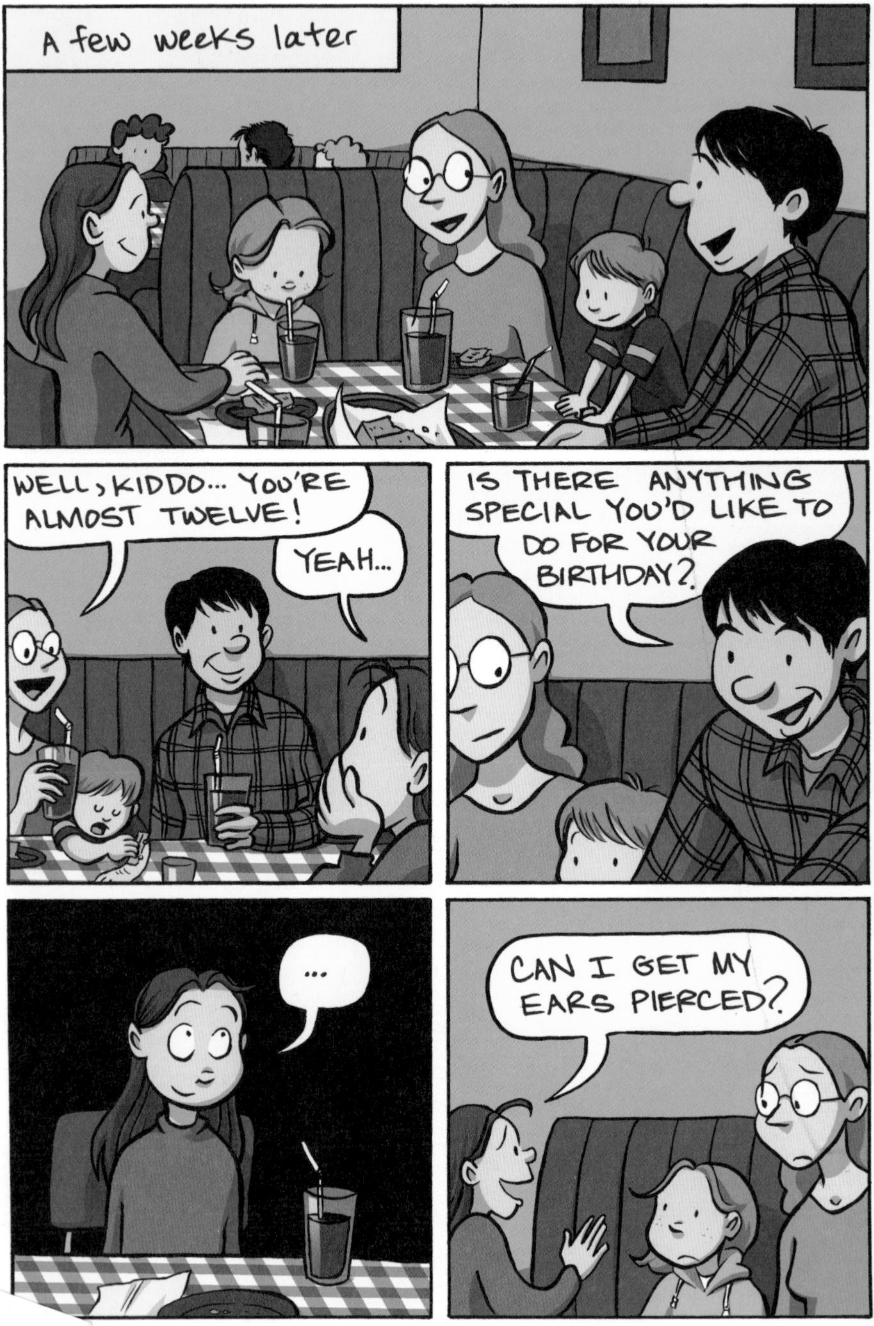
A few weeks later
WELL, KIDDO... YOU'RE ALMOST TWELVE!
YEAH...
IS THERE ANYTHING SPECIAL YOU'D LIKE TO DO FOR YOUR BIRTHDAY?
...
CAN I GET MY EARS PIERCED?

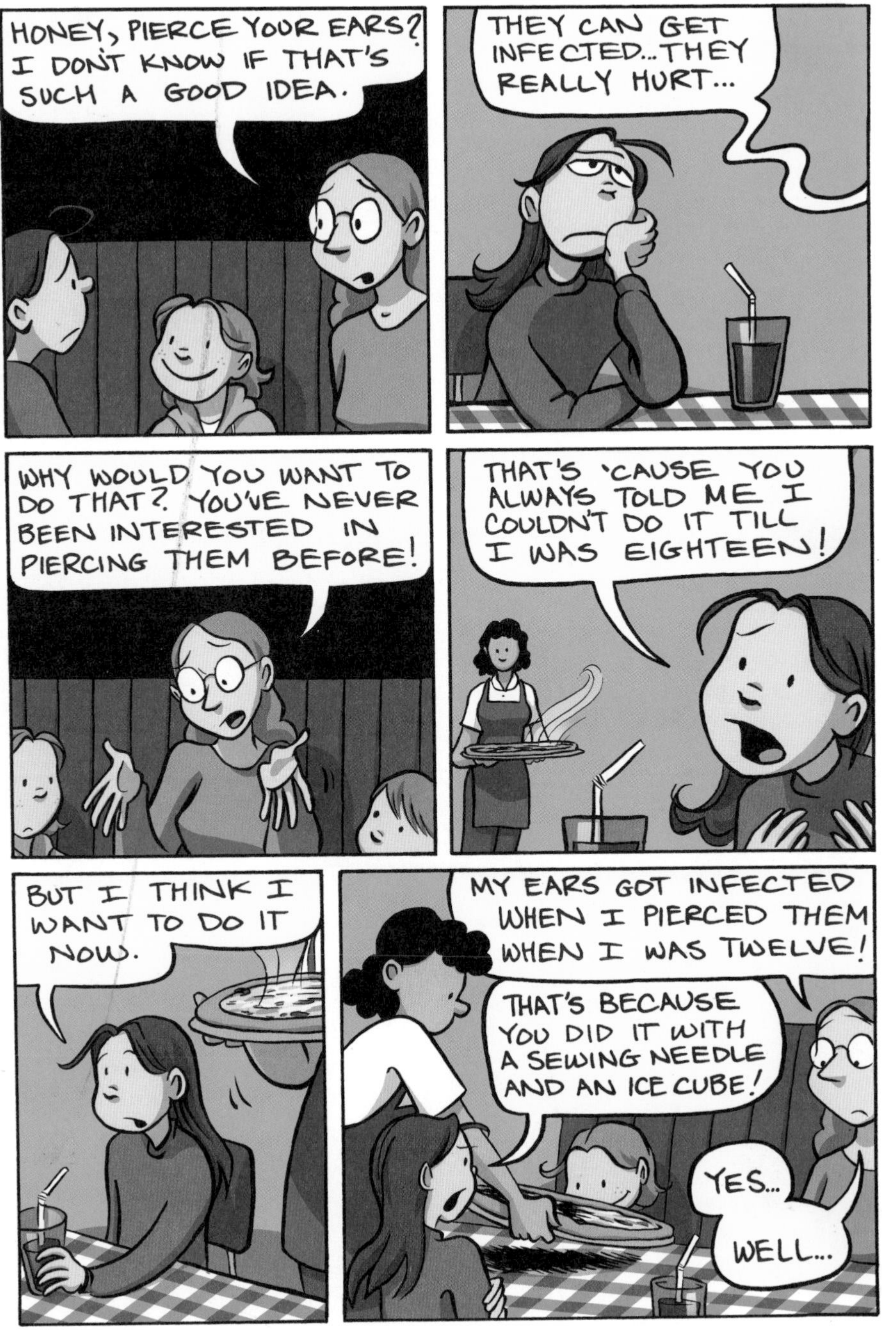
HONEY, PIERCE YOUR EARS? I DON'T KNOW IF THAT'S SUCH A GOOD IDEA.
THEY CAN GET INFECTED... THEY REALLY HURT...
WHY WOULD YOU WANT TO DO THAT? YOU'VE NEVER BEEN INTERESTED IN PIERCING THEM BEFORE!
THAT'S 'CAUSE YOU ALWAYS TOLD ME I COULDN'T DO IT TILL I WAS EIGHTEEN!
BUT I THINK I WANT TO DO IT NOW.
MY EARS GOT INFECTED WHEN I PIERCED THEM WHEN I WAS TWELVE!
THAT'S BECAUSE YOU DID IT WITH A SEWING NEEDLE AND AN ICE CUBE!
YES...
WELL...

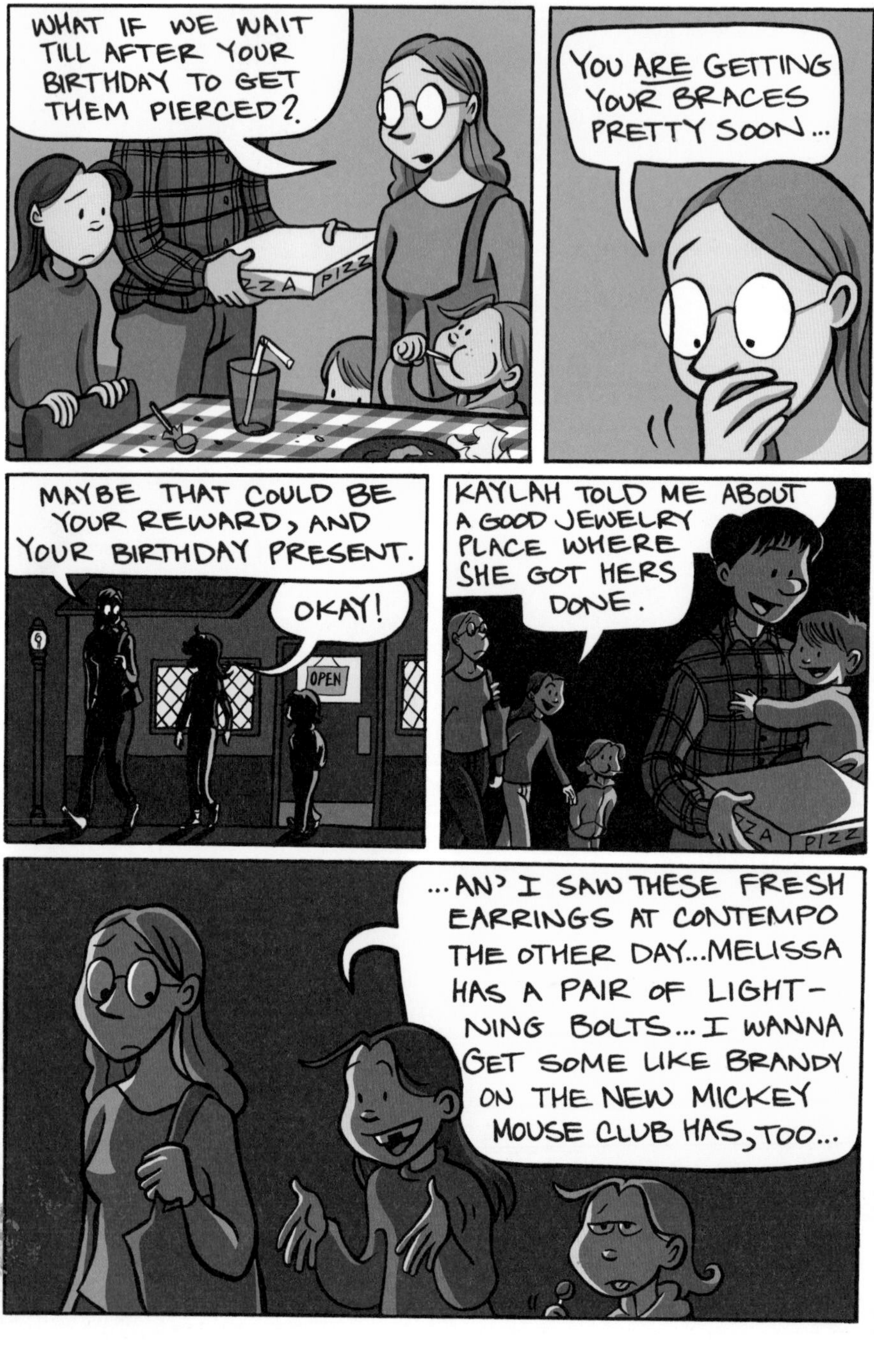
WHAT IF WE WAIT TILL AFTER YOUR BIRTHDAY TO GET THEM PIERCED?
YOU ARE GETTING YOUR BRACES PRETTY SOON...
MAYBE THAT COULD BE YOUR REWARD, AND YOUR BIRTHDAY PRESENT.
OKAY!
OPEN
KAYLAH TOLD ME ABOUT A GOOD JEWELRY PLACE WHERE SHE GOT HERS DONE.
...AN' I SAW THESE FRESH EARRINGS AT CONTEMPO THE OTHER DAY...MELISSA HAS A PAIR OF LIGHTNING BOLTS... I WANNA GET SOME LIKE BRANDY ON THE NEW MICKEY MOUSE CLUB HAS, TOO...

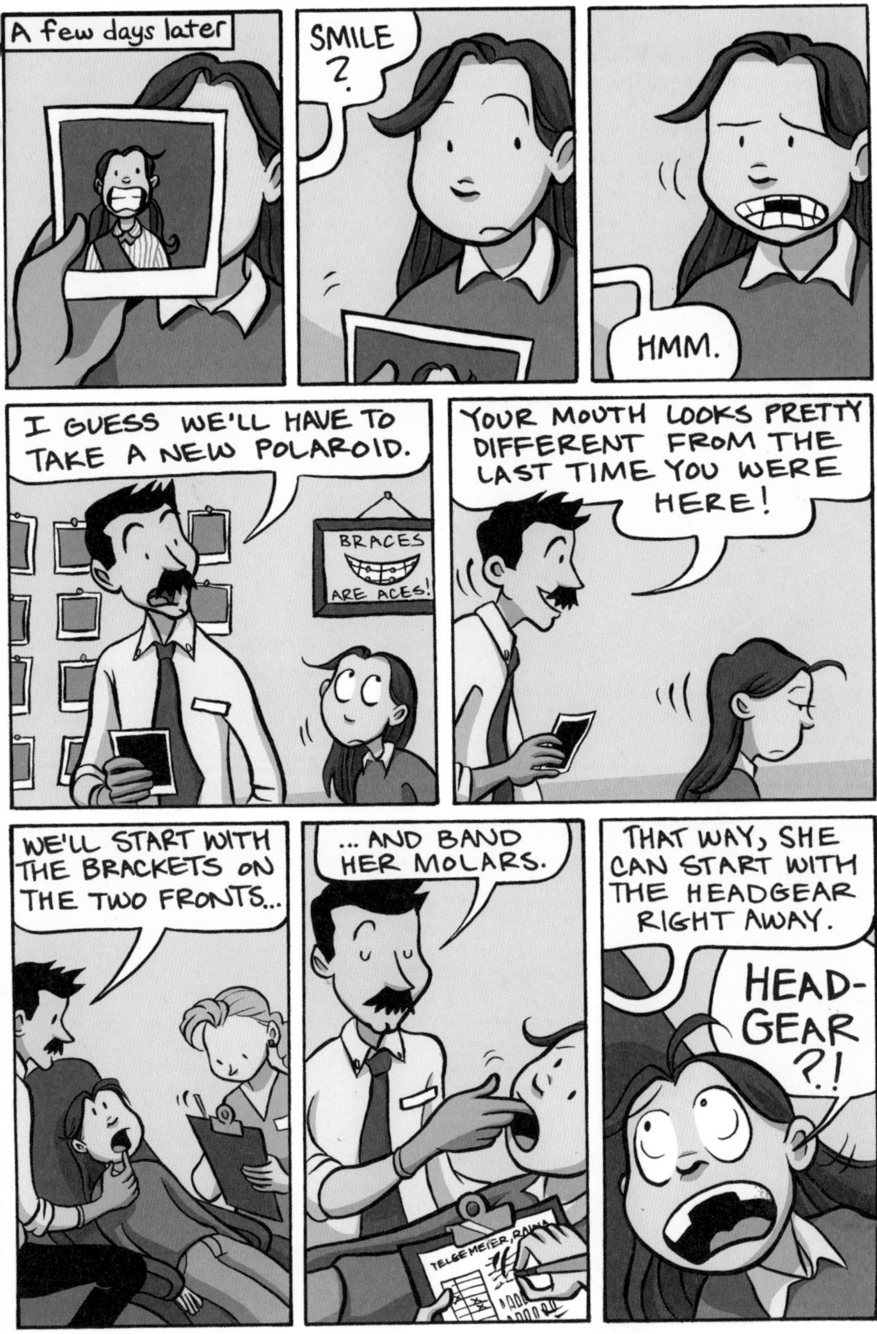
A few days later
SMILE ?
HMM.
I GUESS WE'LL HAVE TO TAKE A NEW POLAROID.
BRACES ARE ACES!
YOUR MOUTH LOOKS PRETTY DIFFERENT FROM THE LAST TIME YOU WERE HERE!
WE'LL START WITH THE BRACKETS ON THE TWO FRONTS...
... AND BAND HER MOLARS.
TELGEMEIER, RAINA
THAT WAY, SHE CAN START WITH THE HEADGEAR RIGHT AWAY.
HEAD-GEAR ?!

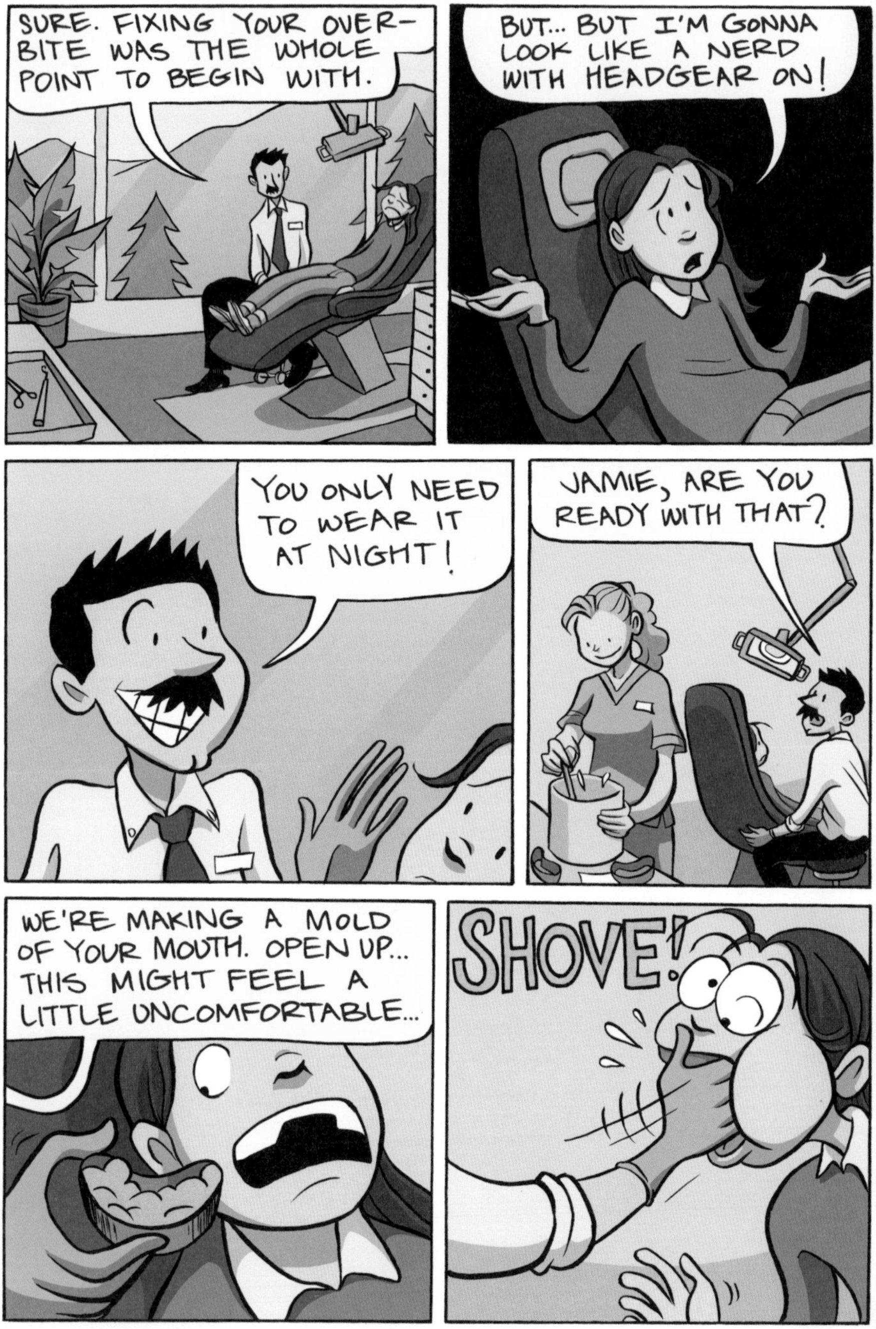
SURE. FIXING YOUR OVER-BITE WAS THE WHOLE POINT TO BEGIN WITH.
BUT... BUT I'M GONNA LOOK LIKE A NERD WITH HEADGEAR ON!
YOU ONLY NEED TO WEAR IT AT NIGHT!
JAMIE, ARE YOU READY WITH THAT?
WE'RE MAKING A MOLD OF YOUR MOUTH. OPEN UP... THIS MIGHT FEEL A LITTLE UNCOMFORTABLE...
SHOVE!

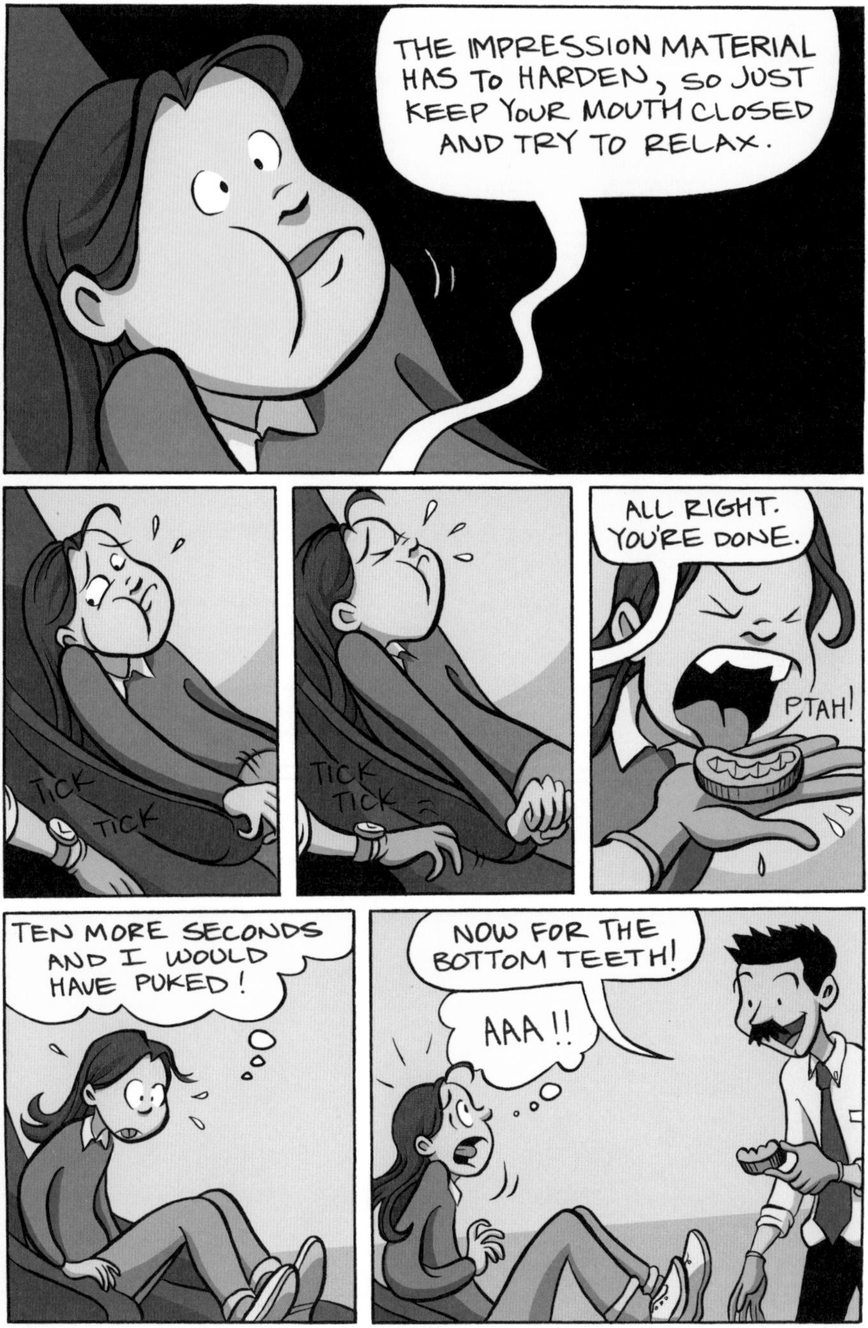
THE IMPRESSION MATERIAL HAS TO HARDEN, SO JUST KEEP YOUR MOUTH CLOSED AND TRY TO RELAX.
TICK
TICK
TICK
TICK
ALL RIGHT. YOU'RE DONE.
PTAH!
TEN MORE SECONDS AND I WOULD HAVE PUKED!
NOW FOR THE BOTTOM TEETH!
AAA!!

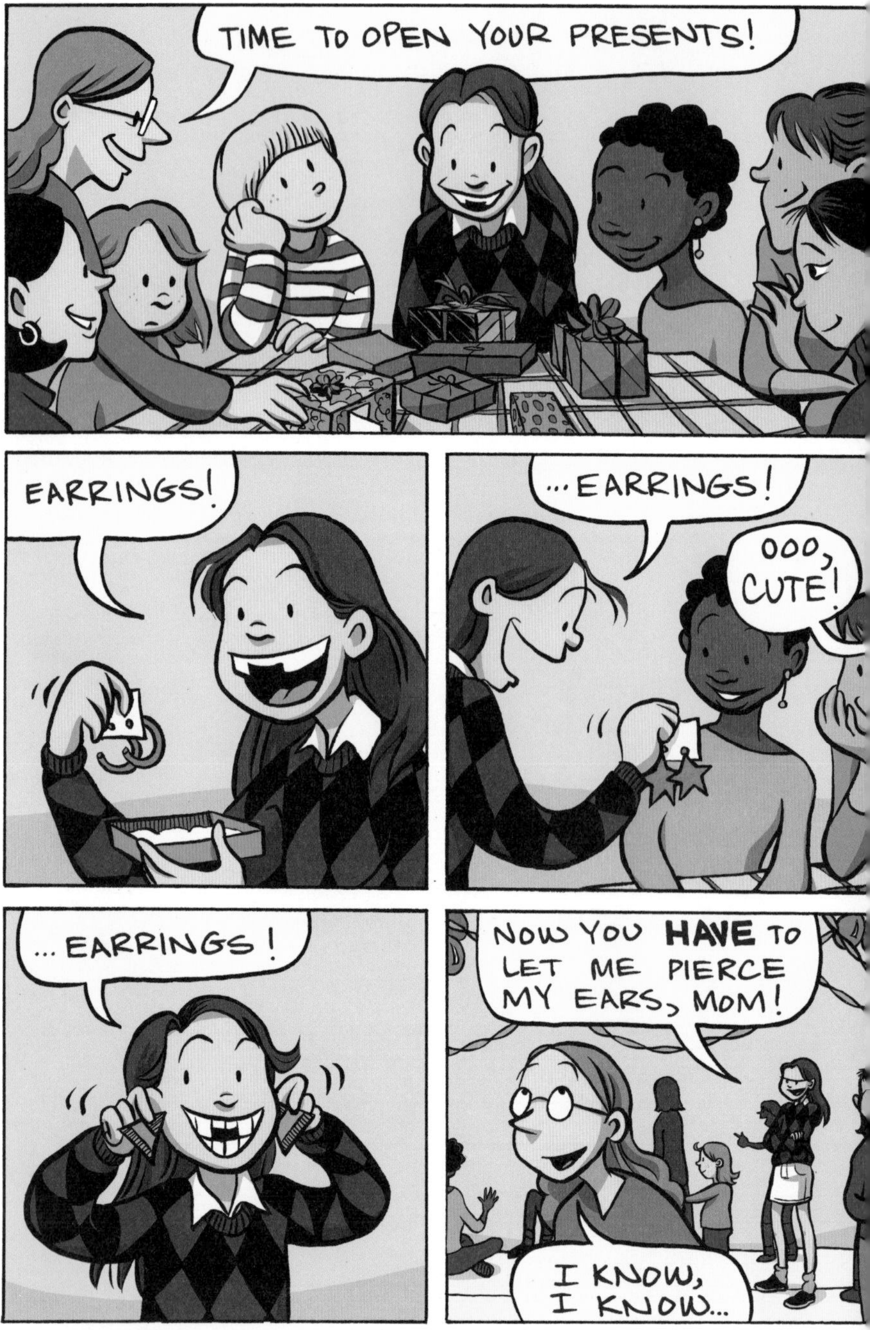
TIME TO OPEN YOUR PRESENTS!
EARRINGS!
...EARRINGS!
OOO, CUTE!
...EARRINGS!
NOW YOU **HAVE** TO LET ME PIERCE MY EARS, MOM!
I KNOW, I KNOW...

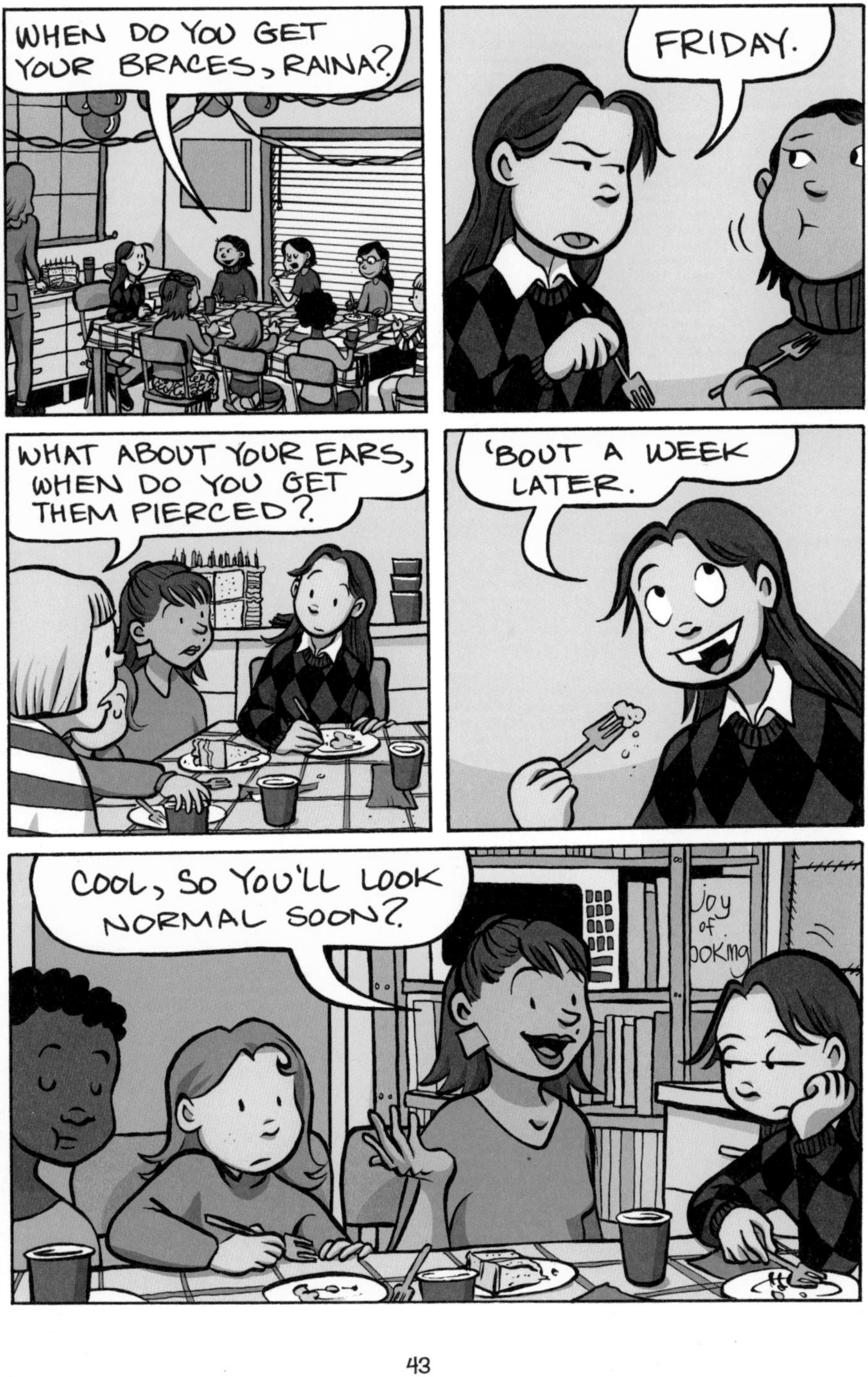

WHEN DO YOU GET YOUR BRACES, RAINA?
FRIDAY.
WHAT ABOUT YOUR EARS, WHEN DO YOU GET THEM PIERCED?
'BOUT A WEEK LATER.
COOL, SO YOU'LL LOOK NORMAL SOON?

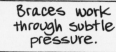

44

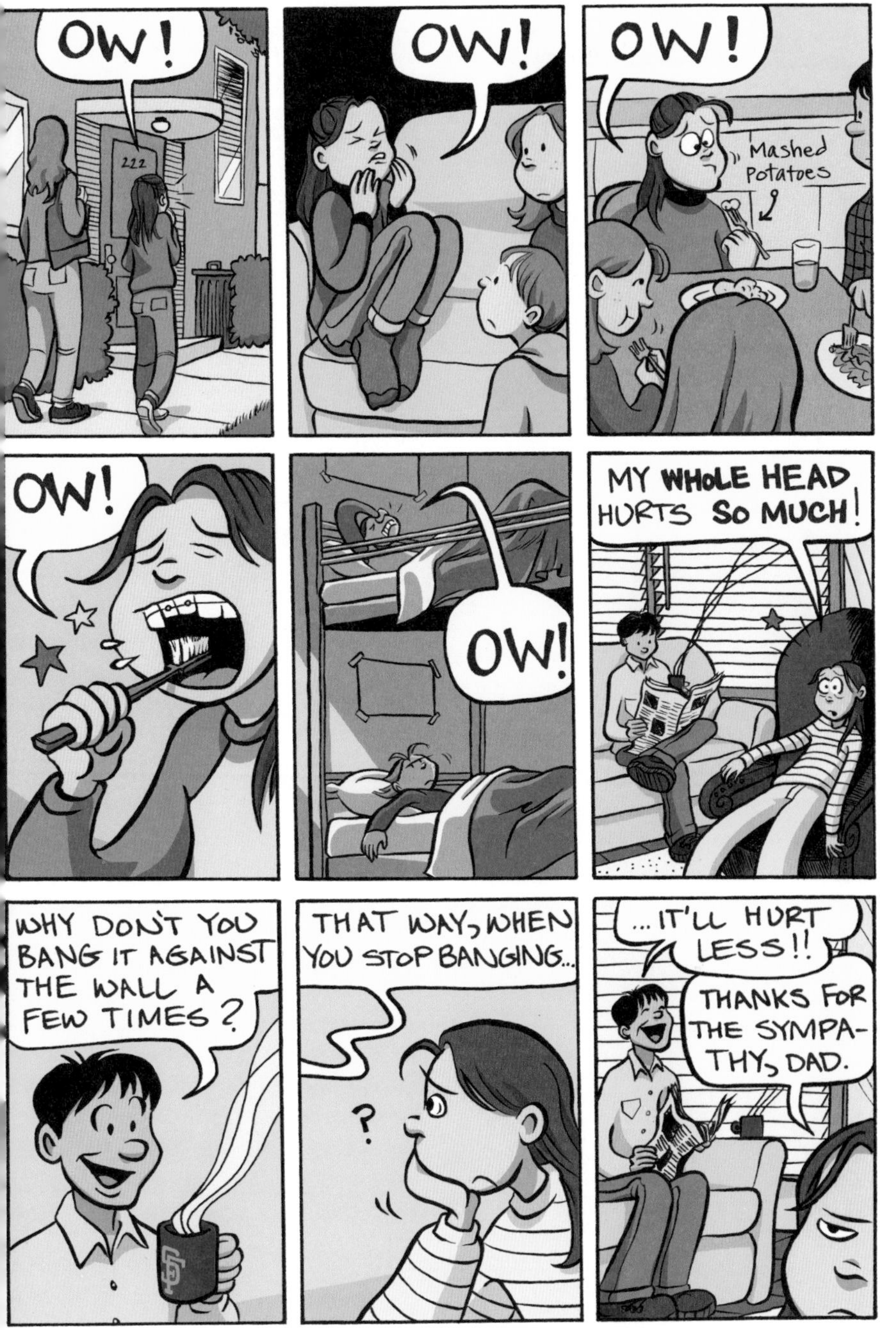
OW!
OW!
OW!
Mashed Potatoes
OW!
OW!
MY WHOLE HEAD HURTS SO MUCH!
WHY DON'T YOU BANG IT AGAINST THE WALL A FEW TIMES?
THAT WAY, WHEN YOU STOP BANGING...
?
...IT'LL HURT LESS!!
THANKS FOR THE SYMPATHY, DAD.

AW, C'MON ... LET'S GO SEE A MOVIE OR SOMETHING. WANT TO COME, WILL?

YEAH!

CAN WE GET POP-CORN, DADDY?

HMM ...

RAINA'S NOT SUPPOSED TO EAT POP-CORN WHILE SHE HAS HER BRACES...

Glaming the Cube   3:30 7:
Troop Beverly Hills   1:00 4:
Police Academy 6   3:00 5:

EH, IT'S OKAY... WILL CAN STILL HAVE SOME.

I'M NOT THAT INTO POPCORN ANYWAY.

OF COURSE, AS SOON AS YOU CAN'T HAVE SOMETHING, IT STARTS TO SMELL AMAZING!!

46

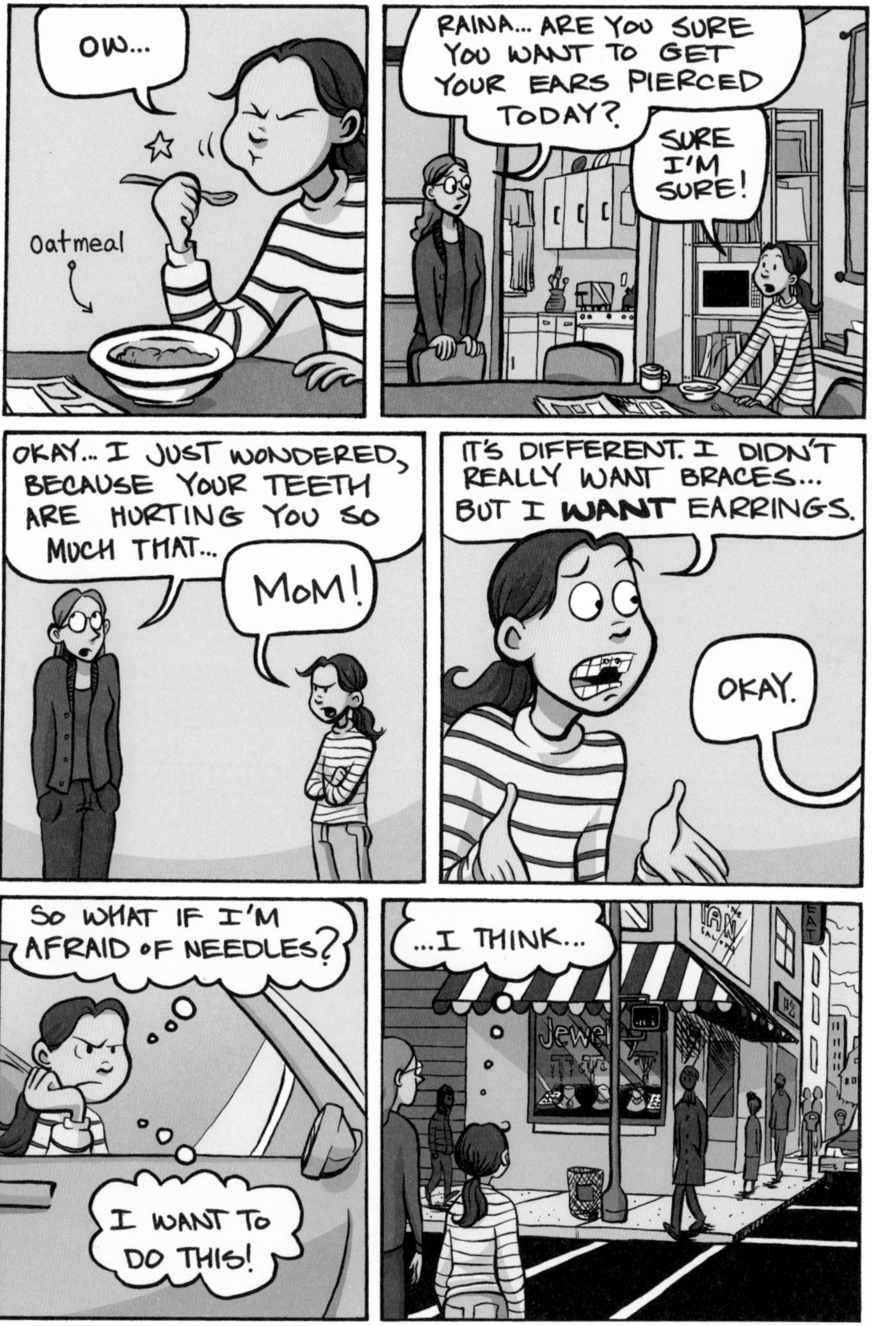
OW...
Oatmeal
RAINA... ARE YOU SURE YOU WANT TO GET YOUR EARS PIERCED TODAY?
SURE I'M SURE!
OKAY... I JUST WONDERED, BECAUSE YOUR TEETH ARE HURTING YOU SO MUCH THAT...
MOM!
IT'S DIFFERENT. I DIDN'T REALLY WANT BRACES... BUT I **WANT** EARRINGS.
OKAY.
SO WHAT IF I'M AFRAID OF NEEDLES?
I WANT TO DO THIS!
...I THINK...
Jewelry

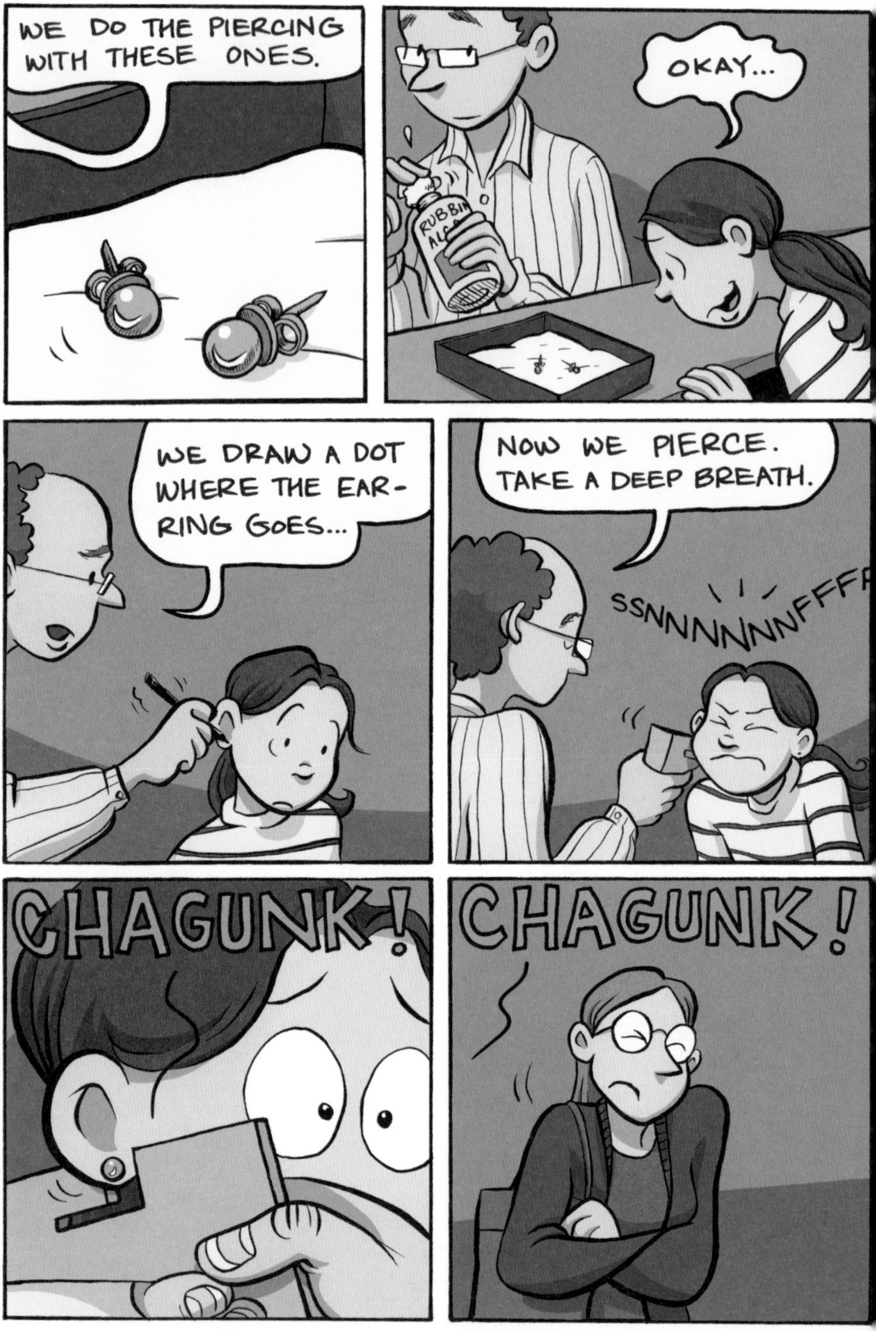
WE DO THE PIERCING WITH THESE ONES.
OKAY...
WE DRAW A DOT WHERE THE EAR-RING GOES...
NOW WE PIERCE. TAKE A DEEP BREATH.
SSNNNNNNNFFFF
CHAGUNK!
CHAGUNK!

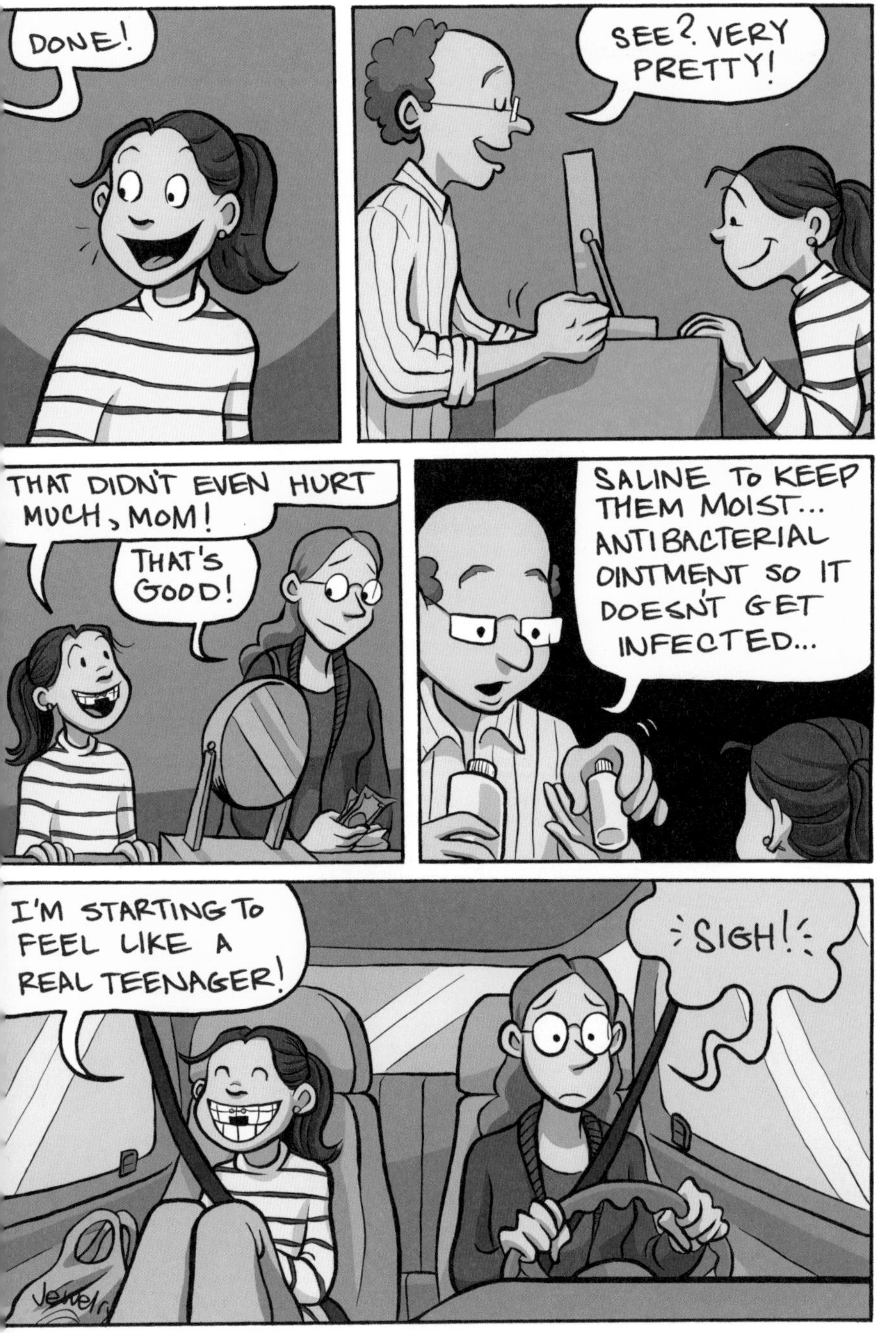
DONE!
SEE? VERY PRETTY!
THAT DIDN'T EVEN HURT MUCH, MOM!
THAT'S GOOD!
SALINE TO KEEP THEM MOIST... ANTIBACTERIAL OINTMENT SO IT DOESN'T GET INFECTED...
I'M STARTING TO FEEL LIKE A REAL TEENAGER!
SIGH!

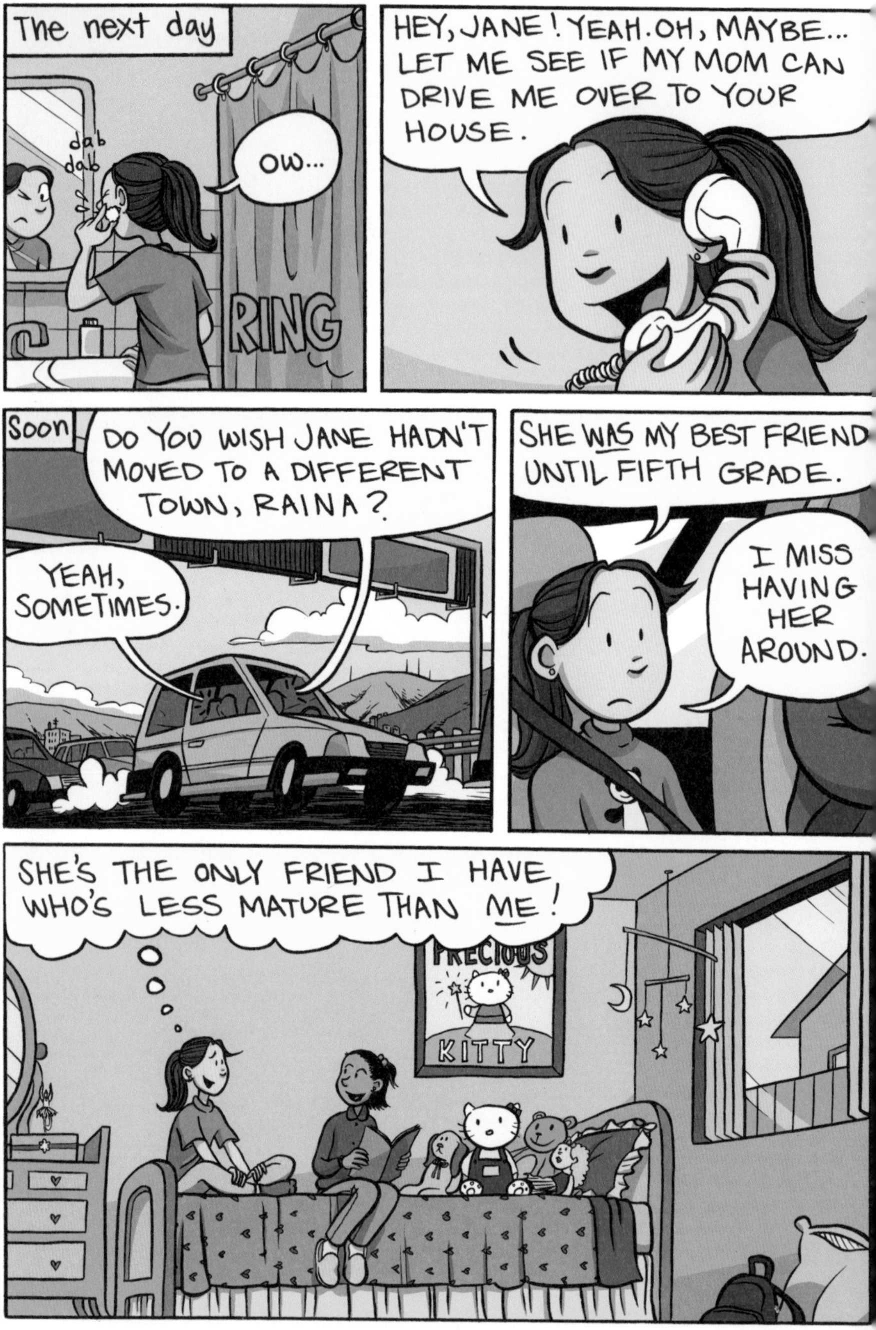
The next day
dab
dab
OW...
RING
HEY, JANE! YEAH. OH, MAYBE... LET ME SEE IF MY MOM CAN DRIVE ME OVER TO YOUR HOUSE.
Soon
DO YOU WISH JANE HADN'T MOVED TO A DIFFERENT TOWN, RAINA?
YEAH, SOMETIMES.
SHE WAS MY BEST FRIEND UNTIL FIFTH GRADE.
I MISS HAVING HER AROUND.
SHE'S THE ONLY FRIEND I HAVE WHO'S LESS MATURE THAN ME!
PRECIOUS
KITTY

SO... WHAT DO YOU THINK?

YOU LOOK ABOUT THE SAME.

AW, C'MON, JANE. DO I LOOK COOLER? OLDER?

I GUESS.

HEY, IS YOUR DAD HERE? MAYBE HE COULD DRIVE US TO THE MALL!

HE'S AT WORK.

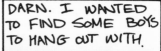

DARN. I WANTED TO FIND SOME BOYS TO HANG OUT WITH.

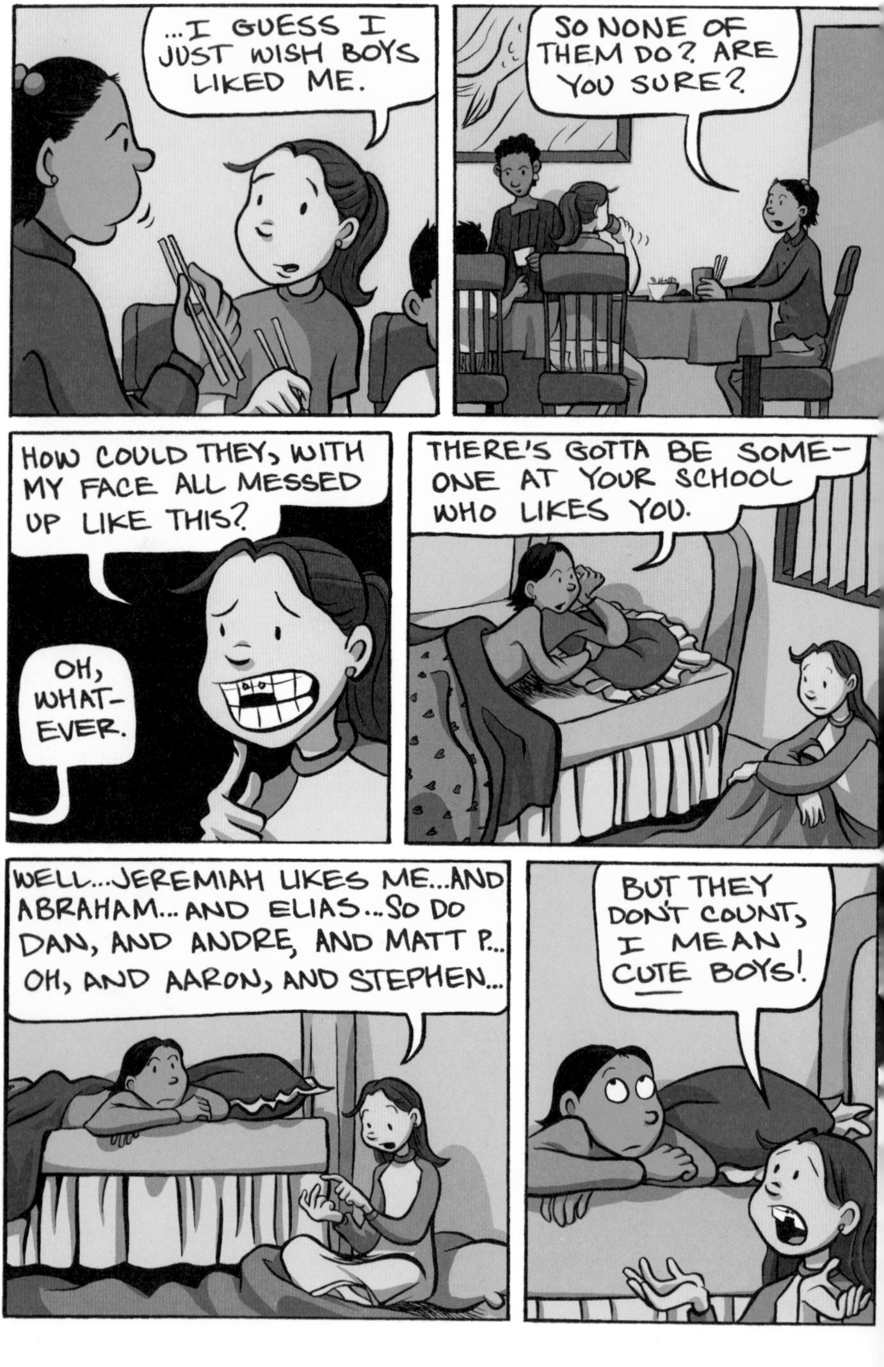
...I GUESS I JUST WISH BOYS LIKED ME.
SO NONE OF THEM DO? ARE YOU SURE?
HOW COULD THEY, WITH MY FACE ALL MESSED UP LIKE THIS?
OH, WHAT-EVER.
THERE'S GOTTA BE SOME-ONE AT YOUR SCHOOL WHO LIKES YOU.
WELL...JEREMIAH LIKES ME...AND ABRAHAM... AND ELIAS...SO DO DAN, AND ANDRE, AND MATT P... OH, AND AARON, AND STEPHEN...
BUT THEY DON'T COUNT, I MEAN CUTE BOYS!

CHAPTER THREE

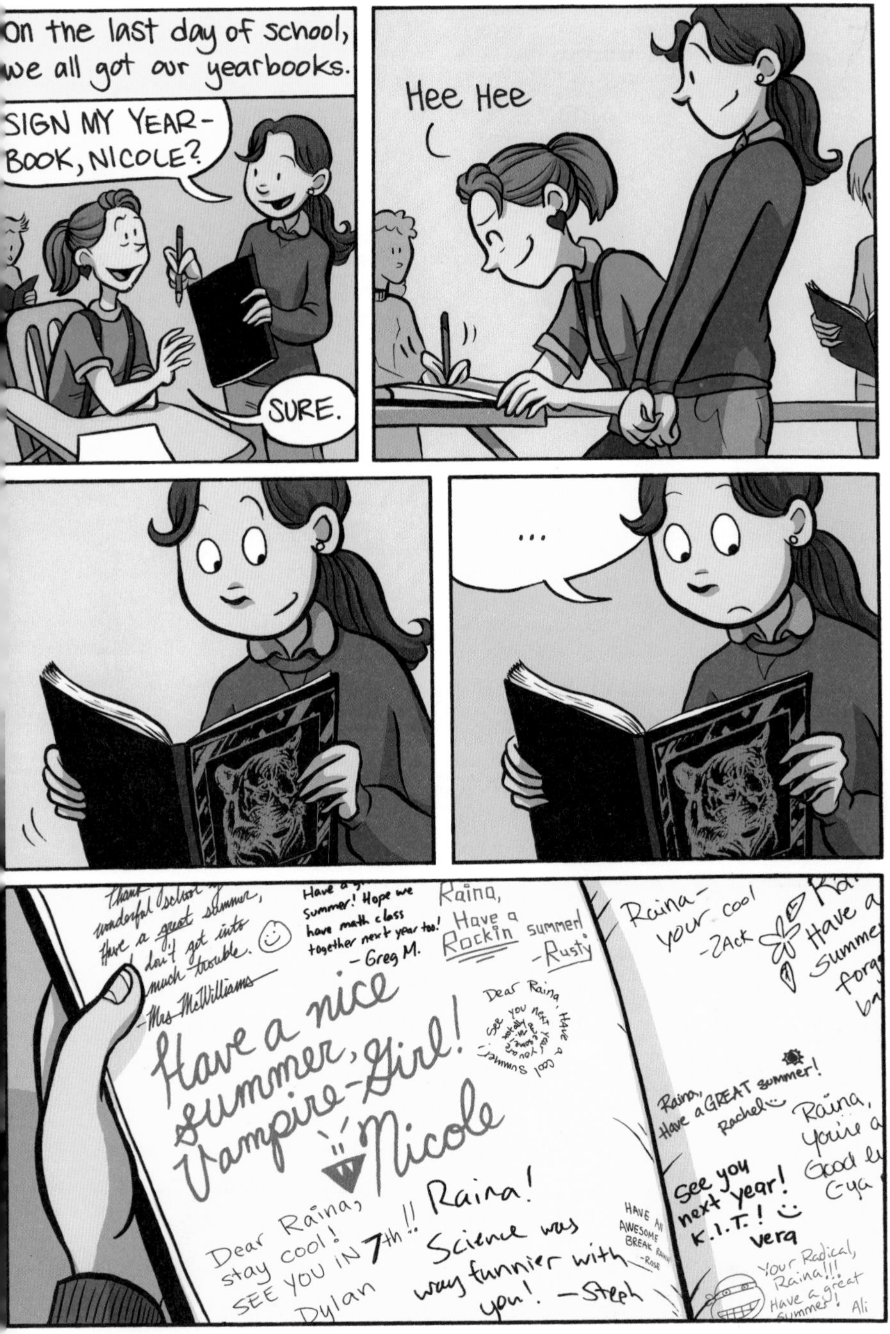

On the last day of school, we all got our yearbooks.
SIGN MY YEAR-BOOK, NICOLE?
SURE.
Hee Hee
...
Have a great summer,
don't get into much trouble.
-Mrs McWilliams
Summer! Hope we have math class together next year too!
-Greg M.
Raina, Have a Rockin summer!
-Rusty
Have a nice summer, Vampire-Girl!
Nicole
Dear Raina, Have a cool summer!
Dear Raina, stay cool! SEE YOU IN 7th!!
Dylan
Raina! Science was way funnier with you! —Steph
HAVE AN AWESOME BREAK RAINA!
-ROSE
Raina- your cool
-ZACK
Raina, Have a GREAT summer!
Rachel
See you next year! K.I.T.!
vera
Your Radical, Raina!!! Have a great summer!
Ali

That summer was pretty normal, as summers go.

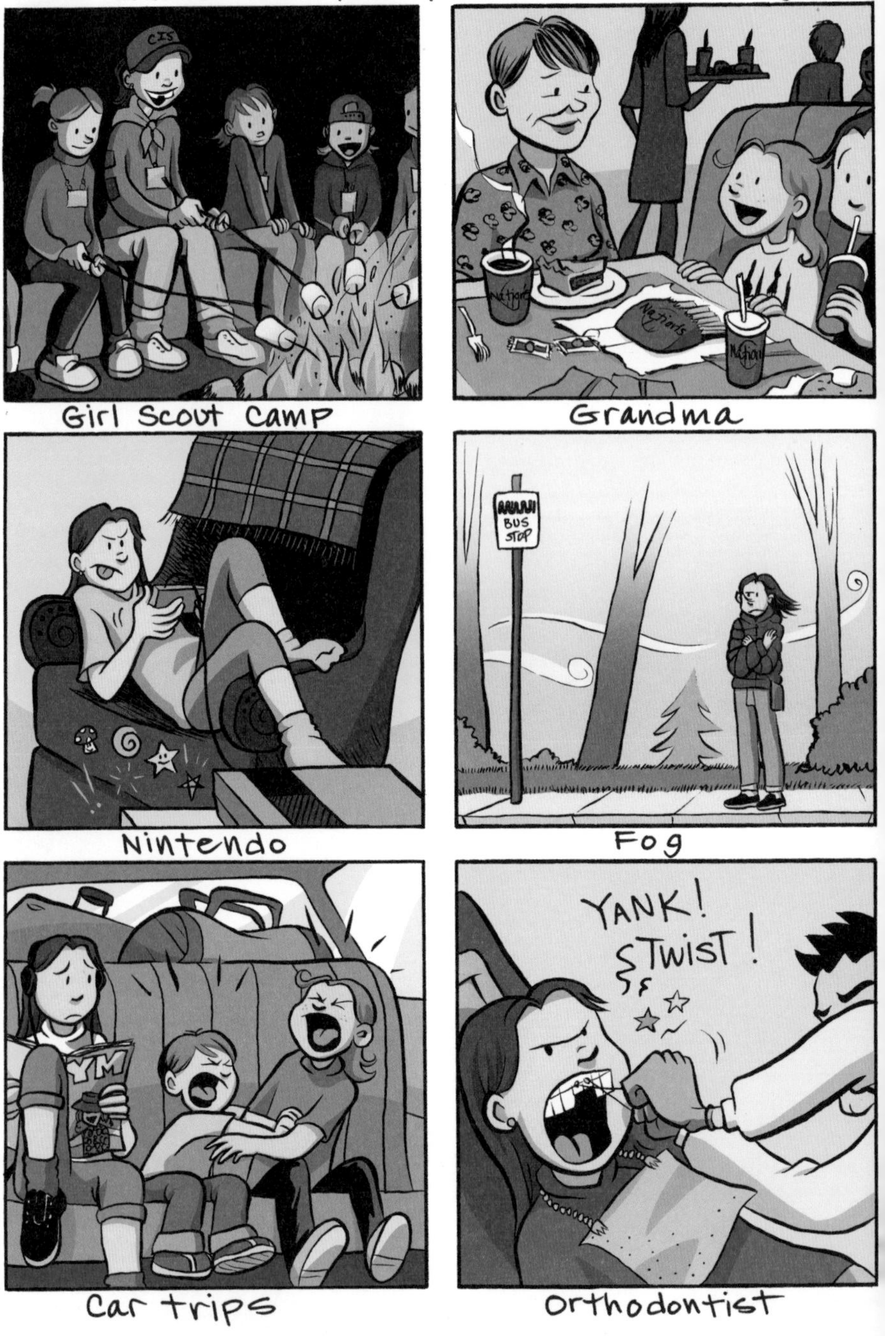
CIS
Girl Scout Camp
Nations
Grandma
Nintendo
BUS STOP
Fog
YM
Car trips
YANK!
TWIST!
Orthodontist

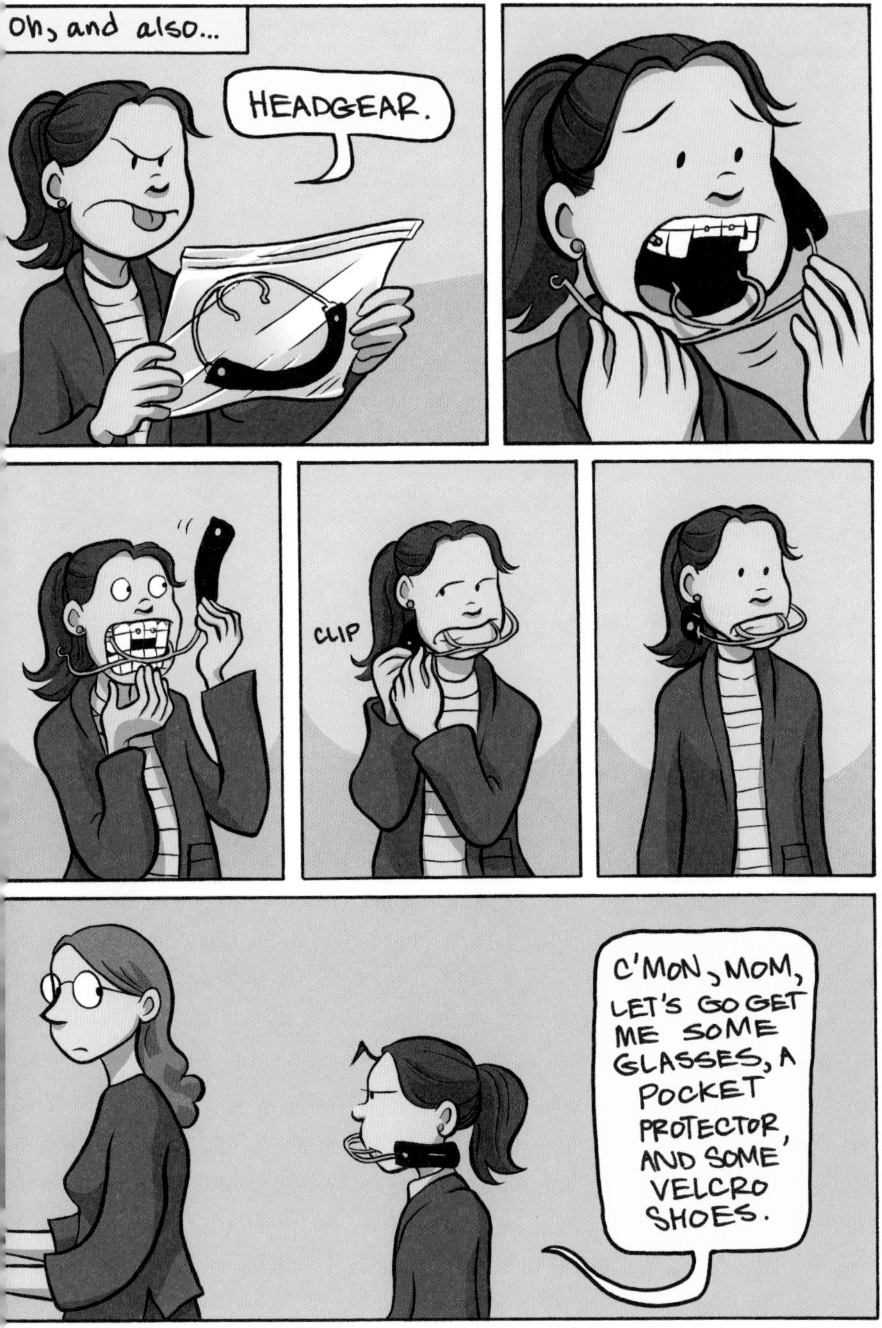
Oh, and also...
HEADGEAR.
CLIP
C'MON, MOM, LET'S GO GET ME SOME GLASSES, A POCKET PROTECTOR, AND SOME VELCRO SHOES.

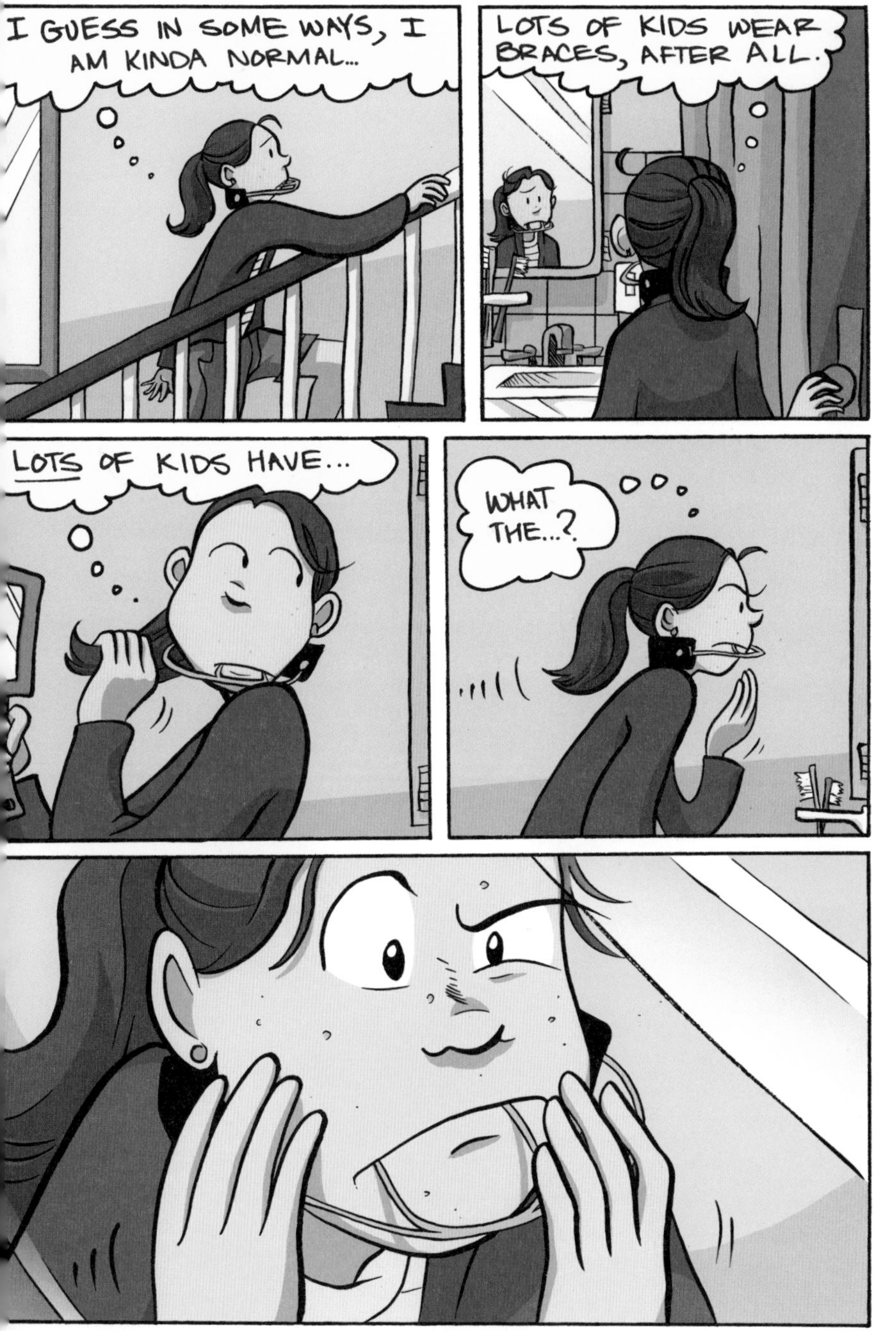
I GUESS IN SOME WAYS, I AM KINDA NORMAL...
LOTS OF KIDS WEAR BRACES, AFTER ALL.
LOTS OF KIDS HAVE...
WHAT THE...?

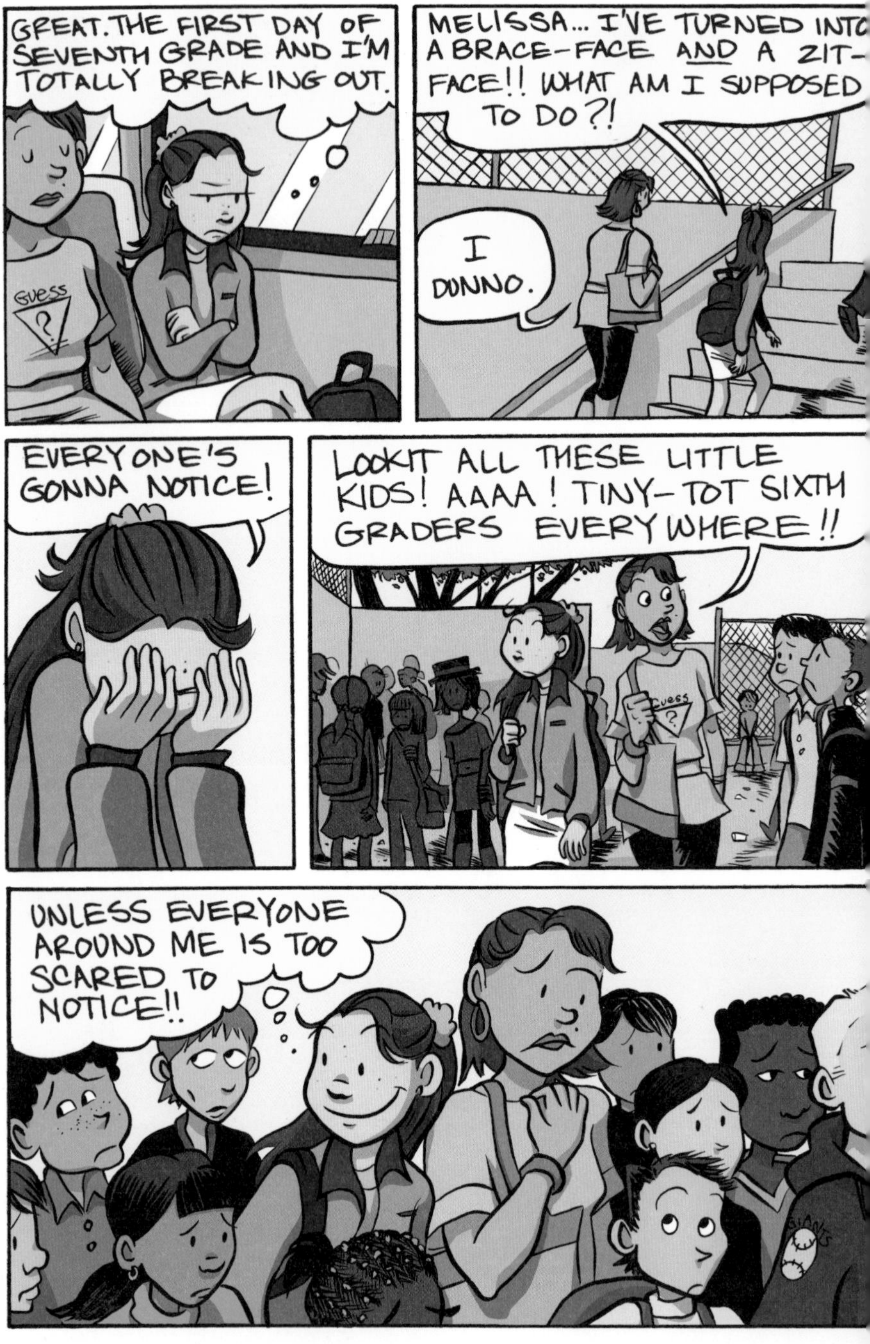
GREAT. THE FIRST DAY OF SEVENTH GRADE AND I'M TOTALLY BREAKING OUT.
MELISSA... I'VE TURNED INTO A BRACE-FACE AND A ZIT-FACE!! WHAT AM I SUPPOSED TO DO?!
I DUNNO.
GUESS
EVERYONE'S GONNA NOTICE!
LOOKIT ALL THESE LITTLE KIDS! AAAA! TINY-TOT SIXTH GRADERS EVERYWHERE!!
UNLESS EVERYONE AROUND ME IS TOO SCARED TO NOTICE!!
GIANTS

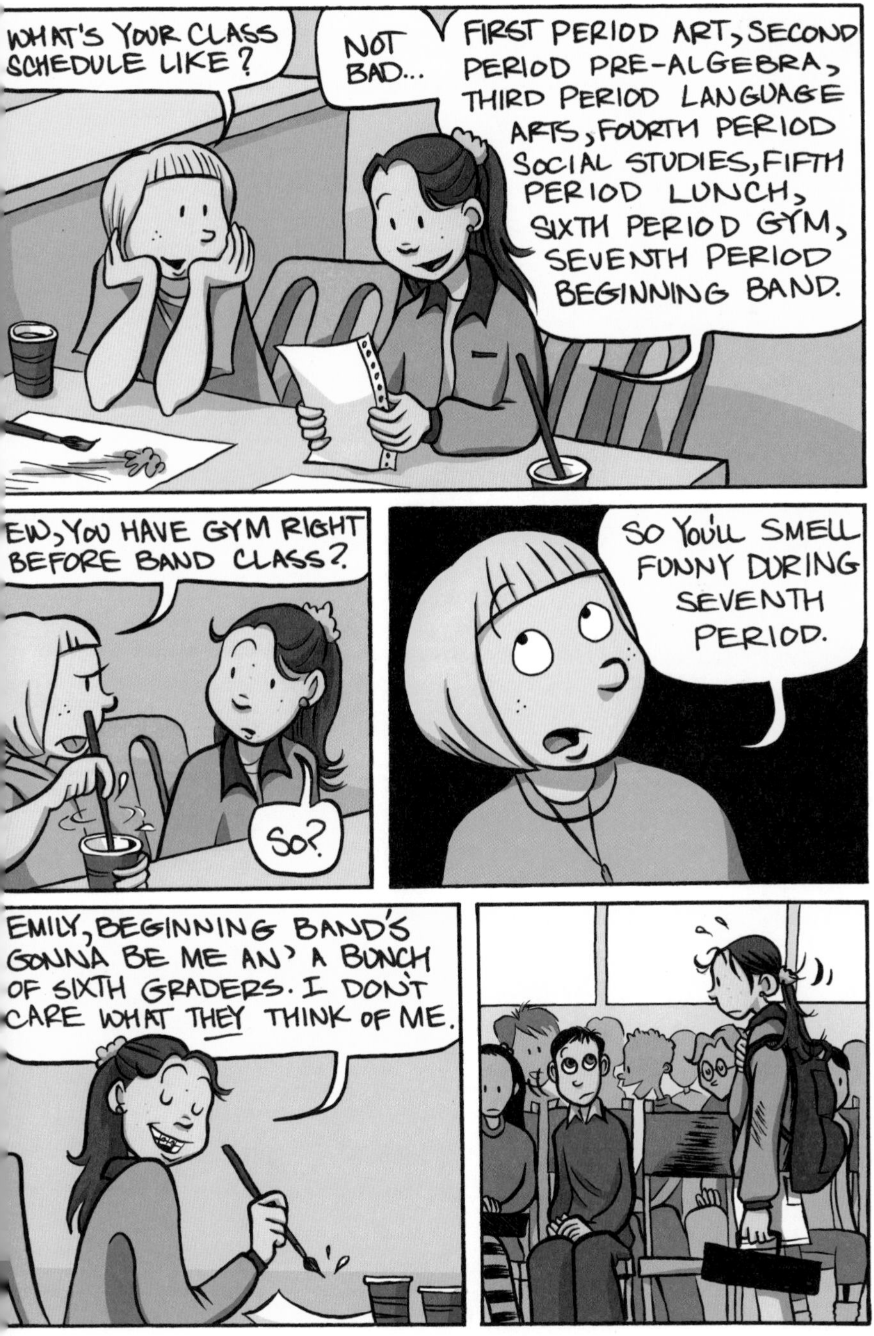
WHAT'S YOUR CLASS SCHEDULE LIKE?
NOT BAD...
FIRST PERIOD ART, SECOND PERIOD PRE-ALGEBRA, THIRD PERIOD LANGUAGE ARTS, FOURTH PERIOD SOCIAL STUDIES, FIFTH PERIOD LUNCH, SIXTH PERIOD GYM, SEVENTH PERIOD BEGINNING BAND.
EW, YOU HAVE GYM RIGHT BEFORE BAND CLASS?
SO?
SO YOU'LL SMELL FUNNY DURING SEVENTH PERIOD.
EMILY, BEGINNING BAND'S GONNA BE ME AN' A BUNCH OF SIXTH GRADERS. I DON'T CARE WHAT THEY THINK OF ME.

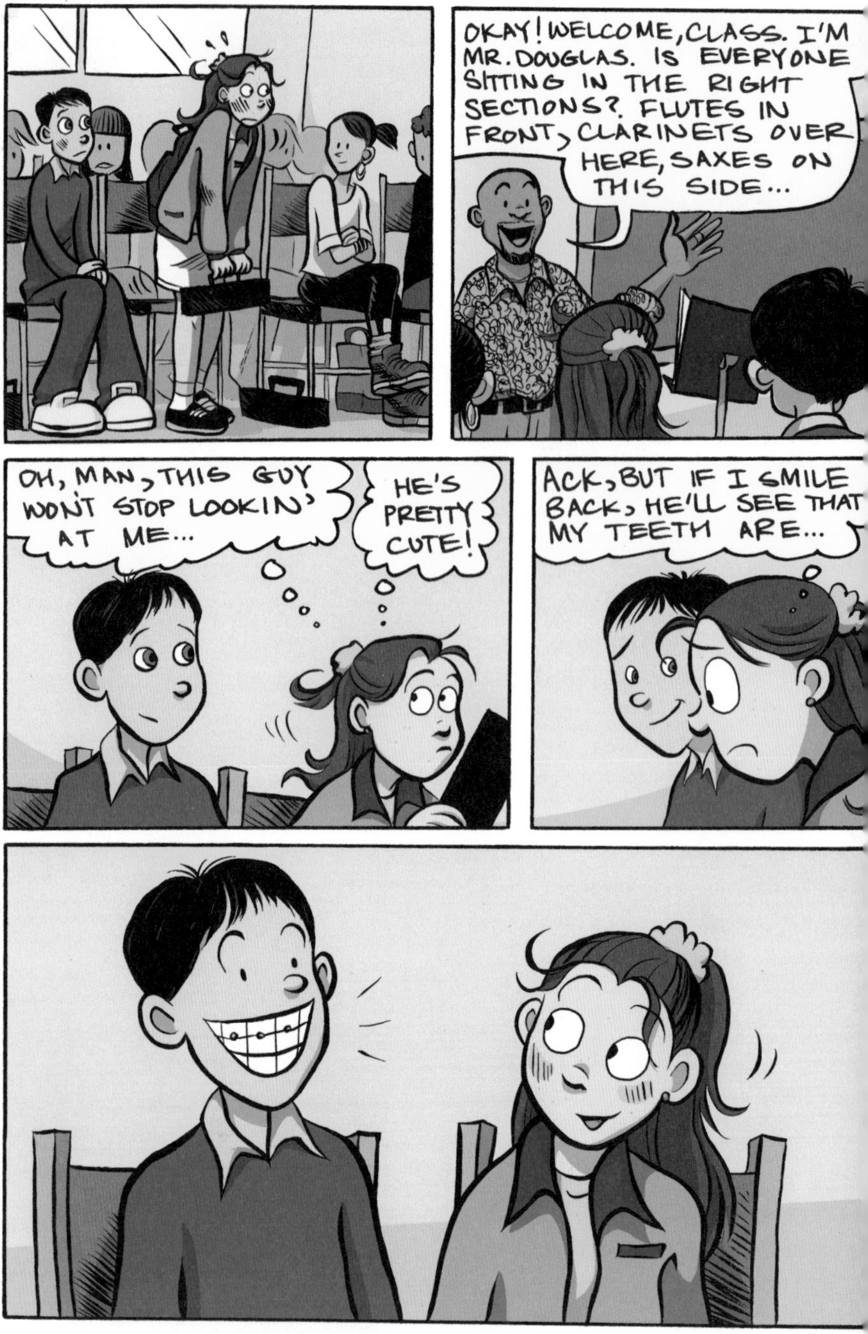
OKAY! WELCOME, CLASS. I'M MR. DOUGLAS. IS EVERYONE SITTING IN THE RIGHT SECTIONS? FLUTES IN FRONT, CLARINETS OVER HERE, SAXES ON THIS SIDE...
OH, MAN, THIS GUY WON'T STOP LOOKIN' AT ME...
HE'S PRETTY CUTE!
ACK, BUT IF I SMILE BACK, HE'LL SEE THAT MY TEETH ARE...

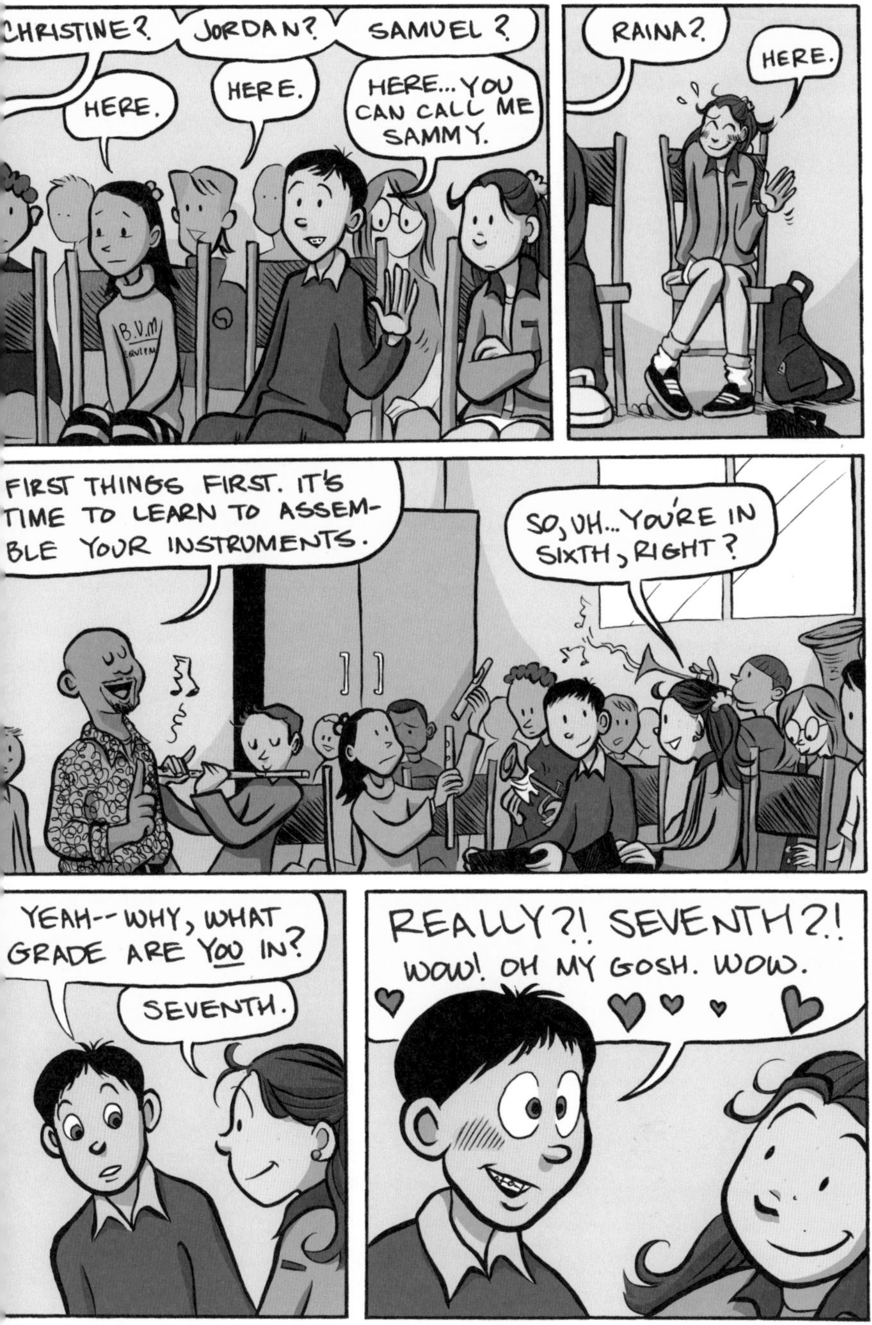
CHRISTINE?
HERE.
JORDAN?
HERE.
SAMUEL?
HERE... YOU CAN CALL ME SAMMY.
RAINA?
HERE.
FIRST THINGS FIRST. IT'S TIME TO LEARN TO ASSEMBLE YOUR INSTRUMENTS.
SO, UH... YOU'RE IN SIXTH, RIGHT?
YEAH-- WHY, WHAT GRADE ARE YOU IN?
SEVENTH.
REALLY?! SEVENTH?!
WOW! OH MY GOSH. WOW.

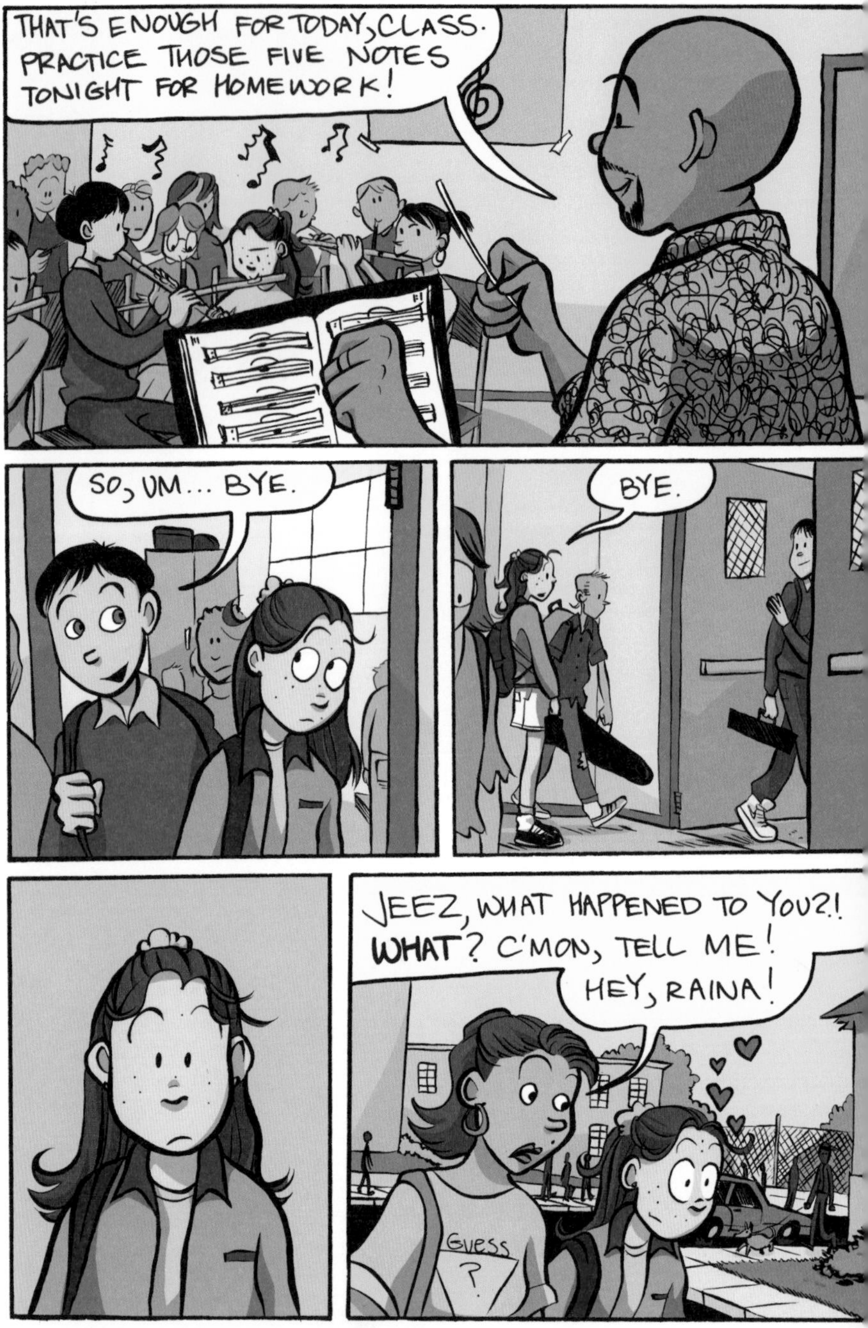
THAT'S ENOUGH FOR TODAY, CLASS. PRACTICE THOSE FIVE NOTES TONIGHT FOR HOMEWORK!
SO, UM... BYE.
BYE.
JEEZ, WHAT HAPPENED TO YOU?!
WHAT? C'MON, TELL ME!
HEY, RAINA!
GUESS ?

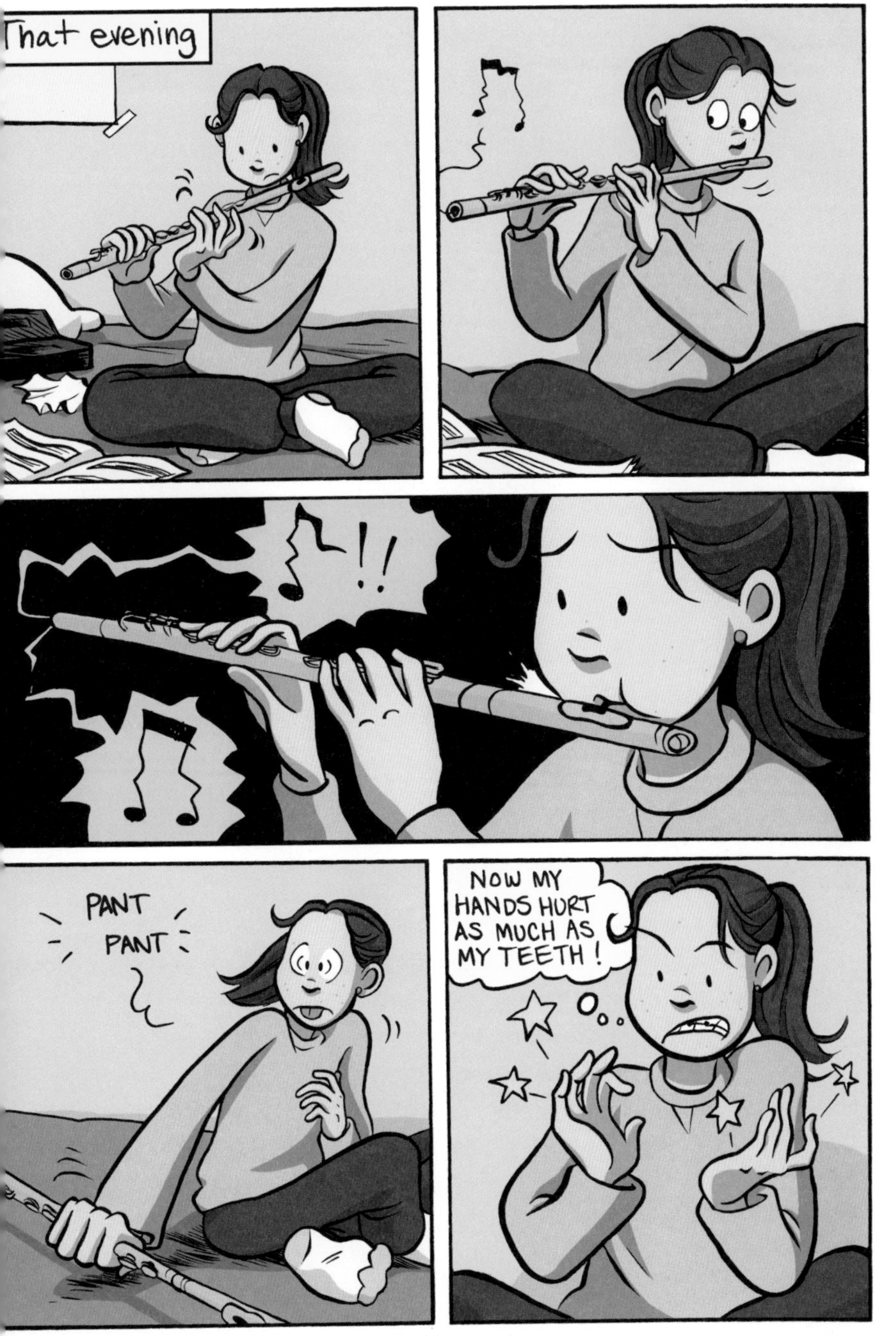

That evening
PANT
PANT
NOW MY HANDS HURT AS MUCH AS MY TEETH!

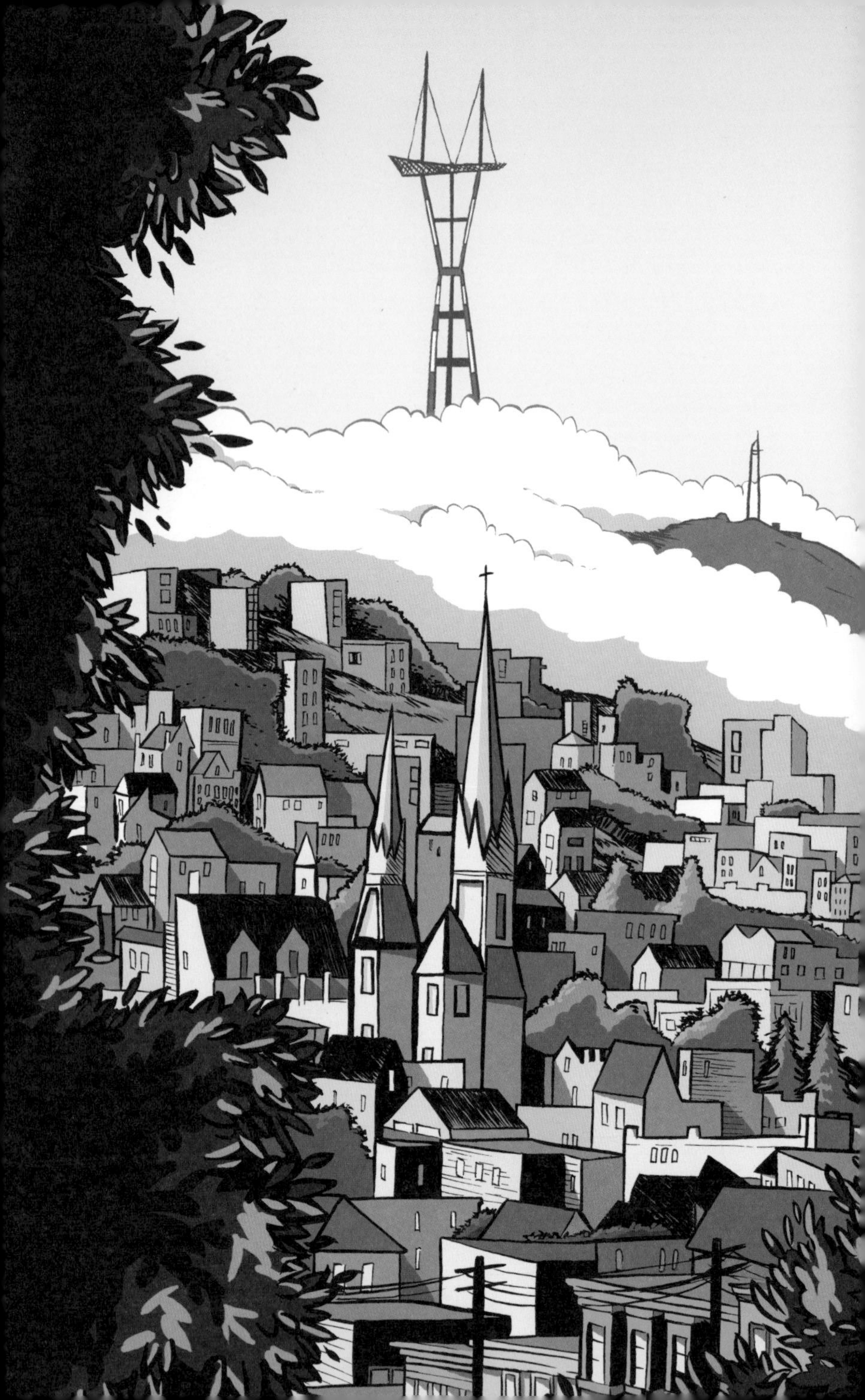

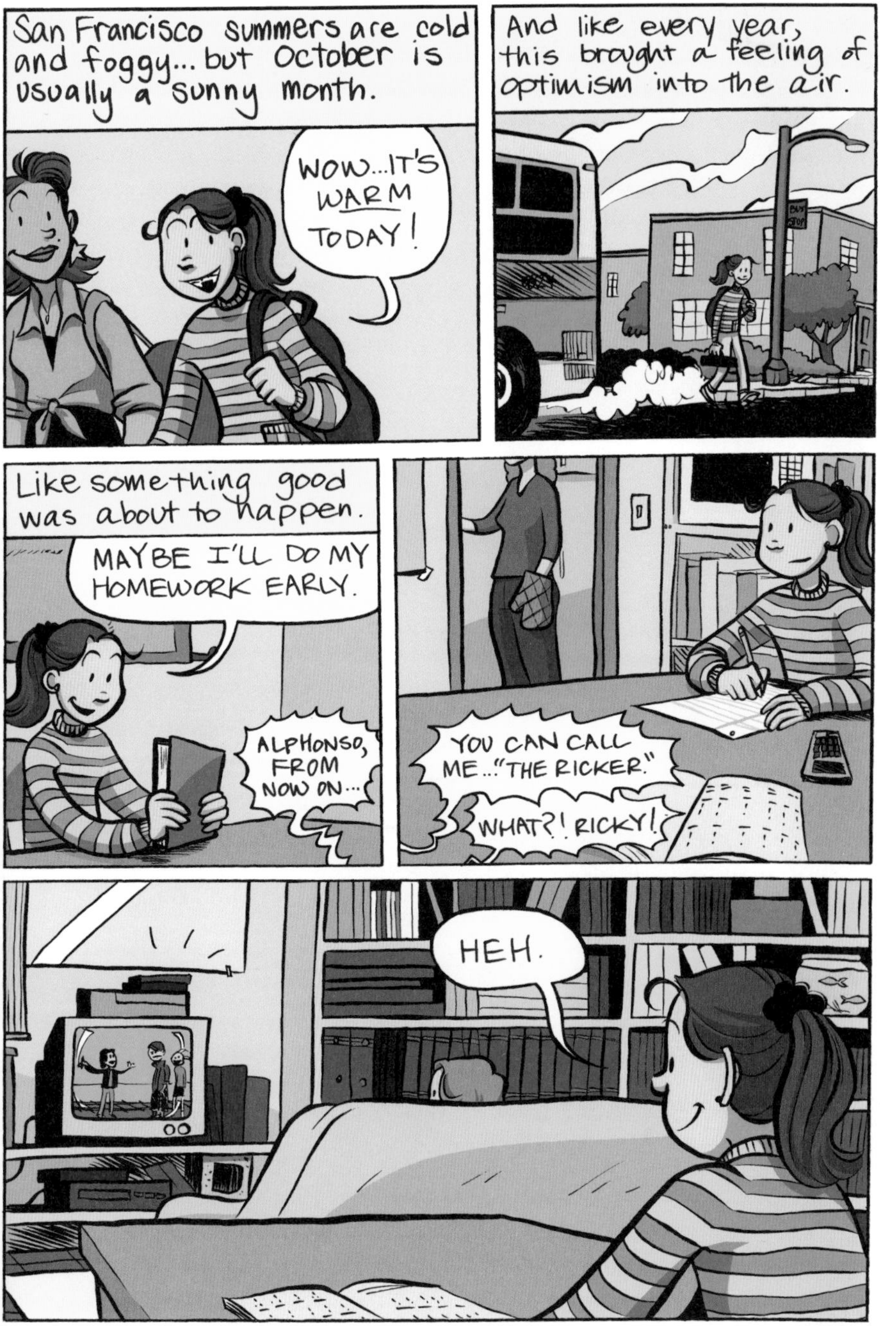
San Francisco summers are cold and foggy... but October is usually a sunny month.
WOW...IT'S WARM TODAY!
And like every year, this brought a feeling of optimism into the air.
BUS STOP
Like something good was about to happen.
MAYBE I'LL DO MY HOMEWORK EARLY.
ALPHONSO, FROM NOW ON...
YOU CAN CALL ME..."THE RICKER."
WHAT?! RICKY!
HEH.

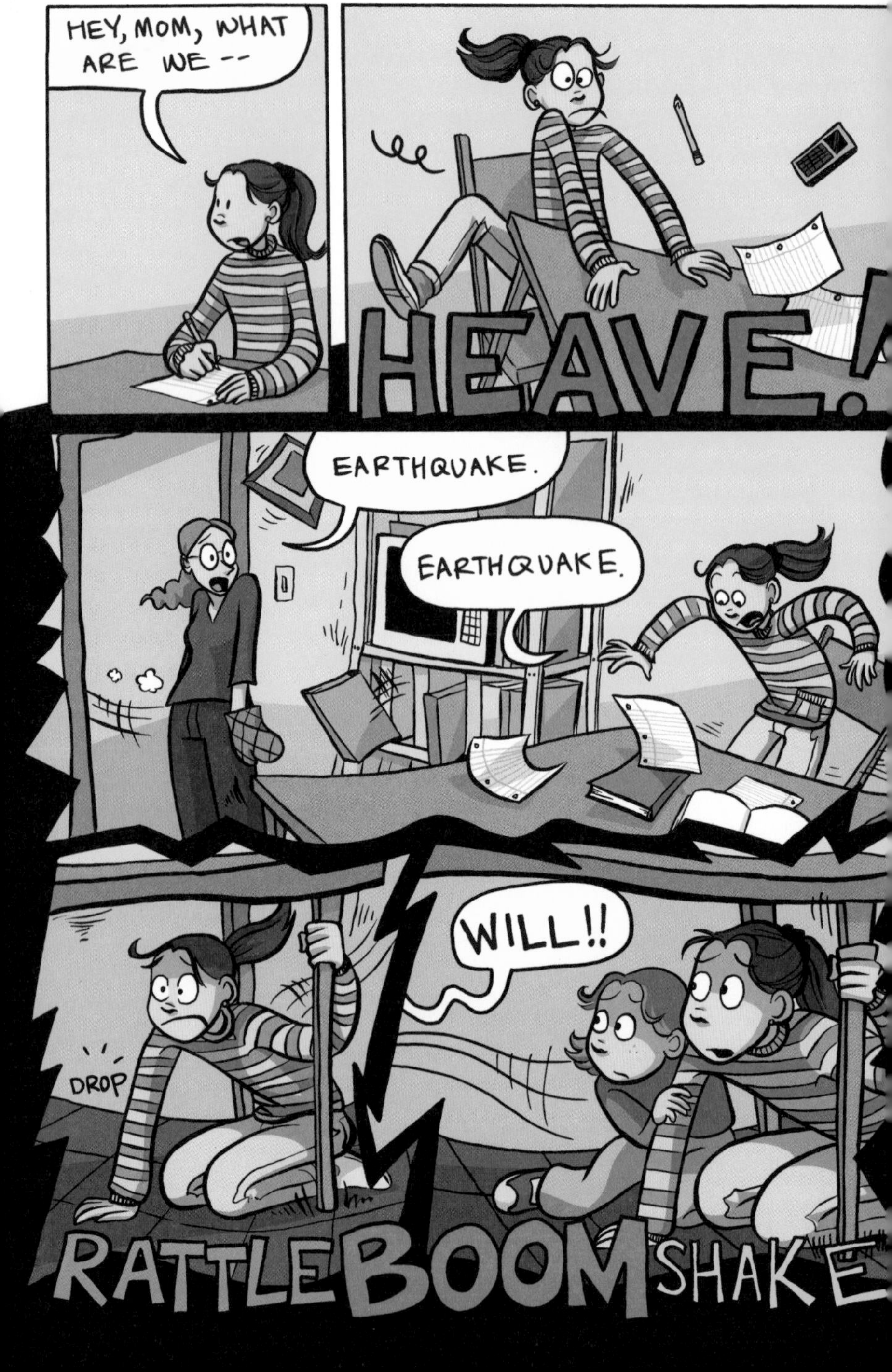

HEY, MOM, WHAT ARE WE --
HEAVE!
EARTHQUAKE.
EARTHQUAKE.
WILL!!
DROP
RATTLE BOOM SHAKE

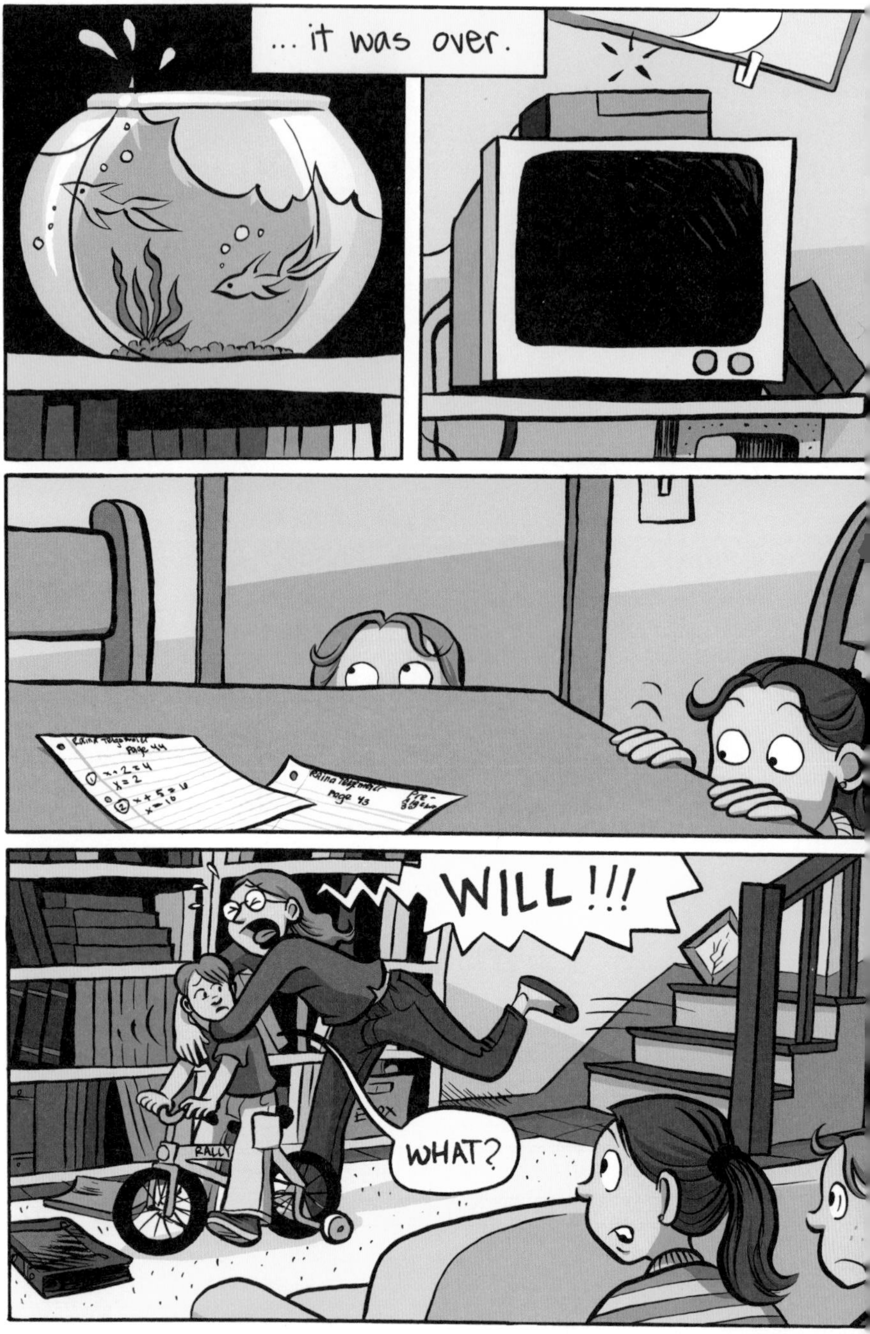
... it was over.
WILL!!!
WHAT?
RALLY

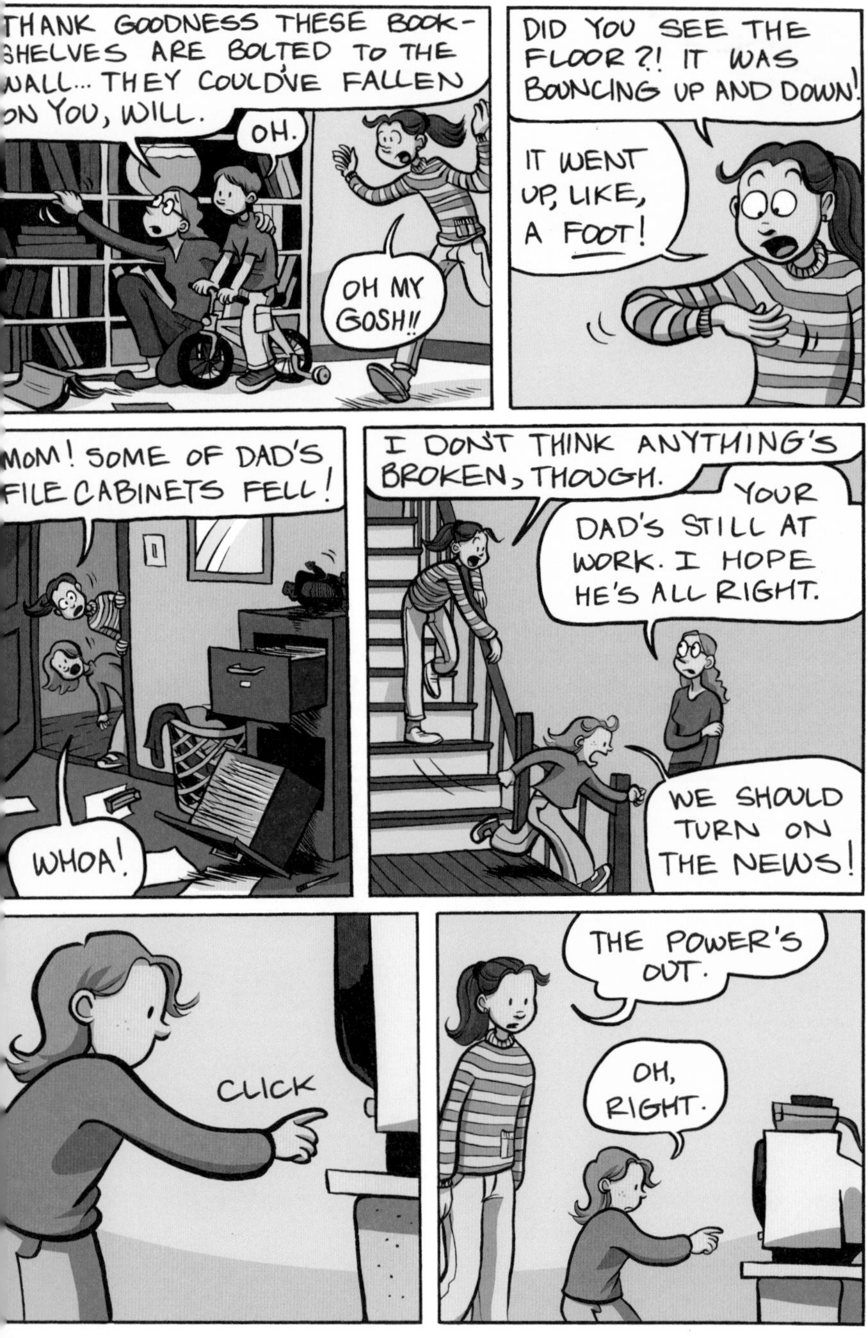
THANK GOODNESS THESE BOOK-SHELVES ARE BOLTED TO THE WALL... THEY COULD'VE FALLEN ON YOU, WILL.
OH.
OH MY GOSH!!
DID YOU SEE THE FLOOR?! IT WAS BOUNCING UP AND DOWN!
IT WENT UP, LIKE, A FOOT!
MOM! SOME OF DAD'S FILE CABINETS FELL!
WHOA!
I DON'T THINK ANYTHING'S BROKEN, THOUGH.
YOUR DAD'S STILL AT WORK. I HOPE HE'S ALL RIGHT.
WE SHOULD TURN ON THE NEWS!
CLICK
THE POWER'S OUT.
OH, RIGHT.

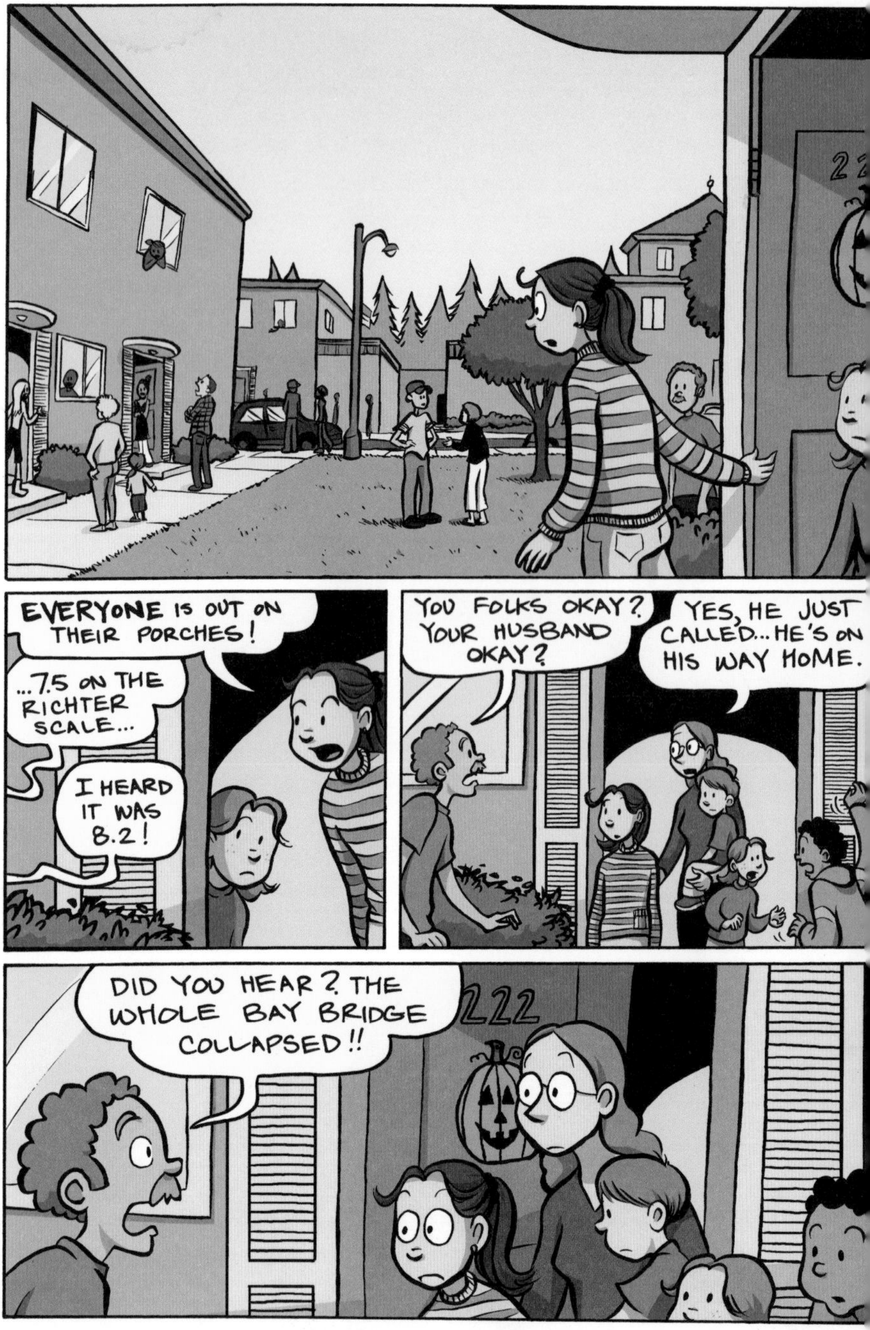
EVERYONE IS OUT ON THEIR PORCHES!
...7.5 ON THE RICHTER SCALE...
I HEARD IT WAS 8.2!
YOU FOLKS OKAY? YOUR HUSBAND OKAY?
YES, HE JUST CALLED... HE'S ON HIS WAY HOME.
DID YOU HEAR? THE WHOLE BAY BRIDGE COLLAPSED!!
222

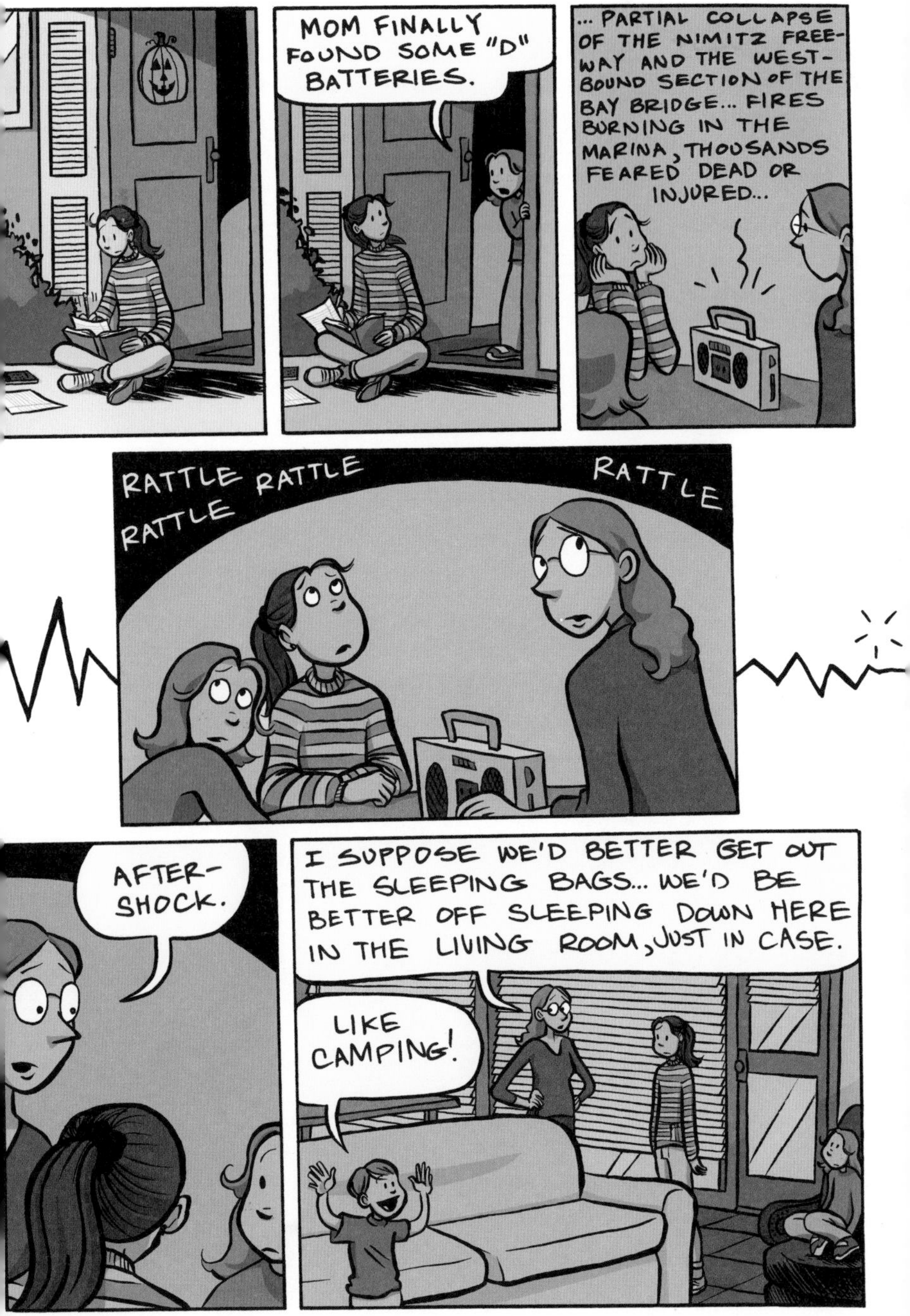
MOM FINALLY FOUND SOME "D" BATTERIES.
... PARTIAL COLLAPSE OF THE NIMITZ FREEWAY AND THE WEST-BOUND SECTION OF THE BAY BRIDGE... FIRES BURNING IN THE MARINA, THOUSANDS FEARED DEAD OR INJURED...
RATTLE RATTLE
RATTLE
RATTLE
AFTER-SHOCK.
I SUPPOSE WE'D BETTER GET OUT THE SLEEPING BAGS... WE'D BE BETTER OFF SLEEPING DOWN HERE IN THE LIVING ROOM, JUST IN CASE.
LIKE CAMPING!

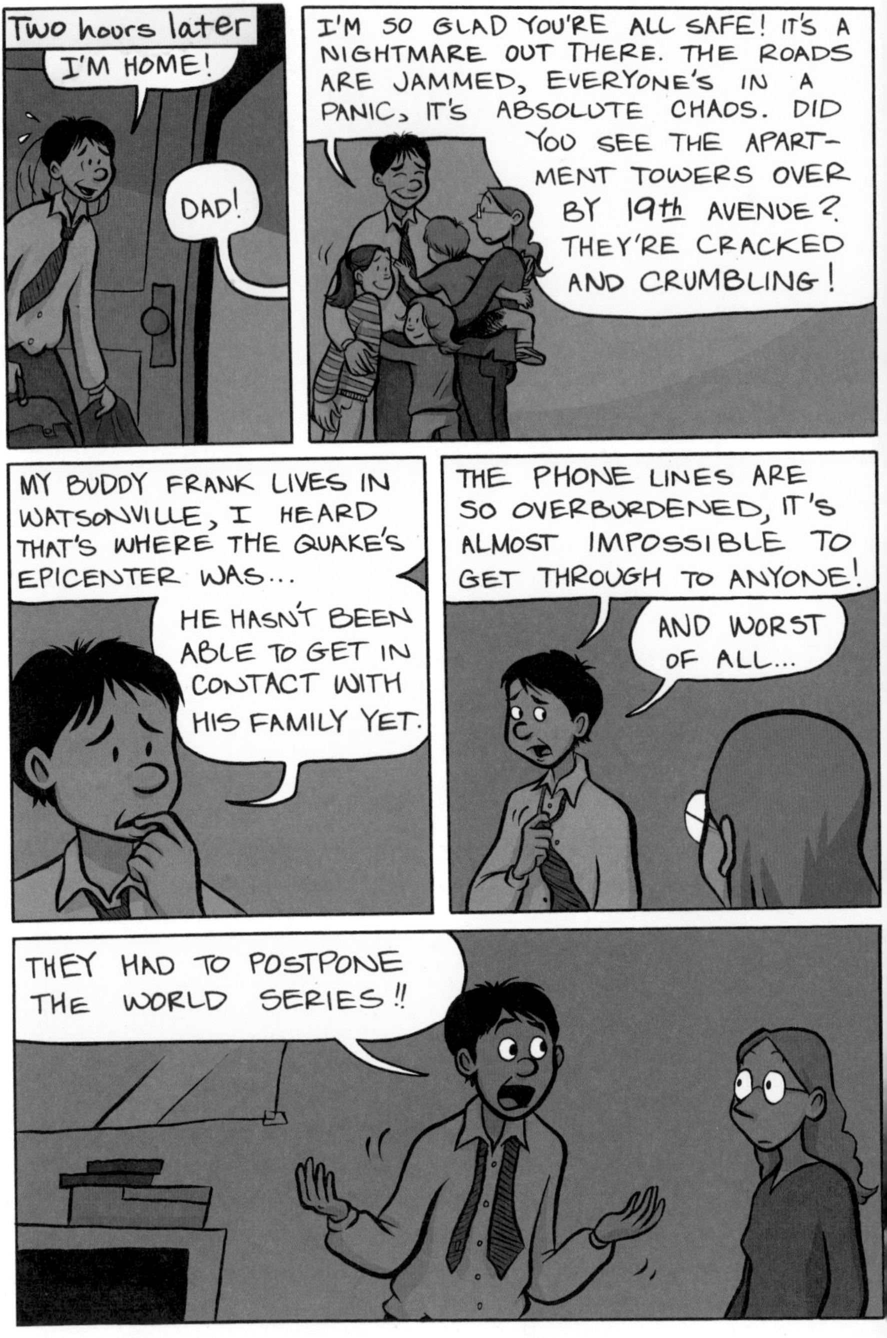
Two hours later
I'M HOME!
DAD!
I'M SO GLAD YOU'RE ALL SAFE! IT'S A NIGHTMARE OUT THERE. THE ROADS ARE JAMMED, EVERYONE'S IN A PANIC, IT'S ABSOLUTE CHAOS. DID YOU SEE THE APARTMENT TOWERS OVER BY 19th AVENUE? THEY'RE CRACKED AND CRUMBLING!
MY BUDDY FRANK LIVES IN WATSONVILLE, I HEARD THAT'S WHERE THE QUAKE'S EPICENTER WAS...
HE HASN'T BEEN ABLE TO GET IN CONTACT WITH HIS FAMILY YET.
THE PHONE LINES ARE SO OVERBURDENED, IT'S ALMOST IMPOSSIBLE TO GET THROUGH TO ANYONE!
AND WORST OF ALL...
THEY HAD TO POSTPONE THE WORLD SERIES!!

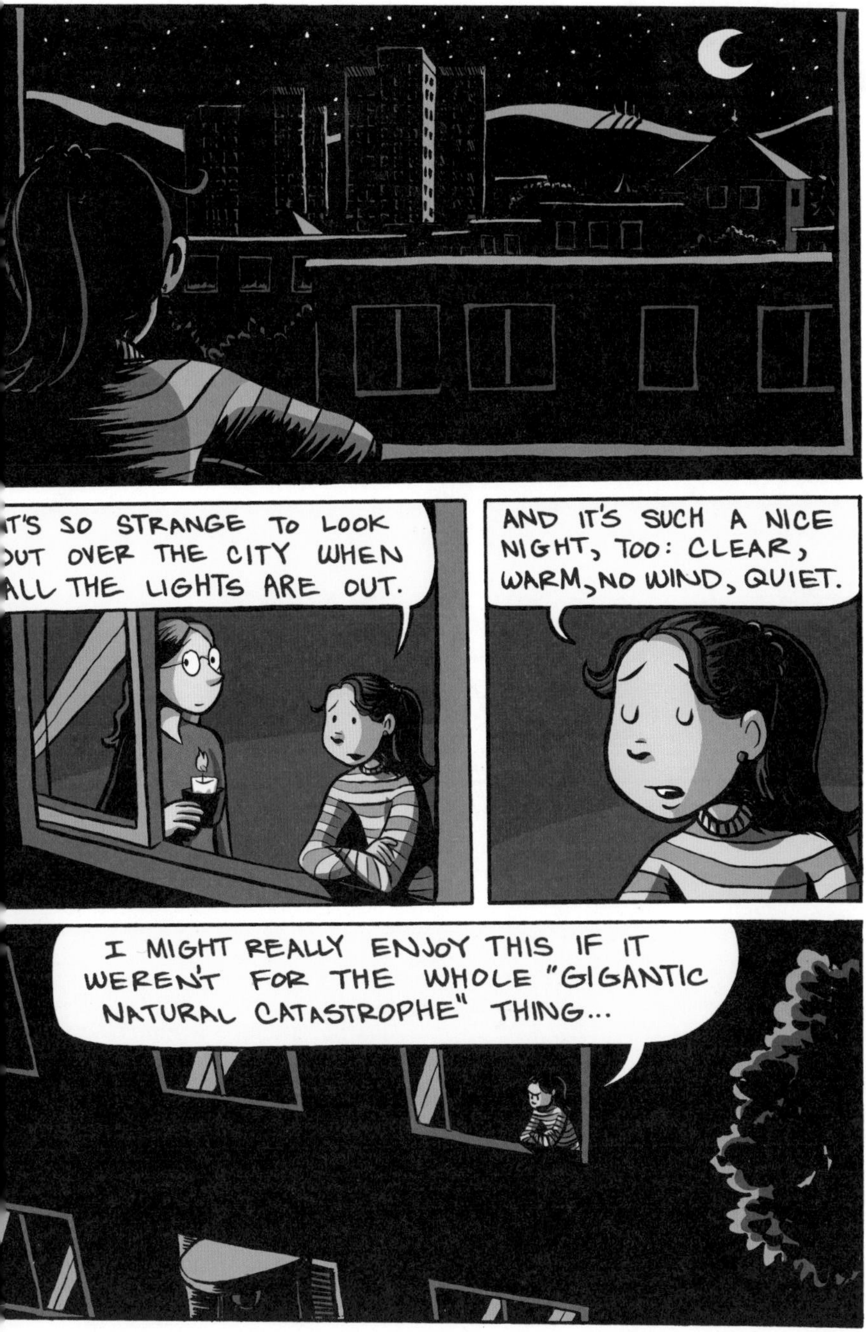
T'S SO STRANGE TO LOOK UT OVER THE CITY WHEN LL THE LIGHTS ARE OUT.
AND IT'S SUCH A NICE NIGHT, TOO: CLEAR, WARM, NO WIND, QUIET.
I MIGHT REALLY ENJOY THIS IF IT WEREN'T FOR THE WHOLE "GIGANTIC NATURAL CATASTROPHE" THING...

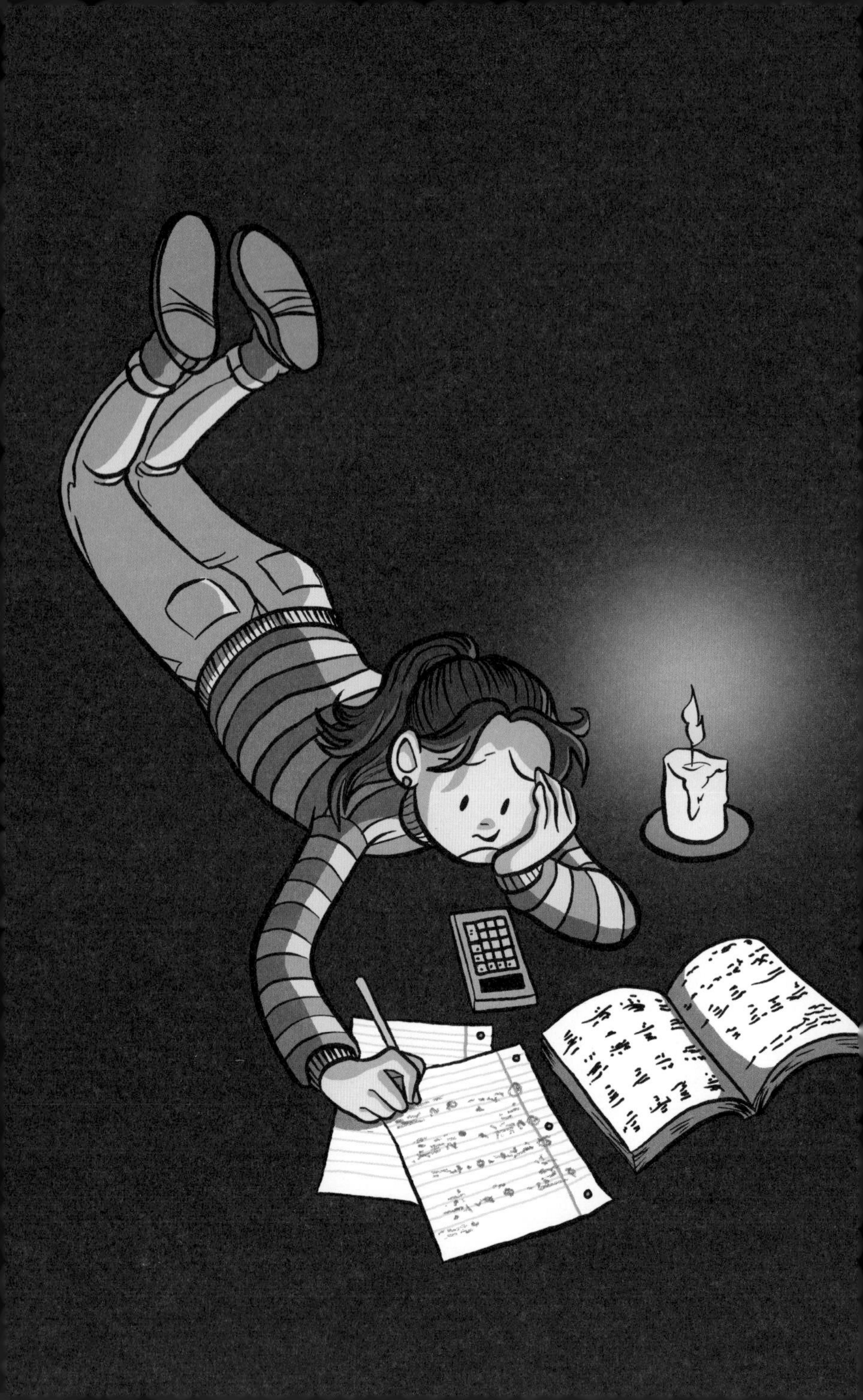

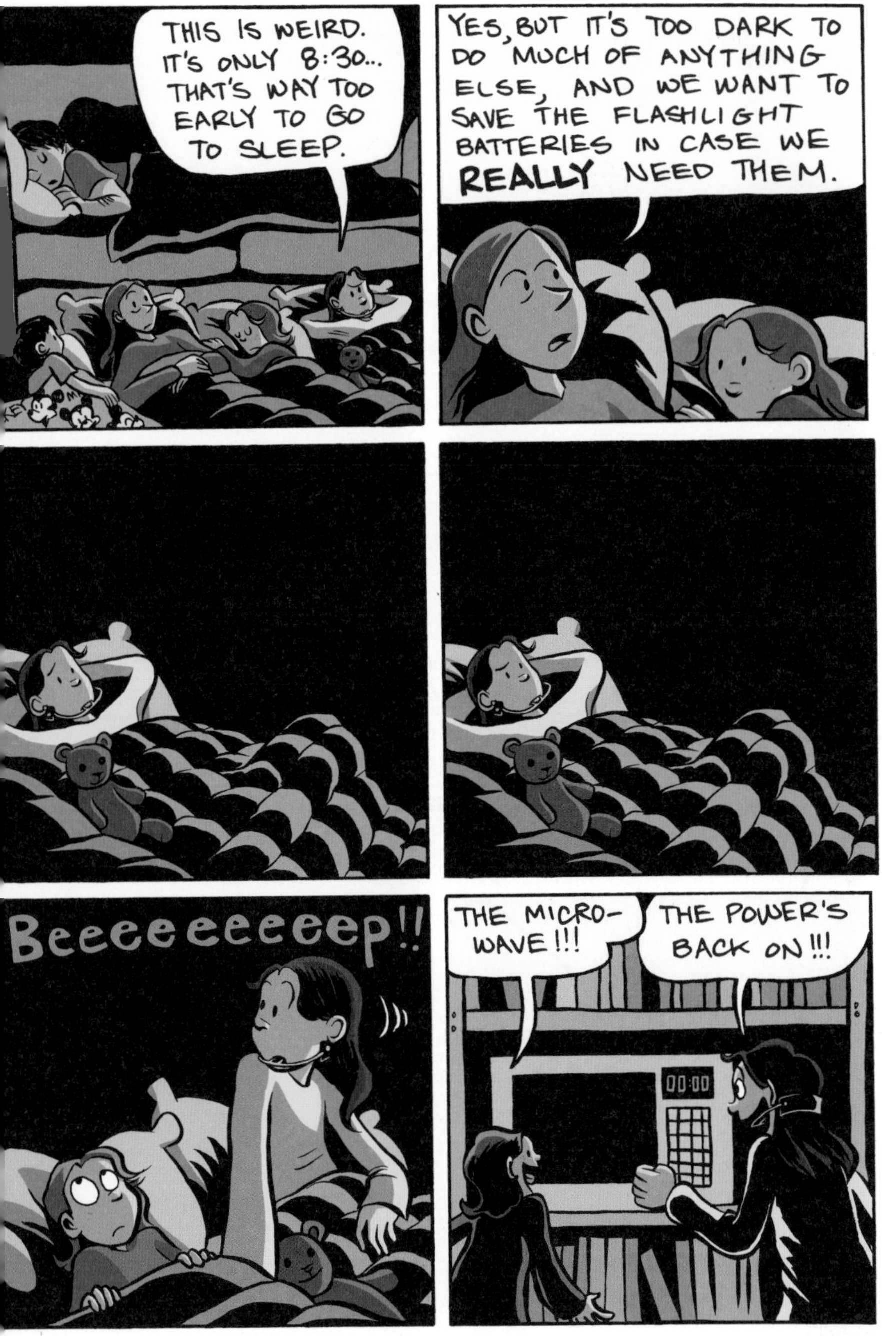
THIS IS WEIRD. IT'S ONLY 8:30... THAT'S WAY TOO EARLY TO GO TO SLEEP.
YES, BUT IT'S TOO DARK TO DO MUCH OF ANYTHING ELSE, AND WE WANT TO SAVE THE FLASHLIGHT BATTERIES IN CASE WE REALLY NEED THEM.
Beeeeeeeeep!!
THE MICRO-WAVE!!!
THE POWER'S BACK ON!!!
00:00

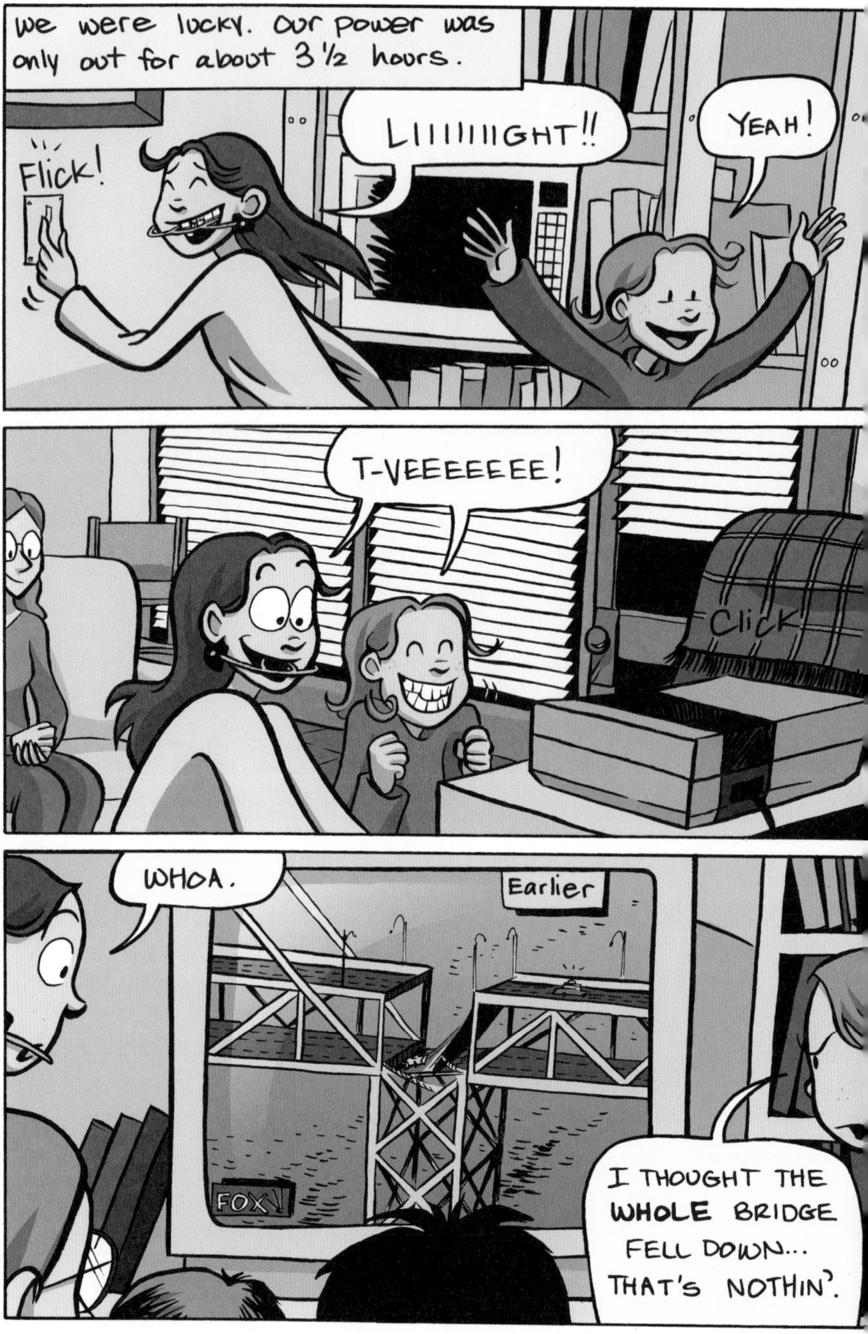

we were lucky. Our power was only out for about 3 ½ hours.
Flick!
LIIIIIIGHT!!
YEAH!
T-VEEEEEEE!
Click!
WHOA.
Earlier
FOX
I THOUGHT THE WHOLE BRIDGE FELL DOWN... THAT'S NOTHIN'.

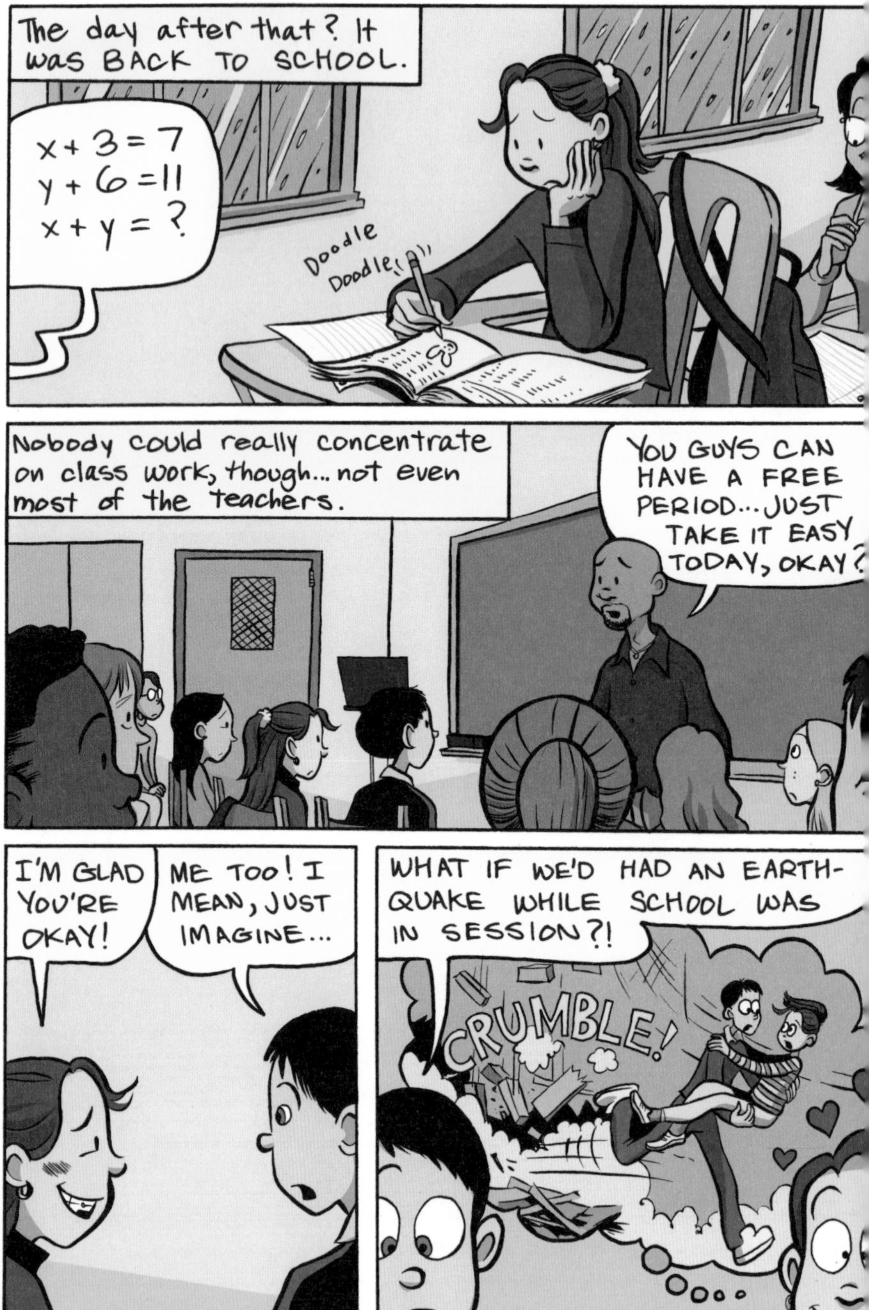
The day after that? It was BACK TO SCHOOL.
x + 3 = 7
y + 6 = 11
x + y = ?
Doodle Doodle
Nobody could really concentrate on class work, though... not even most of the teachers.
YOU GUYS CAN HAVE A FREE PERIOD... JUST TAKE IT EASY TODAY, OKAY?
I'M GLAD YOU'RE OKAY!
ME TOO! I MEAN, JUST IMAGINE...
WHAT IF WE'D HAD AN EARTHQUAKE WHILE SCHOOL WAS IN SESSION?!
CRUMBLE!

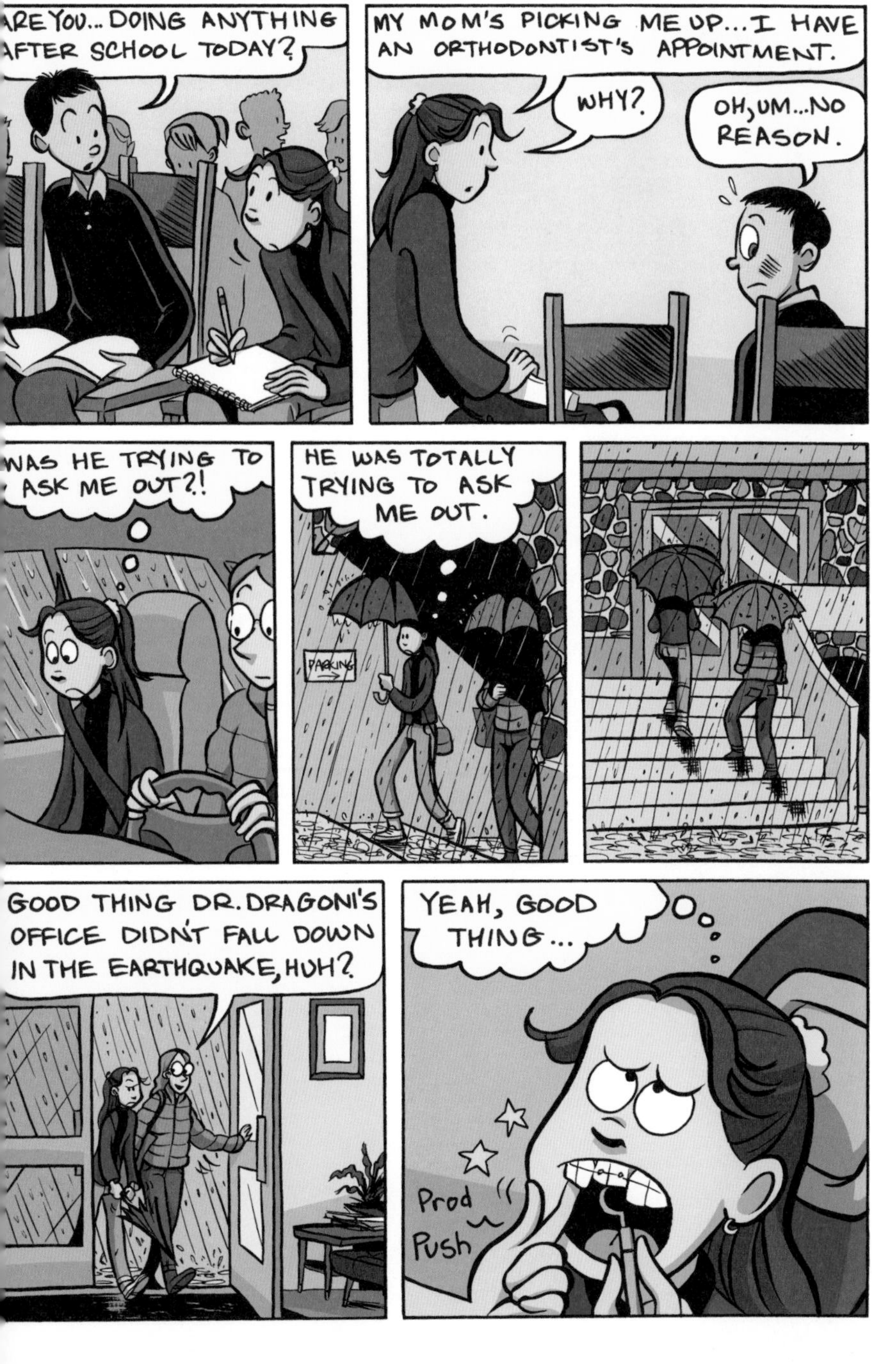
ARE YOU... DOING ANYTHING AFTER SCHOOL TODAY?
MY MOM'S PICKING ME UP... I HAVE AN ORTHODONTIST'S APPOINTMENT.
WHY?
OH, UM... NO REASON.
WAS HE TRYING TO ASK ME OUT?!
HE WAS TOTALLY TRYING TO ASK ME OUT.
PARKING
GOOD THING DR. DRAGONI'S OFFICE DIDN'T FALL DOWN IN THE EARTHQUAKE, HUH?
YEAH, GOOD THING...
Prod
Push

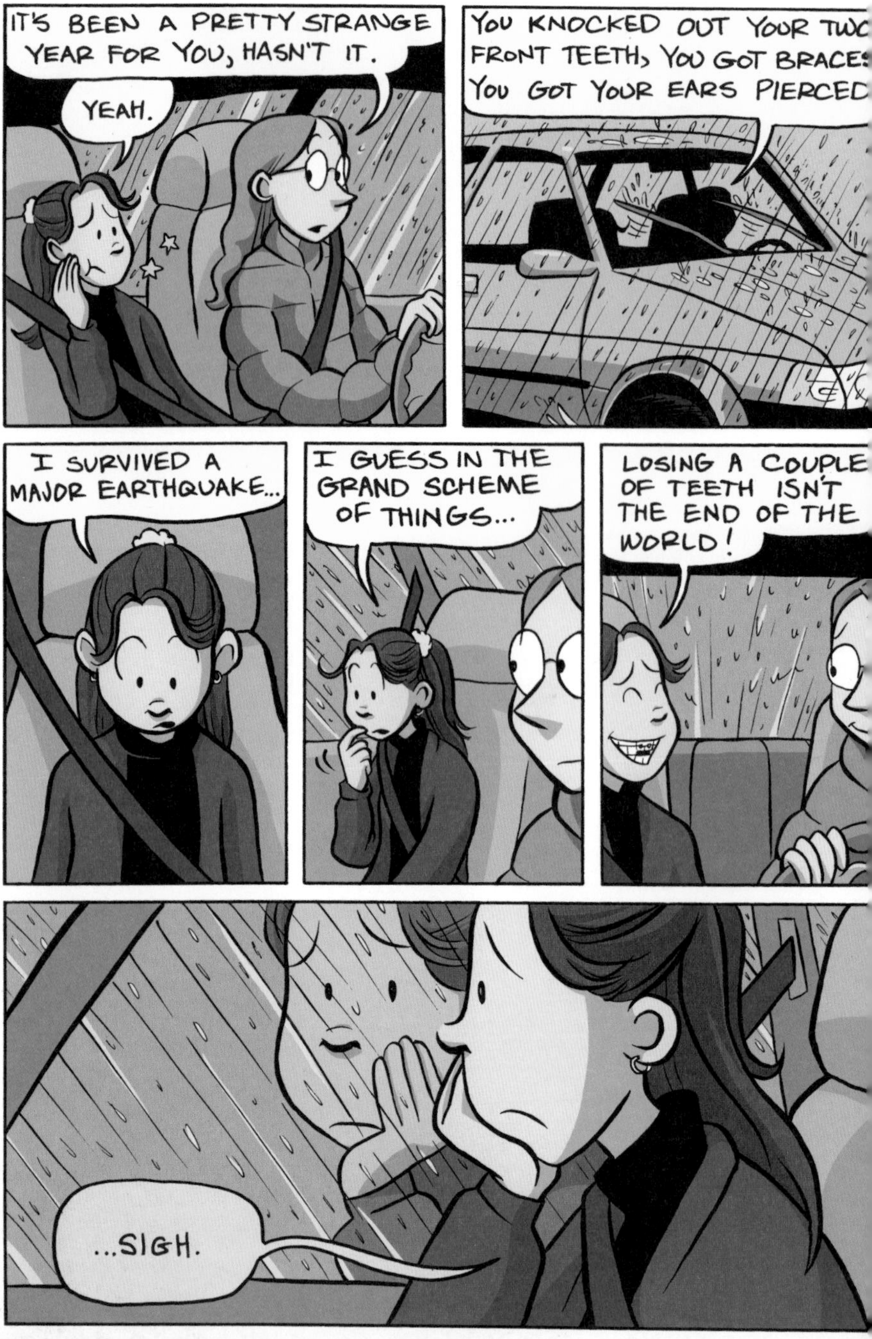
IT'S BEEN A PRETTY STRANGE YEAR FOR YOU, HASN'T IT.
YEAH.
YOU KNOCKED OUT YOUR TWO FRONT TEETH, YOU GOT BRACES, YOU GOT YOUR EARS PIERCED
I SURVIVED A MAJOR EARTHQUAKE...
I GUESS IN THE GRAND SCHEME OF THINGS...
LOSING A COUPLE OF TEETH ISN'T THE END OF THE WORLD!
...SIGH.

CHAPTER FOUR

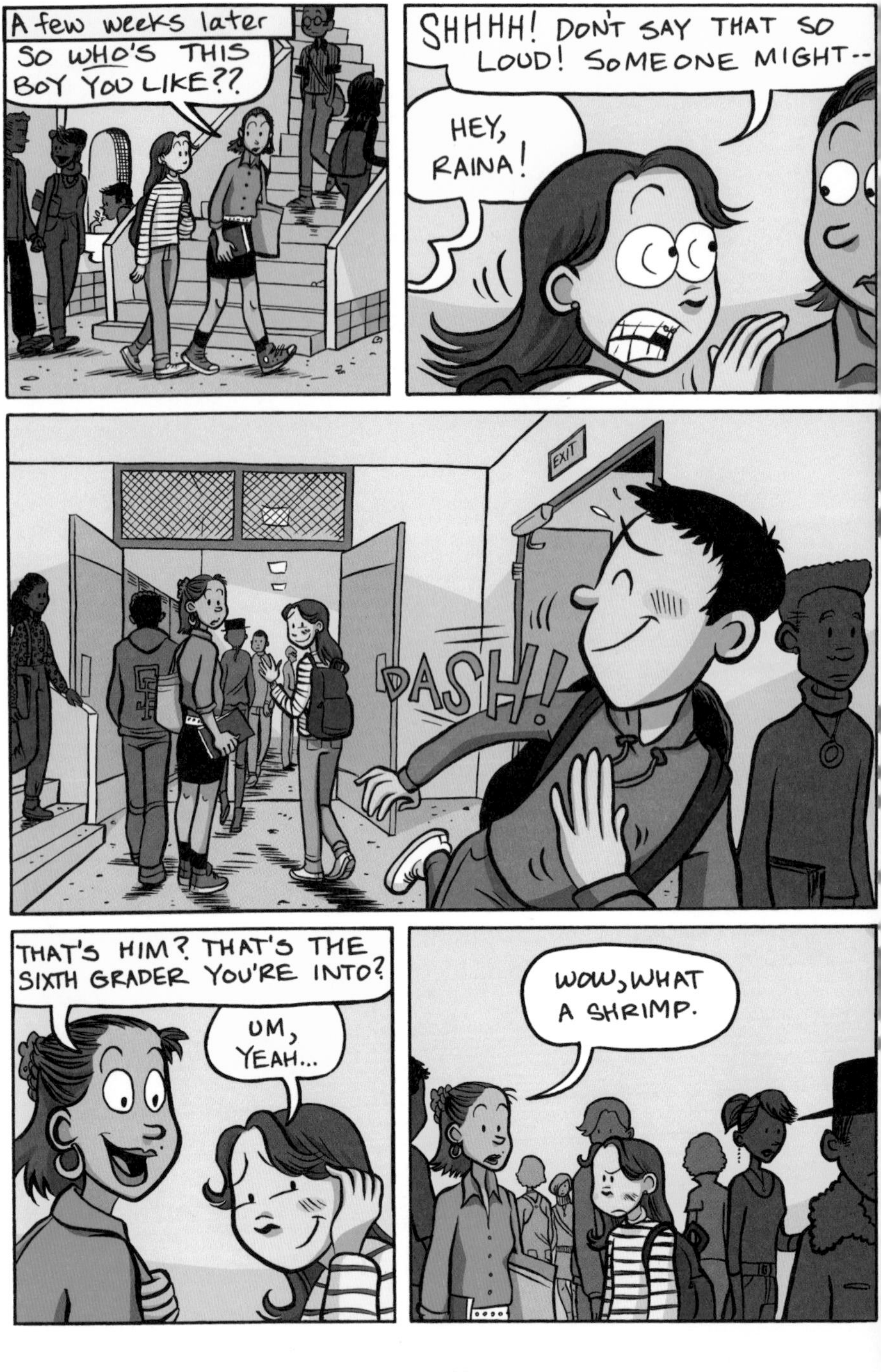
A few weeks later
SO WHO'S THIS BOY YOU LIKE??
SHHHH! DON'T SAY THAT SO LOUD! SOMEONE MIGHT--
HEY, RAINA!
EXIT
DASH!
THAT'S HIM? THAT'S THE SIXTH GRADER YOU'RE INTO?
UM, YEAH...
WOW, WHAT A SHRIMP.

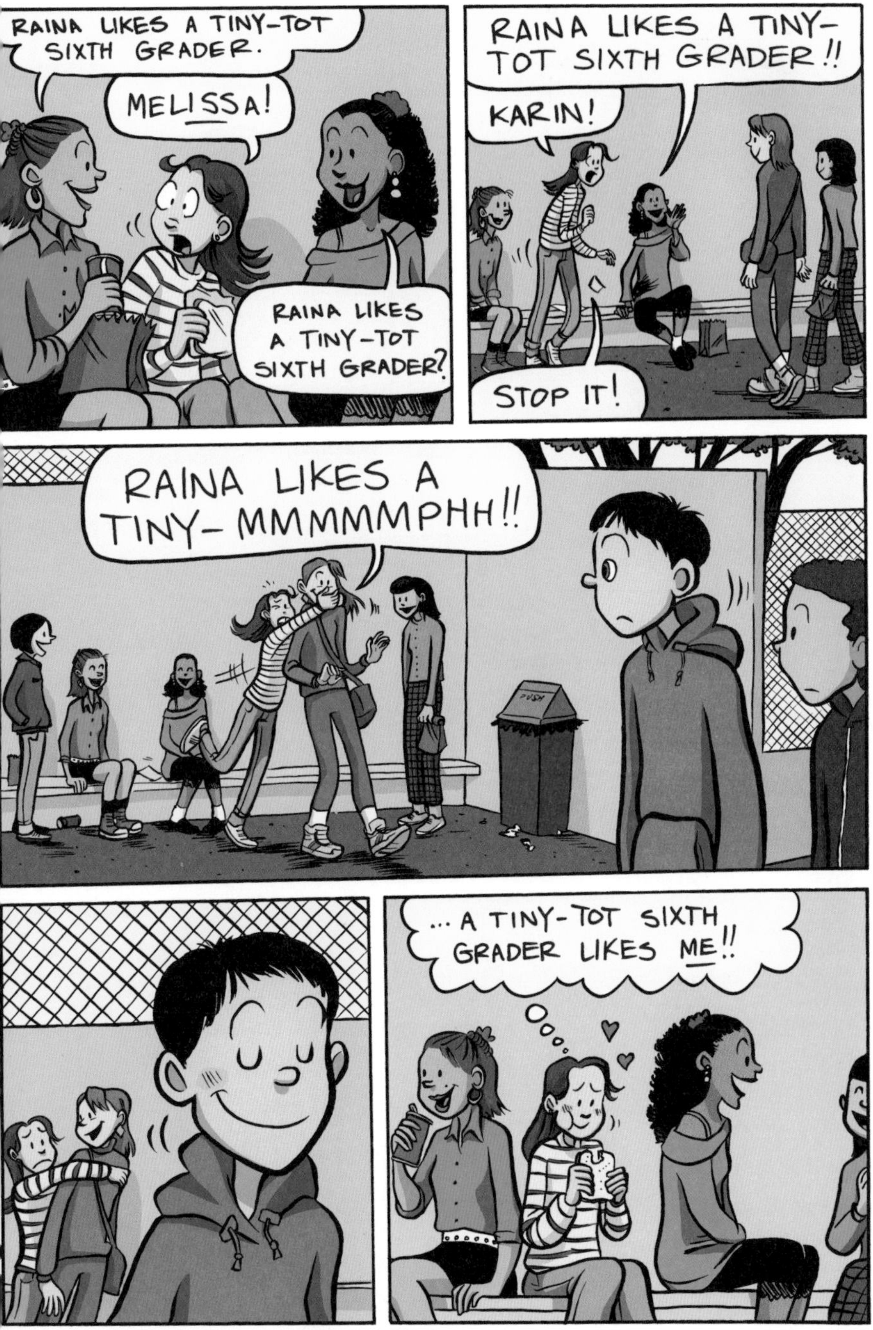
RAINA LIKES A TINY-TOT SIXTH GRADER.
MELISSA!
RAINA LIKES A TINY-TOT SIXTH GRADER?
RAINA LIKES A TINY-TOT SIXTH GRADER!!
KARIN!
STOP IT!
RAINA LIKES A TINY- MMMMMPHH!!
PUSH
... A TINY-TOT SIXTH GRADER LIKES ME!!

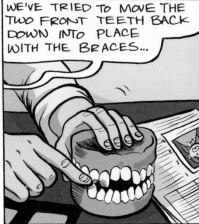

A few days before Thanksgiving

SO, THE BAD NEWS IS, YOUR TEETH AREN'T REALLY RESPONDING TO THE TREATMENT.

WE'VE TRIED TO MOVE THE TWO FRONT TEETH BACK DOWN INTO PLACE WITH THE BRACES...

...BUT AFTER SEVERAL MONTHS, IT JUST DOESN'T SEEM TO BE WORKING.

SO AM I GONNA LOOK LIKE A VAMPIRE FOREVER ??

NO... AND THAT'S THE GOOD NEWS. I THINK WE SHOULD GIVE YOU A TEMPORARY SET OF FAKE TEETH!

IT WOULD FIRST REQUIRE A SIMPLE EXTRACTION.

"EXTRACTION"... AS IN, PULLING SOMETHING OUT?

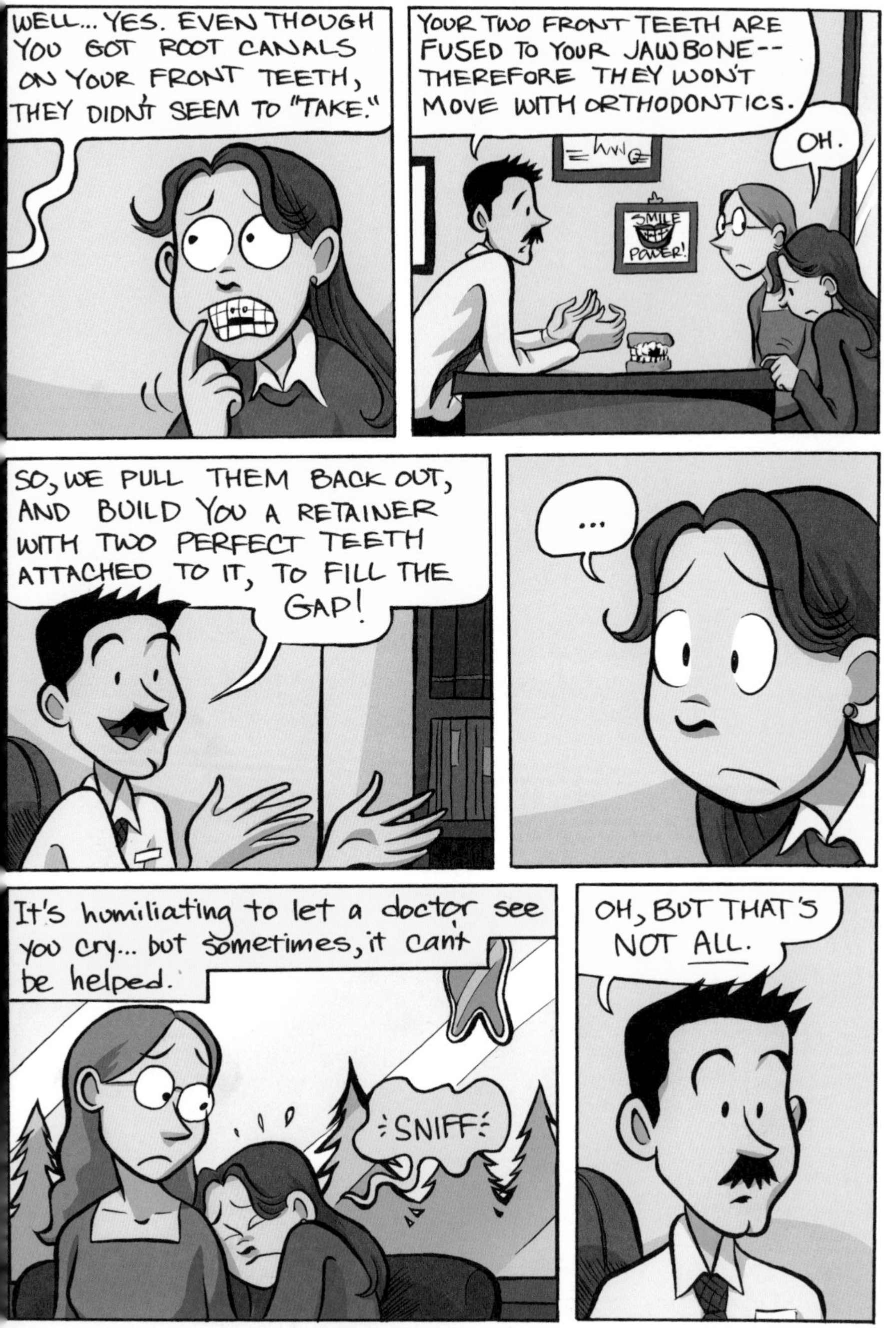
WELL... YES. EVEN THOUGH YOU GOT ROOT CANALS ON YOUR FRONT TEETH, THEY DIDN'T SEEM TO "TAKE."
YOUR TWO FRONT TEETH ARE FUSED TO YOUR JAWBONE-- THEREFORE THEY WON'T MOVE WITH ORTHODONTICS.
OH.
SMILE POWER!
SO, WE PULL THEM BACK OUT, AND BUILD YOU A RETAINER WITH TWO PERFECT TEETH ATTACHED TO IT, TO FILL THE GAP!
...
It's humiliating to let a doctor see you cry... but sometimes, it can't be helped.
SNIFF
OH, BUT THAT'S NOT ALL.

RAINA, WE WANT YOU TO HAVE A FULL MOUTH OF HEALTHY TEETH.

THIS IS WHAT I PROPOSE.

THE REST OF YOUR TEETH ARE STILL FINE.

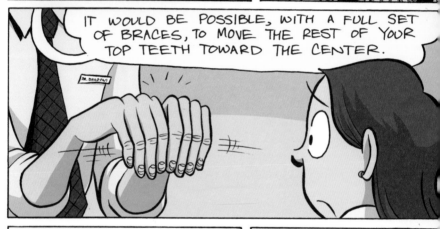

IT WOULD BE POSSIBLE, WITH A FULL SET OF BRACES, TO MOVE THE REST OF YOUR TOP TEETH TOWARD THE CENTER.

IT WOULD TAKE A COUPLE OF YEARS, AND IT WOULDN'T BE COSMETICALLY PERFECT, BUT IT WOULD BE VERY CLOSE.

WHAT DO YOU THINK ABOUT THAT?

WAAAAAAAAHH!!

I GUESS WE CAN TALK IT OVER LATER.

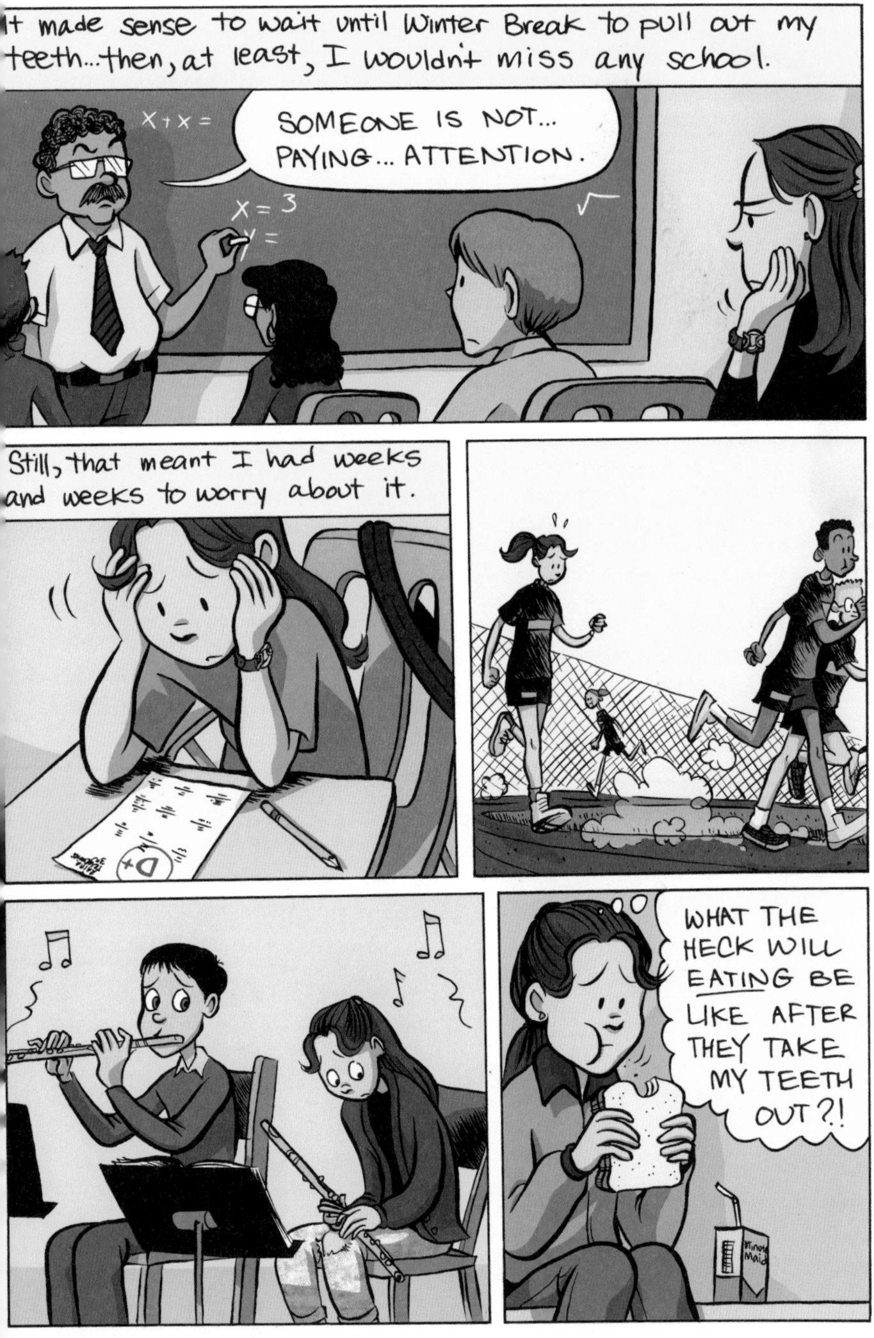
It made sense to wait until Winter Break to pull out my teeth...then, at least, I wouldn't miss any school.
X + X =
SOMEONE IS NOT... PAYING... ATTENTION.
X = 3
Still, that meant I had weeks and weeks to worry about it.
D+
WHAT THE HECK WILL EATING BE LIKE AFTER THEY TAKE MY TEETH OUT?!
Minute Maid

I even worried during art class, which was usually my escape from reality.

HEY, MY DAD TOOK ME TO SEE "THE LITTLE MER-MAID" LAST NIGHT. IT WAS REALLY GOOD.

OH, YEAH?

YEAH. YOU SHOULD DEFINITELY GO SEE IT.

...MAYBE I WILL.

I'M TAKING YOUR SISTER AND HER FRIEND TO SEE "THE LITTLE MERMAID" TO-MORROW, RAINA... WANT TO COME WITH US?

I GUESS.

BUT **ONLY** 'CAUSE EMILY TOLD ME IT WAS GOOD.

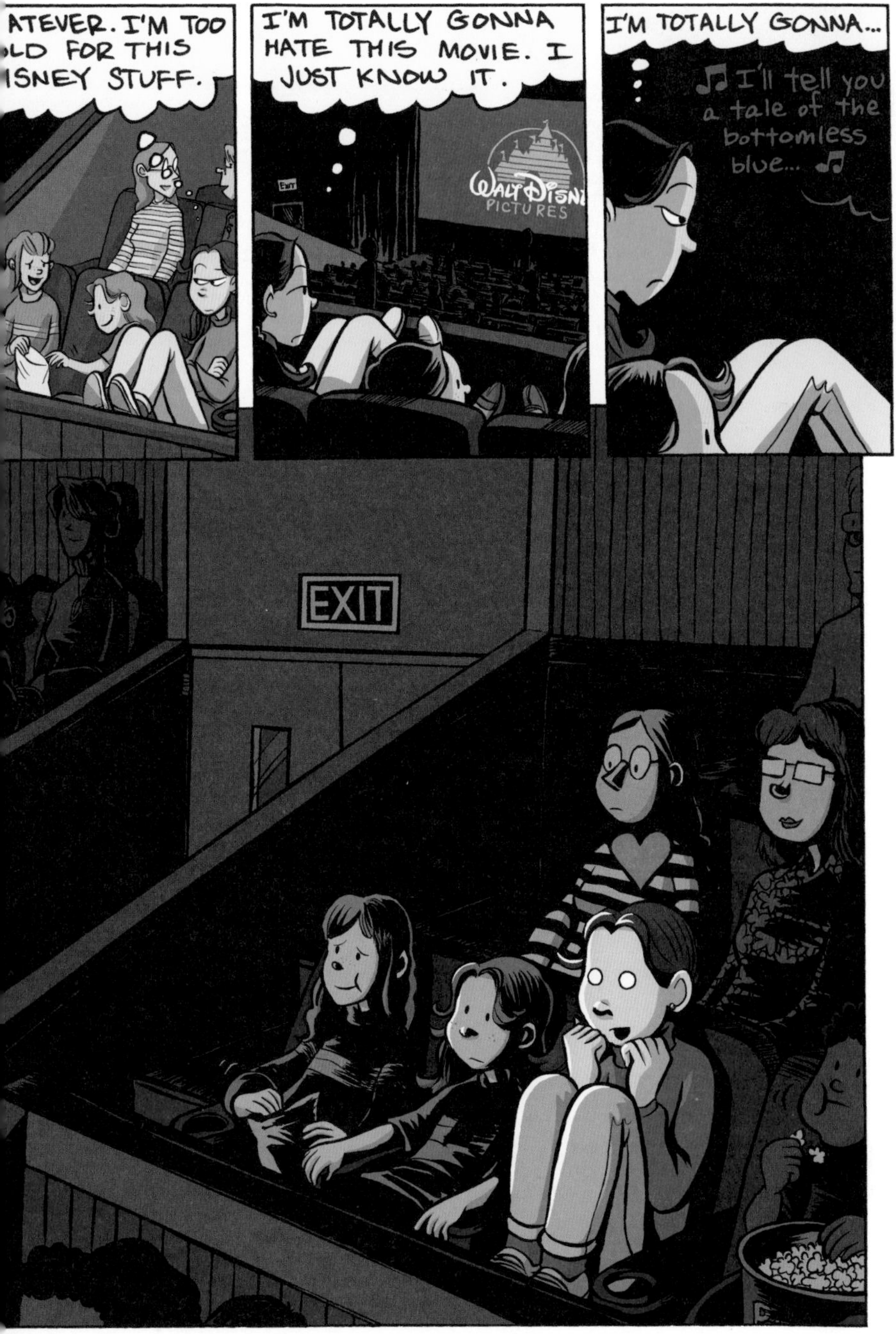
ATEVER. I'M TOO
LD FOR THIS
ISNEY STUFF.
I'M TOTALLY GONNA HATE THIS MOVIE. I JUST KNOW IT.
EXIT
WALT DISNEY PICTURES
I'M TOTALLY GONNA...
♫ I'll tell you a tale of the bottomless blue... ♫
EXIT

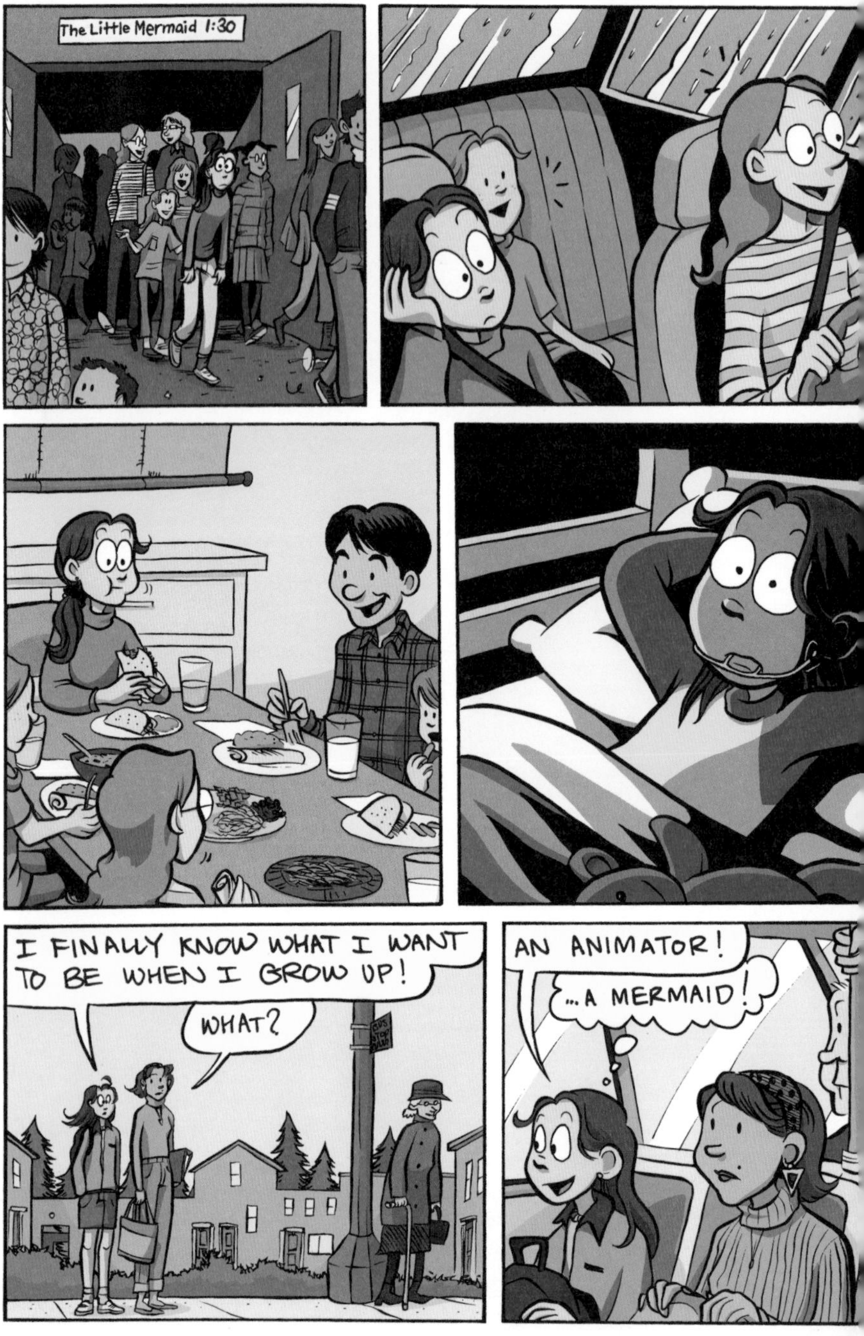
The Little Mermaid 1:30
I FINALLY KNOW WHAT I WANT TO BE WHEN I GROW UP!
WHAT?
AN ANIMATOR!
...A MERMAID!

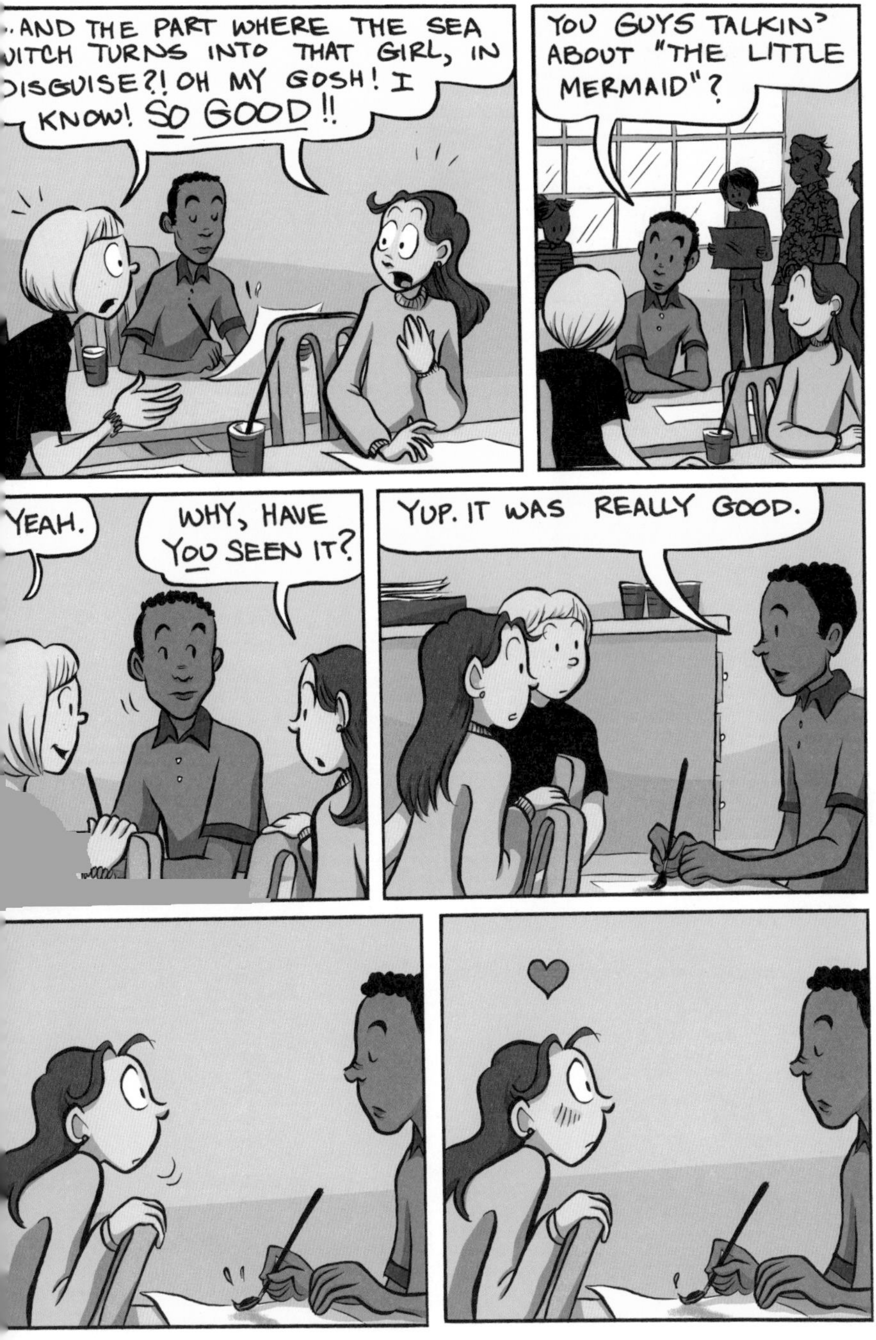

..AND THE PART WHERE THE SEA WITCH TURNS INTO THAT GIRL, IN DISGUISE?! OH MY GOSH! I KNOW! SO GOOD!!
YOU GUYS TALKIN' ABOUT "THE LITTLE MERMAID"?
YEAH.
WHY, HAVE YOU SEEN IT?
YUP. IT WAS REALLY GOOD.

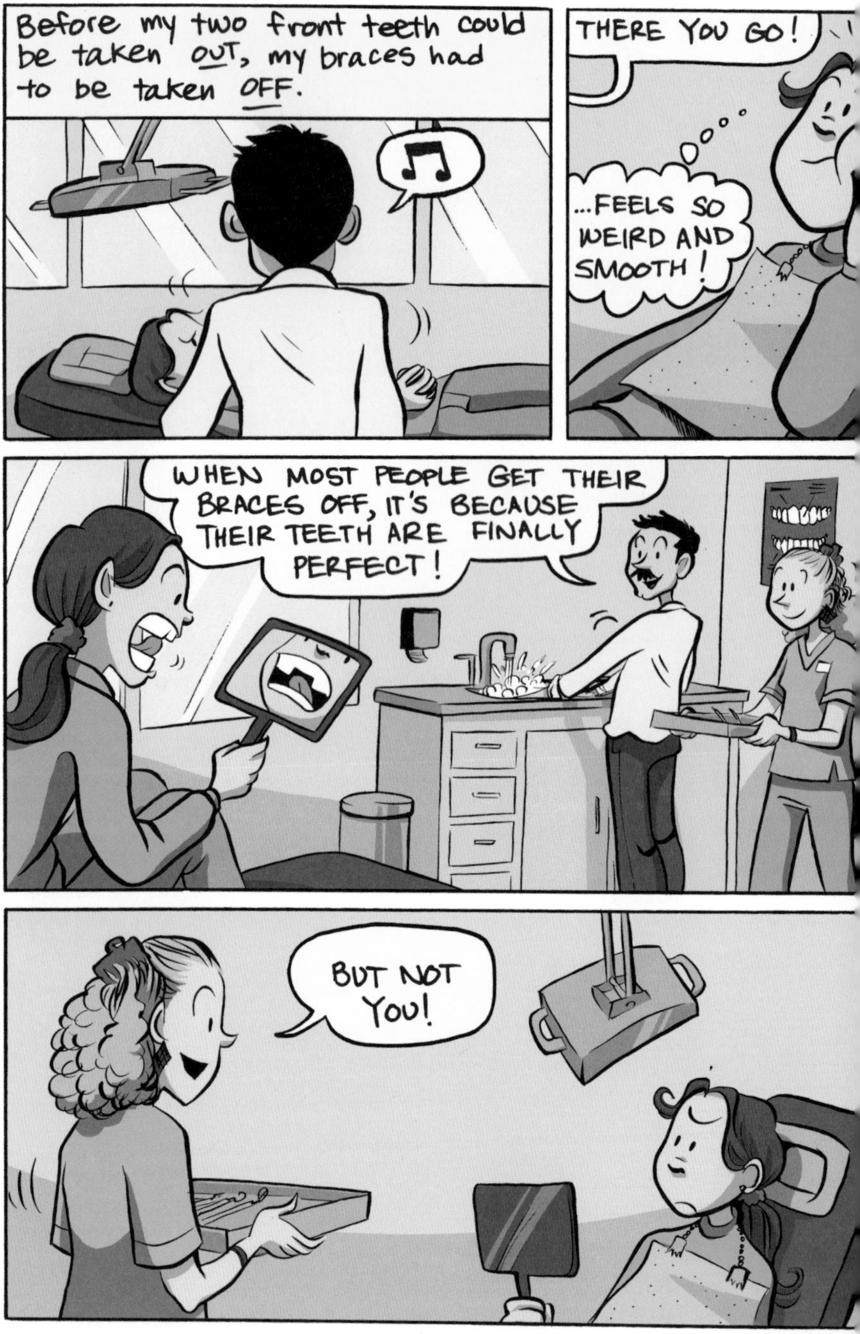

Before my two front teeth could be taken OUT, my braces had to be taken OFF.
♫
THERE YOU GO!
...FEELS SO WEIRD AND SMOOTH!
WHEN MOST PEOPLE GET THEIR BRACES OFF, IT'S BECAUSE THEIR TEETH ARE FINALLY PERFECT!
BUT NOT YOU!

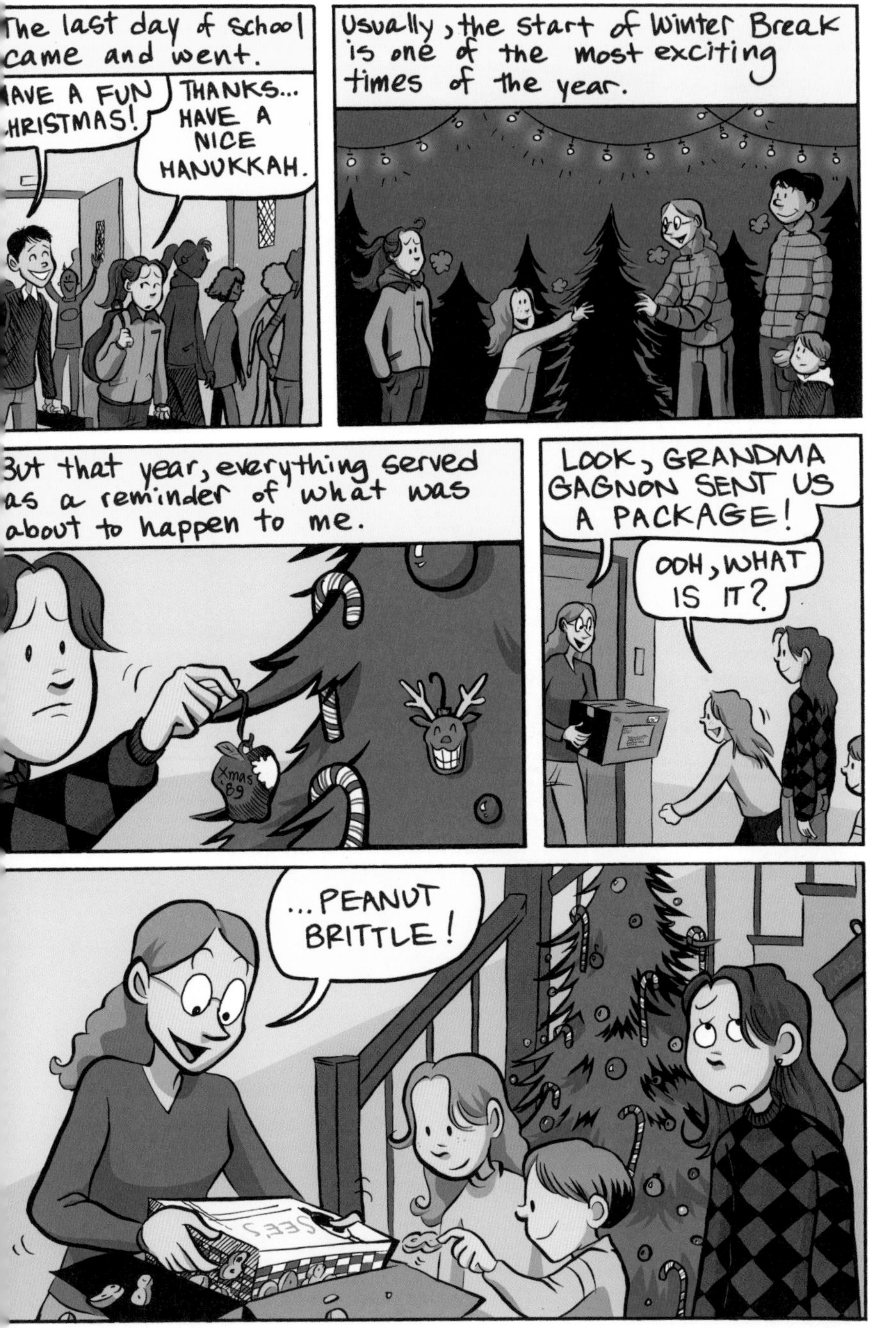
The last day of school came and went.
HAVE A FUN CHRISTMAS!
THANKS... HAVE A NICE HANUKKAH.
Usually, the start of Winter Break is one of the most exciting times of the year.
But that year, everything served as a reminder of what was about to happen to me.
Xmas '89
LOOK, GRANDMA GAGNON SENT US A PACKAGE!
OOH, WHAT IS IT?
...PEANUT BRITTLE!
SEE'S

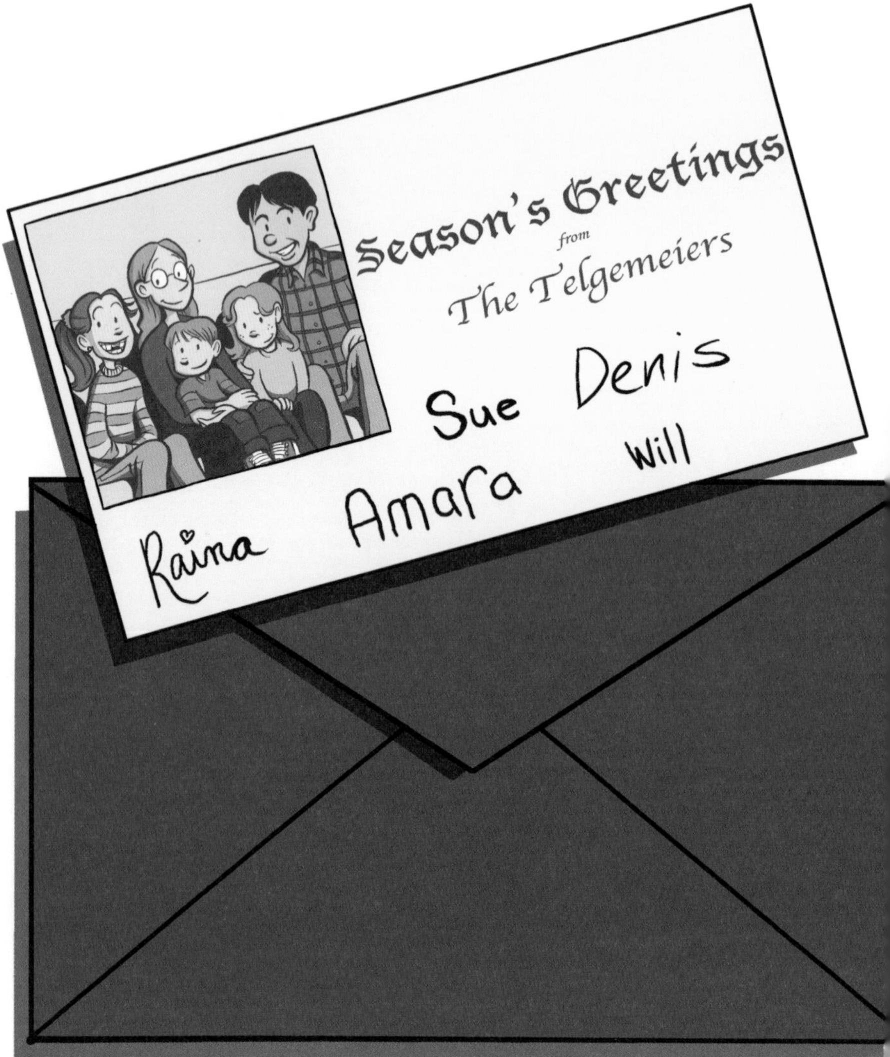

Season's Greetings
from
The Telgemeiers
Sue
Denis
Will
Amara
Raina

Finally, right before Christmas, the dreaded day arrived.

OKAY, RAINA. JUST TRY AND RELAX.

IT'S GOING TO BE FINE.

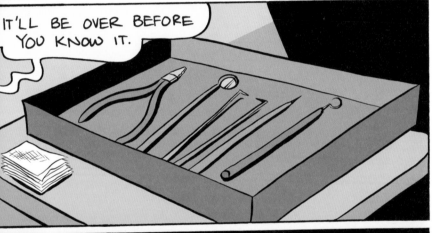

IT'LL BE OVER BEFORE YOU KNOW IT.

JUST TRY TO RELAX...

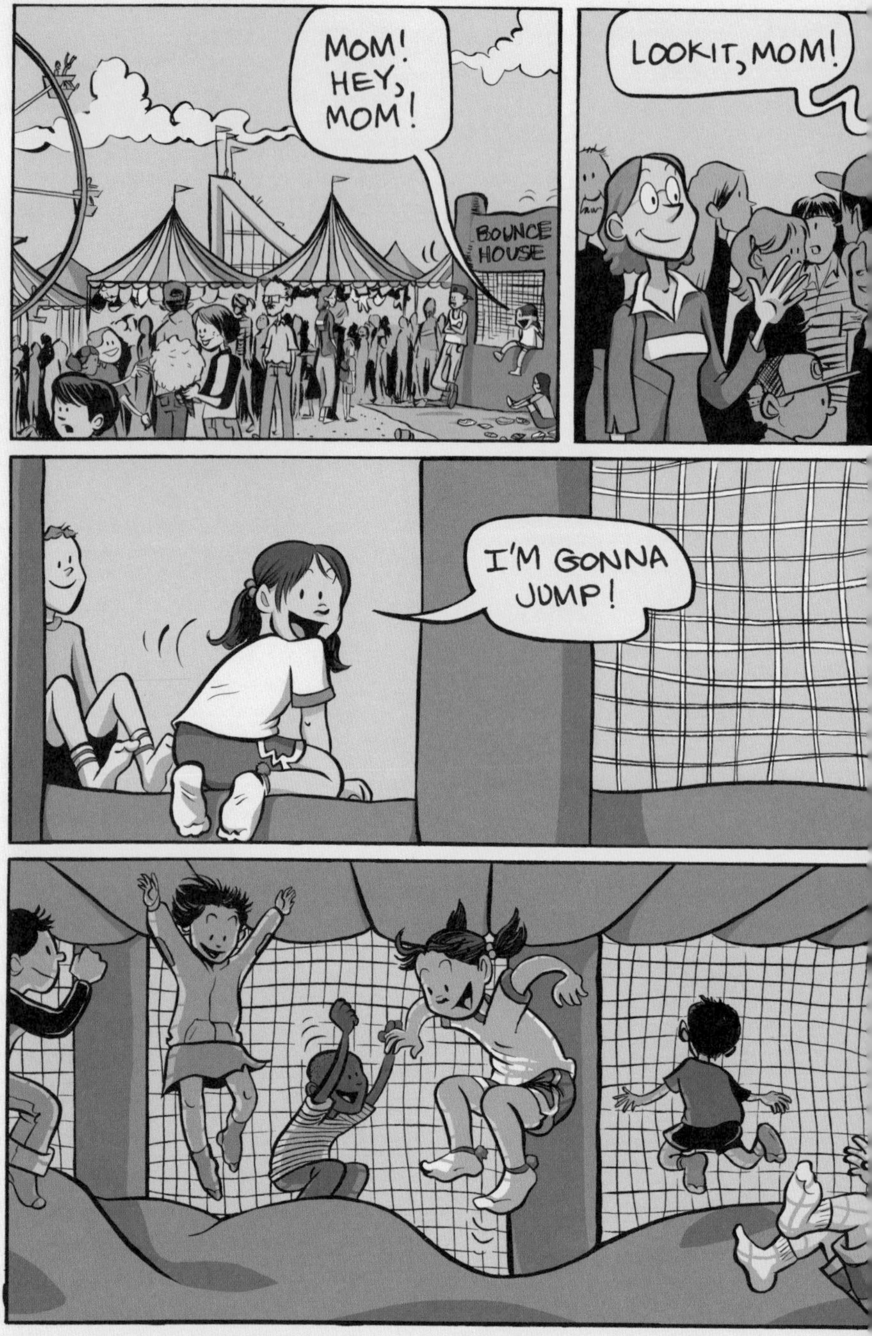
MOM! HEY, MOM!
BOUNCE HOUSE
LOOKIT, MOM!
I'M GONNA JUMP!

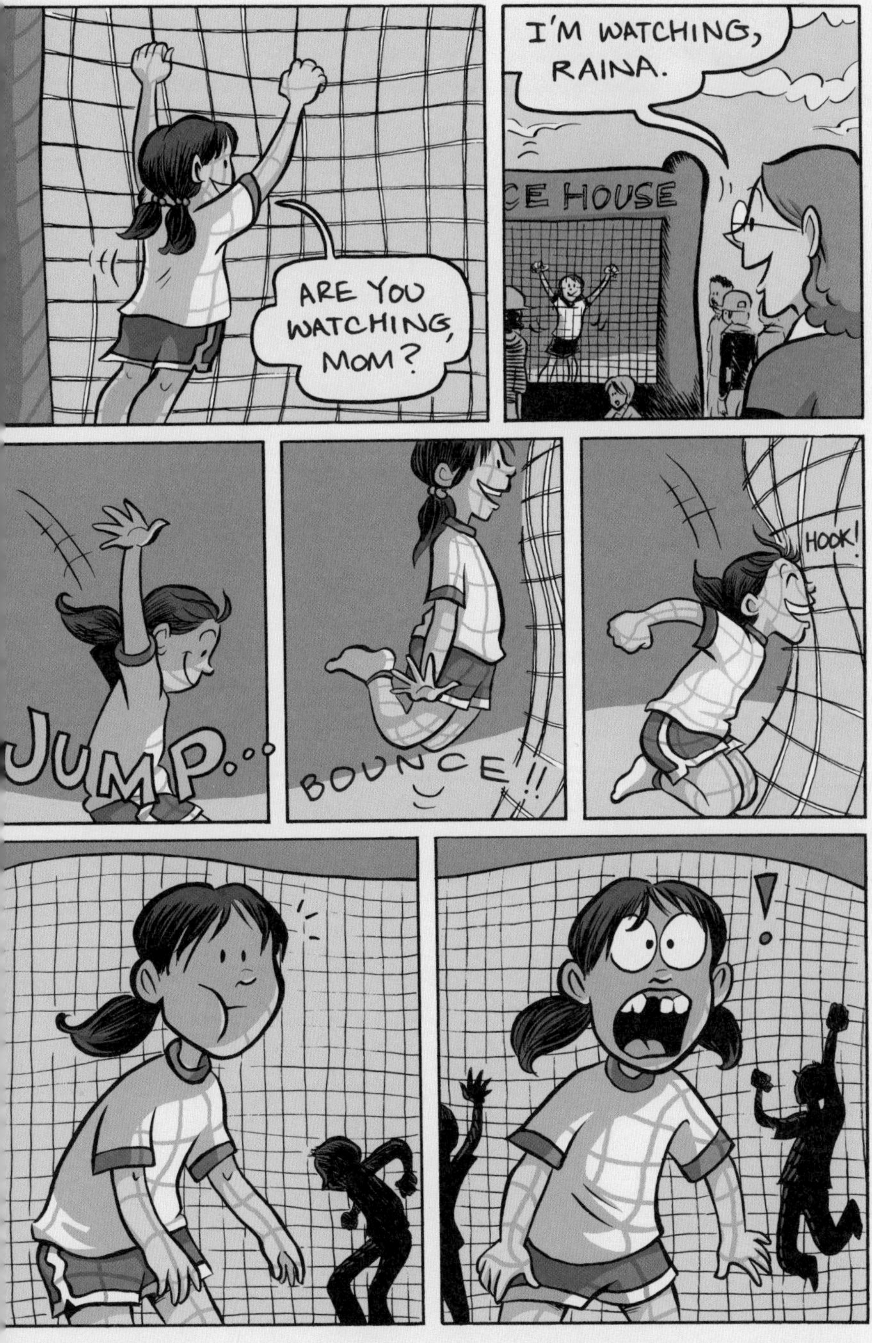
ARE YOU WATCHING, MOM?
I'M WATCHING, RAINA.
CE HOUSE
JUMP...
BOUNCE!!
HOOK!
!

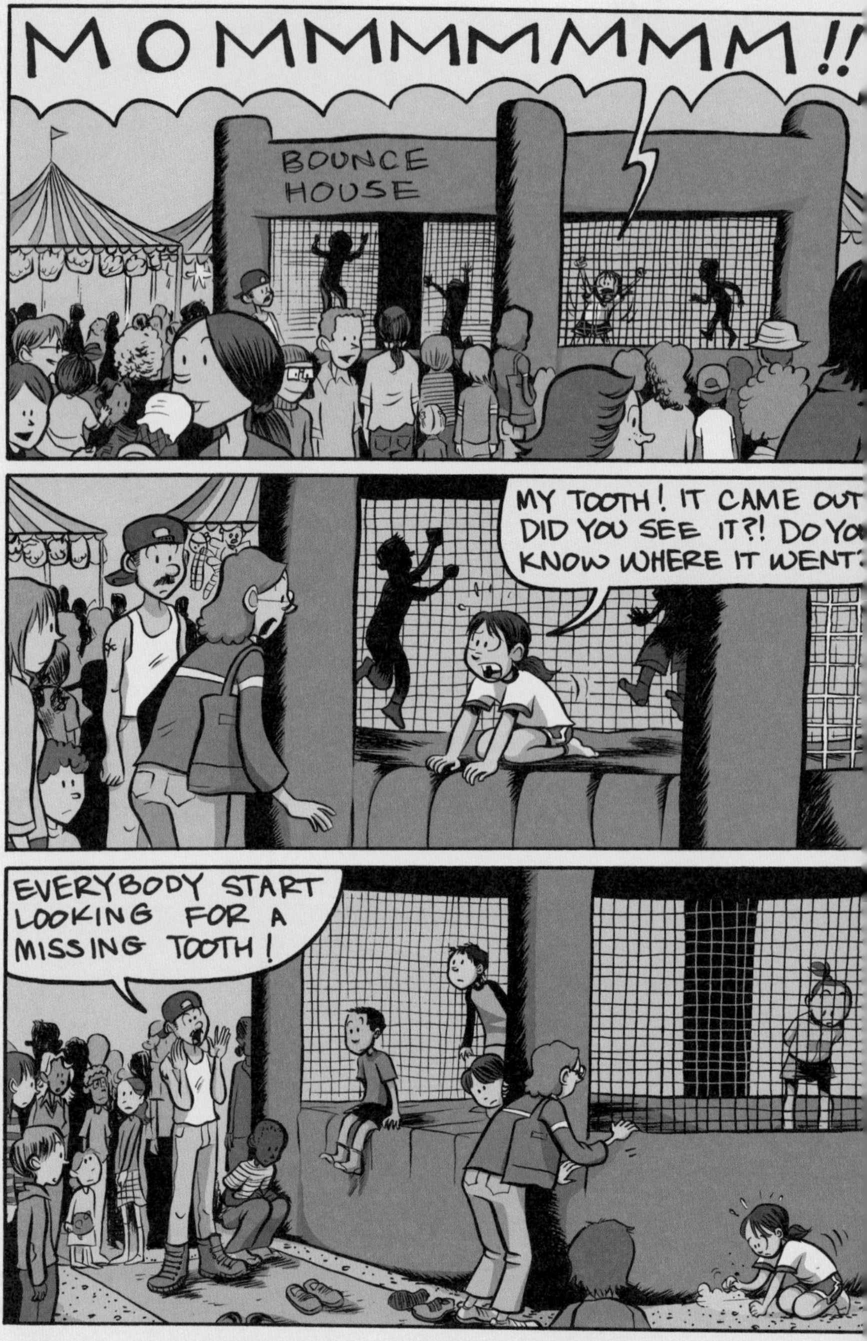
MOMMMMMMM!!
BOUNCE HOUSE
MY TOOTH! IT CAME OUT DID YOU SEE IT?! DO YOU KNOW WHERE IT WENT?
EVERYBODY START LOOKING FOR A MISSING TOOTH!

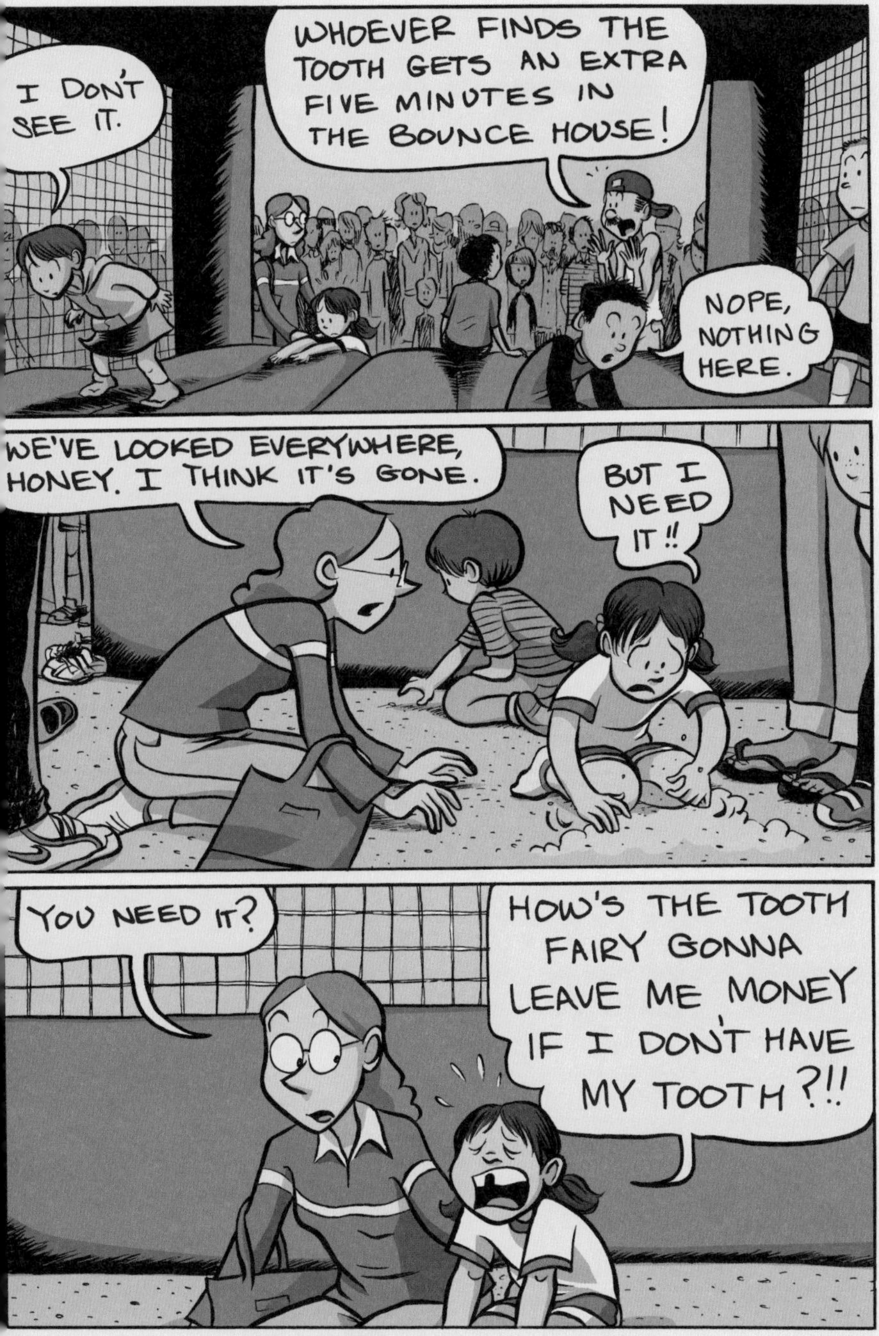
I DON'T SEE IT.
WHOEVER FINDS THE TOOTH GETS AN EXTRA FIVE MINUTES IN THE BOUNCE HOUSE!
NOPE, NOTHING HERE.
WE'VE LOOKED EVERYWHERE, HONEY. I THINK IT'S GONE.
BUT I NEED IT!!
YOU NEED IT?
HOW'S THE TOOTH FAIRY GONNA LEAVE ME MONEY IF I DON'T HAVE MY TOOTH?!!

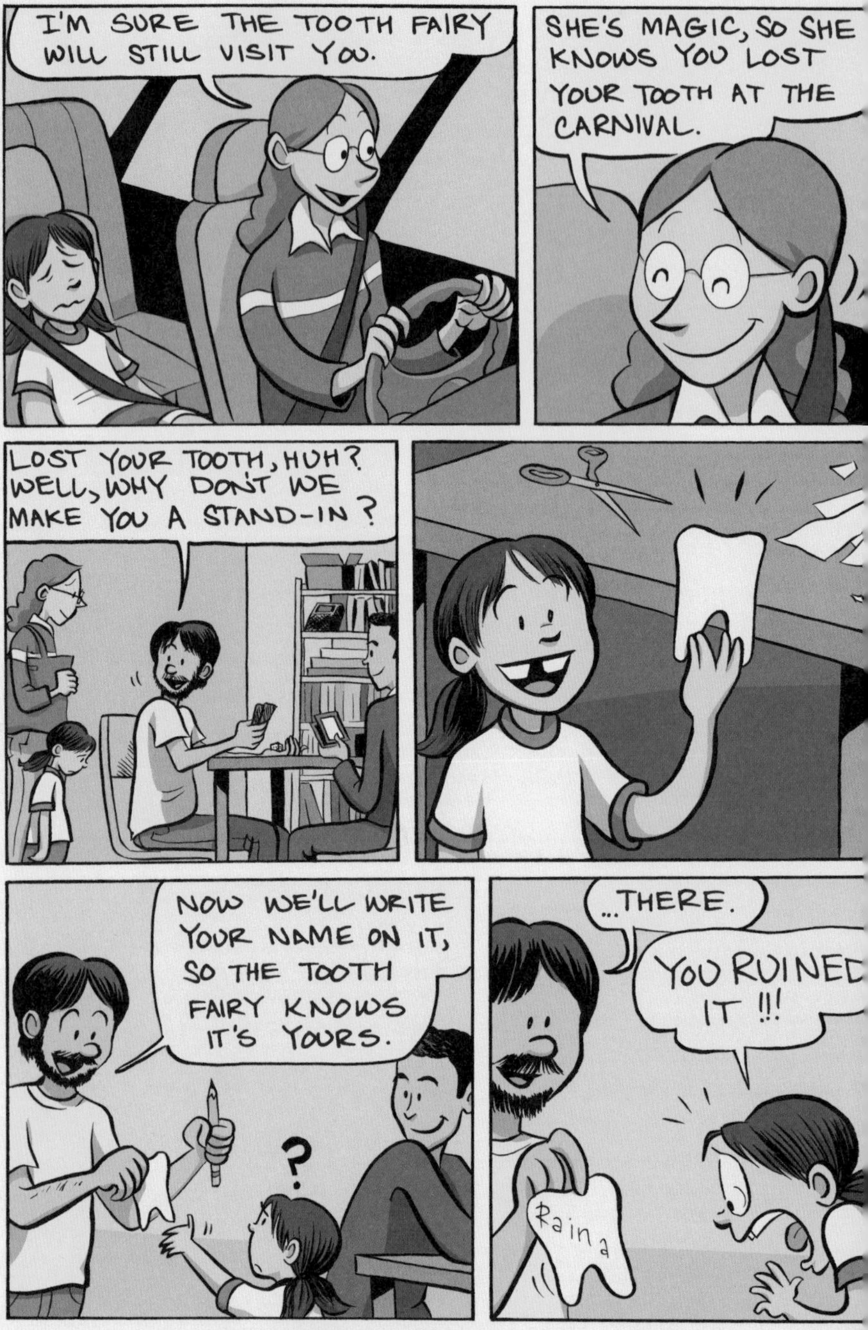
I'M SURE THE TOOTH FAIRY WILL STILL VISIT YOU.
SHE'S MAGIC, SO SHE KNOWS YOU LOST YOUR TOOTH AT THE CARNIVAL.
LOST YOUR TOOTH, HUH? WELL, WHY DON'T WE MAKE YOU A STAND-IN?
NOW WE'LL WRITE YOUR NAME ON IT, SO THE TOOTH FAIRY KNOWS IT'S YOURS.
?
...THERE.
Raina
YOU RUINED IT !!!

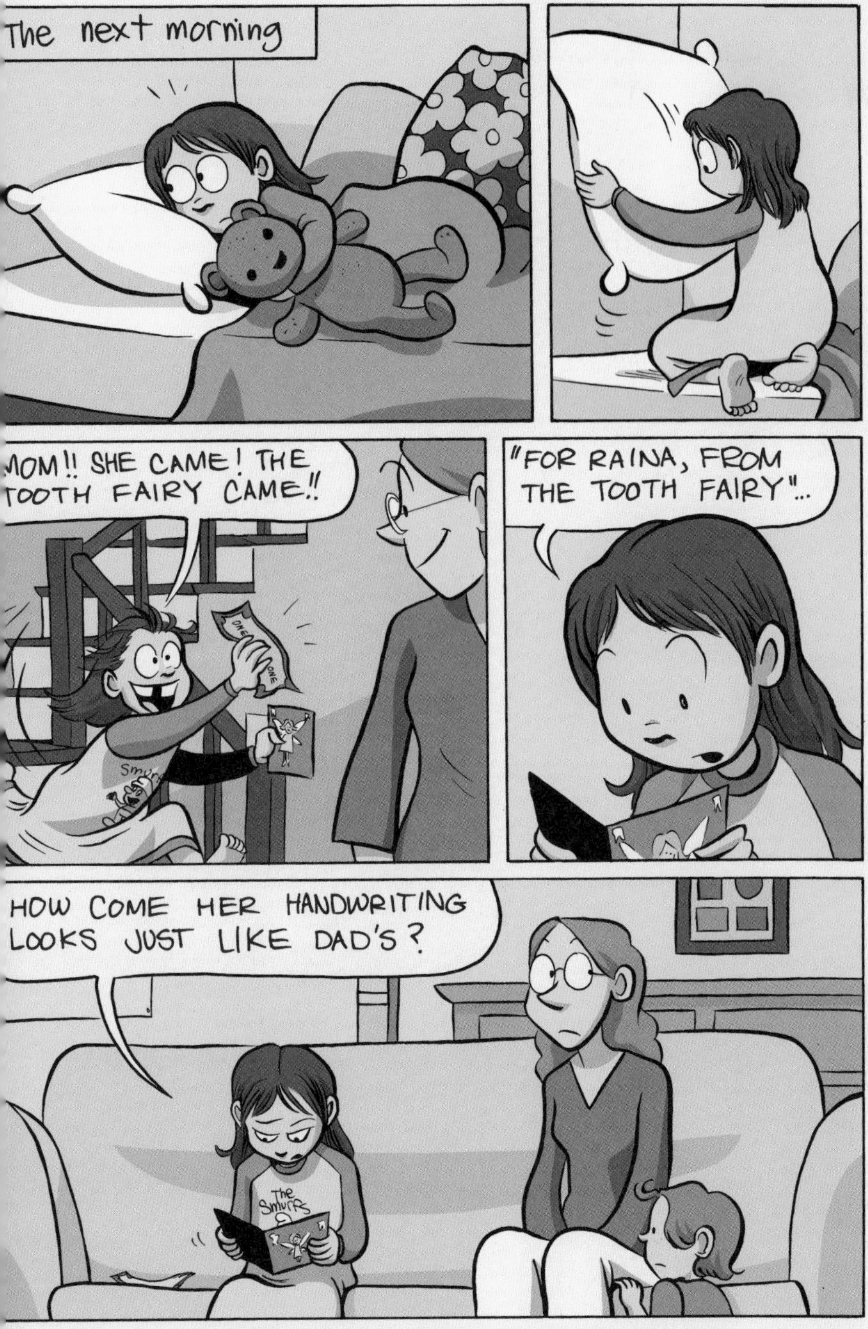

The next morning
MOM!! SHE CAME! THE TOOTH FAIRY CAME!!
ONE
"FOR RAINA, FROM THE TOOTH FAIRY"...
HOW COME HER HANDWRITING LOOKS JUST LIKE DAD'S?
The Smurfs

Blink

YOU'RE ALL DONE, RAINA. HOW DO YOU FEEL?

Ha
Heal

HHK.

JUST MAKE SURE SHE KEEPS THE GAUZE IN TONIGHT, OKAY? ONLY SOFT FOODS, TYLENOL, YOU KNOW THE DRILL.

THANKS, DR. GOLDEN.

I'LL SEE YOU IN A WEEK FOR THE FOLLOW-UP.

KKH.

DR. GOLDEN DDS

HAVE A MERRY CHRISTMAS!!

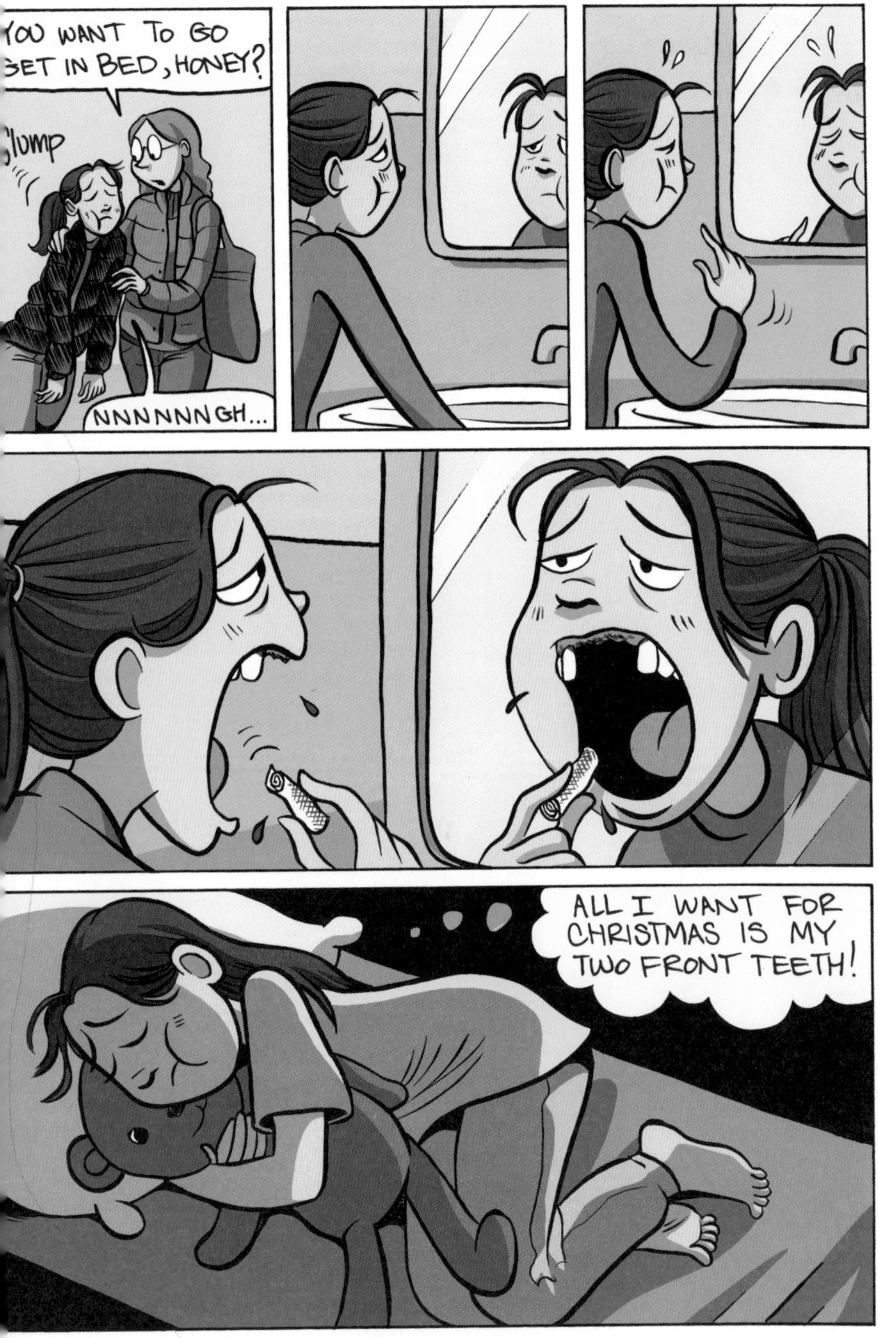
YOU WANT TO GO
GET IN BED, HONEY?
SLUMP
NNNNNNGH...
ALL I WANT FOR
CHRISTMAS IS MY
TWO FRONT TEETH!

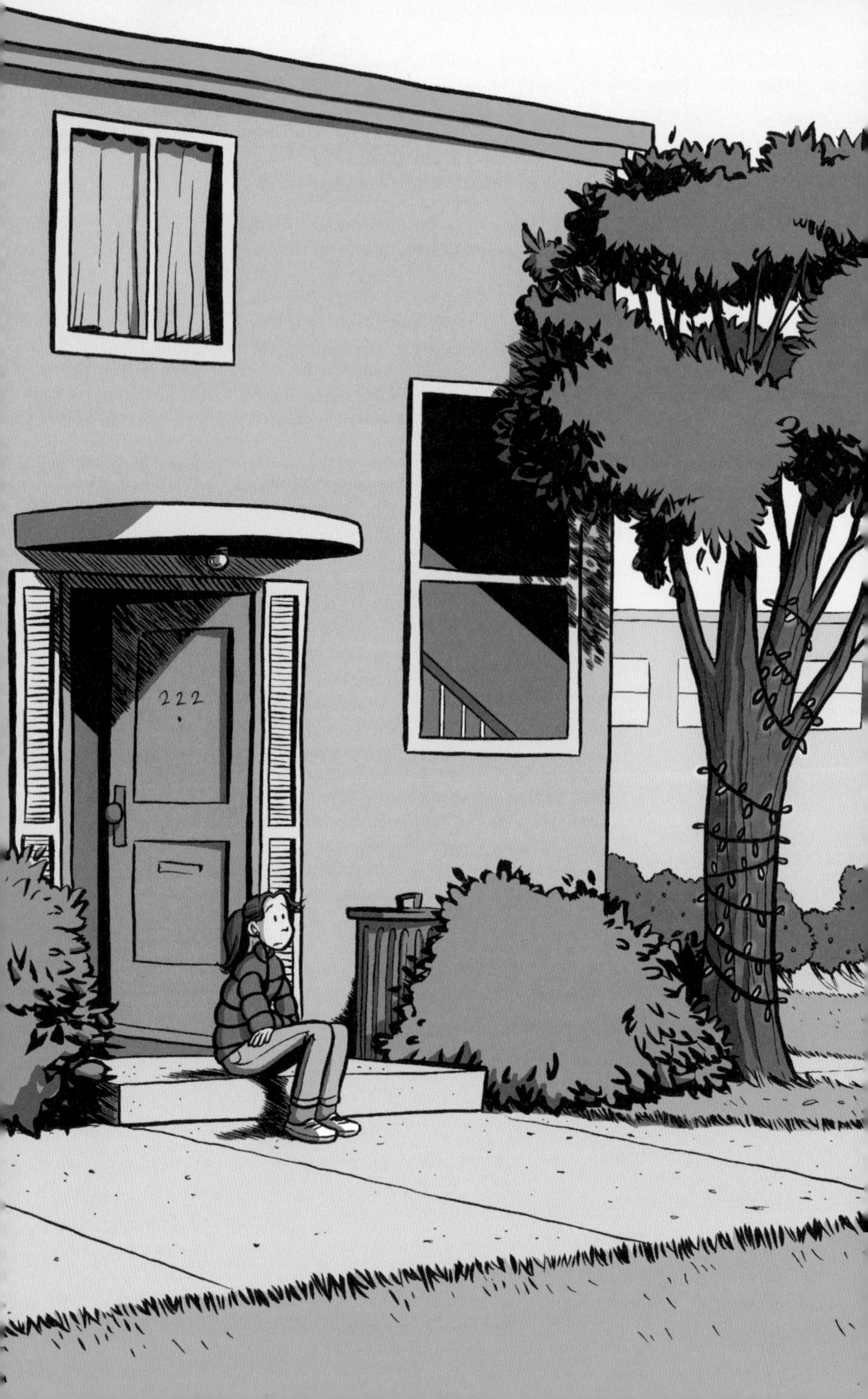
222

A few days later

YOUR NEW RETAINER IS HERE!

GET READY...

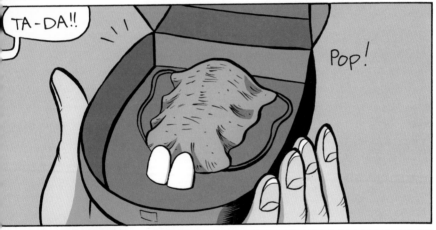

TA-DA!!

POP!

TRY IT ON!

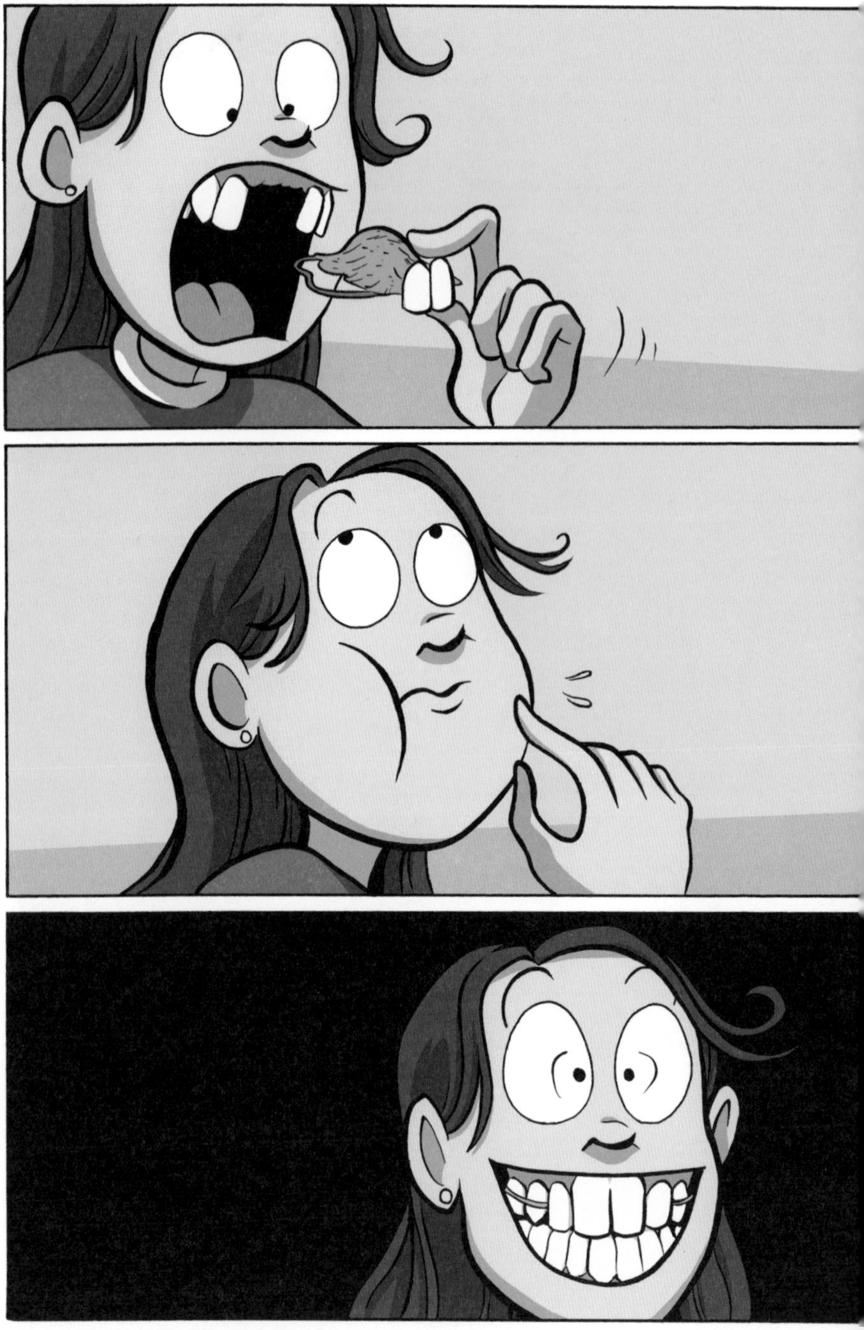

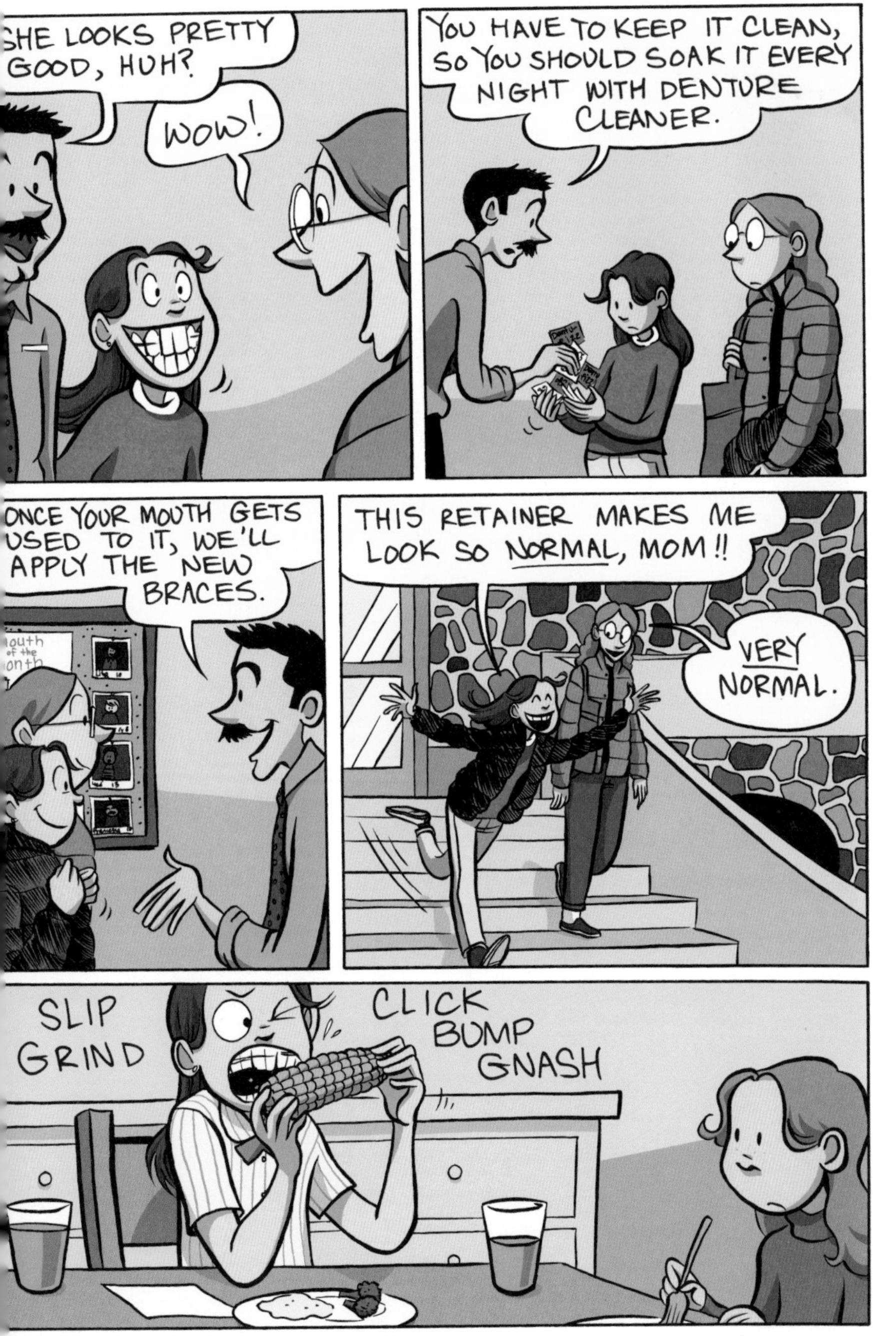
SHE LOOKS PRETTY GOOD, HUH?
WOW!
YOU HAVE TO KEEP IT CLEAN, SO YOU SHOULD SOAK IT EVERY NIGHT WITH DENTURE CLEANER.
ONCE YOUR MOUTH GETS USED TO IT, WE'LL APPLY THE NEW BRACES.
THIS RETAINER MAKES ME LOOK SO NORMAL, MOM!!
VERY NORMAL.
SLIP
GRIND
CLICK
BUMP
GNASH

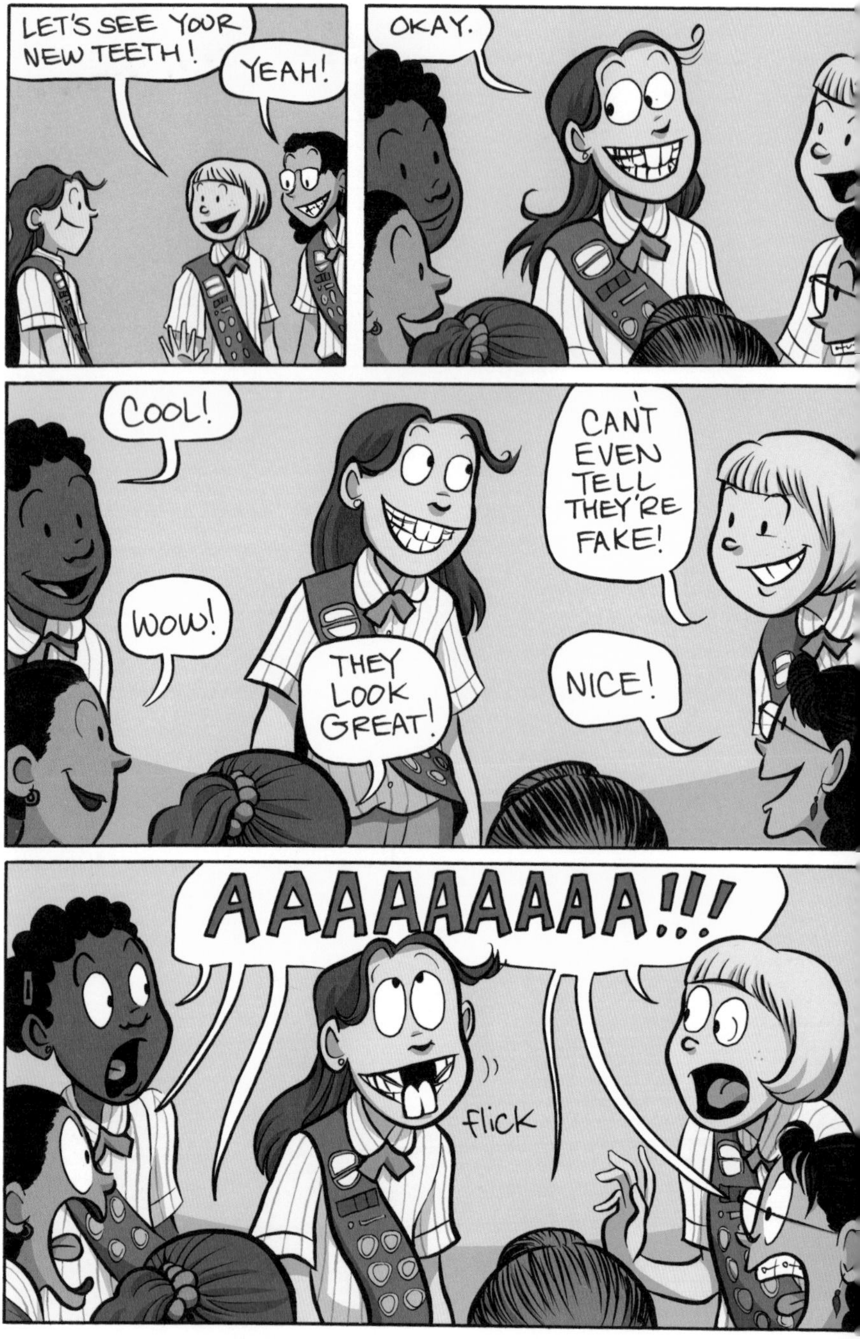
LET'S SEE YOUR NEW TEETH!
YEAH!
OKAY.
COOL!
CAN'T EVEN TELL THEY'RE FAKE!
WOW!
THEY LOOK GREAT!
NICE!
AAAAAAAAA!!!
flick

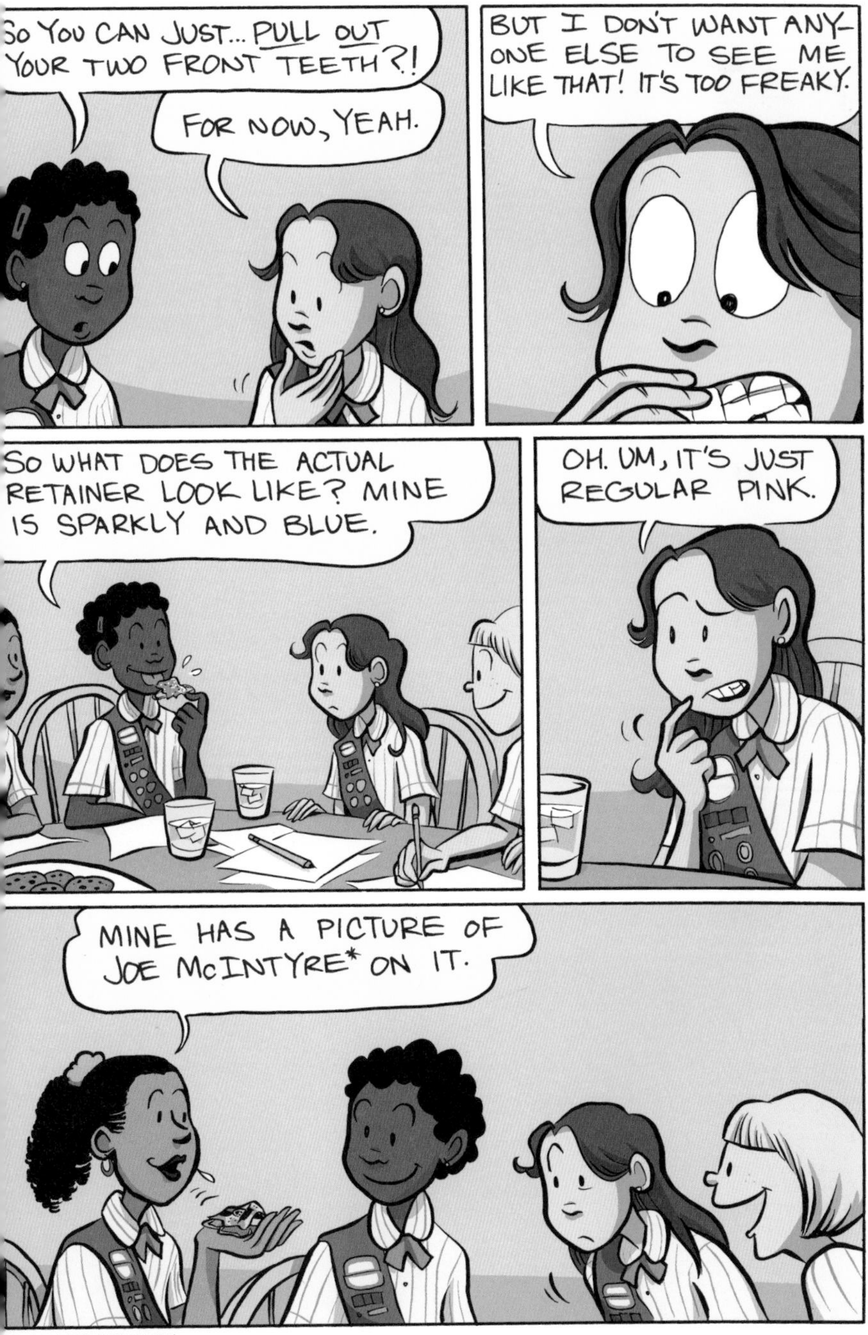
SO YOU CAN JUST... PULL OUT YOUR TWO FRONT TEETH?!
FOR NOW, YEAH.
BUT I DON'T WANT ANY-ONE ELSE TO SEE ME LIKE THAT! IT'S TOO FREAKY.
SO WHAT DOES THE ACTUAL RETAINER LOOK LIKE? MINE IS SPARKLY AND BLUE.
OH. UM, IT'S JUST REGULAR PINK.
MINE HAS A PICTURE OF JOE McINTYRE* ON IT.
*FROM NEW KIDS ON THE BLOCK!

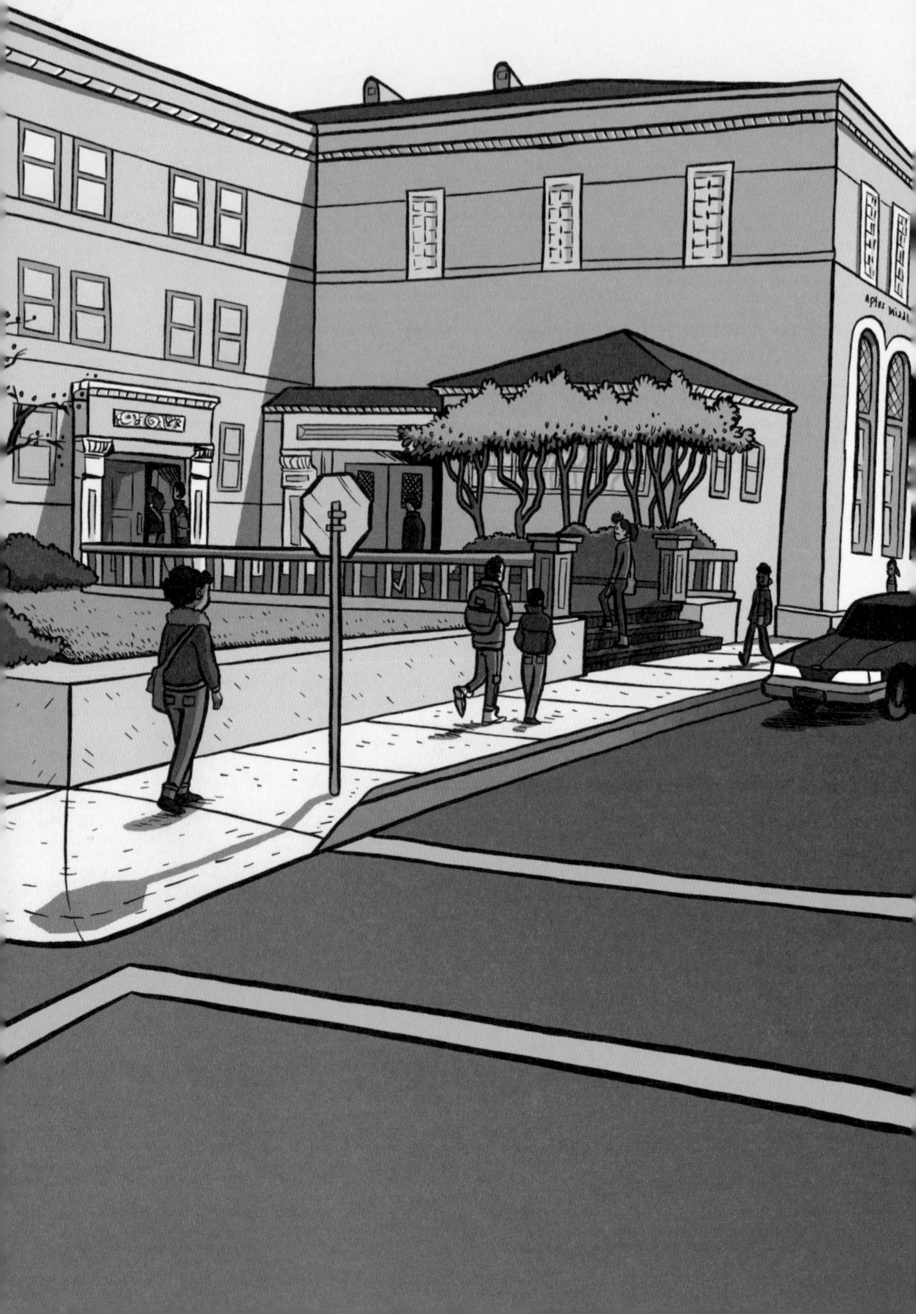

Aptos

CHAPTER FIVE

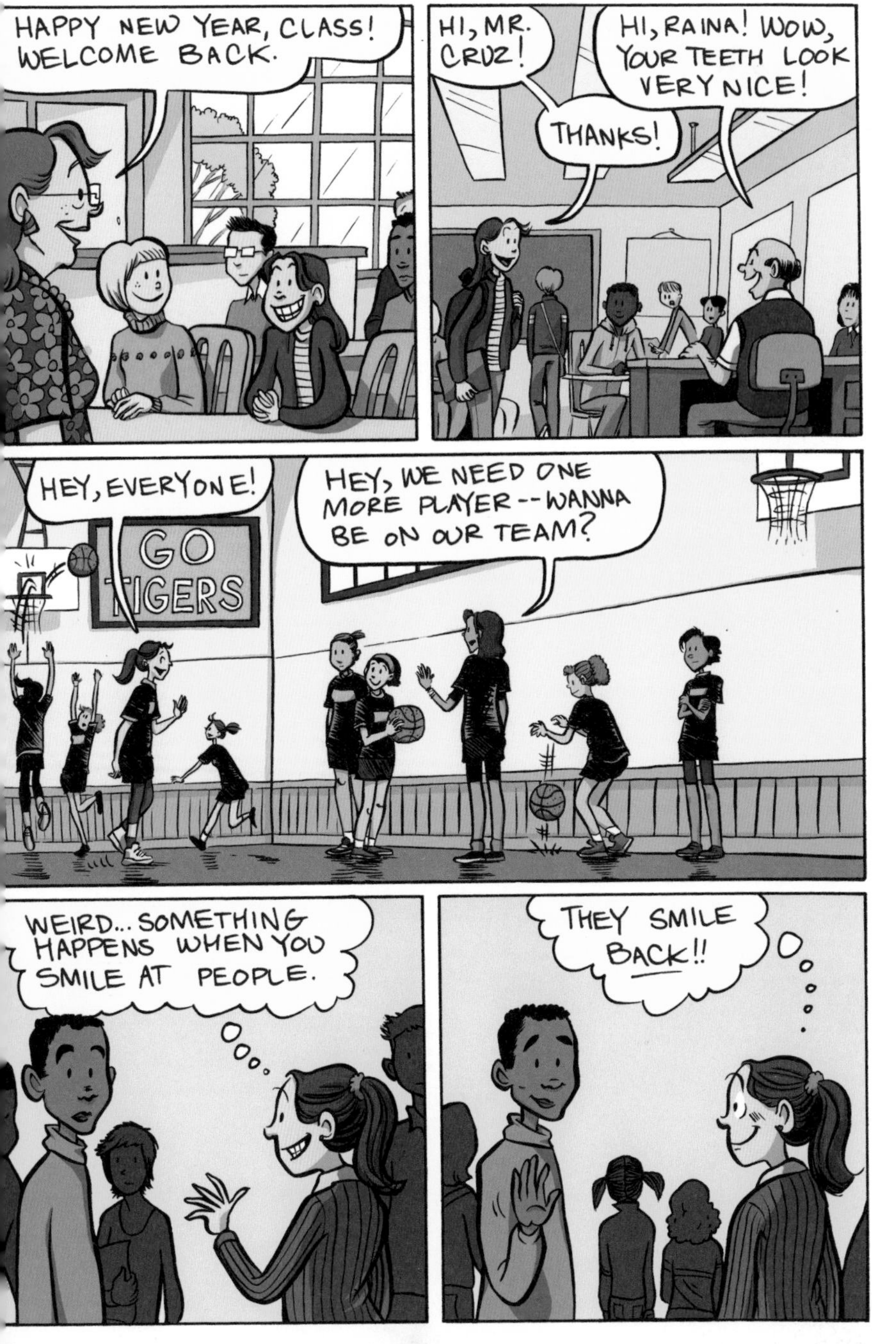
HAPPY NEW YEAR, CLASS! WELCOME BACK.
HI, MR. CRUZ!
HI, RAINA! WOW, YOUR TEETH LOOK VERY NICE!
THANKS!
HEY, EVERYONE!
GO TIGERS
HEY, WE NEED ONE MORE PLAYER--WANNA BE ON OUR TEAM?
WEIRD... SOMETHING HAPPENS WHEN YOU SMILE AT PEOPLE.
THEY SMILE BACK!!

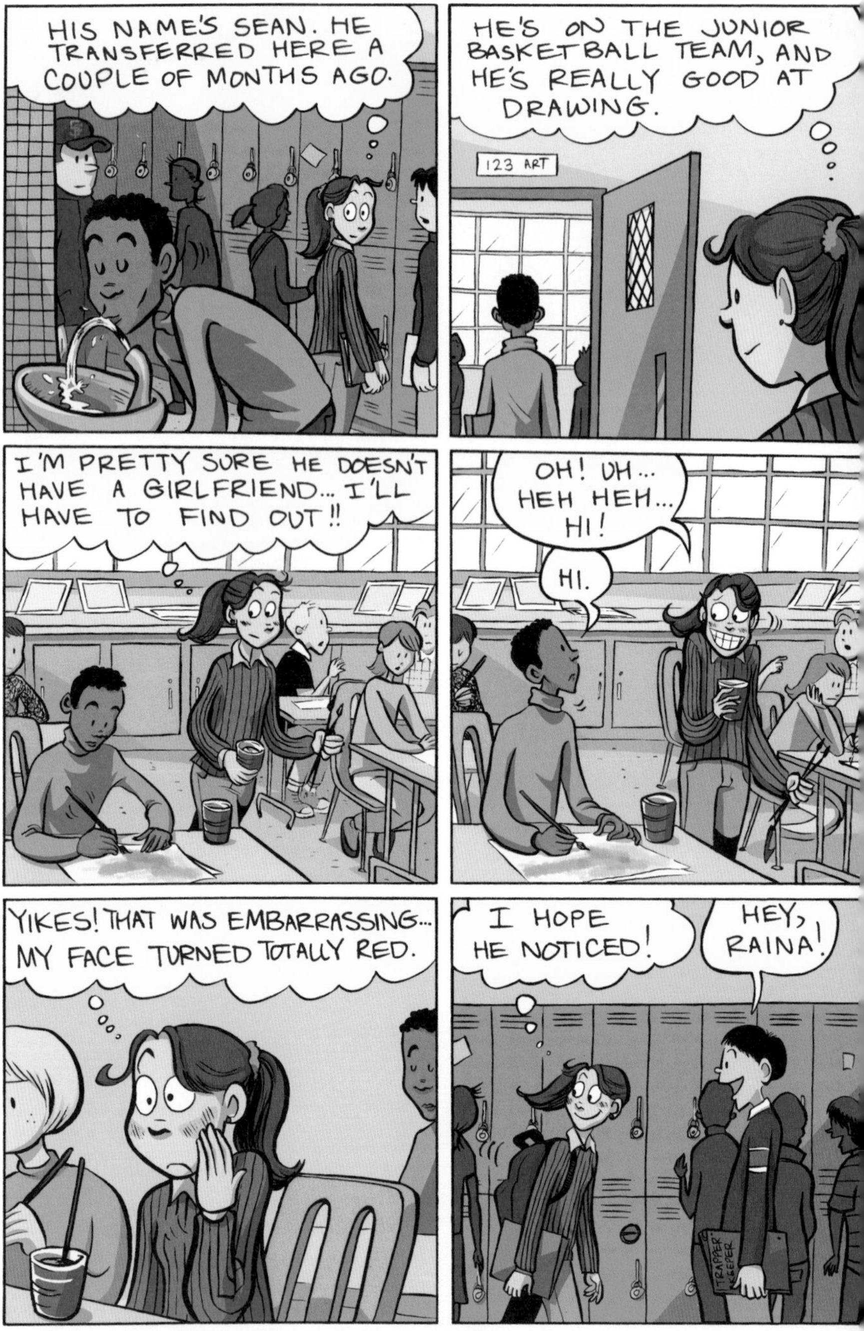
HIS NAME'S SEAN. HE TRANSFERRED HERE A COUPLE OF MONTHS AGO.
HE'S ON THE JUNIOR BASKETBALL TEAM, AND HE'S REALLY GOOD AT DRAWING.
123 ART
I'M PRETTY SURE HE DOESN'T HAVE A GIRLFRIEND... I'LL HAVE TO FIND OUT!!
OH! UH... HEH HEH... HI!
HI.
YIKES! THAT WAS EMBARRASSING... MY FACE TURNED TOTALLY RED.
I HOPE HE NOTICED!
HEY, RAINA!
TRAPPER KEEPER

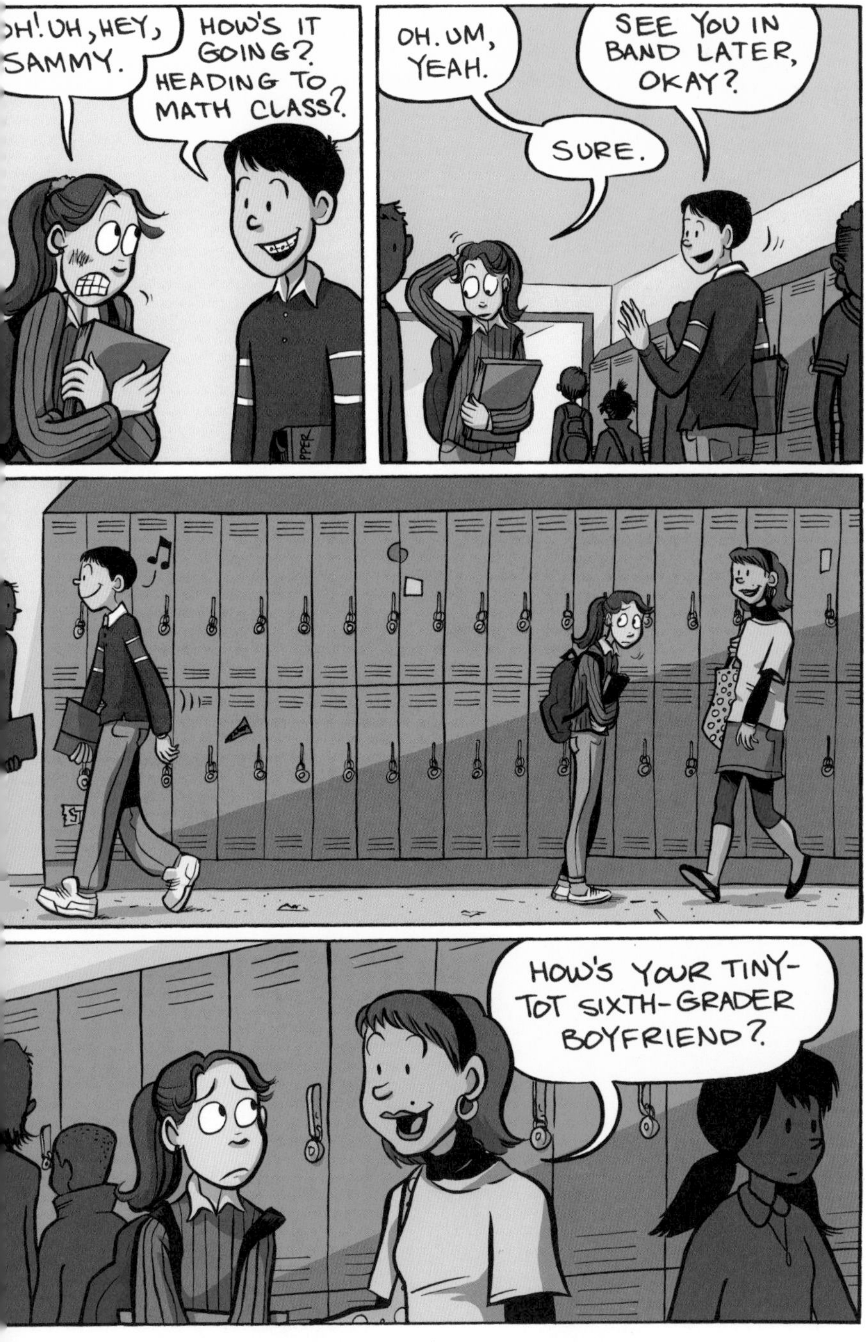
OH! UH, HEY, SAMMY.
HOW'S IT GOING? HEADING TO MATH CLASS?
OH. UM, YEAH.
SEE YOU IN BAND LATER, OKAY?
SURE.
HOW'S YOUR TINY-TOT SIXTH-GRADER BOYFRIEND?

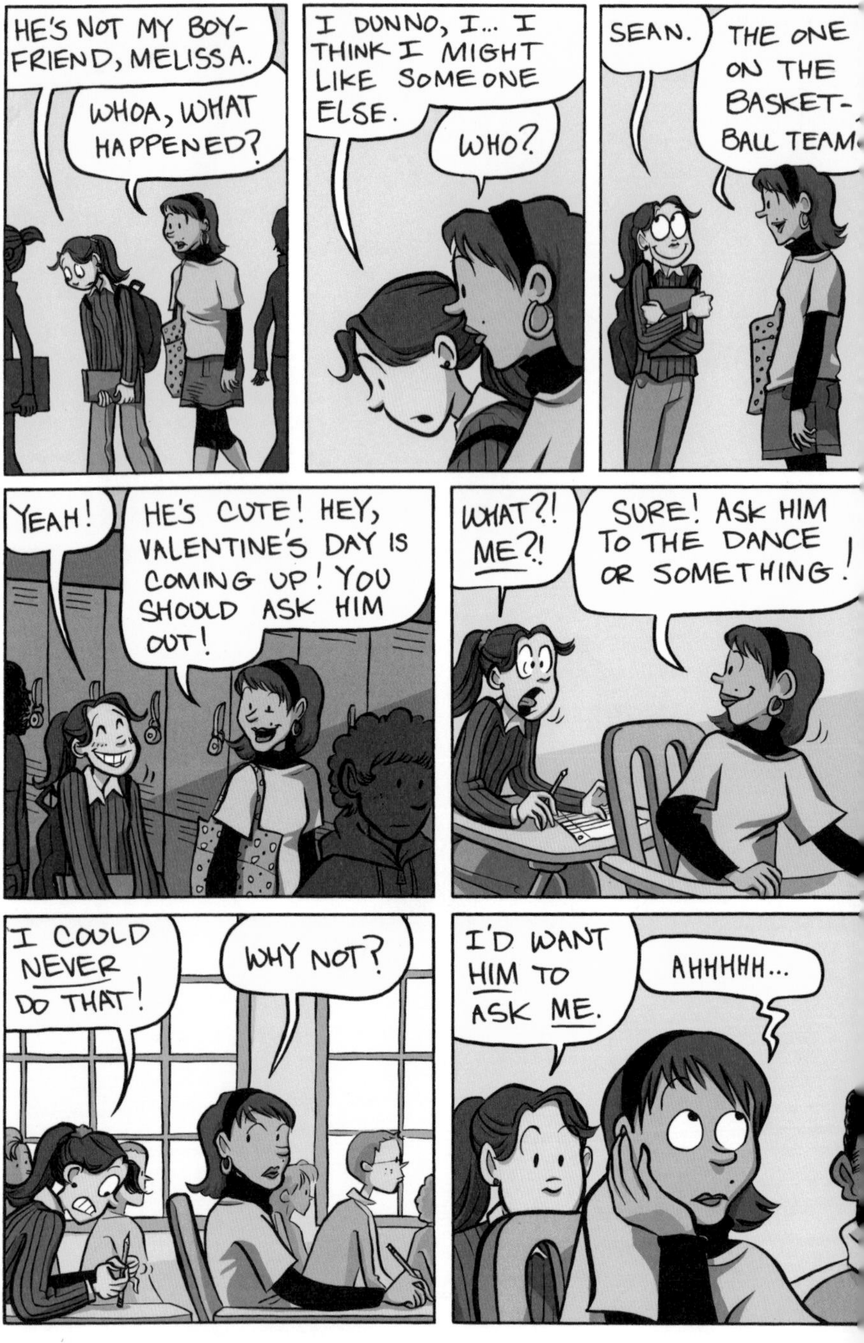
HE'S NOT MY BOY-FRIEND, MELISSA.
WHOA, WHAT HAPPENED?
I DUNNO, I... I THINK I MIGHT LIKE SOMEONE ELSE.
WHO?
SEAN.
THE ONE ON THE BASKET-BALL TEAM?
YEAH!
HE'S CUTE! HEY, VALENTINE'S DAY IS COMING UP! YOU SHOULD ASK HIM OUT!
WHAT?! ME?!
SURE! ASK HIM TO THE DANCE OR SOMETHING!
I COULD NEVER DO THAT!
WHY NOT?
I'D WANT HIM TO ASK ME.
AHHHHH...

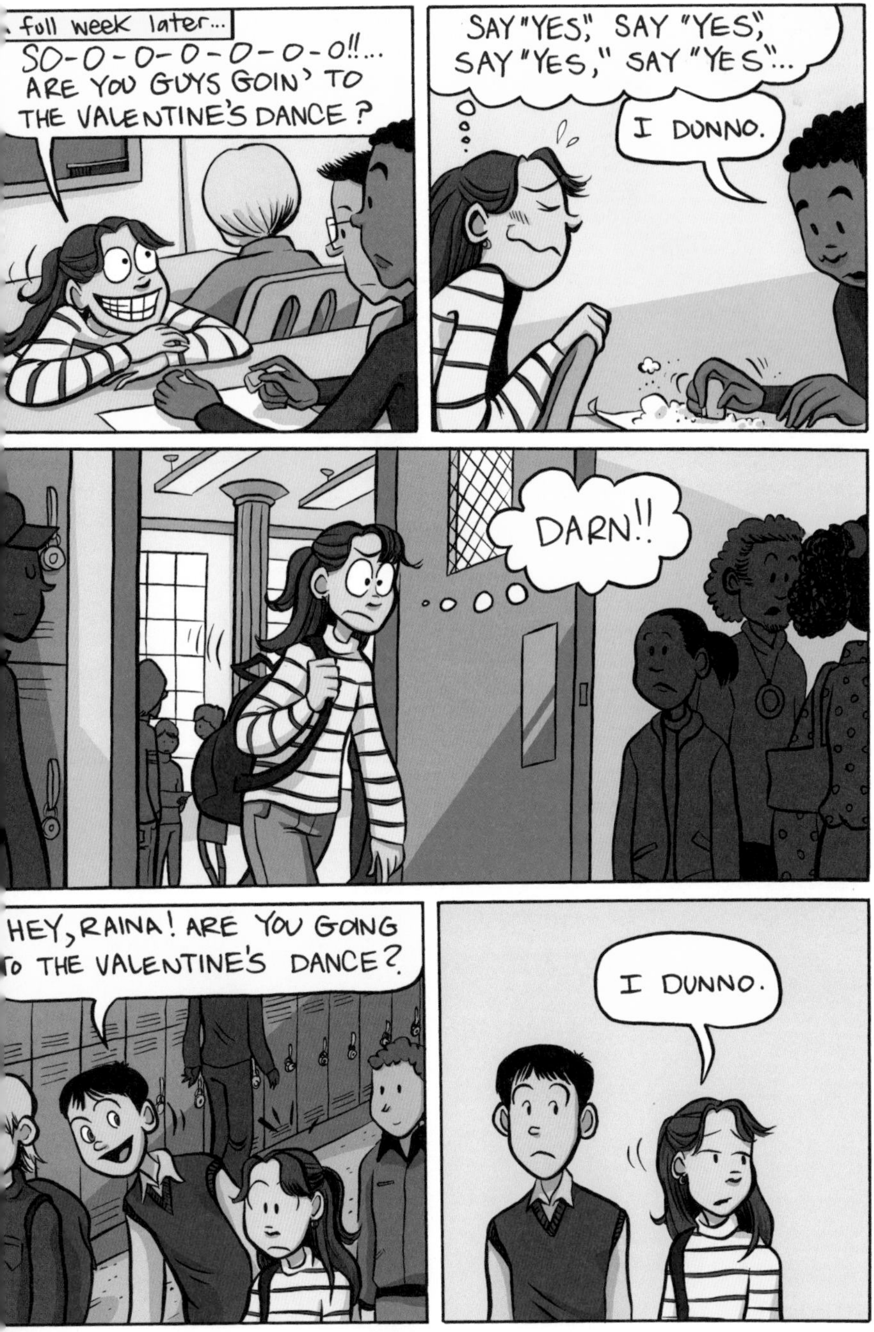
. full week later...
SO-O-O-O-O-O-O-O!!... ARE YOU GUYS GOIN' TO THE VALENTINE'S DANCE?
SAY "YES," SAY "YES," SAY "YES," SAY "YES"...
I DUNNO.
DARN!!
HEY, RAINA! ARE YOU GOING TO THE VALENTINE'S DANCE?
I DUNNO.

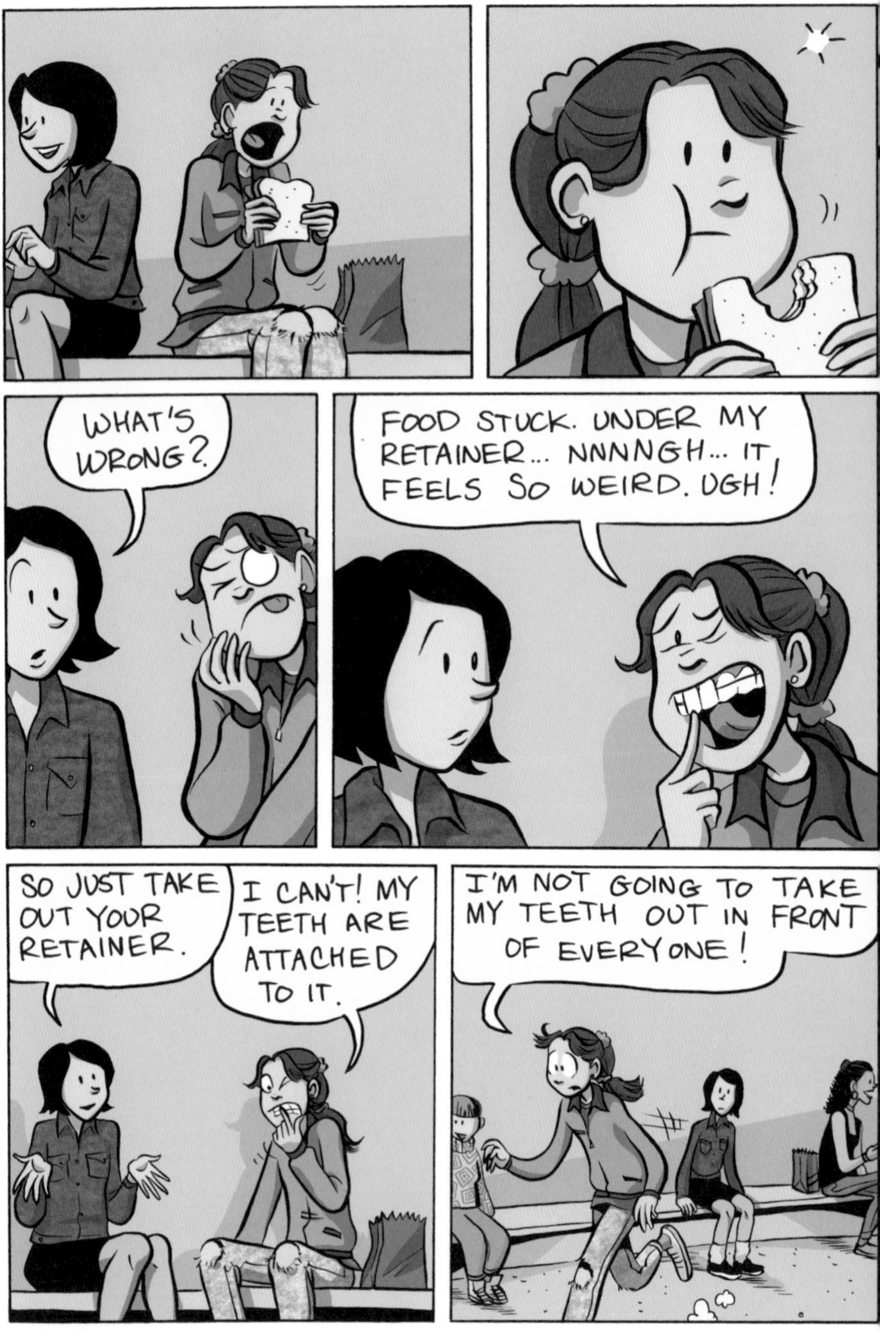
WHAT'S WRONG?
FOOD STUCK. UNDER MY RETAINER... NNNNGH... IT FEELS SO WEIRD. UGH!
SO JUST TAKE OUT YOUR RETAINER.
I CAN'T! MY TEETH ARE ATTACHED TO IT.
I'M NOT GOING TO TAKE MY TEETH OUT IN FRONT OF EVERYONE!

POP!

GSHHHHHHHHHHHHHHHHHHH!

SLRRRRRP

PTOO

MUCH BETTER.

CLNKL!

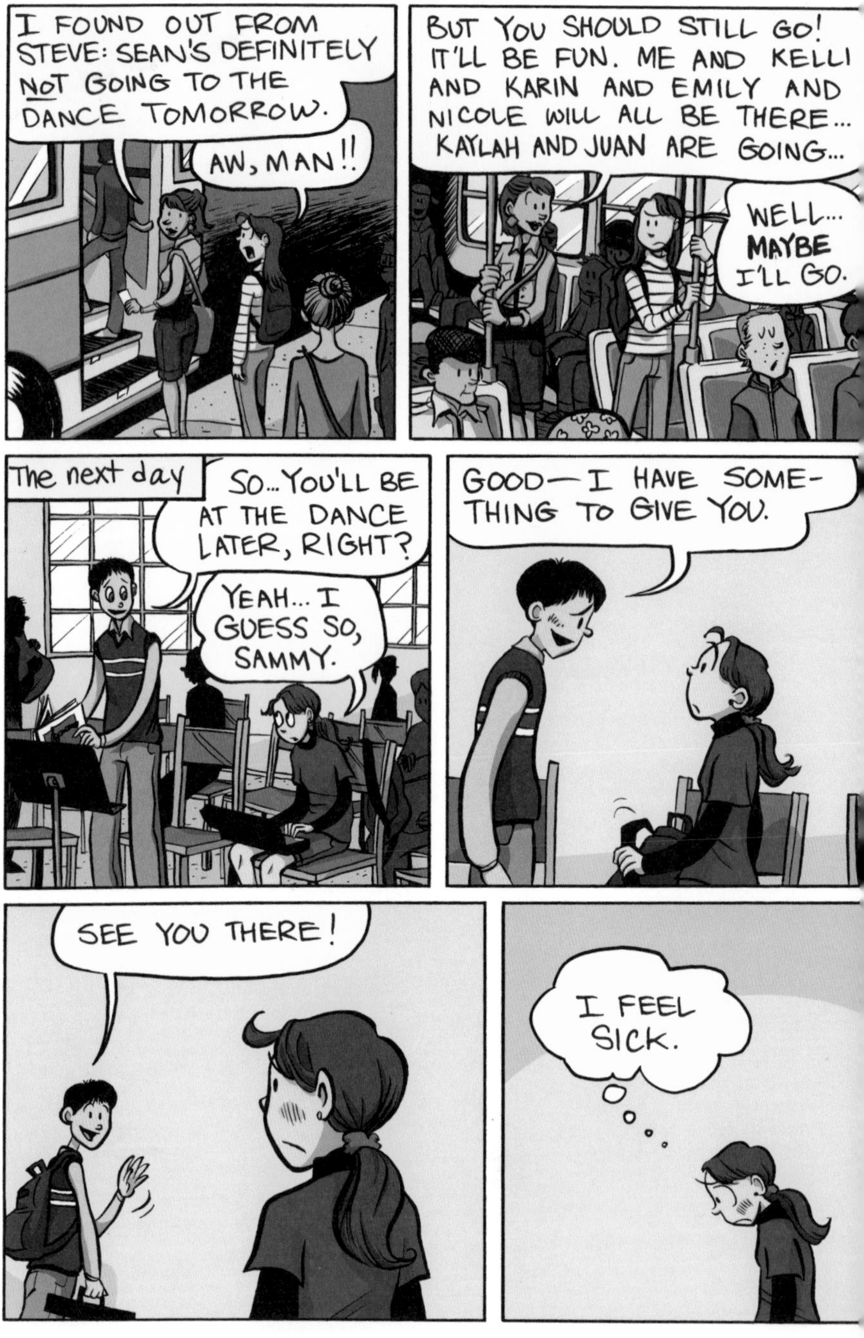
I FOUND OUT FROM STEVE: SEAN'S DEFINITELY NOT GOING TO THE DANCE TOMORROW.
AW, MAN!!
BUT YOU SHOULD STILL GO! IT'LL BE FUN. ME AND KELLI AND KARIN AND EMILY AND NICOLE WILL ALL BE THERE... KAYLAH AND JUAN ARE GOING...
WELL... MAYBE I'LL GO.
The next day
SO... YOU'LL BE AT THE DANCE LATER, RIGHT?
YEAH... I GUESS SO, SAMMY.
GOOD—I HAVE SOME-THING TO GIVE YOU.
SEE YOU THERE!
I FEEL SICK.

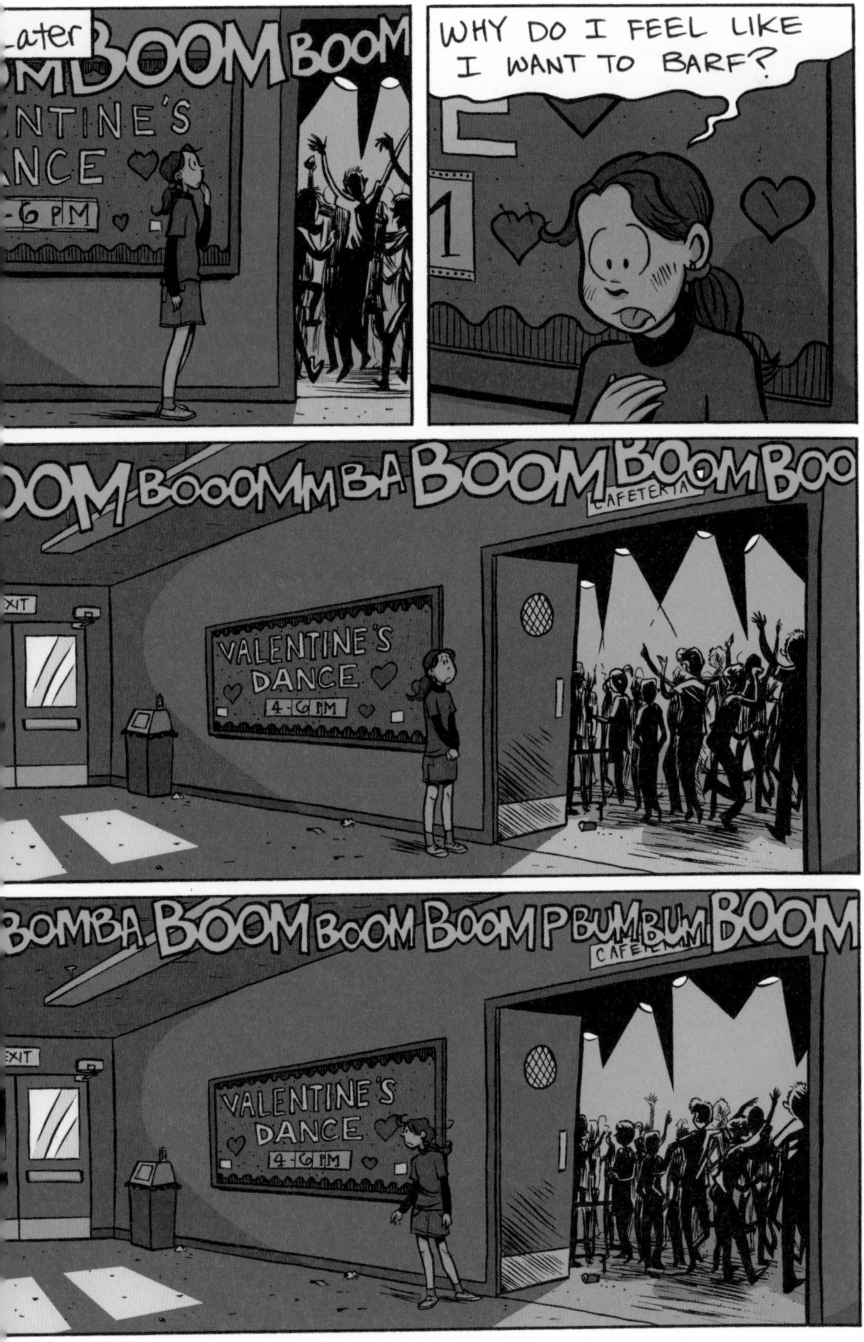
Later
BOOM BOOM
NTINE'S
NCE
6 PM
WHY DO I FEEL LIKE I WANT TO BARF?
OOM BOOOMMBA BOOM BOOM BOO
CAFETERIA
EXIT
VALENTINE'S DANCE
4-6 PM
BOMBA BOOM BOOM BOOM P BUM BUM BOOM
CAFE
EXIT
VALENTINE'S DANCE
4-6 PM

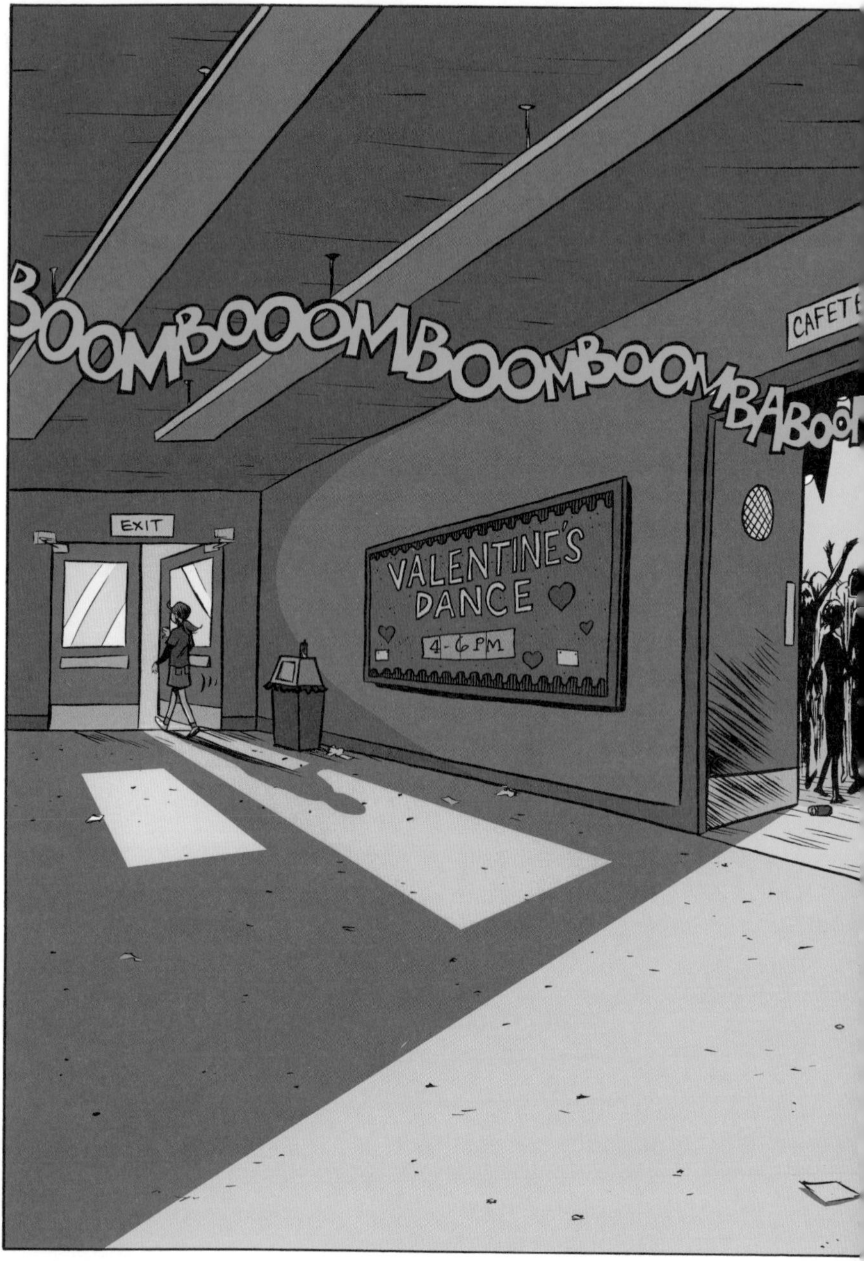
BOOMBOOOMBOOOMBOOOMBABOO
CAFETE
EXIT
VALENTINE'S DANCE
4-6 PM

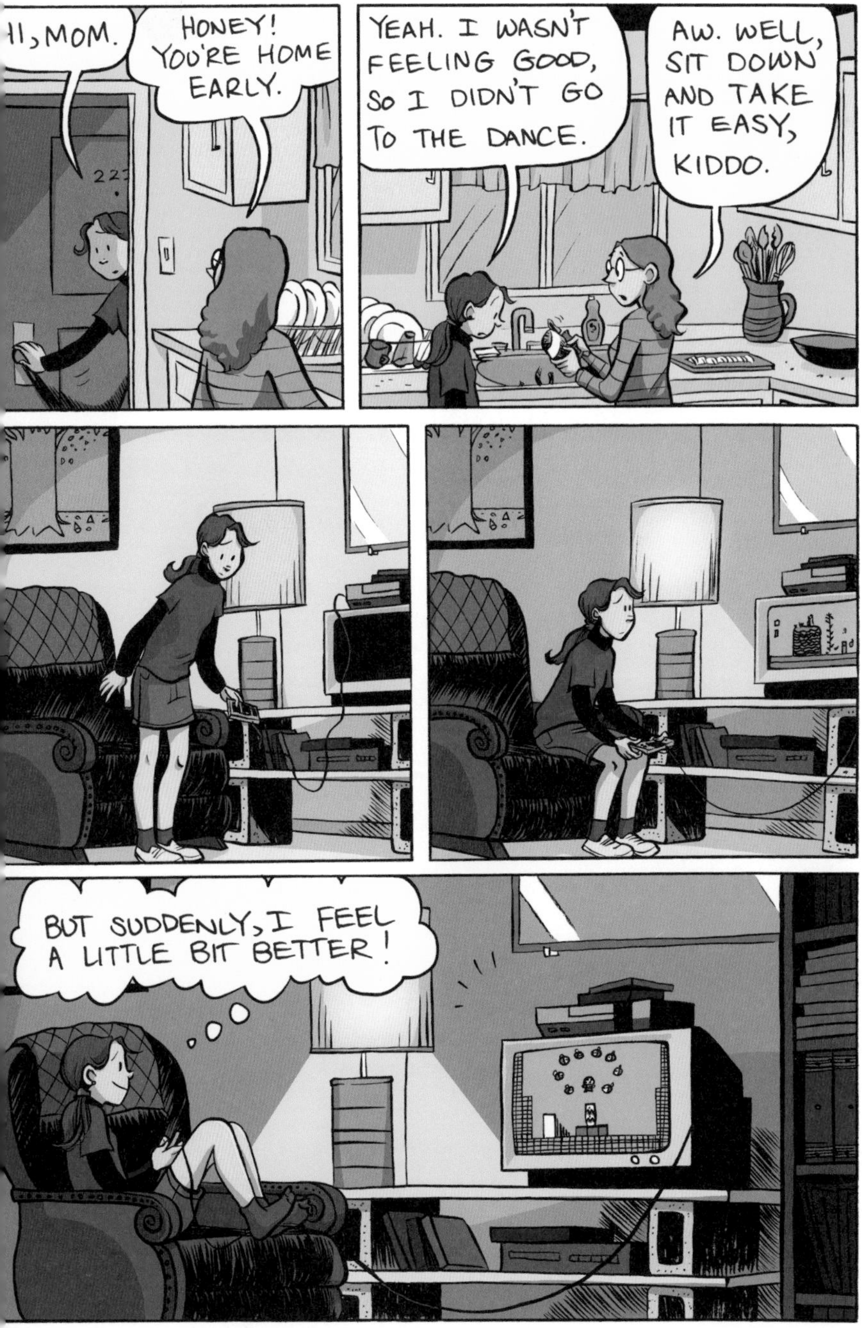
HI, MOM.
HONEY! YOU'RE HOME EARLY.
YEAH. I WASN'T FEELING GOOD, SO I DIDN'T GO TO THE DANCE.
AW. WELL, SIT DOWN AND TAKE IT EASY, KIDDO.
BUT SUDDENLY, I FEEL A LITTLE BIT BETTER!

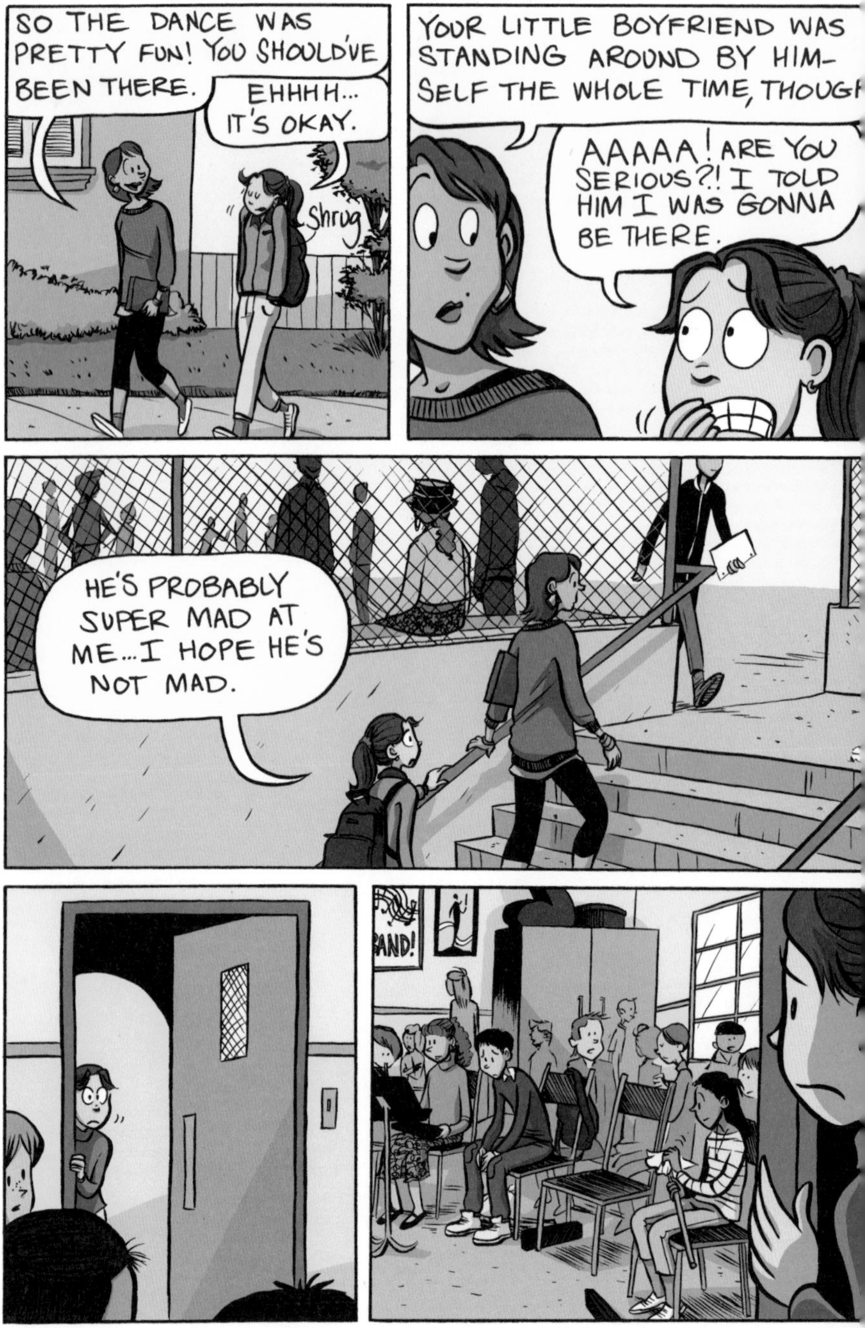
SO THE DANCE WAS PRETTY FUN! YOU SHOULD'VE BEEN THERE.
EHHHH... IT'S OKAY.
Shrug
YOUR LITTLE BOYFRIEND WAS STANDING AROUND BY HIMSELF THE WHOLE TIME, THOUGH
AAAAA! ARE YOU SERIOUS?! I TOLD HIM I WAS GONNA BE THERE.
HE'S PROBABLY SUPER MAD AT ME...I HOPE HE'S NOT MAD.
BAND!

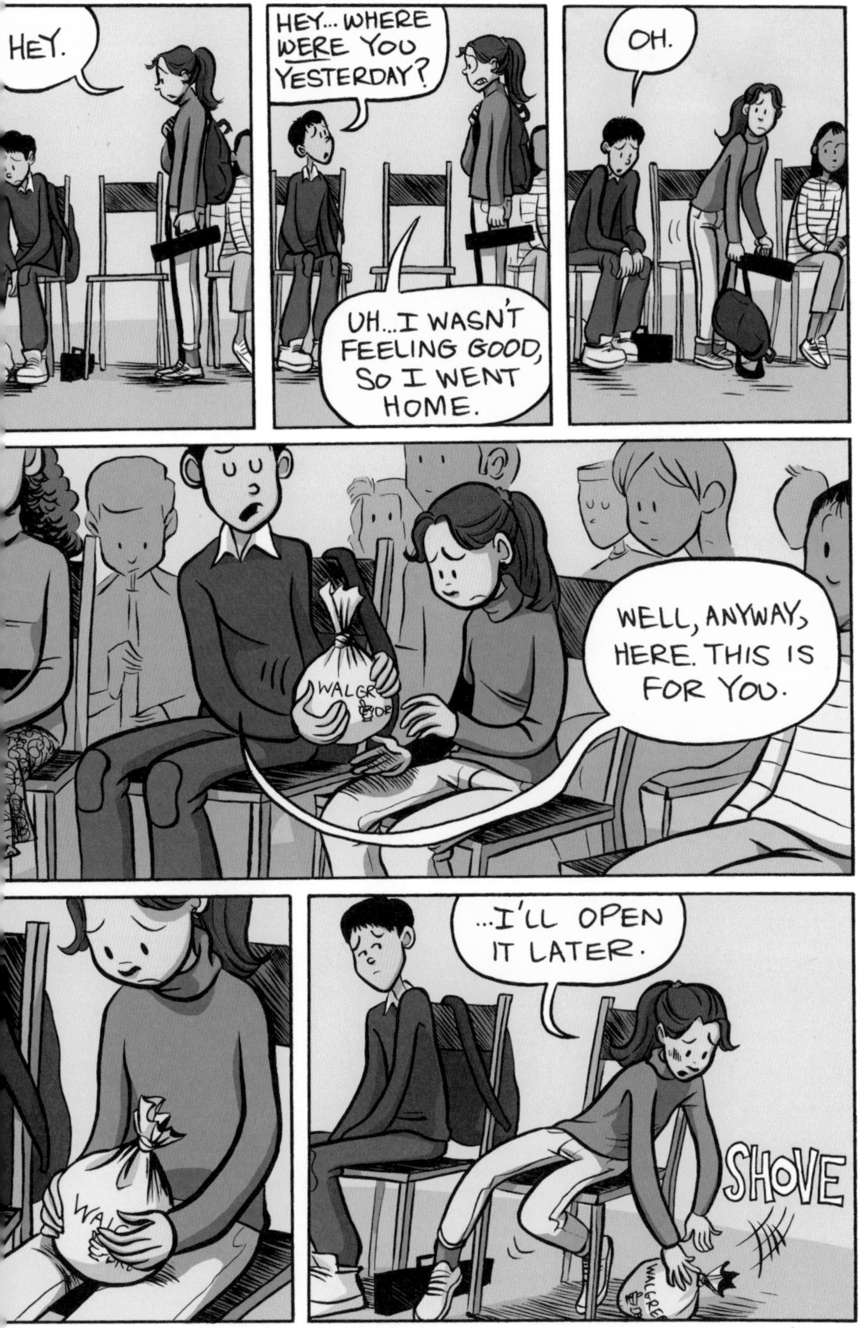
HEY.
HEY... WHERE WERE YOU YESTERDAY?
UH... I WASN'T FEELING GOOD, SO I WENT HOME.
OH.
WELL, ANYWAY, HERE. THIS IS FOR YOU.
...I'LL OPEN IT LATER.
SHOVE

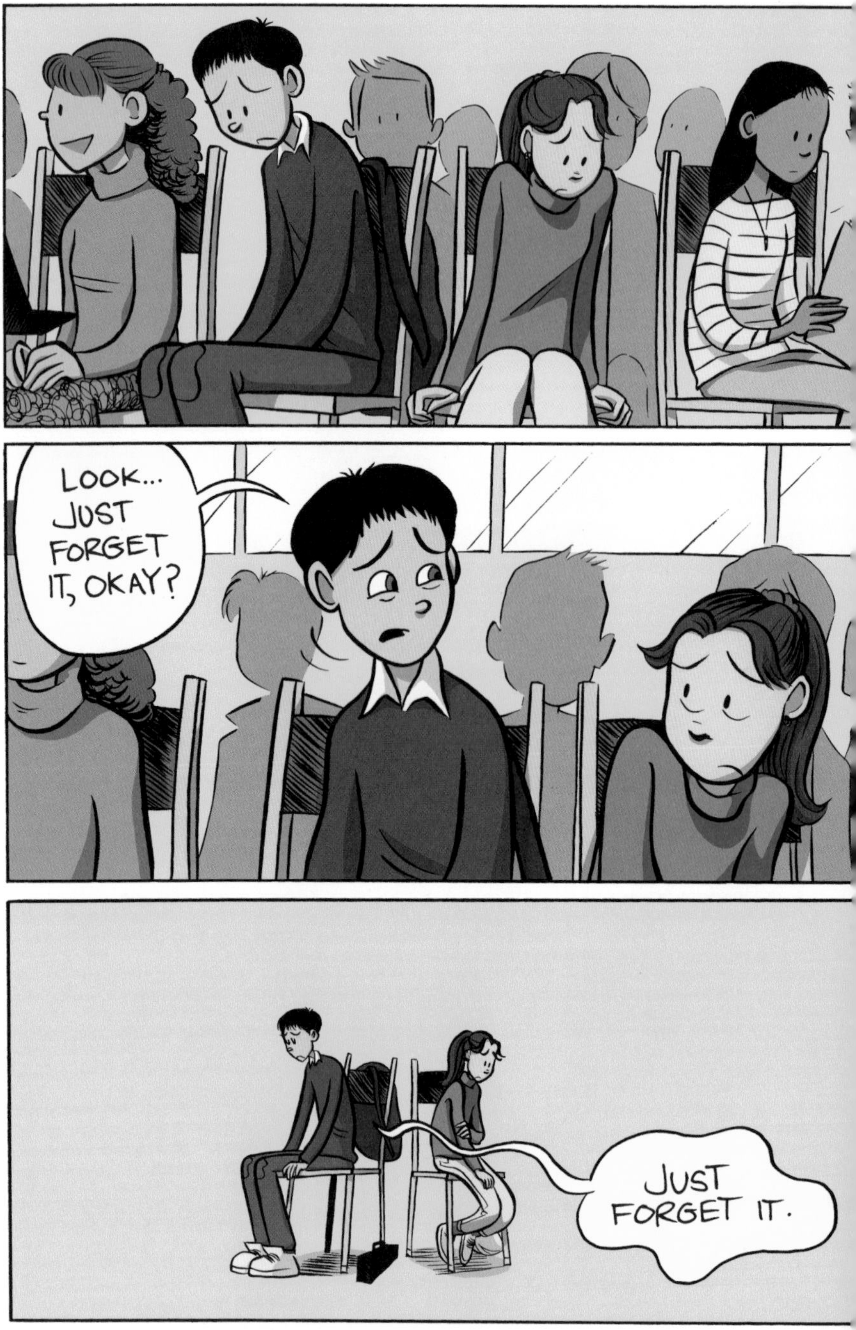
LOOK... JUST FORGET IT, OKAY?
JUST FORGET IT.

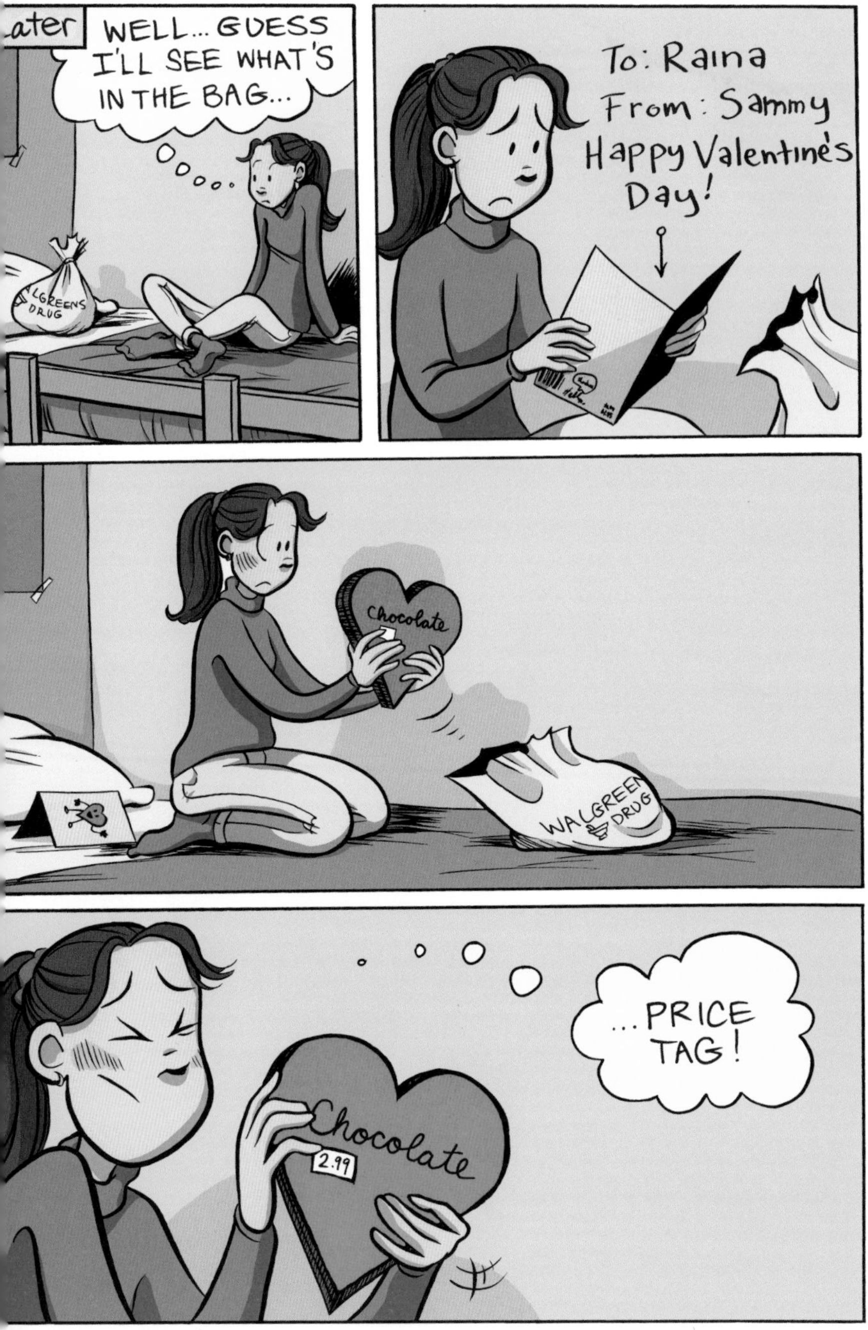
Later
WELL... GUESS I'LL SEE WHAT'S IN THE BAG...
WALGREENS DRUG
To: Raina
From: Sammy
Happy Valentine's Day!
Chocolate
WALGREENS DRUG
...PRICE TAG!
Chocolate
2.99

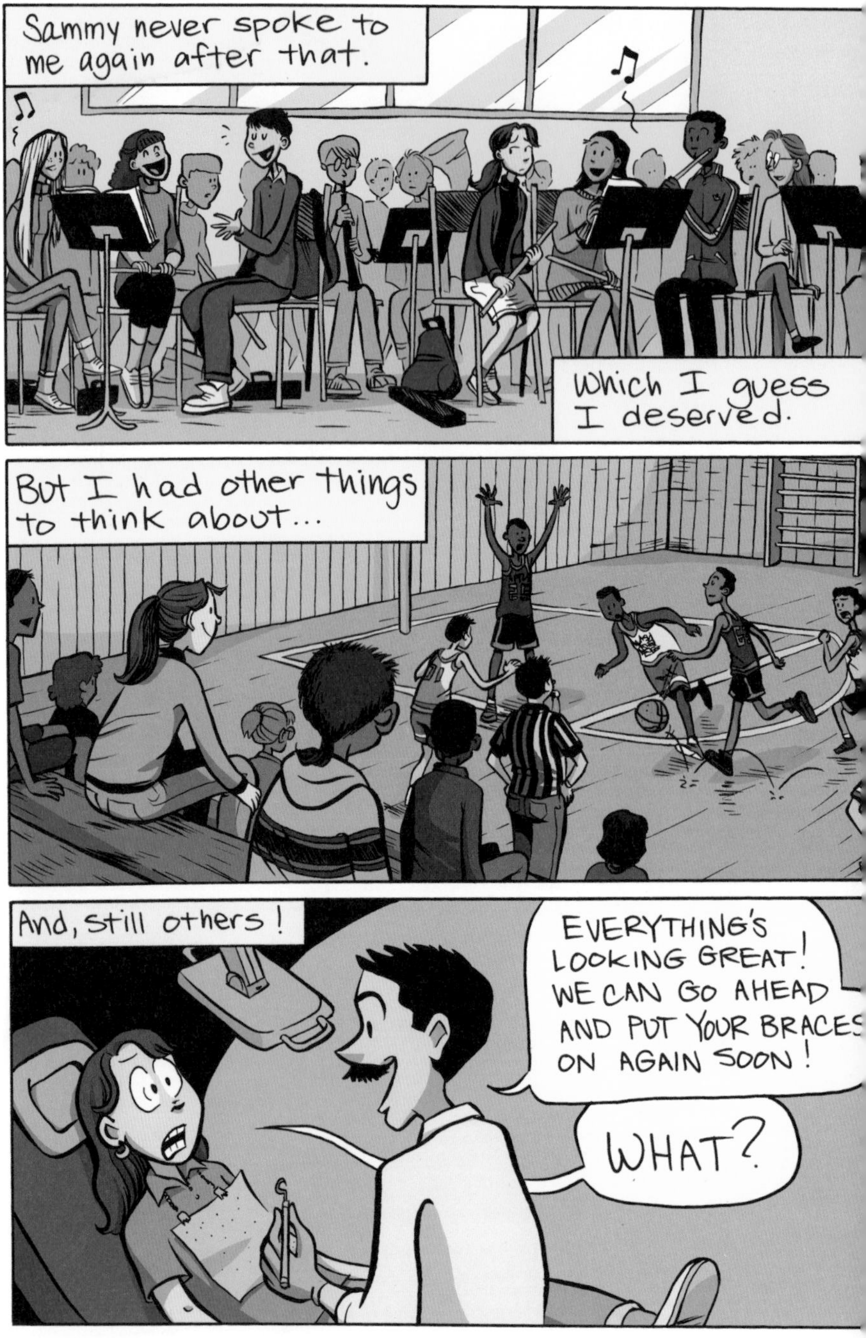
Sammy never spoke to me again after that.
Which I guess I deserved.
But I had other things to think about...
And, still others!
EVERYTHING'S LOOKING GREAT! WE CAN GO AHEAD AND PUT YOUR BRACES ON AGAIN SOON!
WHAT?

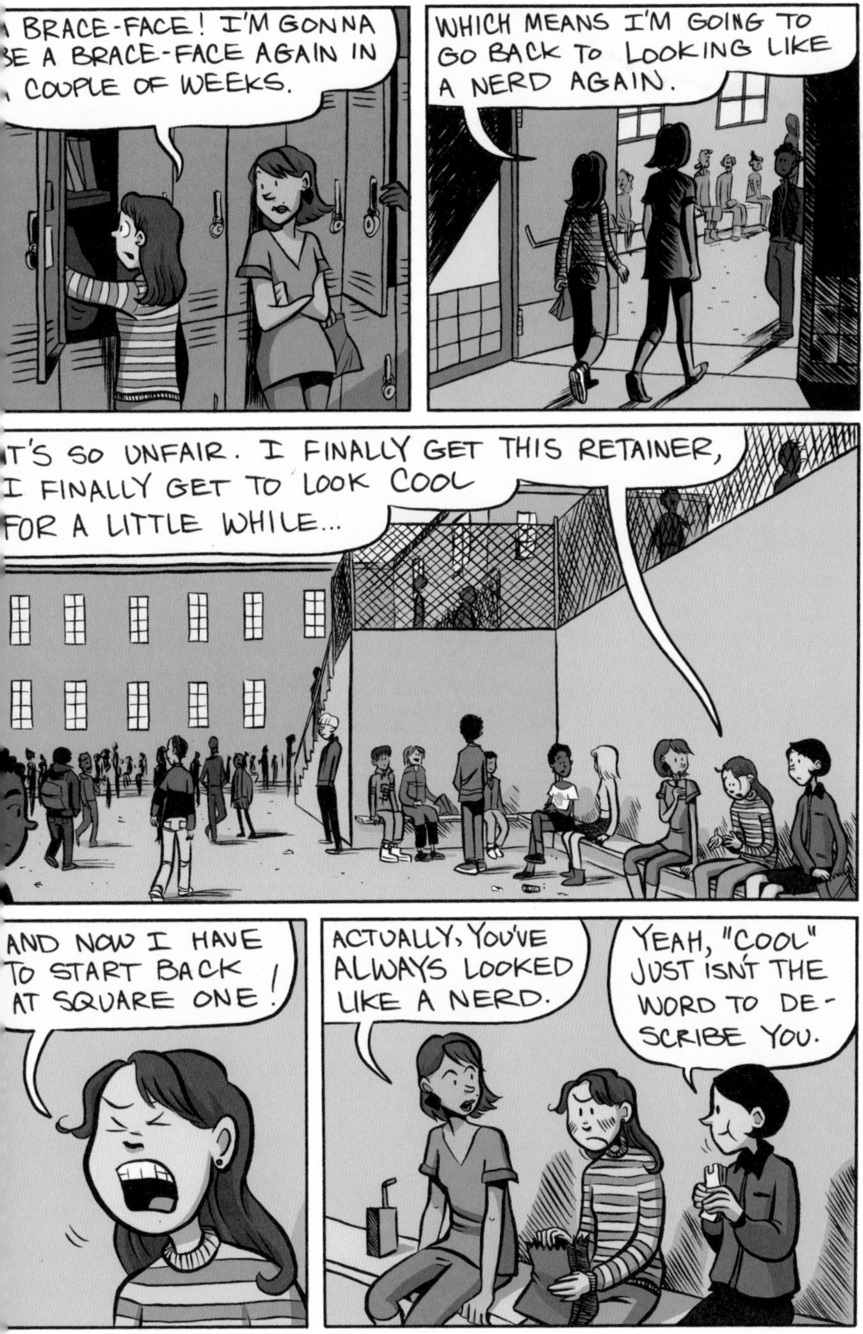

A BRACE-FACE! I'M GONNA BE A BRACE-FACE AGAIN IN A COUPLE OF WEEKS.
WHICH MEANS I'M GOING TO GO BACK TO LOOKING LIKE A NERD AGAIN.
IT'S SO UNFAIR. I FINALLY GET THIS RETAINER, I FINALLY GET TO LOOK COOL FOR A LITTLE WHILE...
AND NOW I HAVE TO START BACK AT SQUARE ONE!
ACTUALLY, YOU'VE ALWAYS LOOKED LIKE A NERD.
YEAH, "COOL" JUST ISN'T THE WORD TO DE-SCRIBE YOU.

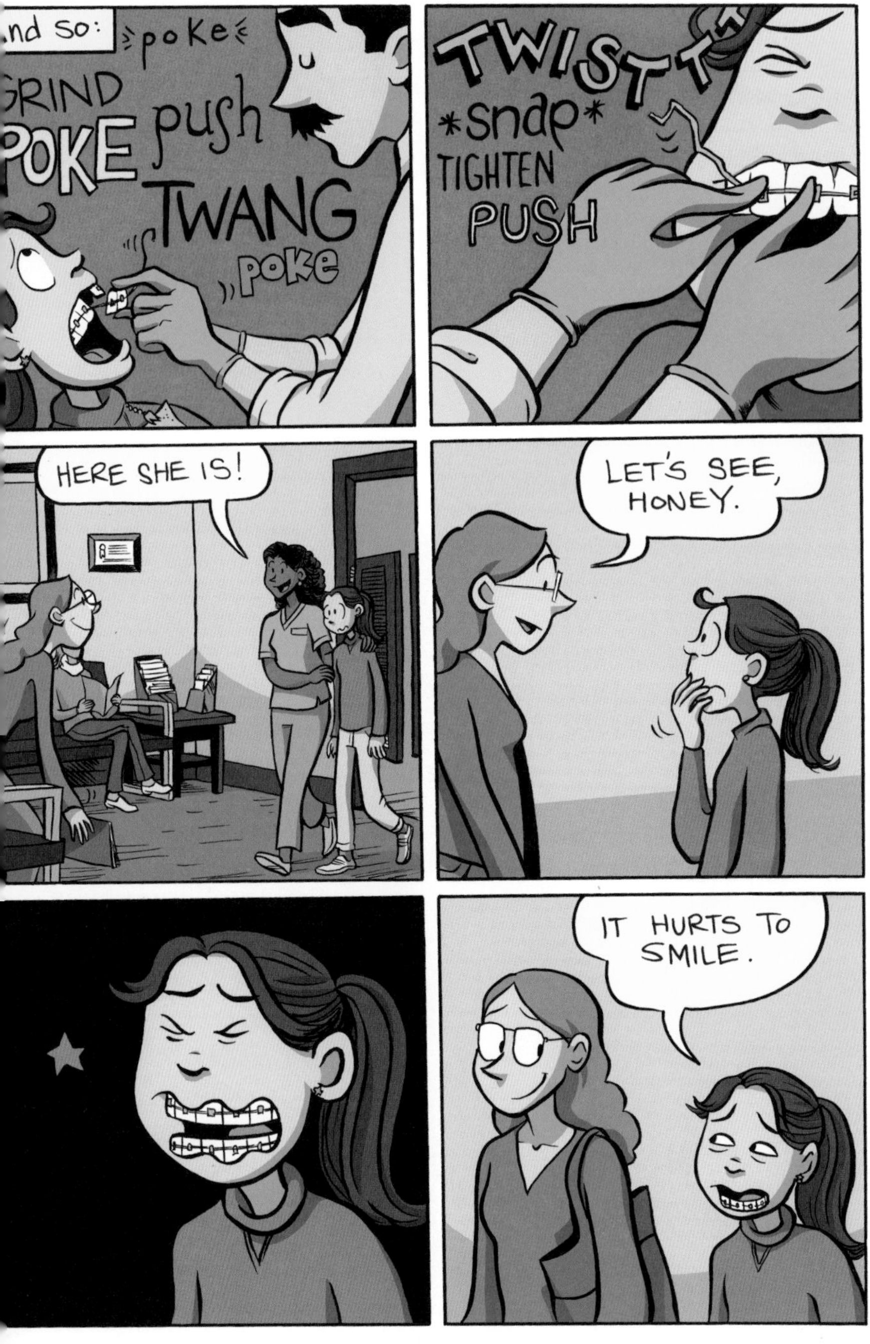
...nd so:
poke
GRIND
POKE
push
TWANG
poke
TWIST
snap
TIGHTEN
PUSH
HERE SHE IS!
LET'S SEE, HONEY.
IT HURTS TO SMILE.

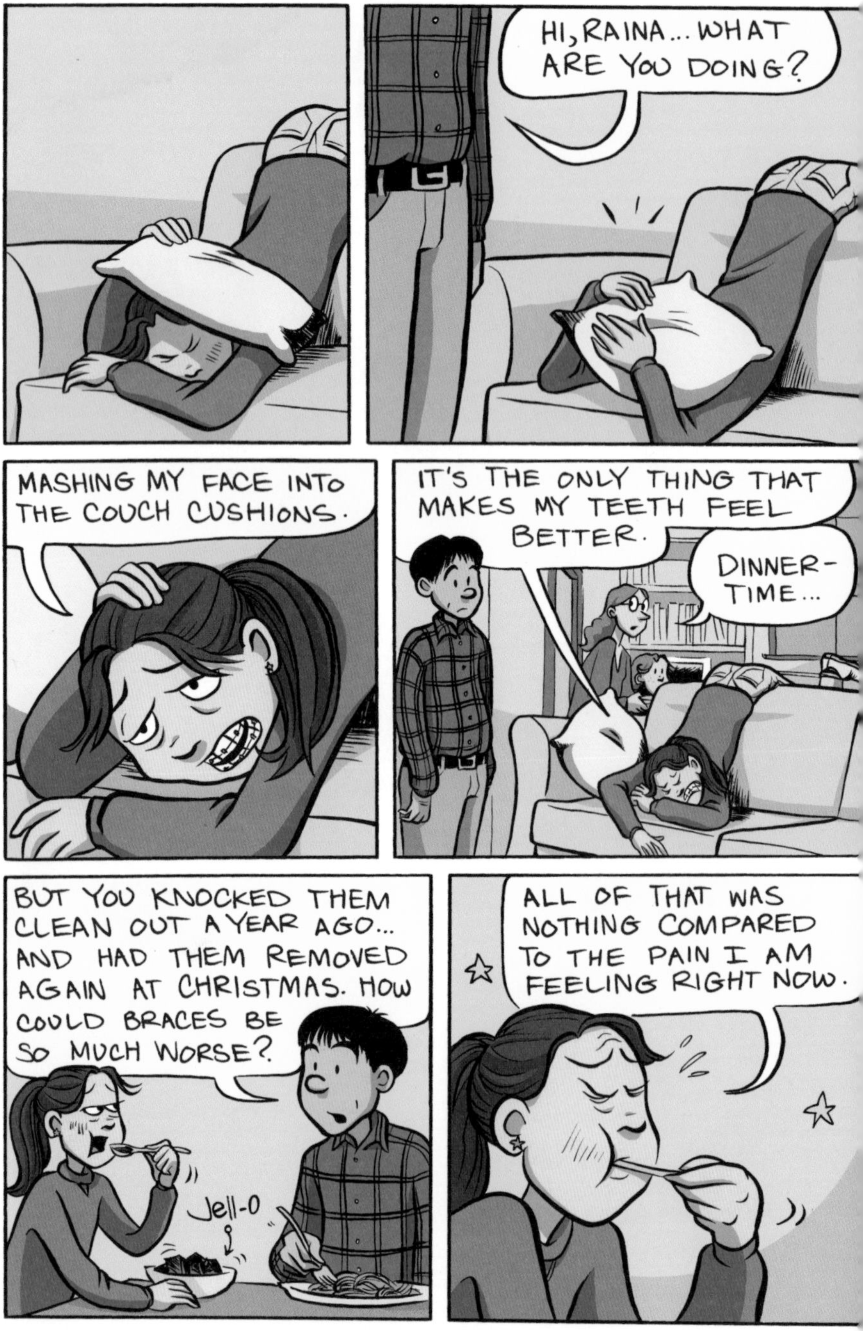
HI, RAINA... WHAT ARE YOU DOING?
MASHING MY FACE INTO THE COUCH CUSHIONS.
IT'S THE ONLY THING THAT MAKES MY TEETH FEEL BETTER.
DINNER-TIME...
BUT YOU KNOCKED THEM CLEAN OUT A YEAR AGO... AND HAD THEM REMOVED AGAIN AT CHRISTMAS. HOW COULD BRACES BE SO MUCH WORSE?
Jell-O
ALL OF THAT WAS NOTHING COMPARED TO THE PAIN I AM FEELING RIGHT NOW.

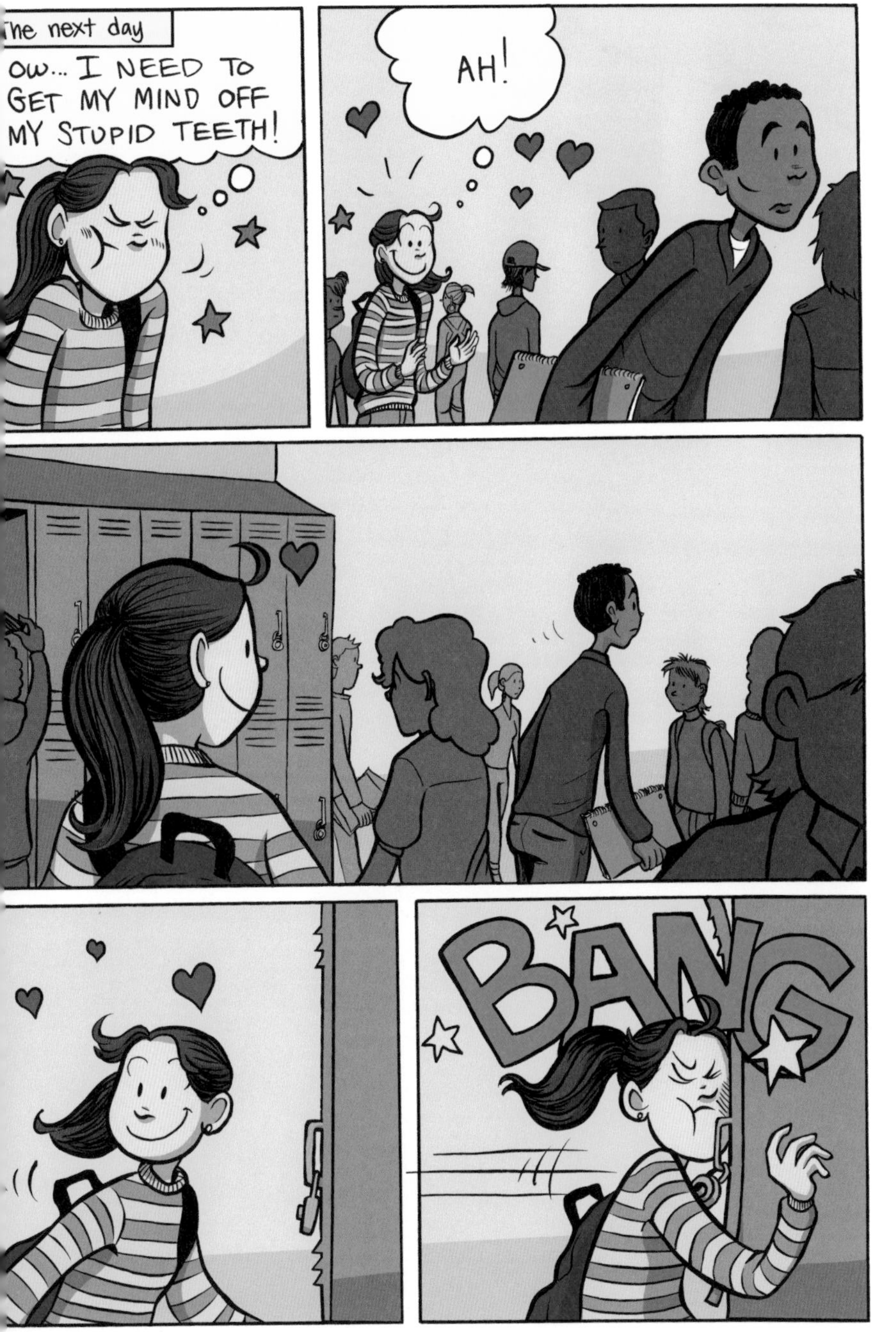
The next day
OW... I NEED TO GET MY MIND OFF MY STUPID TEETH!
AH!
BANG

Braces <u>DO</u> stop hurting after several days.

I CAN SORT OF CHEW BREAD AGAIN!

But then...

YOU'VE GOT AN APPOINTMENT WITH DR. DRAGONI ON THURSDAY AFTERNOON, HONEY.

AWW...

Every couple of weeks, you go and get them tightened.

380 | 101 | SF Int'l Airport
EXIT 1 MILE

I'M STARTING TO REALLY HATE THIS FREEWAY EXIT.

And then you start all over.

OPEN...

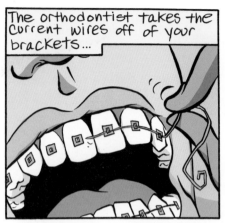

The orthodontist takes the current wires off of your brackets...

...and puts new wires on

wiggle twang

And then he **TIGHTENS THEM**.

TWIST! TWIST! TWIST!

The ends of the wires are clipped off...

Snip!

...AND WE'LL SEE YOU AGAIN IN TWO WEEKS!

Before I knew it, my birth-day rolled around again.

OKAY. YOU ARE THIRTEEN YEARS OLD.

I KNOW. IT'S CRAZY!

'S TIME YOU KISSED YOUR FIRST BOY, I'D SAY.

HUH?!

COME ON, RAINA. EVERYONE KNOWS YOU HAVE THE HOTS FOR SEAN...

EXCEPT FOR SEAN HIMSELF!

'S TIME TO MAKE A OVE. IT'S TIME TO AKE AN IMPRESSION.

IT'S TIME FOR A MAKEOVER!!

AAACK! HANG ON! WAIT!!

CABOODLE

GRAB

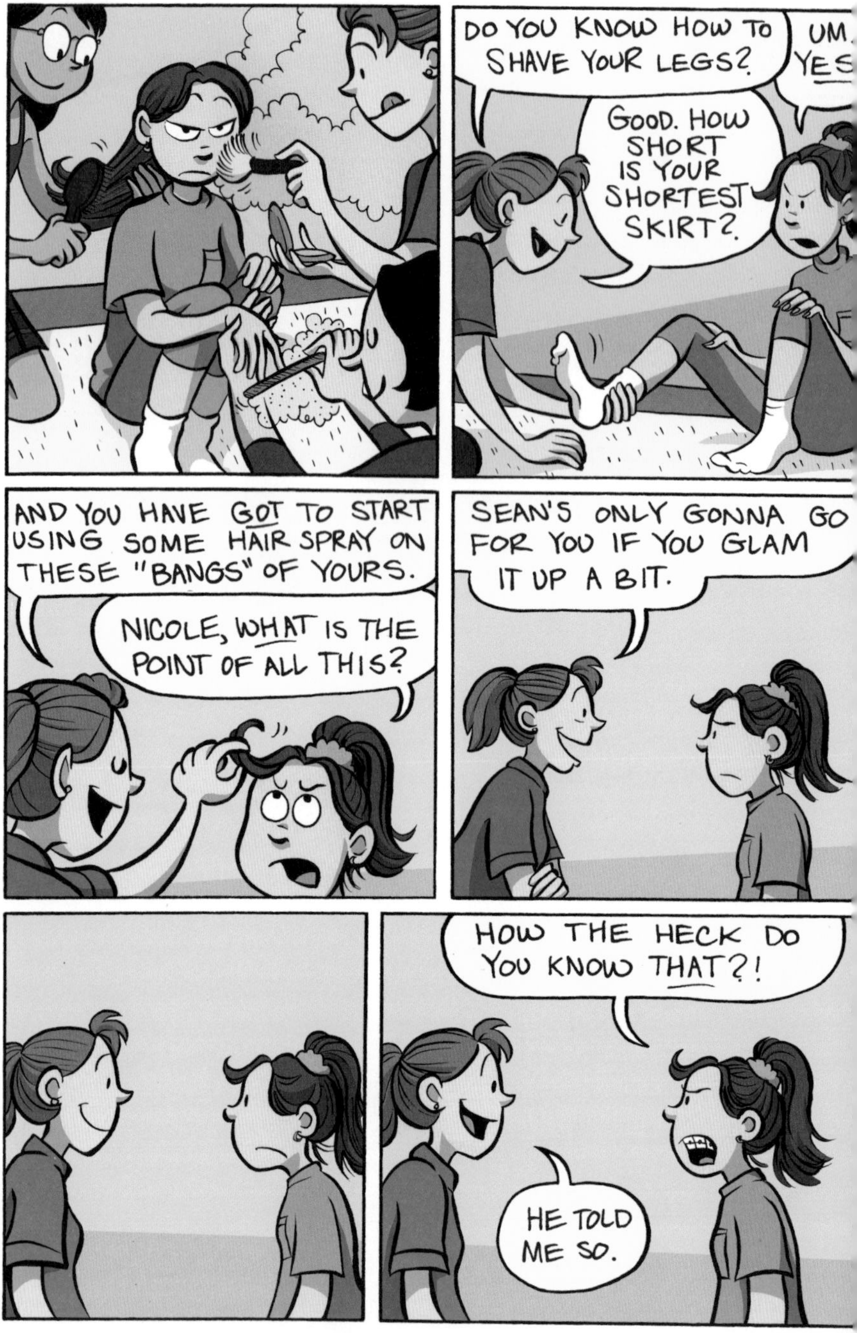
DO YOU KNOW HOW TO SHAVE YOUR LEGS?
UM. YES
GOOD. HOW SHORT IS YOUR SHORTEST SKIRT?
AND YOU HAVE GOT TO START USING SOME HAIR SPRAY ON THESE "BANGS" OF YOURS.
NICOLE, WHAT IS THE POINT OF ALL THIS?
SEAN'S ONLY GONNA GO FOR YOU IF YOU GLAM IT UP A BIT.
HOW THE HECK DO YOU KNOW THAT?!
HE TOLD ME SO.

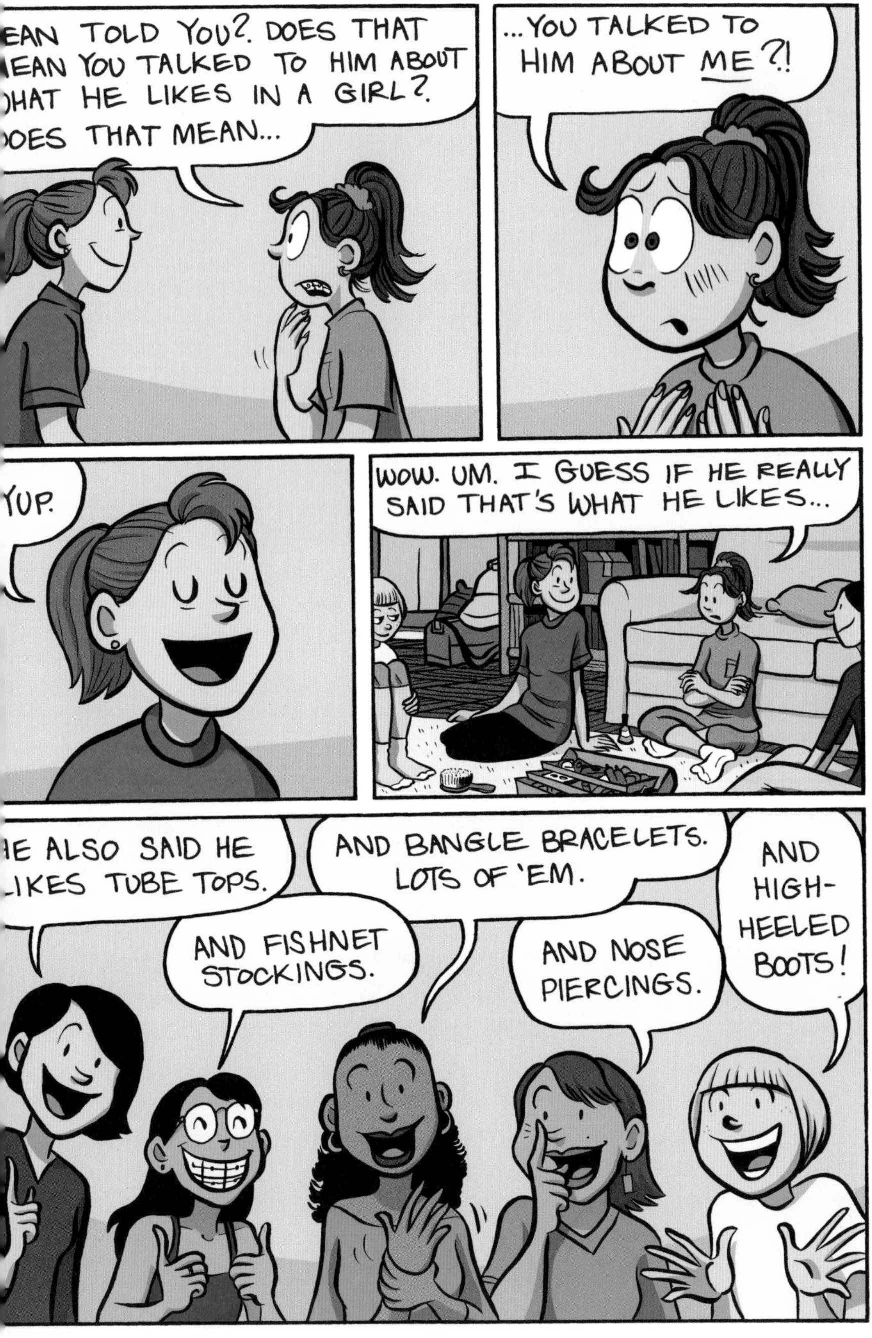
EAN TOLD YOU? DOES THAT EAN YOU TALKED TO HIM ABOUT HAT HE LIKES IN A GIRL? OES THAT MEAN...
...YOU TALKED TO HIM ABOUT ME?!
YUP.
WOW. UM. I GUESS IF HE REALLY SAID THAT'S WHAT HE LIKES...
E ALSO SAID HE IKES TUBE TOPS.
AND BANGLE BRACELETS. LOTS OF 'EM.
AND HIGH-HEELED BOOTS!
AND FISHNET STOCKINGS.
AND NOSE PIERCINGS.

And so:

THERE! SEAN'S GOING TO LOVE IT!!

KKTHPLBBT!!

HA HA HA HA HA HA HA Hee HA HA HA

WAAAAIT A MINUTE...

HAHA HA HA HA HA HA HA HA HA Hoo HA HA HA Hee

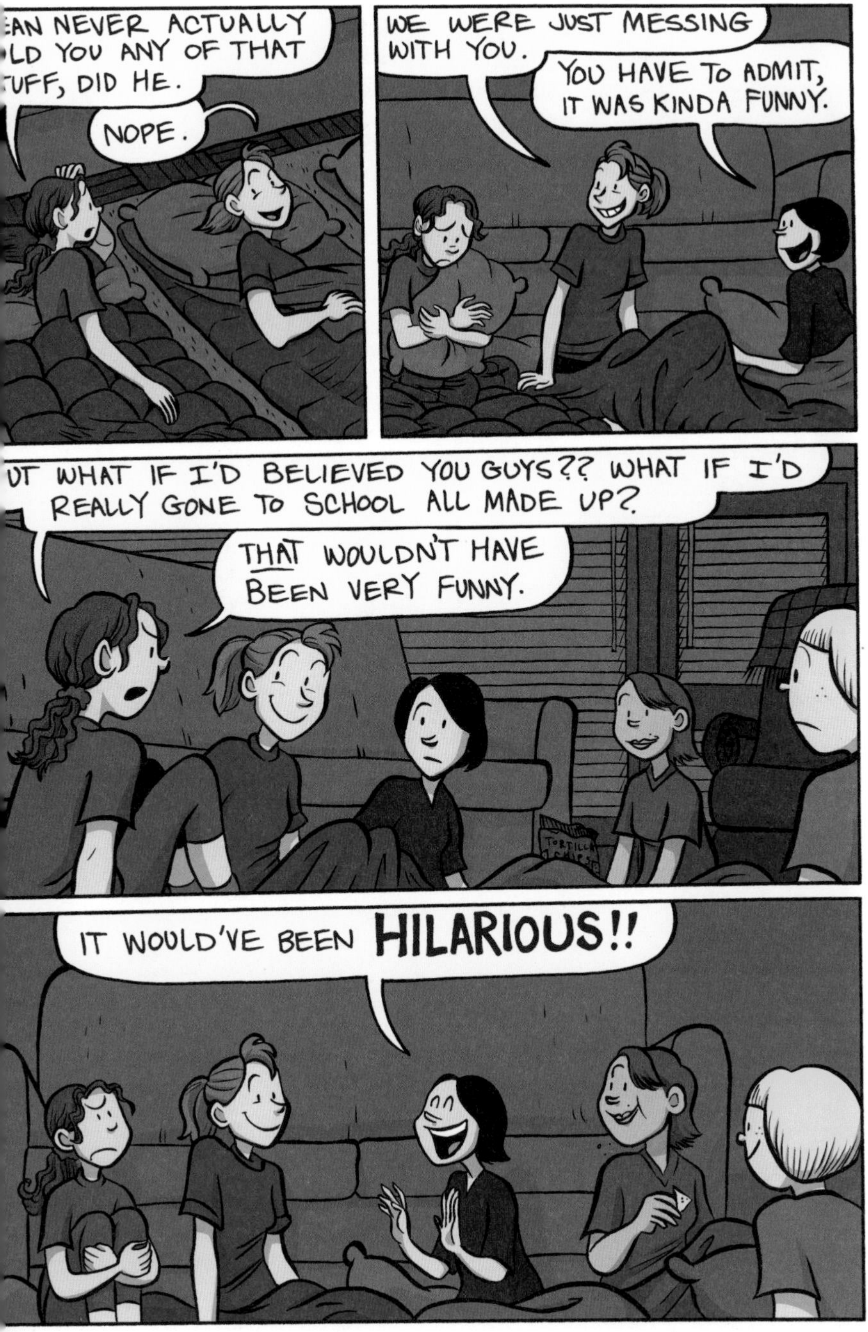
EAN NEVER ACTUALLY LD YOU ANY OF THAT UFF, DID HE.
NOPE.
WE WERE JUST MESSING WITH YOU.
YOU HAVE TO ADMIT, IT WAS KINDA FUNNY.
UT WHAT IF I'D BELIEVED YOU GUYS?? WHAT IF I'D REALLY GONE TO SCHOOL ALL MADE UP?
THAT WOULDN'T HAVE BEEN VERY FUNNY.
TORTILLA CHIPS
IT WOULD'VE BEEN HILARIOUS!!

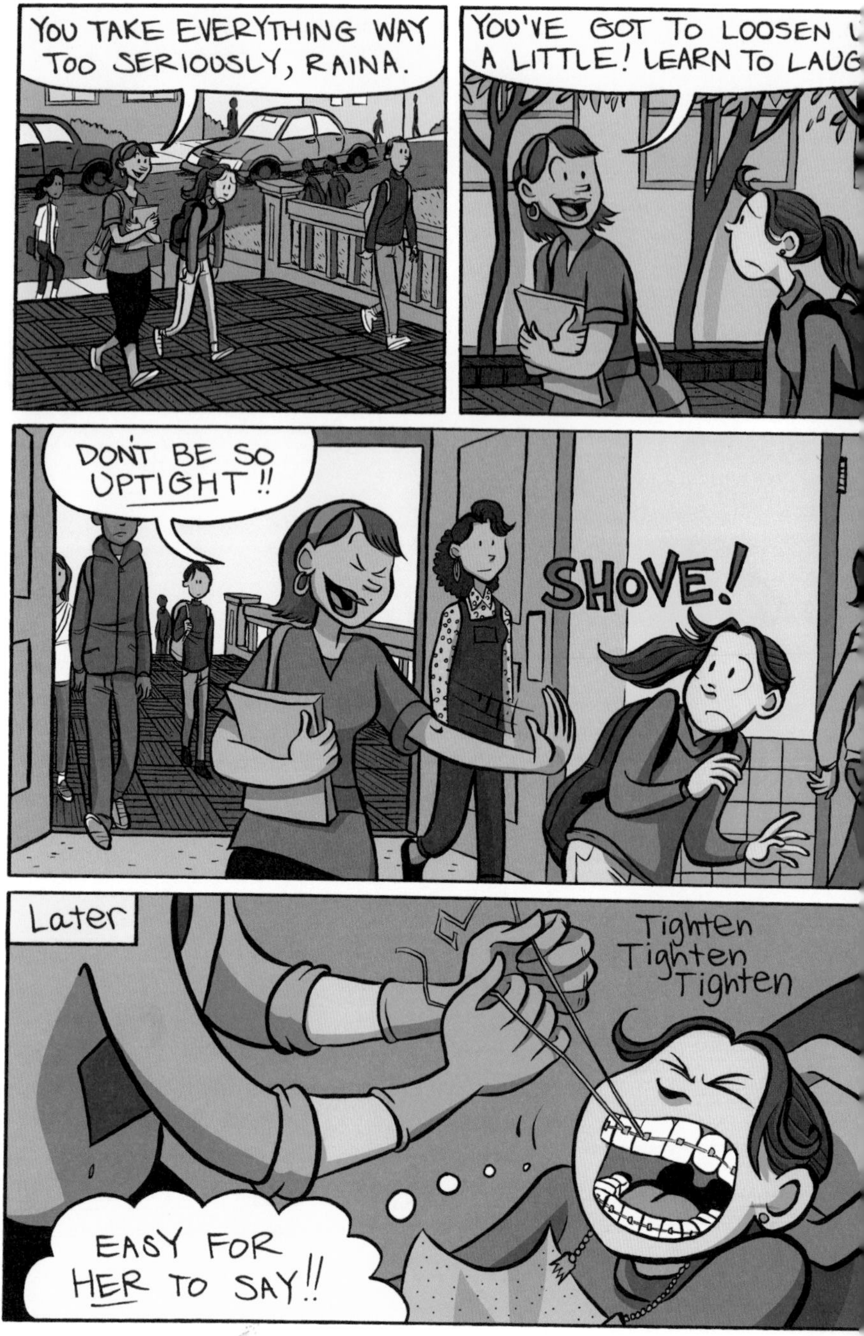

YOU TAKE EVERYTHING WAY TOO SERIOUSLY, RAINA.
YOU'VE GOT TO LOOSEN U
A LITTLE! LEARN TO LAUG
DON'T BE SO UPTIGHT!!
SHOVE!
Later
Tighten Tighten Tighten
EASY FOR HER TO SAY!!

WHAT IF IT WAS TRUE? WHAT IF [S]EAN REALLY *WOULD* NOTICE [M]E IF I DRESSED DIFFERENTLY?

WOULD I BE WILLING TO CHANGE, JUST FOR HIM?

SO FAR, BEING A TEENAGER IS NO FUN AT ALL.

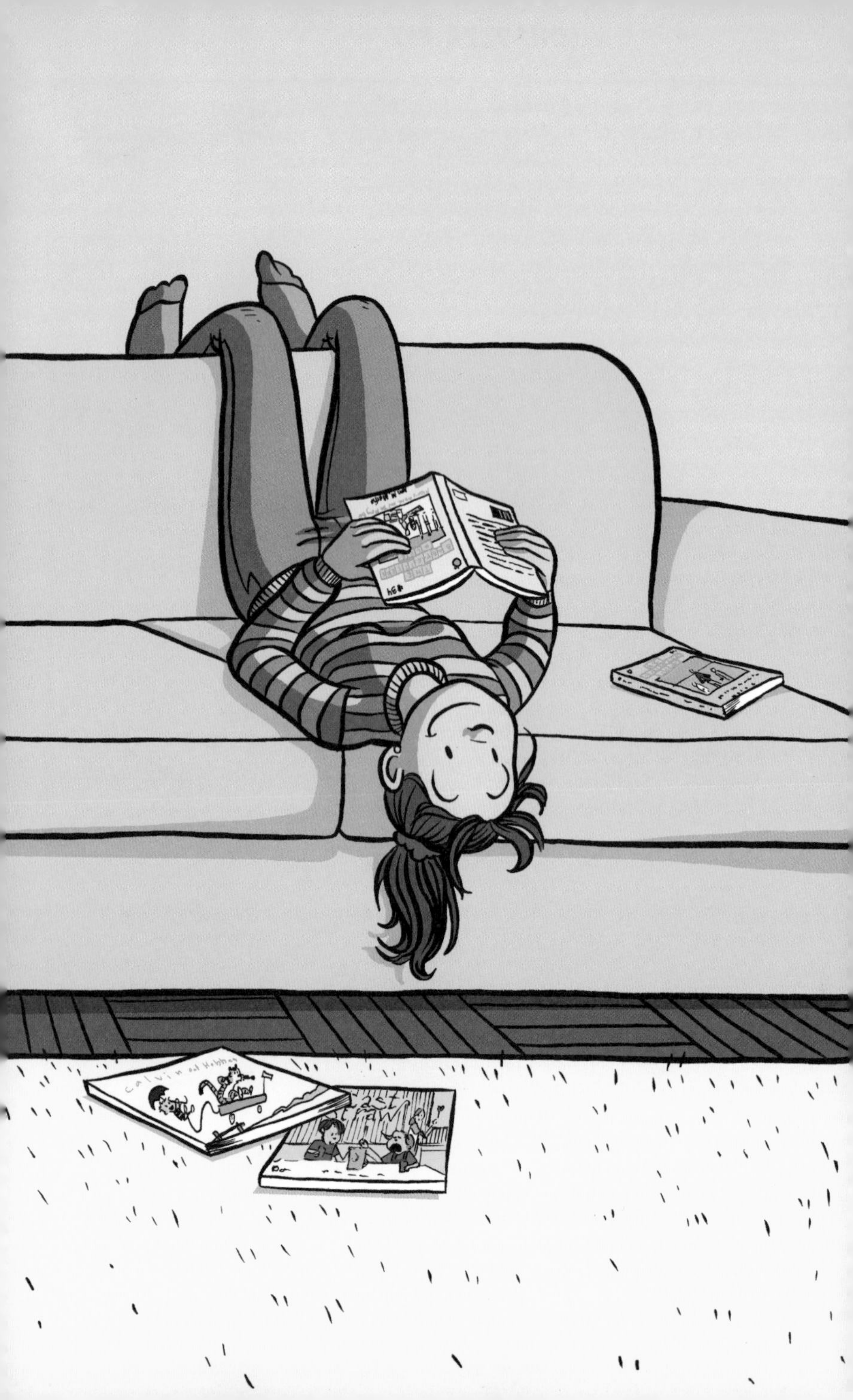
calvin and Hobbes

CHAPTER SIX

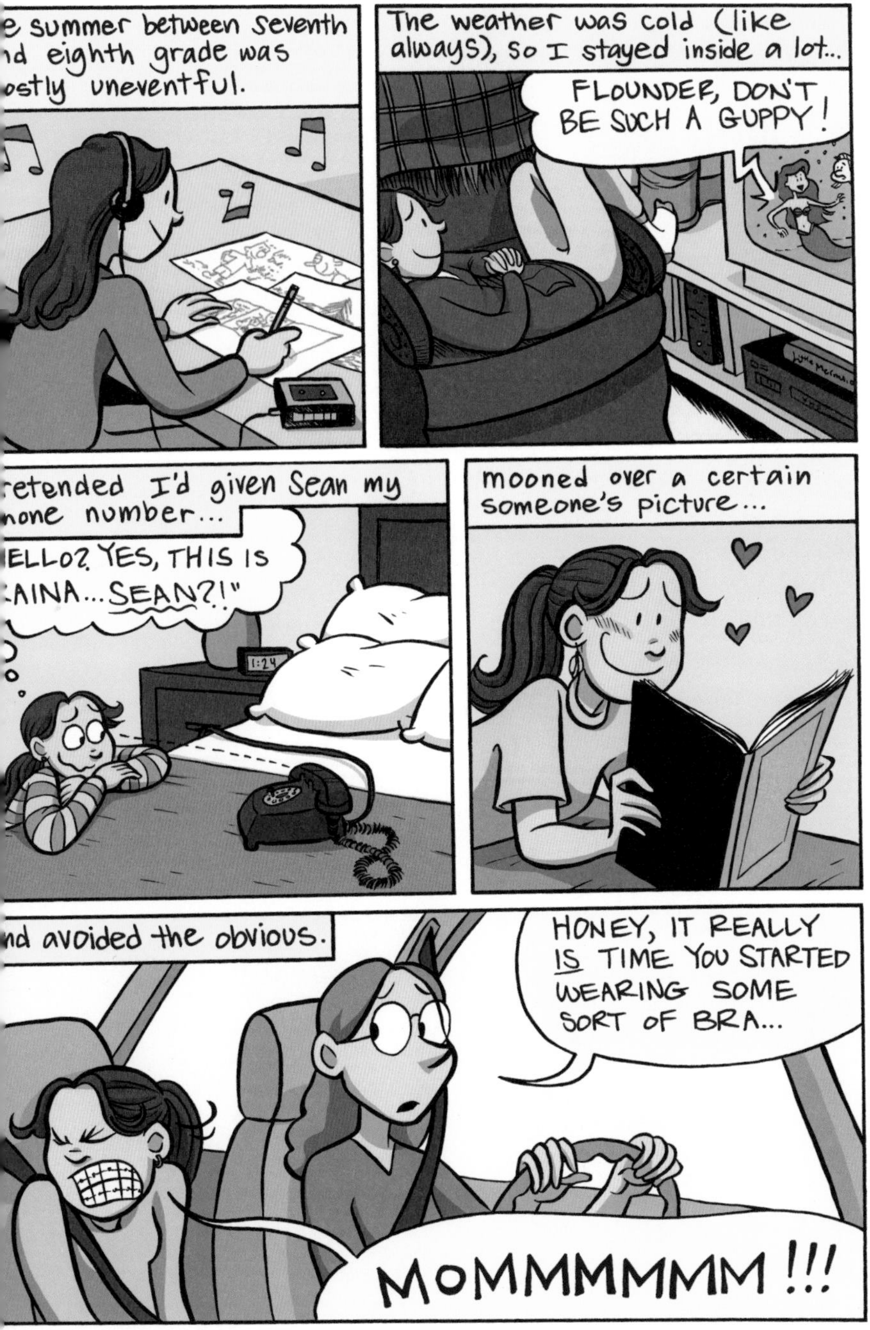
e summer between seventh
nd eighth grade was
ostly uneventful.
The weather was cold (like always), so I stayed inside a lot...
FLOUNDER, DON'T BE SUCH A GUPPY!
retended I'd given Sean my
none number...
ELLO? YES, THIS IS
AINA... SEAN?!"
mooned over a certain someone's picture...
nd avoided the obvious.
HONEY, IT REALLY IS TIME YOU STARTED WEARING SOME SORT OF BRA...
MOMMMMMM!!!

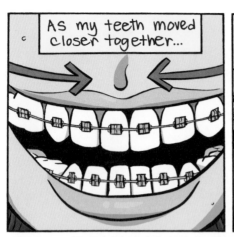

As my teeth moved closer together...

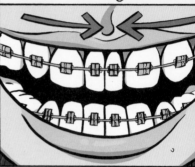

The fake teeth in the empty space were shaved down little by little.

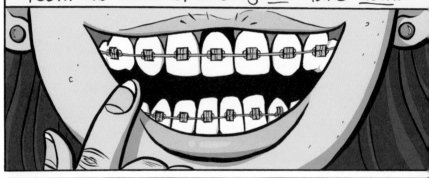

By the time eighth grade started, the two fake teeth had been replaced by one fake tooth.

I just hoped no one could tell.

GIRL, YOU NEED TO START USING A BETTER HAIR CONDITIONER.

MY BROTHER HAS THAT SHIRT... IT'S KIND OF A BOY'S SHIRT.

Eighth grade was weird. We were all going through puberty, and at different rates.

Hair suddenly curly

Taller, hips wider

Chest got huge

Acne

Gloomy

Everyone was very preoccupied.

HAIR

CLOTHES

MAKEUP

PIMPLES

DIETING

ETC.

WHATEVER HAPPENED TO TALKING ABOUT CARTOONS?

But, the boys seemed to notice, and acted accordingly.

W-PWING!!!

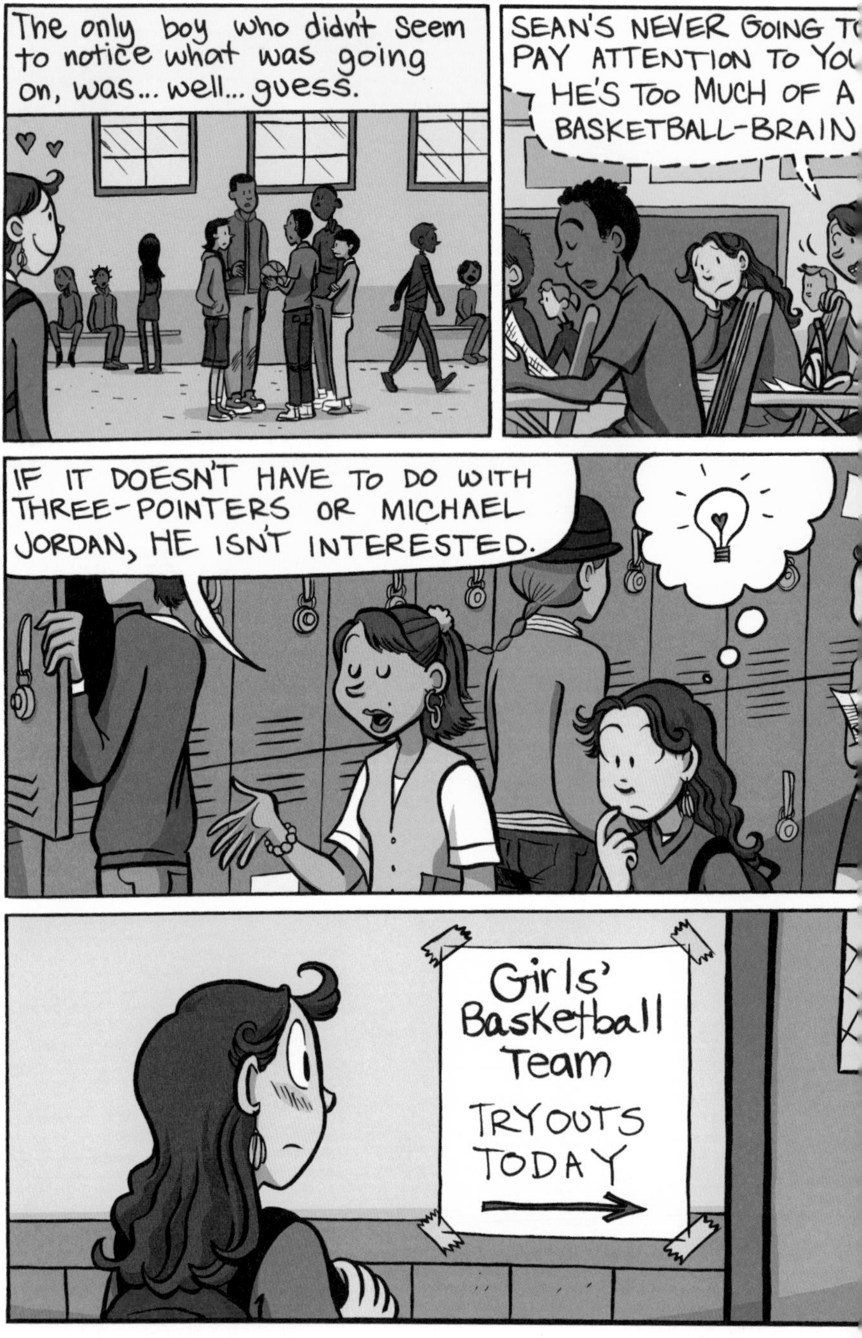

The only boy who didn't seem to notice what was going on, was... well... guess.
SEAN'S NEVER GOING TO PAY ATTENTION TO YOU HE'S TOO MUCH OF A BASKETBALL-BRAIN
IF IT DOESN'T HAVE TO DO WITH THREE-POINTERS OR MICHAEL JORDAN, HE ISN'T INTERESTED.
Girls' Basketball Team TRYOUTS TODAY

YOU WANT TO TRY OUT FOR THE TEAM? SURE. DROP AND GIVE ME 25 PUSH-UPS.

...12 ...13 ...14 ...

PTOOM PTOOM PTOOM

WANG!

WHHHSSHHHL

I THINK I'M DOING... ≤GASP, PANT...≤ PRETTY GOOD!

WOW, THAT WAS REALLY HARD. I'M BEAT.

H'LO.

SLAM DUNK!!

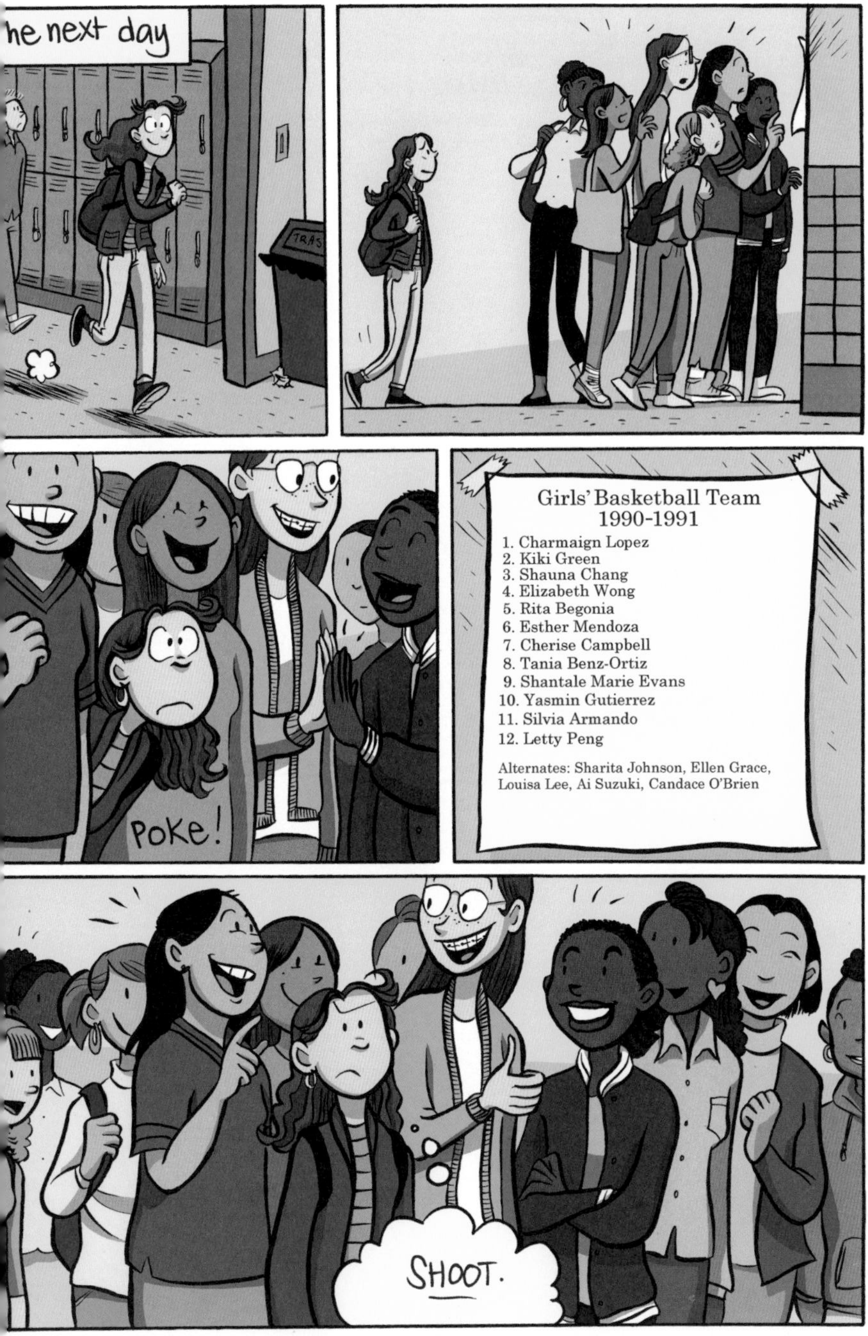
he next day
TRAS
Girls' Basketball Team
1990-1991
1. Charmaign Lopez
2. Kiki Green
3. Shauna Chang
4. Elizabeth Wong
5. Rita Begonia
6. Esther Mendoza
7. Cherise Campbell
8. Tania Benz-Ortiz
9. Shantale Marie Evans
10. Yasmin Gutierrez
11. Silvia Armando
12. Letty Peng
Alternates: Sharita Johnson, Ellen Grace, Louisa Lee, Ai Suzuki, Candace O'Brien
POKE!
SHOOT.

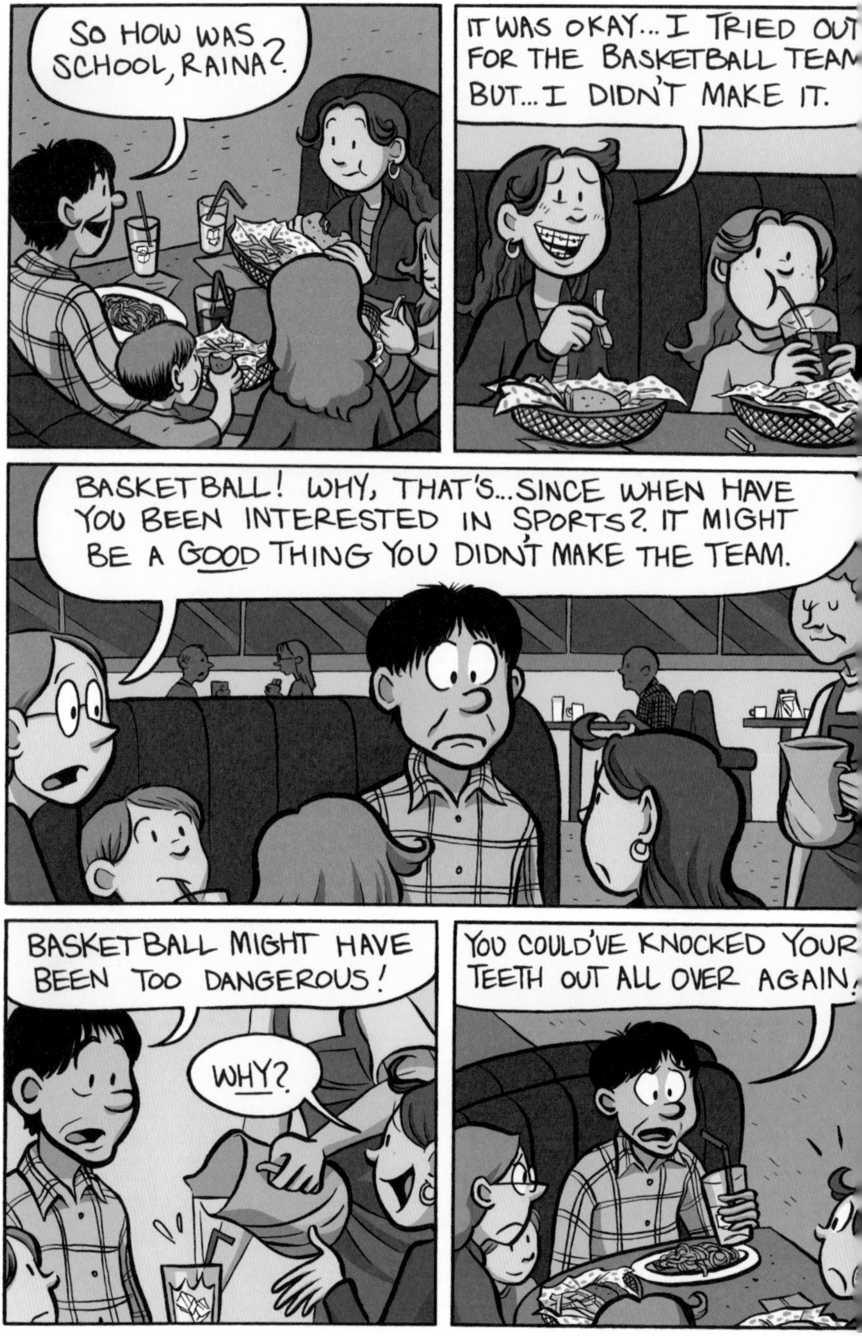
SO HOW WAS SCHOOL, RAINA?
IT WAS OKAY... I TRIED OUT FOR THE BASKETBALL TEAM BUT... I DIDN'T MAKE IT.
BASKETBALL! WHY, THAT'S...SINCE WHEN HAVE YOU BEEN INTERESTED IN SPORTS? IT MIGHT BE A GOOD THING YOU DIDN'T MAKE THE TEAM.
BASKETBALL MIGHT HAVE BEEN TOO DANGEROUS!
WHY?
YOU COULD'VE KNOCKED YOUR TEETH OUT ALL OVER AGAIN.

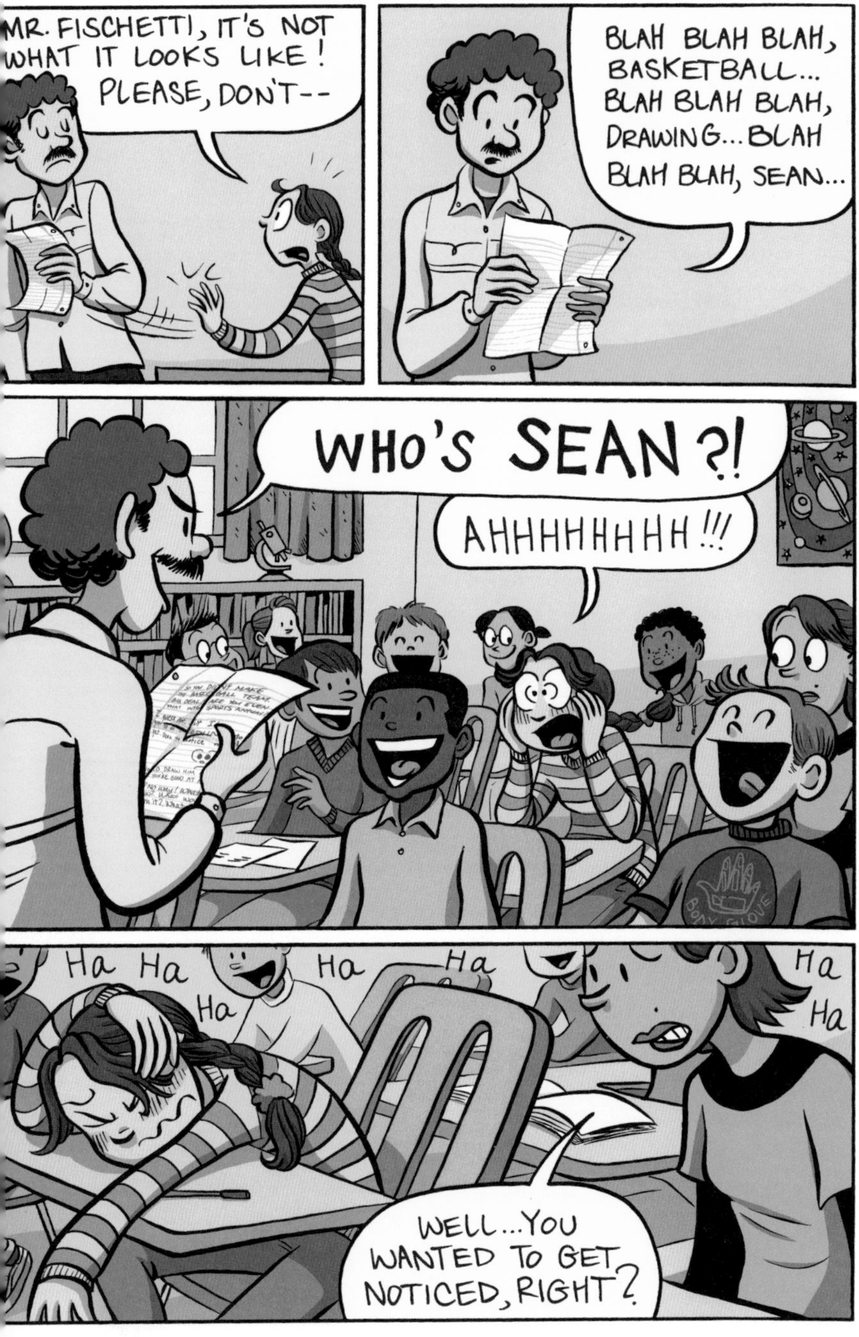
MR. FISCHETTI, IT'S NOT WHAT IT LOOKS LIKE! PLEASE, DON'T--
BLAH BLAH BLAH, BASKETBALL... BLAH BLAH BLAH, DRAWING... BLAH BLAH BLAH, SEAN...
WHO'S SEAN?!
AHHHHHHHH!!!
Ha Ha Ha Ha Ha Ha Ha
WELL... YOU WANTED TO GET NOTICED, RIGHT?

My crush on Sean was old news to everyone else, but still consumed my thoughts a lot of the time.

15...36... SEAN...

However, something interesting was starting to happen.

HEY, RAINA!

HEY, KAYLAH. HEY, EDWARD.

YOU GOIN' TO LUNCH?

YEARBOOK ORDERS MAY 27th

YEAH, WAIT UP.

Some of my friends had kinda-sorta-maybe boyfriends.

Boys who would hang around with us during lunchtime...

... and who would invite their other friends along.

Not all of them were cute, and not all of them were very mature...

WAIT, WHAT'S THIS? NEXT TO MY PEANU BUTTER SANDWICH?

YAAAAARRGH! SPIDER!!

AIIEEE!!

rubber

But they were good fo practice-flirting!

SHOVE!

aybe I liked a few of them, and aybe a few of them liked e... it wasn't that important.

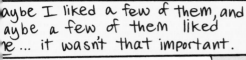

'SST... WHAT'S THE ANSWER TO #6?.

I'M NOT TELLIN' YOU !!

None of them were Sean.

But, boys were good for video game tips.

Boys didn't give me any flack about my appearance.

EVER THINK ABOUT TOOTH-WHITENING, RAINA?. IT MIGHT BE A GOOD IDEA. FOR YOU.

nd, they were willing to talk bout important issues.

So... ARE YOU GUYS READY FOR HIGH SCHOOL?!

HIGH SCHOOL! MAN, IT'S HARD TO BELIEVE WE'RE GRADUATING FROM EIGHTH GRADE IN ONE MONTH...

I KNOW...

LADIES AND GENTLEMEN, I HOP[E] YOU'LL ALL JOIN ME AT MY HOU[SE] NEXT WEEKEND FOR THE END-OF-SCHOOL PARTY TO END ALL PARTIES.

COOL!

THANKS JUAN!

Parties presented a slight problem now that I was friends with boys.

HEY, EVERYONE! WHO WANTS TO PLAY SPIN THE BOTTLE?!

≈ GULP! ≈

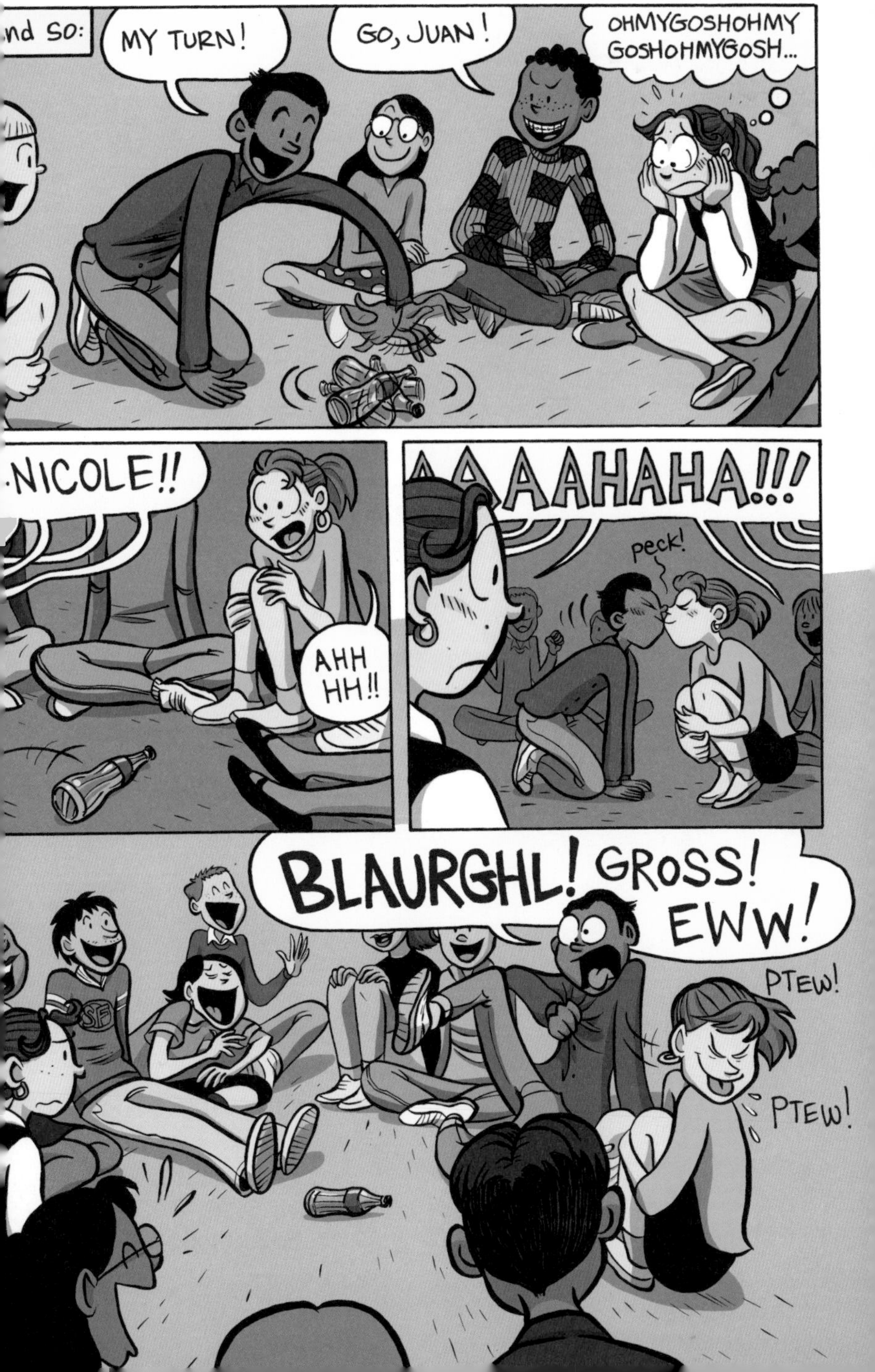
nd so:
MY TURN!
GO, JUAN!
OHMYGOSHOHMY GOSHOHMYGOSH...
NICOLE!!
AHH HH!!
AAAAHAHA!!!
peck!
BLAURGHL! GROSS! EWW!
PTEW!
PTEW!

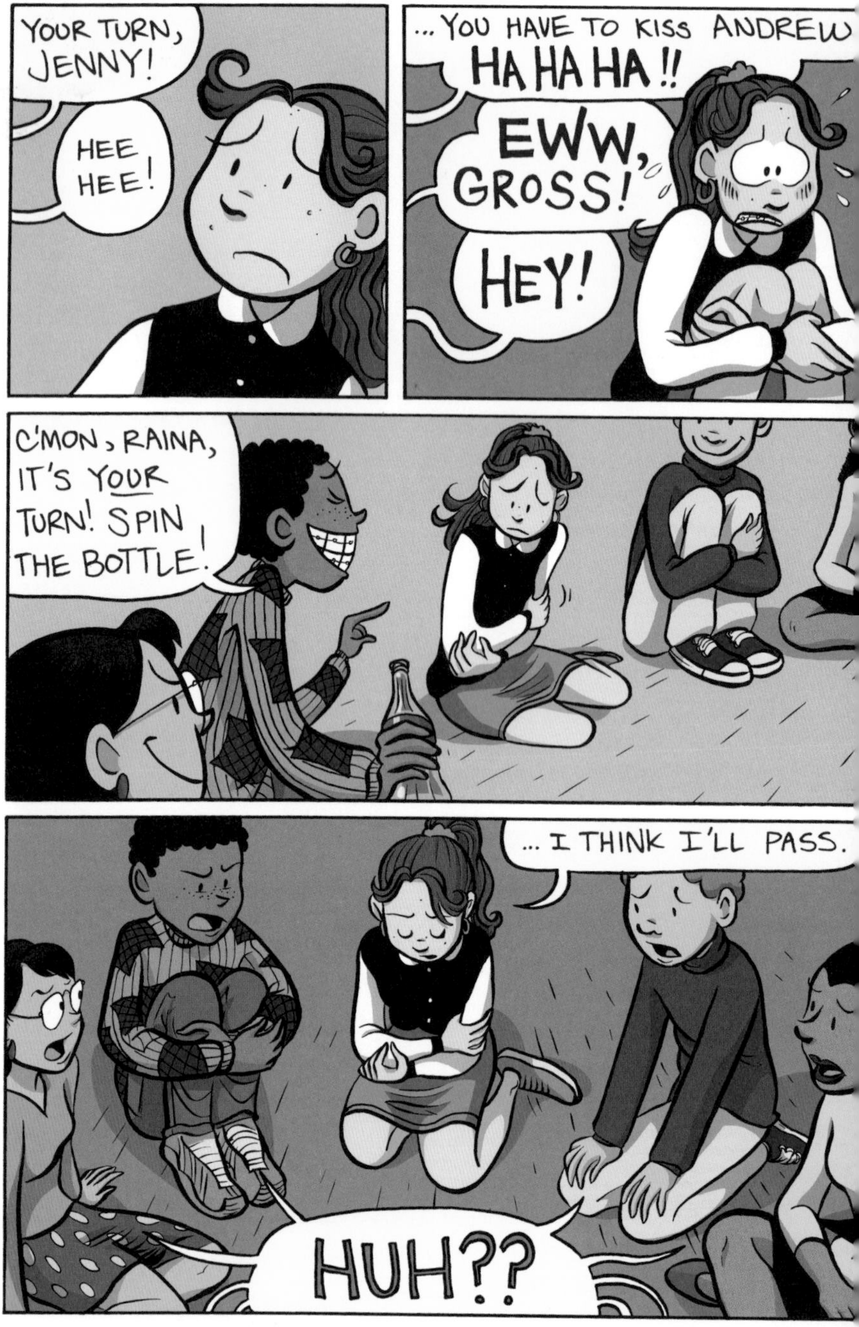
YOUR TURN, JENNY!
HEE HEE!
... YOU HAVE TO KISS ANDREW
HA HA HA!!
EWW, GROSS!
HEY!
C'MON, RAINA, IT'S YOUR TURN! SPIN THE BOTTLE!
... I THINK I'LL PASS.
HUH??

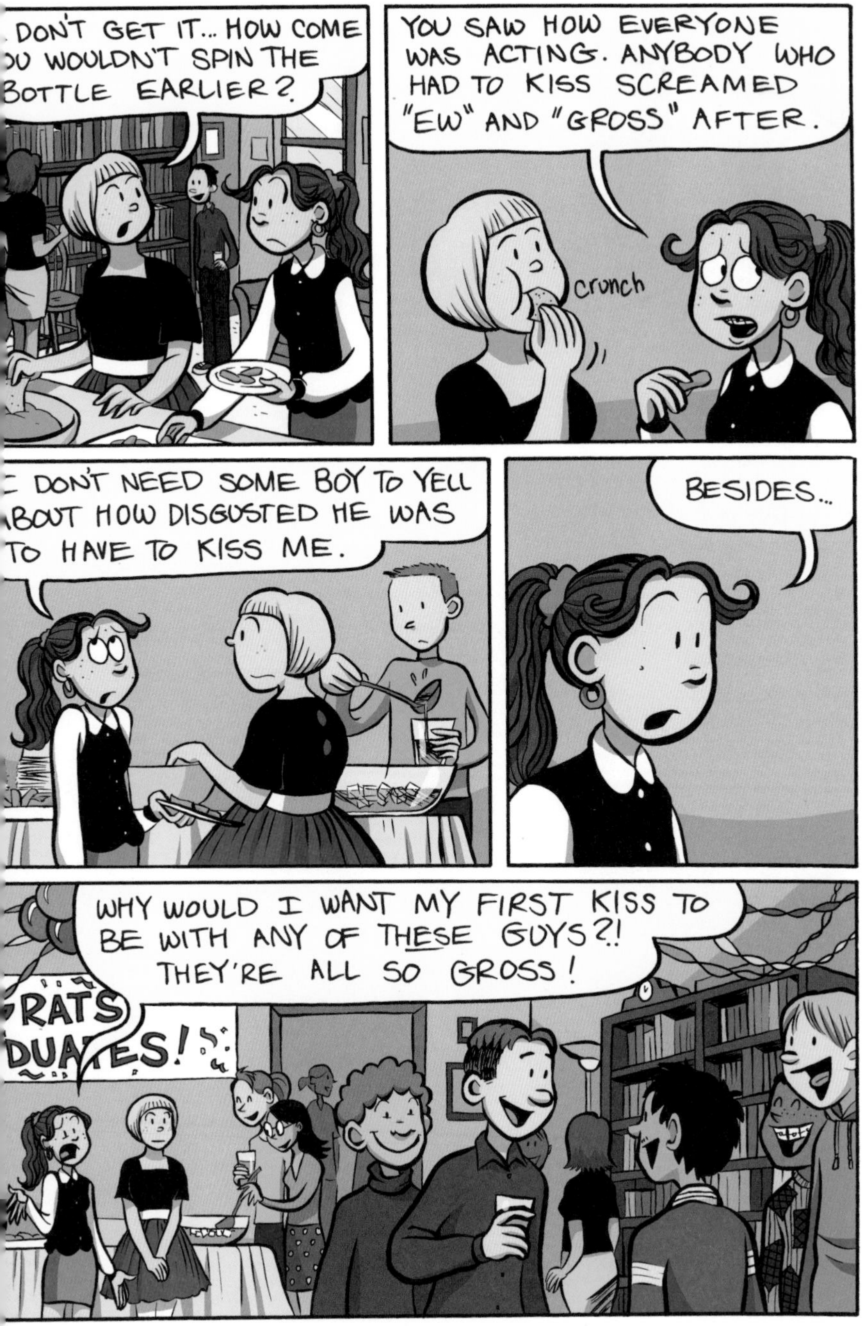
DON'T GET IT... HOW COME
WOULDN'T SPIN THE
BOTTLE EARLIER?
YOU SAW HOW EVERYONE WAS ACTING. ANYBODY WHO HAD TO KISS SCREAMED "EW" AND "GROSS" AFTER.
crunch
DON'T NEED SOME BOY TO YELL
BOUT HOW DISGUSTED HE WAS
TO HAVE TO KISS ME.
BESIDES...
WHY WOULD I WANT MY FIRST KISS TO BE WITH ANY OF THESE GUYS?! THEY'RE ALL SO GROSS!
RATS
DUATES!

THE TRUTH IS ... I WANT MY FIRST KISS TO BE **PERFECT.**

THE PERFECT GUY, THE PERFECT SETTING, THE PERFECT SONG PLAYING

BUT WHEN I IMAGINE ALL OF THOSE THINGS, I IMAGINE MY<u>SELF</u> AS BEING PERFECT, TOO.

Hair

Skin

Teeth

Body

AND I DON'T THINK THAT'S GOING TO HAPPEN ANYTIME SOON!

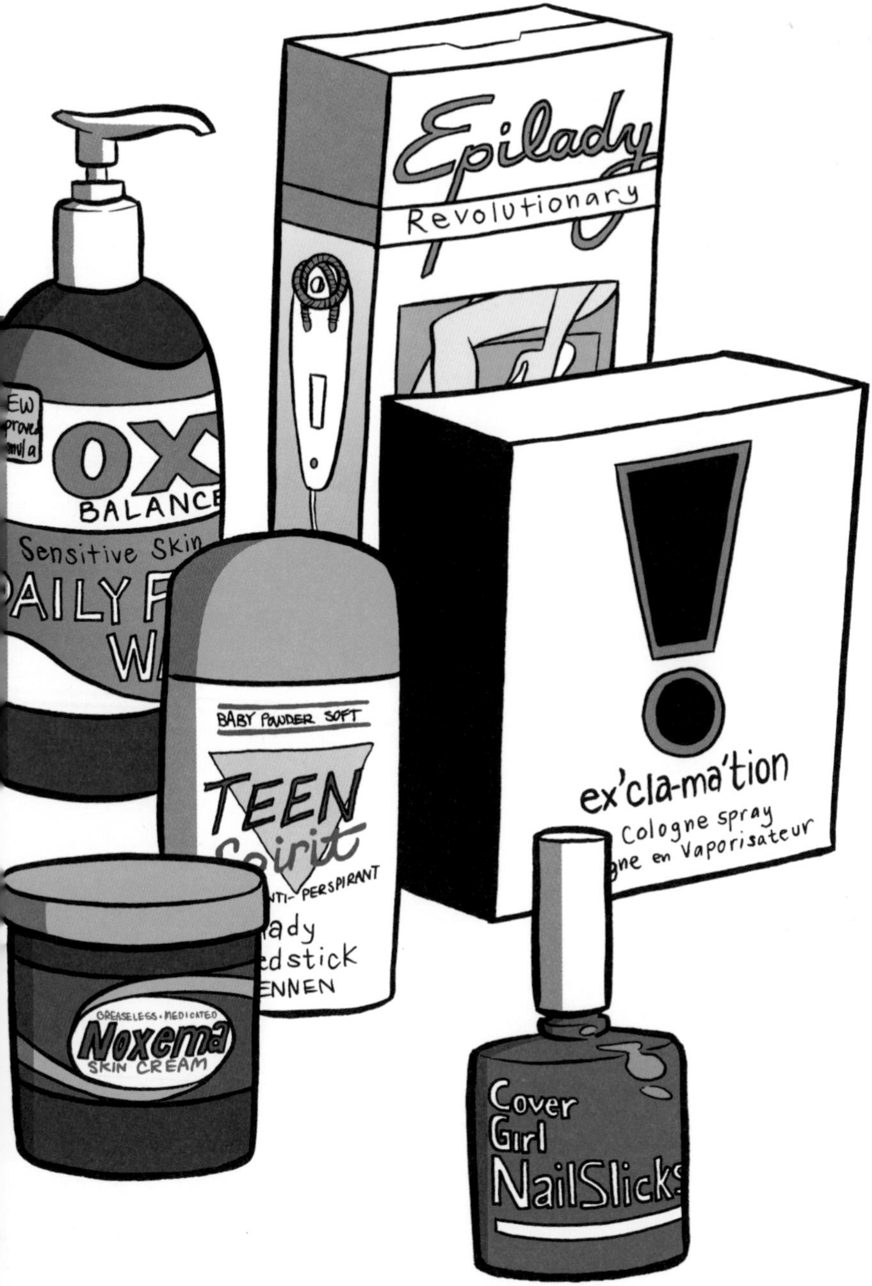

Epilady
Revolutionary
BALANCE
Sensitive Skin
BABY POWDER SOFT
TEEN Spirit
ex'cla-ma'tion
Cologne spray
en Vaporisateur
GREASELESS • MEDICATED
Noxema
SKIN CREAM
Cover Girl
NailSlicks

WELL! GOOD NEWS, RAINA.

YOUR TOP TEETH ARE MOVING TOGETHER NICELY.

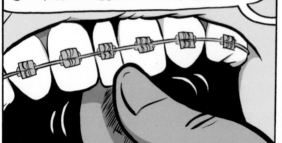

SOON, WE'LL BE ABLE TO REMOVE THIS LITTLE FAKE TOOTH IN THE CENTER, AND WE'LL PUT BONDINGS OVER YOUR NEW "FRONT" TEETH SO THEY LOOK NORMAL.

YOU DO HAVE A LO OF GUM DAMAGE THOUGH...

LET'S MAKE YOU AN APPOINTMENT WITH THE PERIODONTIST -- HE MIGHT BE ABLE TO HELP WITH THAT.

I DIDN'T EVEN KNO THERE WERE THIS MANY KINDS OF "DONTISTS"...

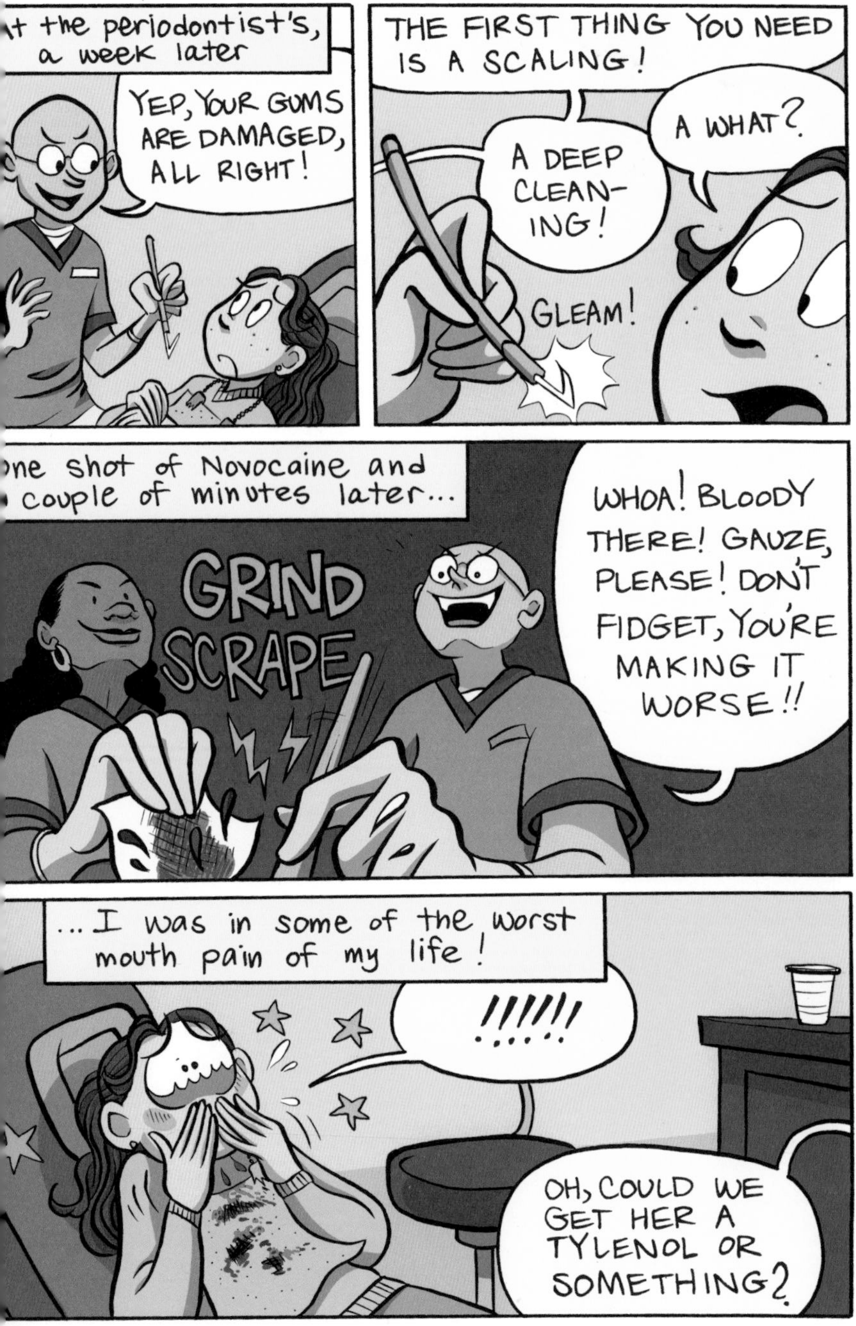
t the periodontist's, a week later
YEP, YOUR GUMS ARE DAMAGED, ALL RIGHT!
THE FIRST THING YOU NEED IS A SCALING!
A WHAT?
A DEEP CLEANING!
GLEAM!
ne shot of Novocaine and couple of minutes later...
GRIND
SCRAPE
WHOA! BLOODY THERE! GAUZE, PLEASE! DON'T FIDGET, YOU'RE MAKING IT WORSE!!
...I was in some of the worst mouth pain of my life!
!!!!!!
OH, COULD WE GET HER A TYLENOL OR SOMETHING?

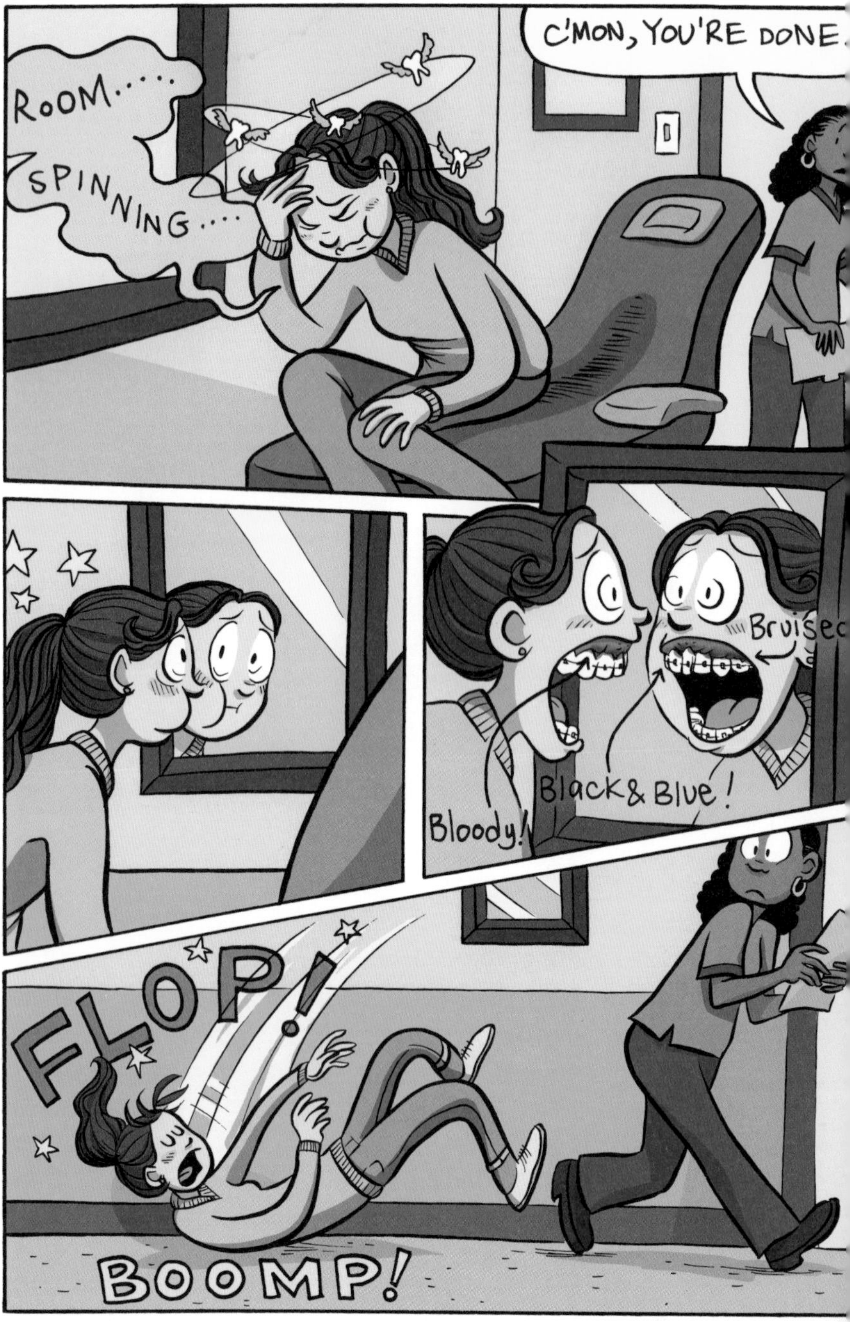
ROOM......
SPINNING.....
C'MON, YOU'RE DONE.
Bloody!
Black & Blue!
Bruisec
FLOP!
BOOMP!

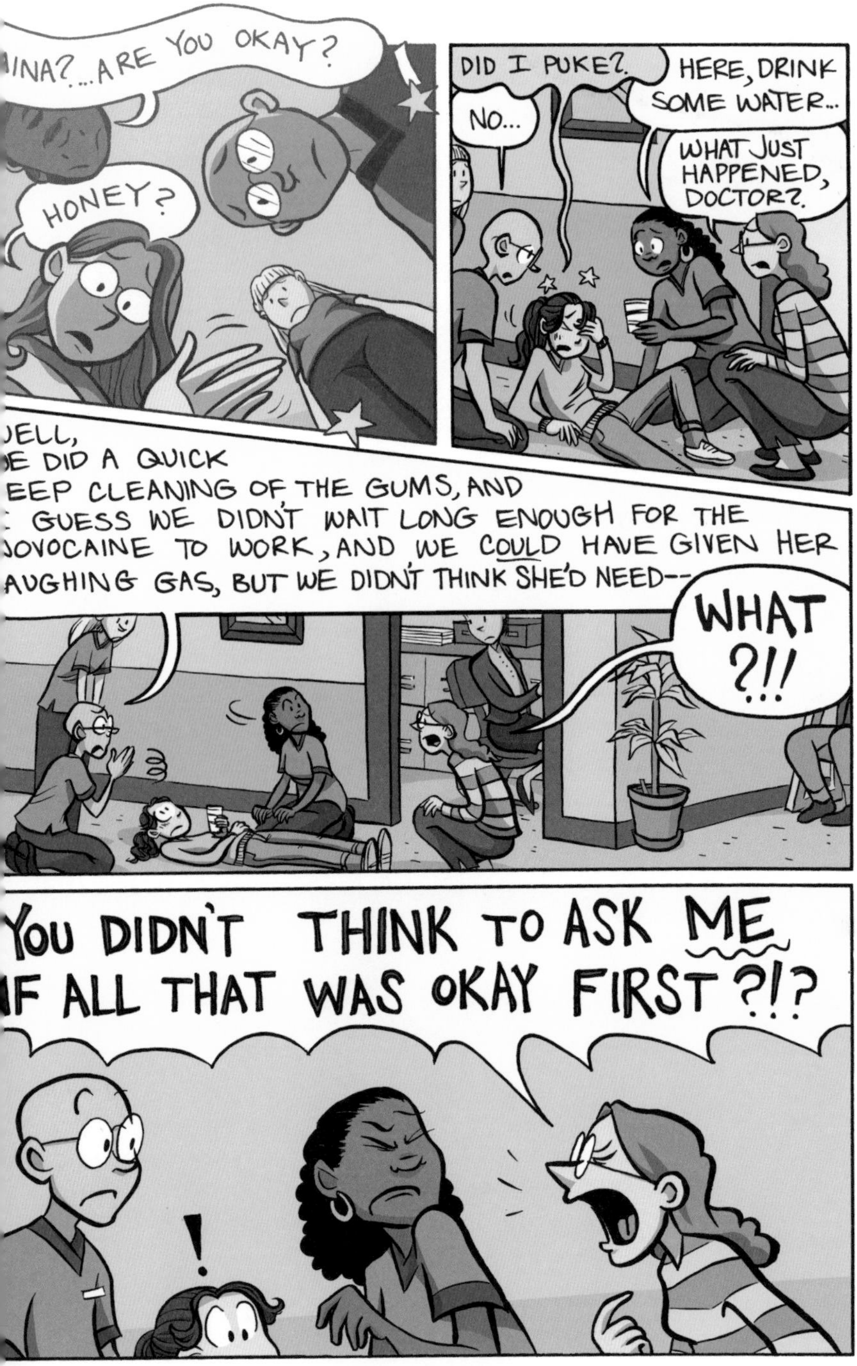

INA?...ARE YOU OKAY?
HONEY?
DID I PUKE?
NO...
HERE, DRINK SOME WATER...
WHAT JUST HAPPENED, DOCTOR?
ELL, E DID A QUICK EEP CLEANING OF THE GUMS, AND GUESS WE DIDN'T WAIT LONG ENOUGH FOR THE OVOCAINE TO WORK, AND WE COULD HAVE GIVEN HER AUGHING GAS, BUT WE DIDN'T THINK SHE'D NEED--
WHAT?!!
YOU DIDN'T THINK TO ASK ME F ALL THAT WAS OKAY FIRST?!?
!

CHAPTER SEVEN

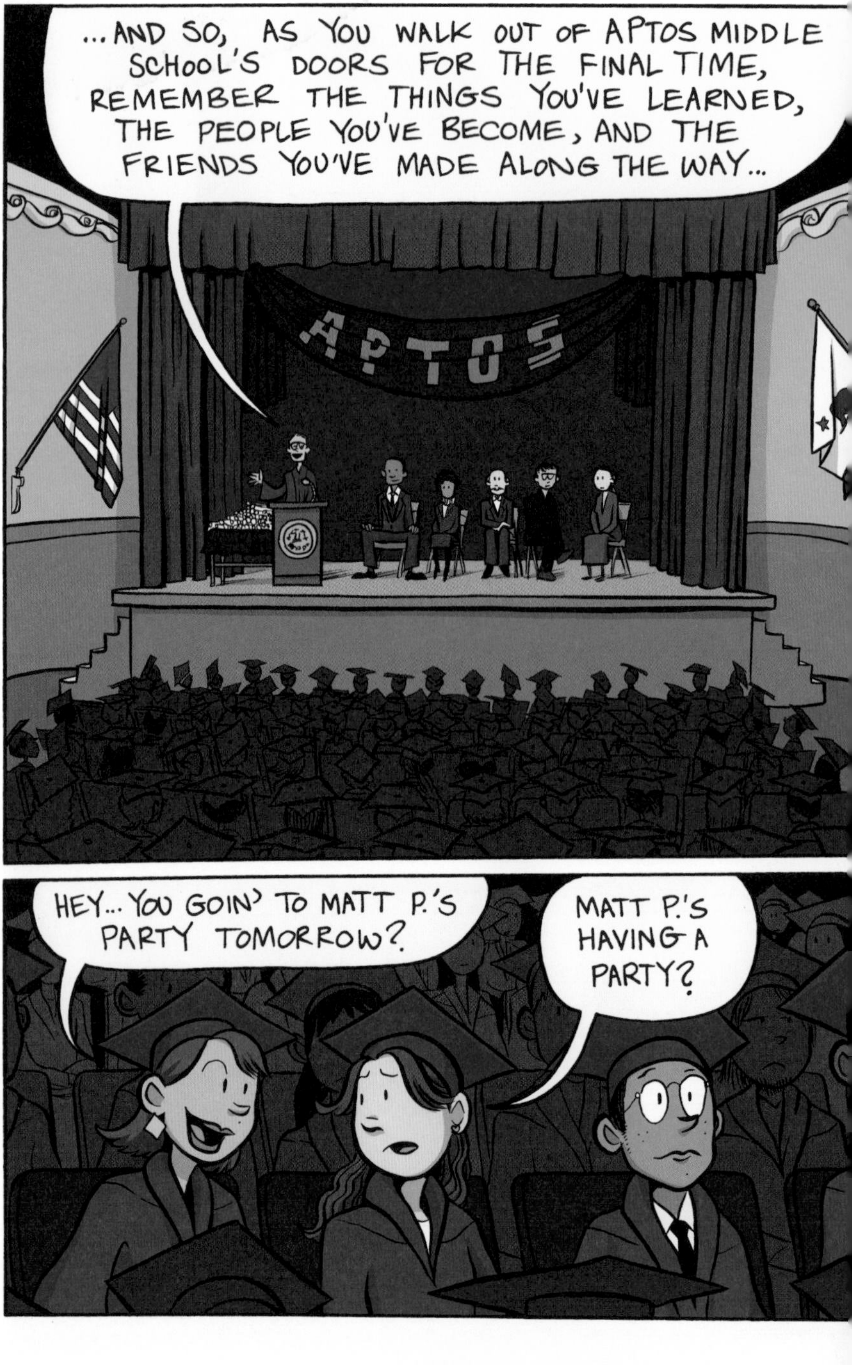
...AND SO, AS YOU WALK OUT OF APTOS MIDDLE SCHOOL'S DOORS FOR THE FINAL TIME, REMEMBER THE THINGS YOU'VE LEARNED, THE PEOPLE YOU'VE BECOME, AND THE FRIENDS YOU'VE MADE ALONG THE WAY...
APTOS
HEY... YOU GOIN' TO MATT P.'S PARTY TOMORROW?
MATT P.'S HAVING A PARTY?

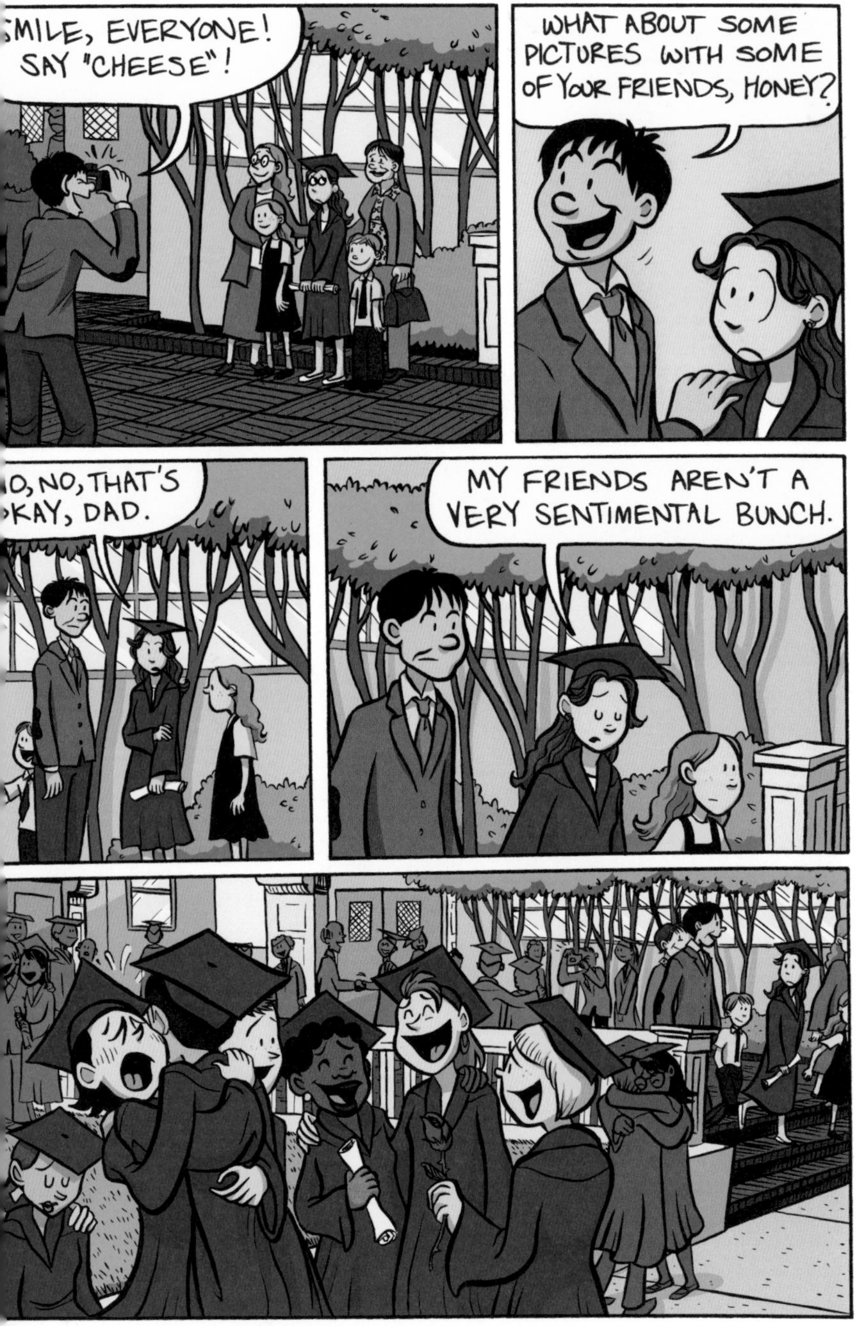
SMILE, EVERYONE! SAY "CHEESE"!
WHAT ABOUT SOME PICTURES WITH SOME OF YOUR FRIENDS, HONEY?
O, NO, THAT'S KAY, DAD.
MY FRIENDS AREN'T A VERY SENTIMENTAL BUNCH.

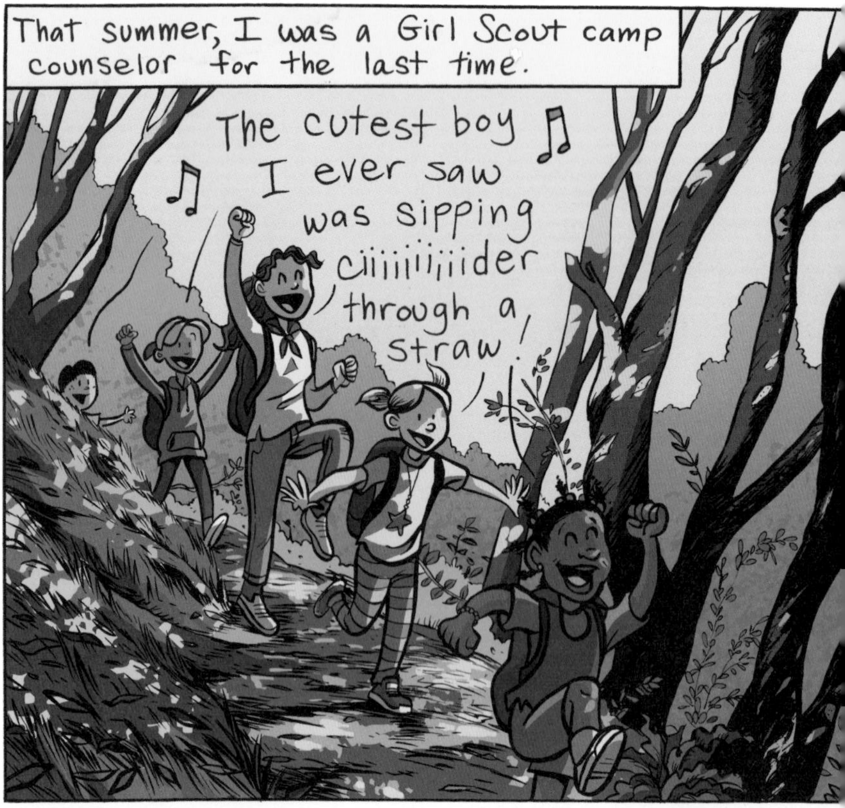
That summer, I was a Girl Scout camp counselor for the last time.
The cutest boy I ever saw was sipping ciiiiiiiiiider through a straw!

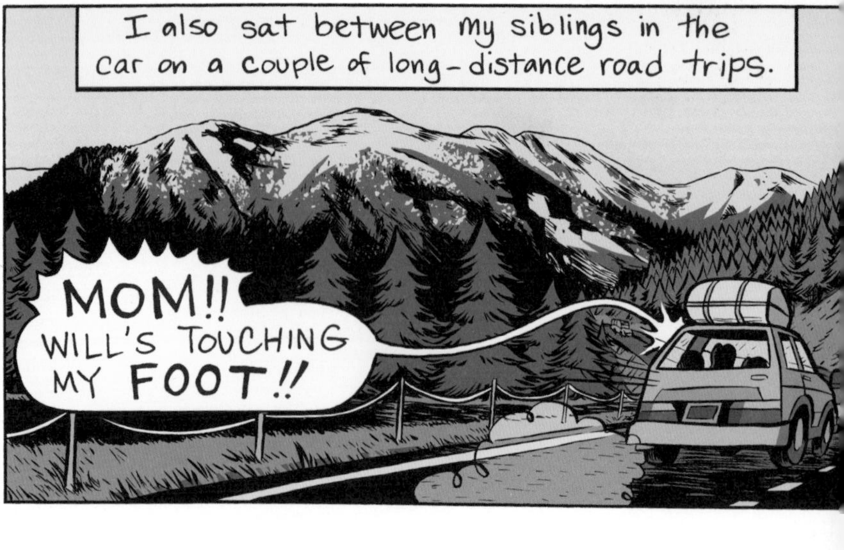
I also sat between my siblings in the car on a couple of long-distance road trips.
MOM!! WILL'S TOUCHING MY FOOT!!

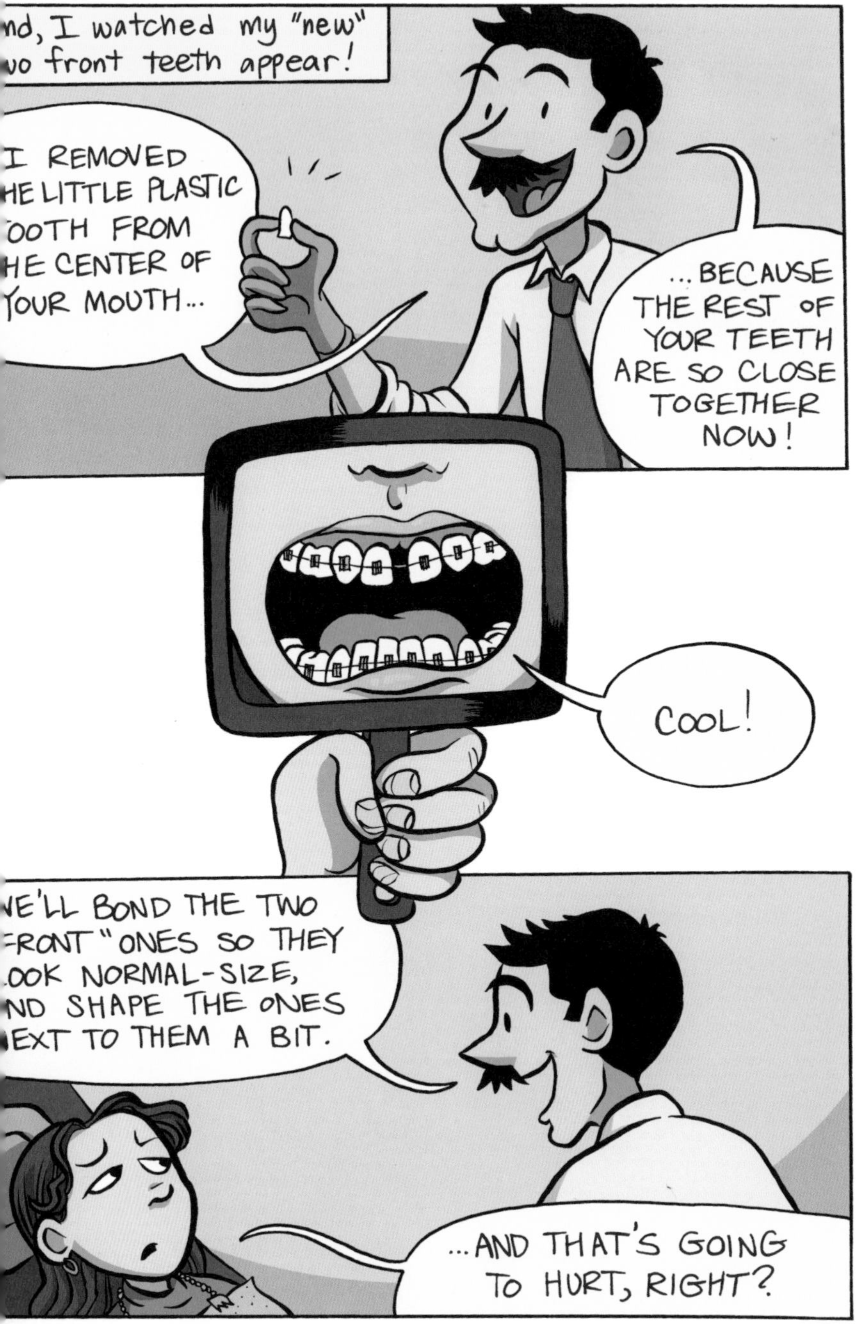
nd, I watched my "new" wo front teeth appear!
I REMOVED HE LITTLE PLASTIC OOTH FROM HE CENTER OF YOUR MOUTH...
...BECAUSE THE REST OF YOUR TEETH ARE SO CLOSE TOGETHER NOW!
COOL!
VE'LL BOND THE TWO FRONT" ONES SO THEY OOK NORMAL-SIZE, ND SHAPE THE ONES EXT TO THEM A BIT.
...AND THAT'S GOING TO HURT, RIGHT?

"ACTUALLY, IT'S NOT! THE DENTIST MATCHES THE COLOR OF YOUR TEETH TO THE BONDING MATERIAL..."

"... APPLIES THE BONDING AS A LIQUID TO YOUR TEETH"

SQUIRT

"... THEN SETS THE LIQUID WITH A SPECIAL LIGHT."

BZZZZZZZZZZ

"THEN, HE USES A LITTLE BUZZING TOOL TO SHAPE AND SMOOTH THE BONDING."

WRZZZZ

WHAT DO YOU THINK? NOT BAD, HUH?
HEY ACTUALLY LOOK... KINDA OKAY.
GLAD YOU THINK SO!
UT REMEMBER, JUST 'CAUSE THEY LOOK NORMAL, DOESN'T MEAN YOU'RE ALLOWED TO START EATING POPCORN AND JAWBREAKERS YET.
I KNOW, I KNOW.

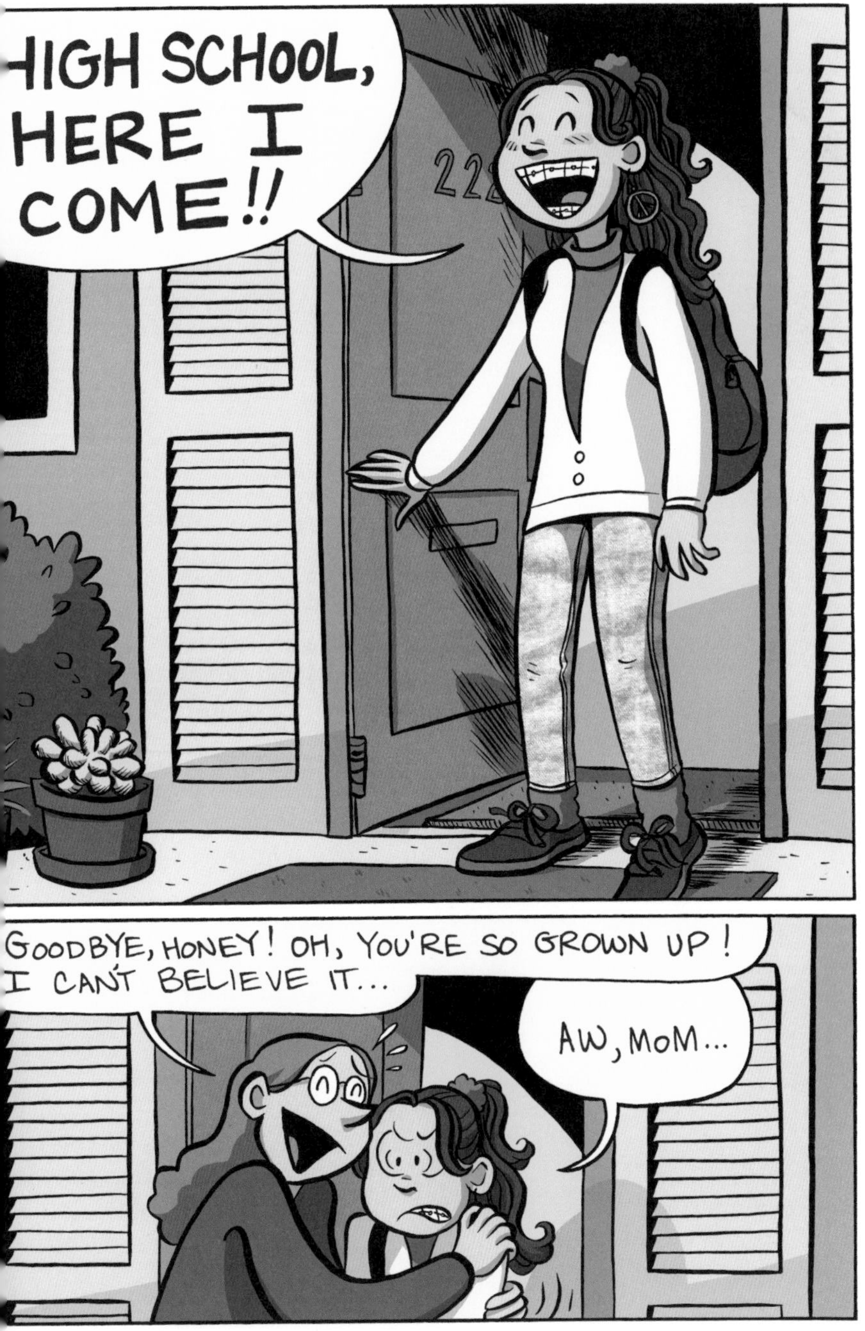
HIGH SCHOOL, HERE I COME!!
GOODBYE, HONEY! OH, YOU'RE SO GROWN UP! I CAN'T BELIEVE IT...
AW, MOM...

OH! HI, MELISSA.

HEY.

IT'S TOO BAD WE'RE NOT GOING TO THE SAME HIGH SCHOOL.

YOU'LL BE OKAY.

SO, YOU'RE NOT NERVOUS? NOT EVEN A LITTLE?

NOPE.

OH!! THIS IS MY STOP. SEE YA LATER!

LATER HEY, RAINA

DON'T FORGET TO SMILE!!

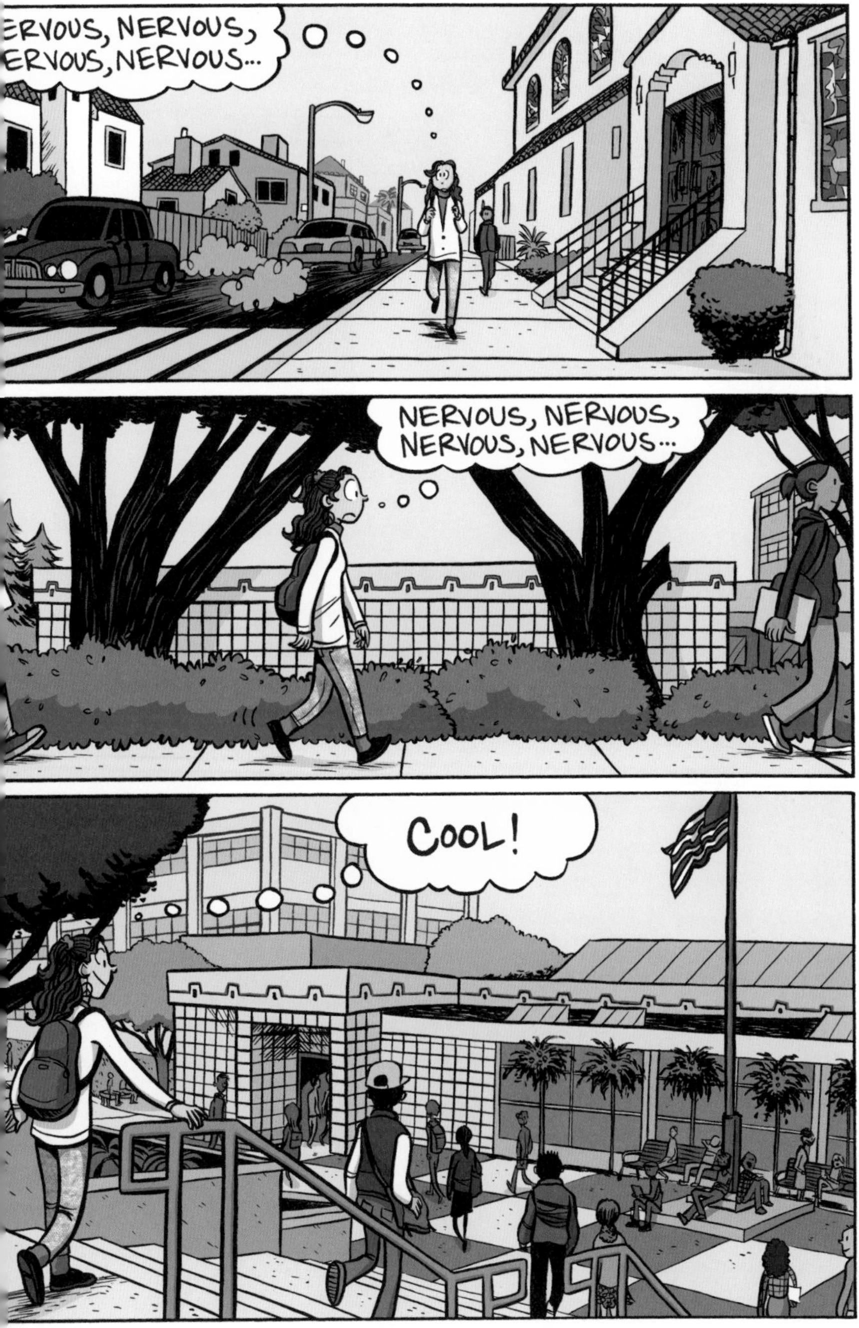
ERVOUS, NERVOUS,
ERVOUS, NERVOUS...
NERVOUS, NERVOUS,
NERVOUS, NERVOUS...
COOL!

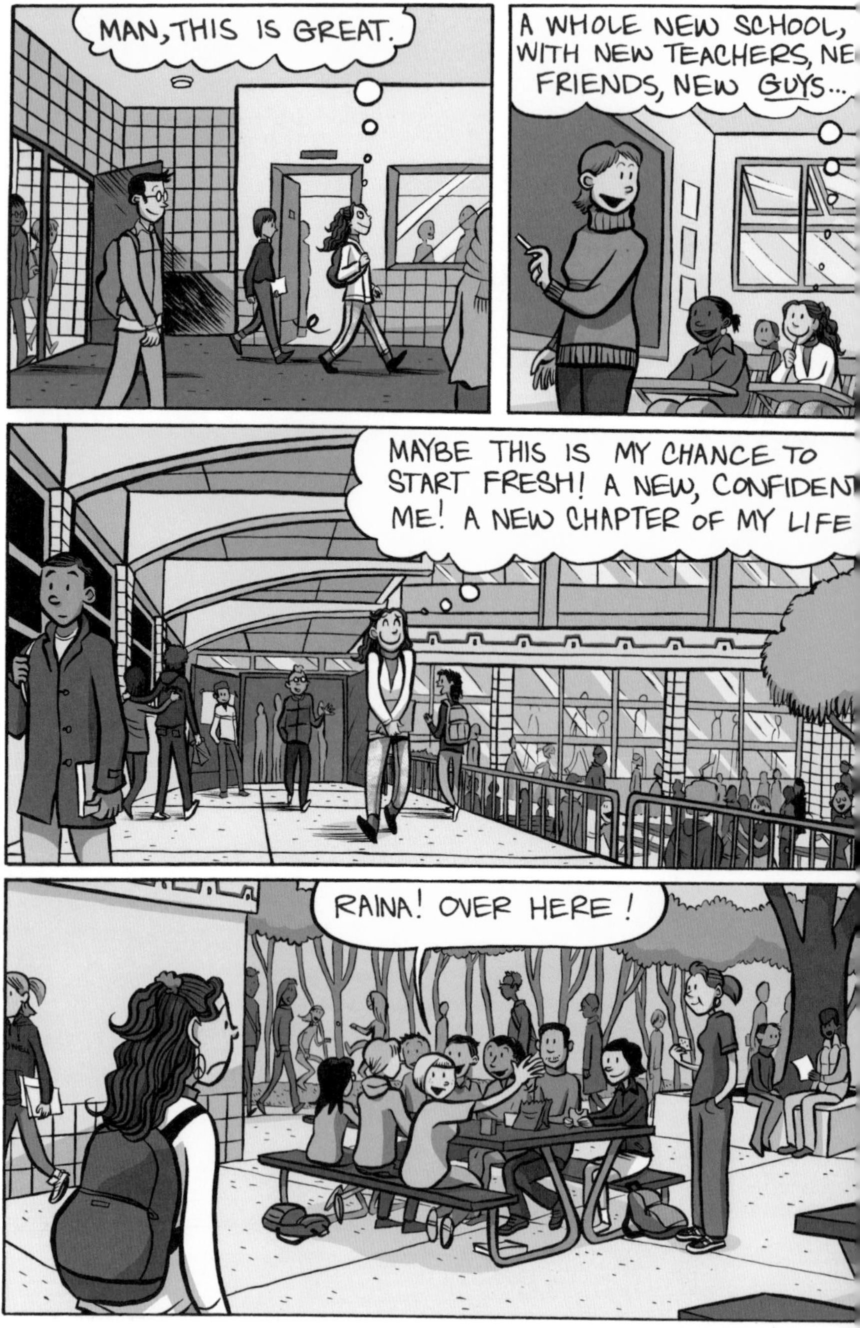
MAN, THIS IS GREAT.
A WHOLE NEW SCHOOL, WITH NEW TEACHERS, NE FRIENDS, NEW GUYS...
MAYBE THIS IS MY CHANCE TO START FRESH! A NEW, CONFIDEN ME! A NEW CHAPTER OF MY LIFE
RAINA! OVER HERE!

EMILY. HI, JENNY, ANDREW, RIN, JUAN, KAYLAH, EDWARD, COLE, AND PERSON-I-DON'T-KNOW.

THAT'S MATT W.

HI.

HOW WAS YOUR SUUUMMER? ♪♫

LOW-KEY.

REALLY?

NE WAS A BLAST! JEN AND ANDREW AND I WENT ALL VER THE CITY TOGETHER. IT WAS SO FUN!!

YEAH, REMEMBER FISHERMAN'S WHARF?

EEE! DON'T TALK ABOUT THAT!!

OH, AND THE TIME YOU GUYS ALL CAME OVER AND WE WATCHED "NIGHT-MARE ON ELM STREET"?

HA HA HA!

ter

RAINA! HOW WAS THE FIRST DAY AT YOUR NEW SCHOOL?!

EXACTLY THE SAME.

DO WE HAVE ANY CHIPS?

The next stage of my orthodontic treatment was a fairly entertaining one, designed to correct my

CROSS-BITE.

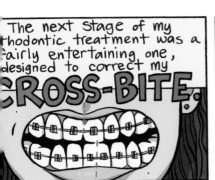

(That's when your top and bottom jaws don't line up.)

To fix this, little hooks are attached to specific brackets on the top and the bottom teeth...

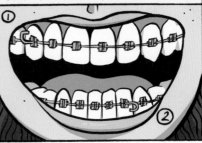

① ②

..and a tiny rubber band is stretched between them.

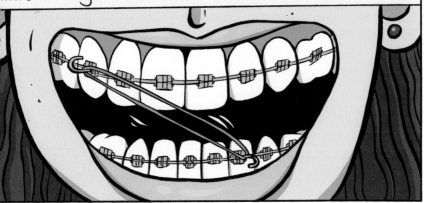

Twannngg!

I CAN' OPEN MA MOUF ALL TH' WEY!

YOU'LL GET USED TO IT!

183

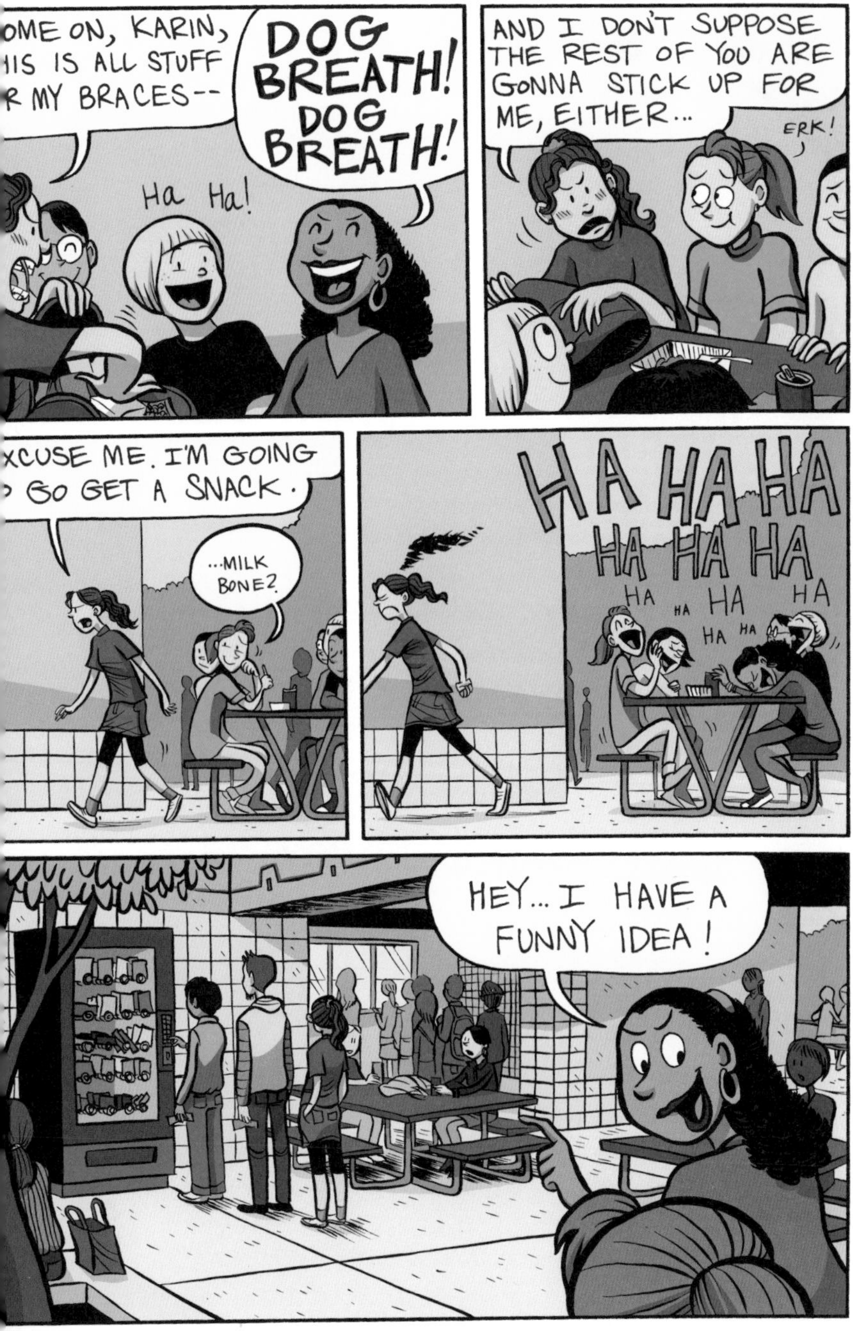
OME ON, KARIN, HIS IS ALL STUFF R MY BRACES--
DOG BREATH! DOG BREATH!
Ha Ha!
AND I DON'T SUPPOSE THE REST OF YOU ARE GONNA STICK UP FOR ME, EITHER...
ERK!
XCUSE ME. I'M GOING GO GET A SNACK.
...MILK BONE?
HA HA HA HA
HA HA HA
HA HA HA HA
HA HA HA
HEY... I HAVE A FUNNY IDEA!

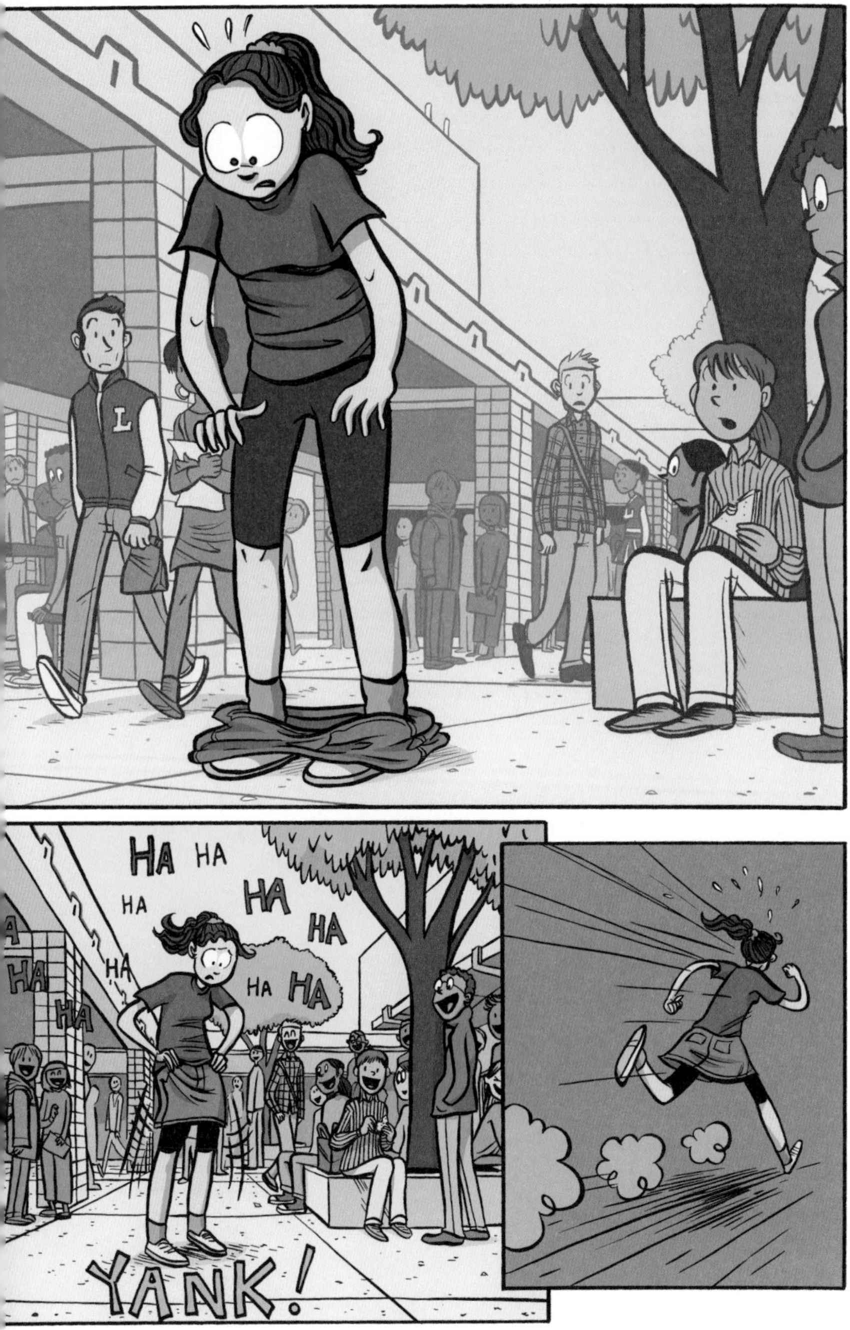
HA HA
HA
HA
HA
HA
HA
HA HA
HA
HA
HA
YANK!

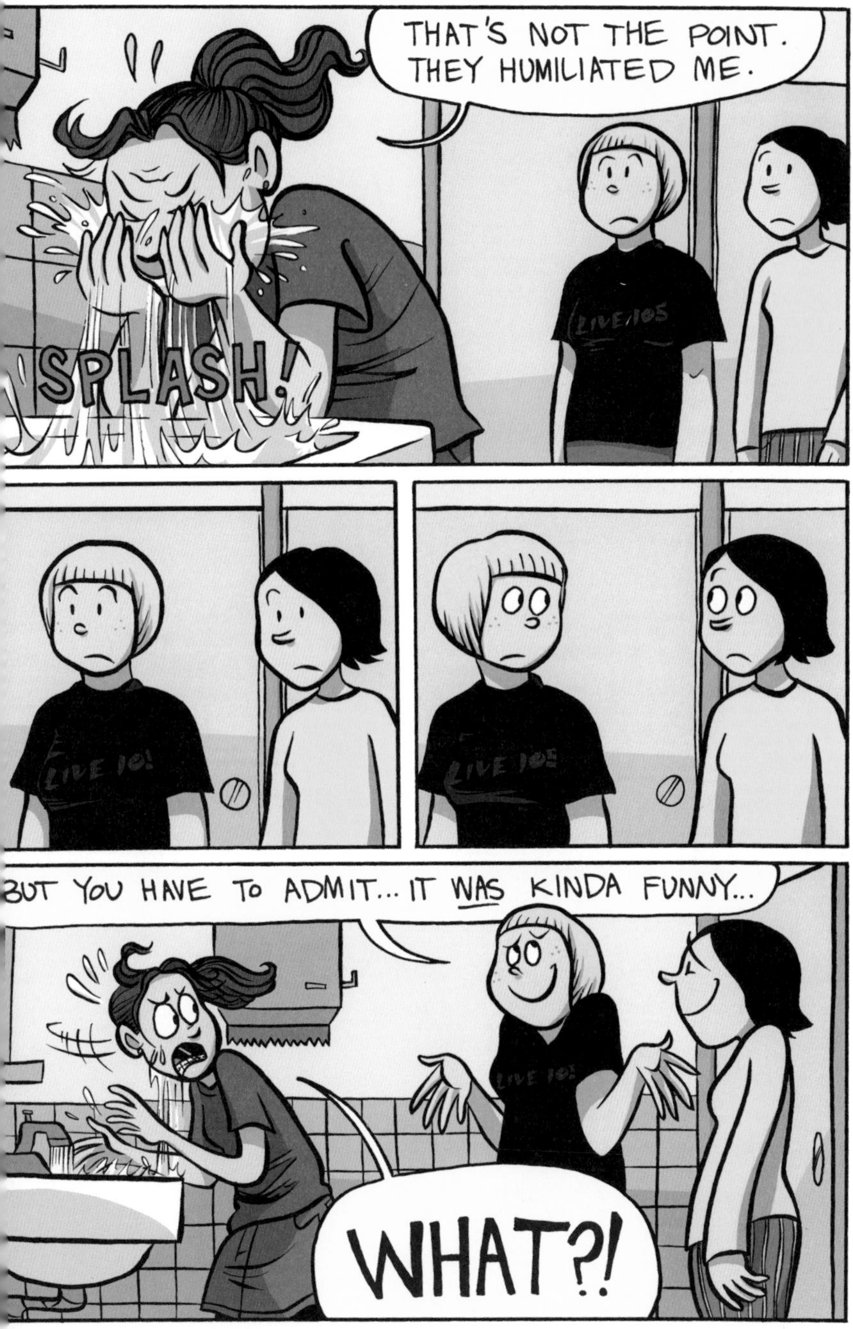
THAT'S NOT THE POINT. THEY HUMILIATED ME.
SPLASH!
LIVE 105
LIVE 105
LIVE 105
BUT YOU HAVE TO ADMIT... IT WAS KINDA FUNNY...
LIVE 105
WHAT?!

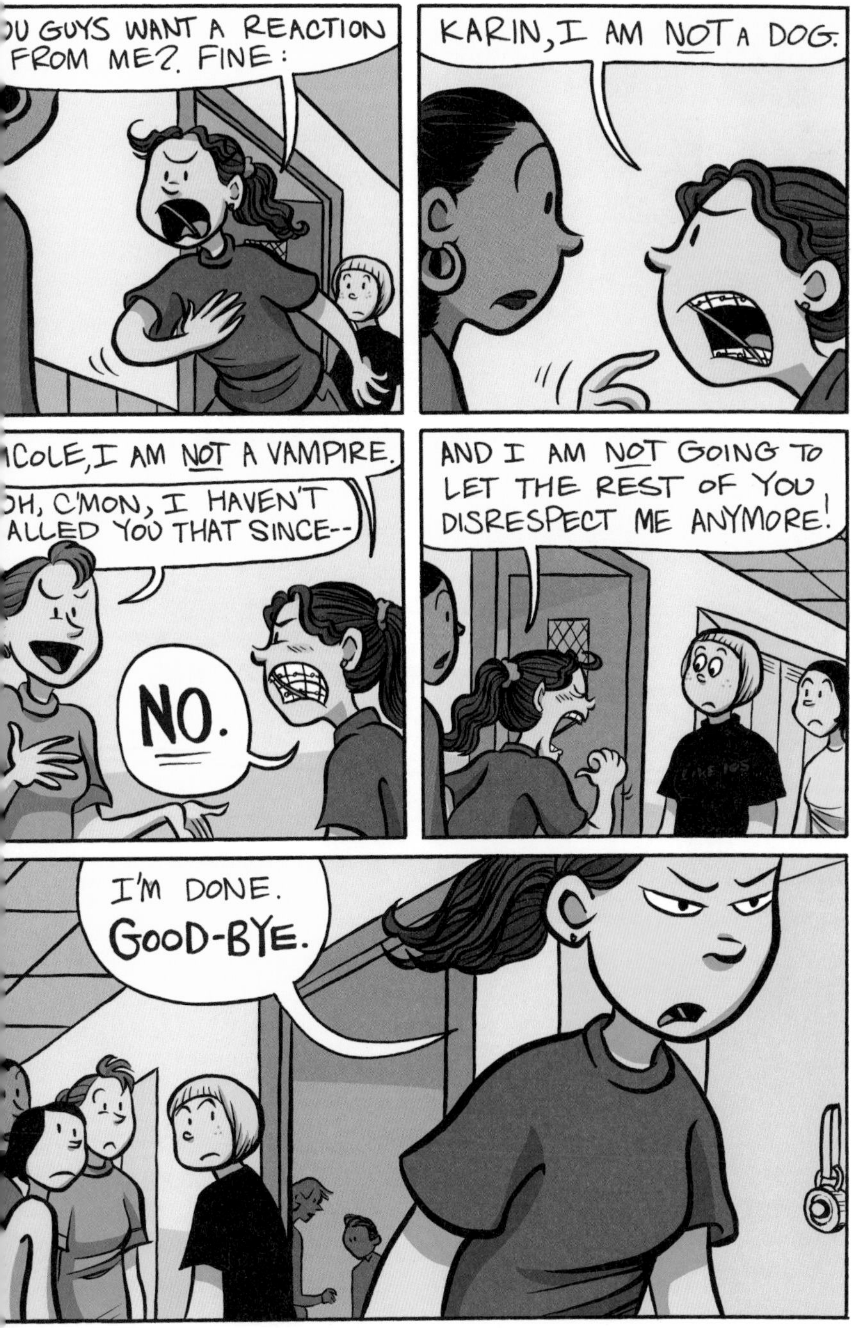

U GUYS WANT A REACTION FROM ME? FINE:
KARIN, I AM NOT A DOG.
ICOLE, I AM NOT A VAMPIRE.
H, C'MON, I HAVEN'T ALLED YOU THAT SINCE--
NO.
AND I AM NOT GOING TO LET THE REST OF YOU DISRESPECT ME ANYMORE!
I'M DONE. GOOD-BYE.

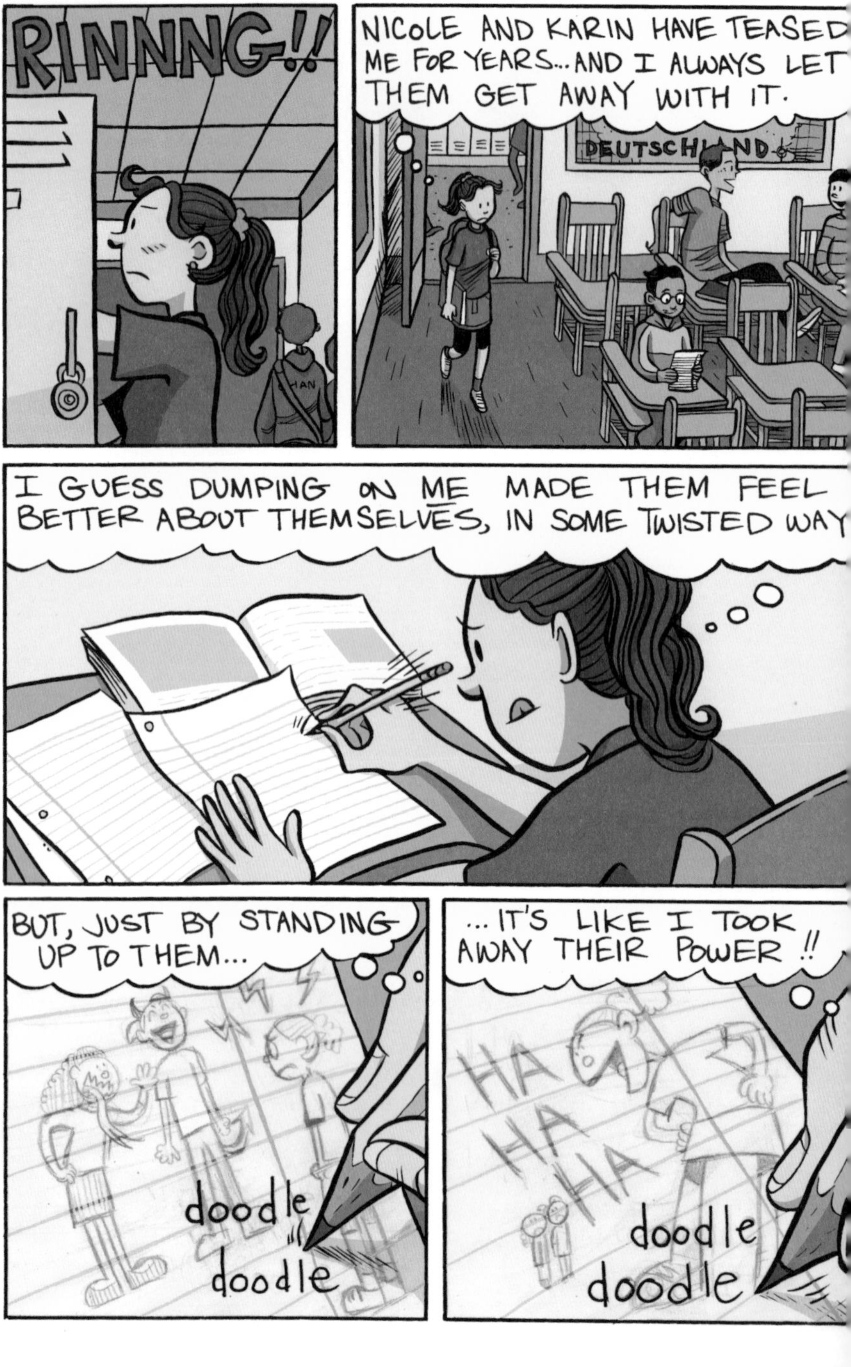
RINNNG!!
NICOLE AND KARIN HAVE TEASED ME FOR YEARS... AND I ALWAYS LET THEM GET AWAY WITH IT.
DEUTSCHLAND
I GUESS DUMPING ON ME MADE THEM FEEL BETTER ABOUT THEMSELVES, IN SOME TWISTED WAY
BUT, JUST BY STANDING UP TO THEM...
doodle
doodle
...IT'S LIKE I TOOK AWAY THEIR POWER!!
HA
HA
HA
doodle
doodle

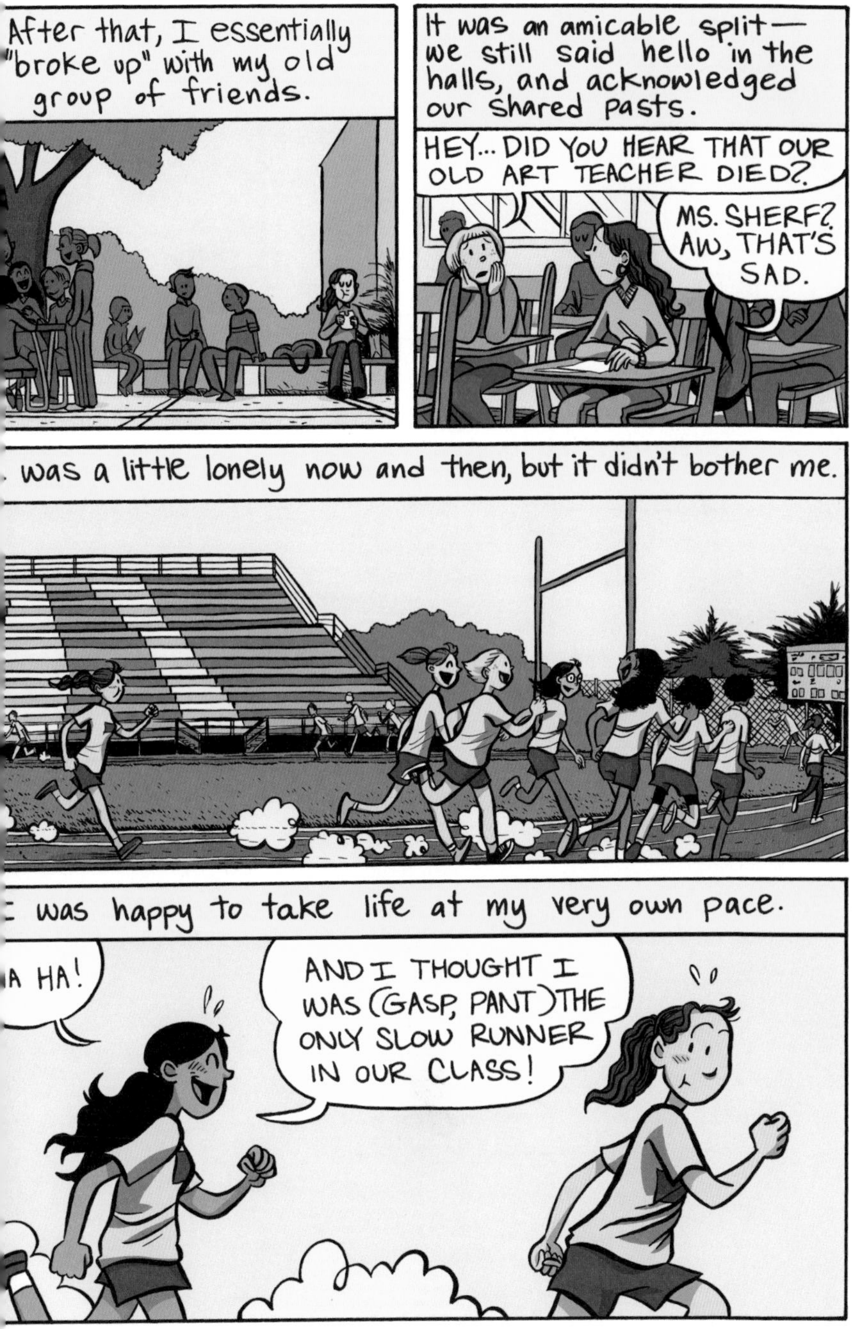
After that, I essentially "broke up" with my old group of friends.
It was an amicable split—we still said hello in the halls, and acknowledged our shared pasts.
HEY... DID YOU HEAR THAT OUR OLD ART TEACHER DIED?
MS. SHERF? AW, THAT'S SAD.
was a little lonely now and then, but it didn't bother me.
was happy to take life at my very own pace.
A HA!
AND I THOUGHT I WAS (GASP, PANT) THE ONLY SLOW RUNNER IN OUR CLASS!

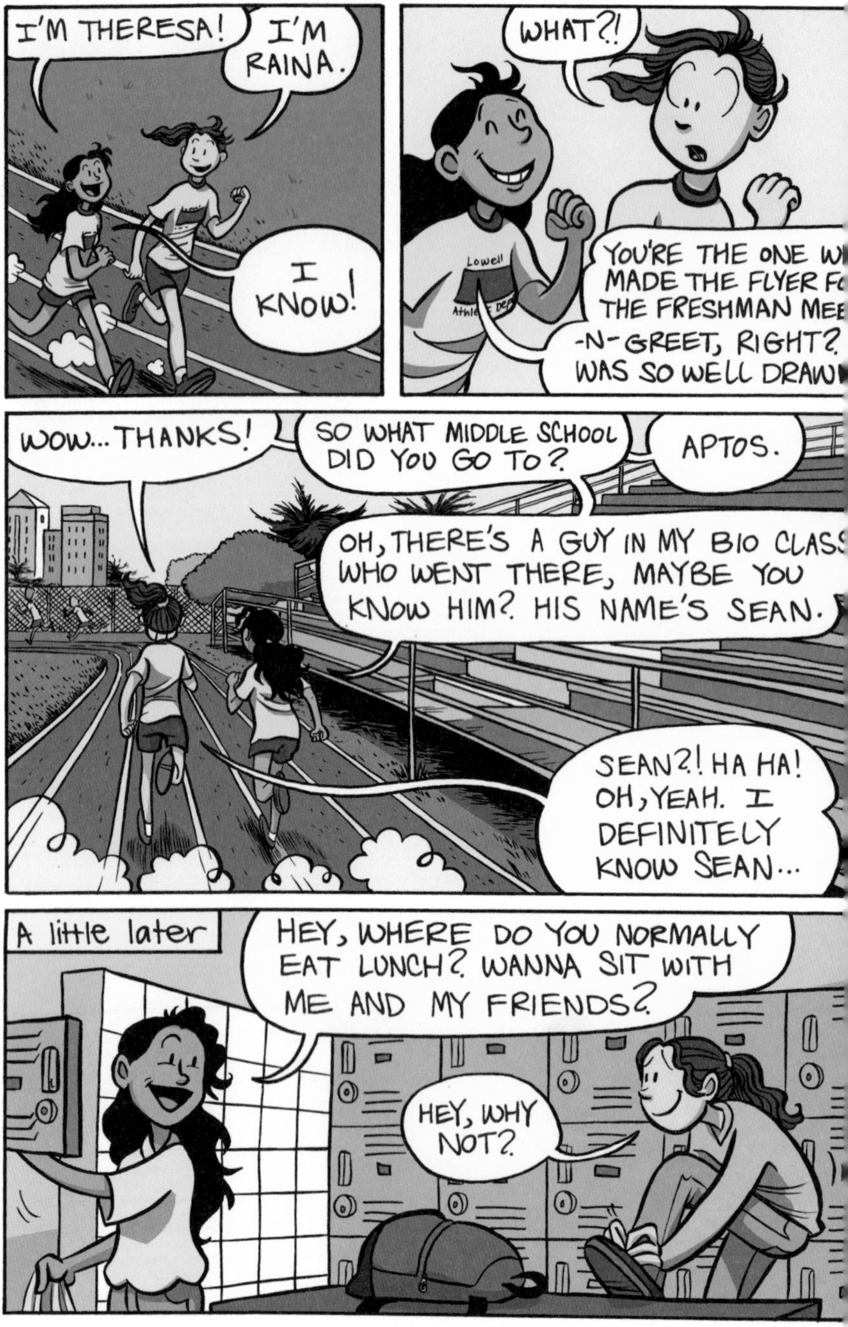
I'M THERESA!
I'M RAINA.
I KNOW!
WHAT?!
YOU'RE THE ONE W
MADE THE FLYER F
THE FRESHMAN ME
-N-GREET, RIGHT?
WAS SO WELL DRAW
WOW... THANKS!
SO WHAT MIDDLE SCHOOL DID YOU GO TO?
APTOS.
OH, THERE'S A GUY IN MY BIO CLAS
WHO WENT THERE, MAYBE YOU KNOW HIM? HIS NAME'S SEAN.
SEAN?! HA HA! OH, YEAH. I DEFINITELY KNOW SEAN...
A little later
HEY, WHERE DO YOU NORMALLY EAT LUNCH? WANNA SIT WITH ME AND MY FRIENDS?
HEY, WHY NOT?

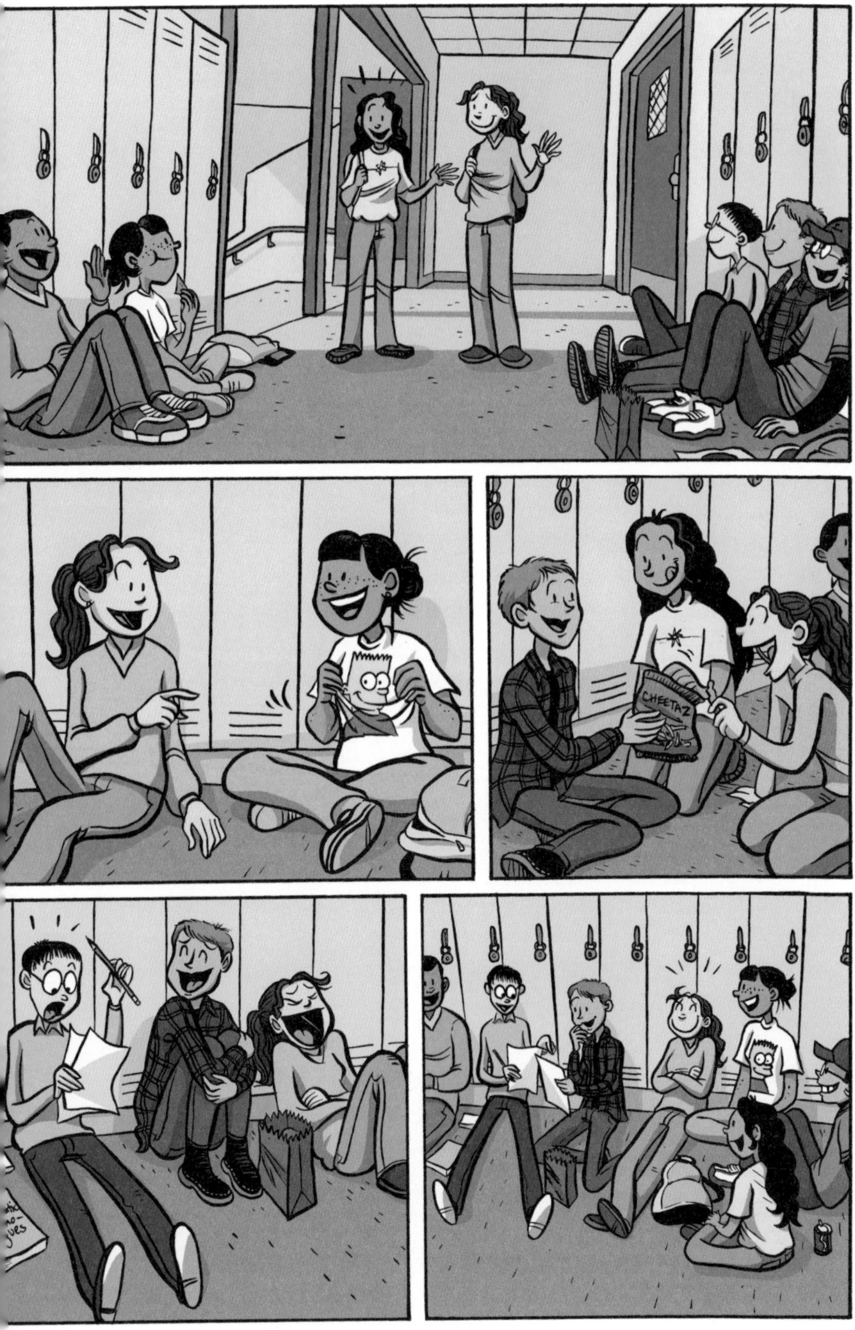
CHEETAZ

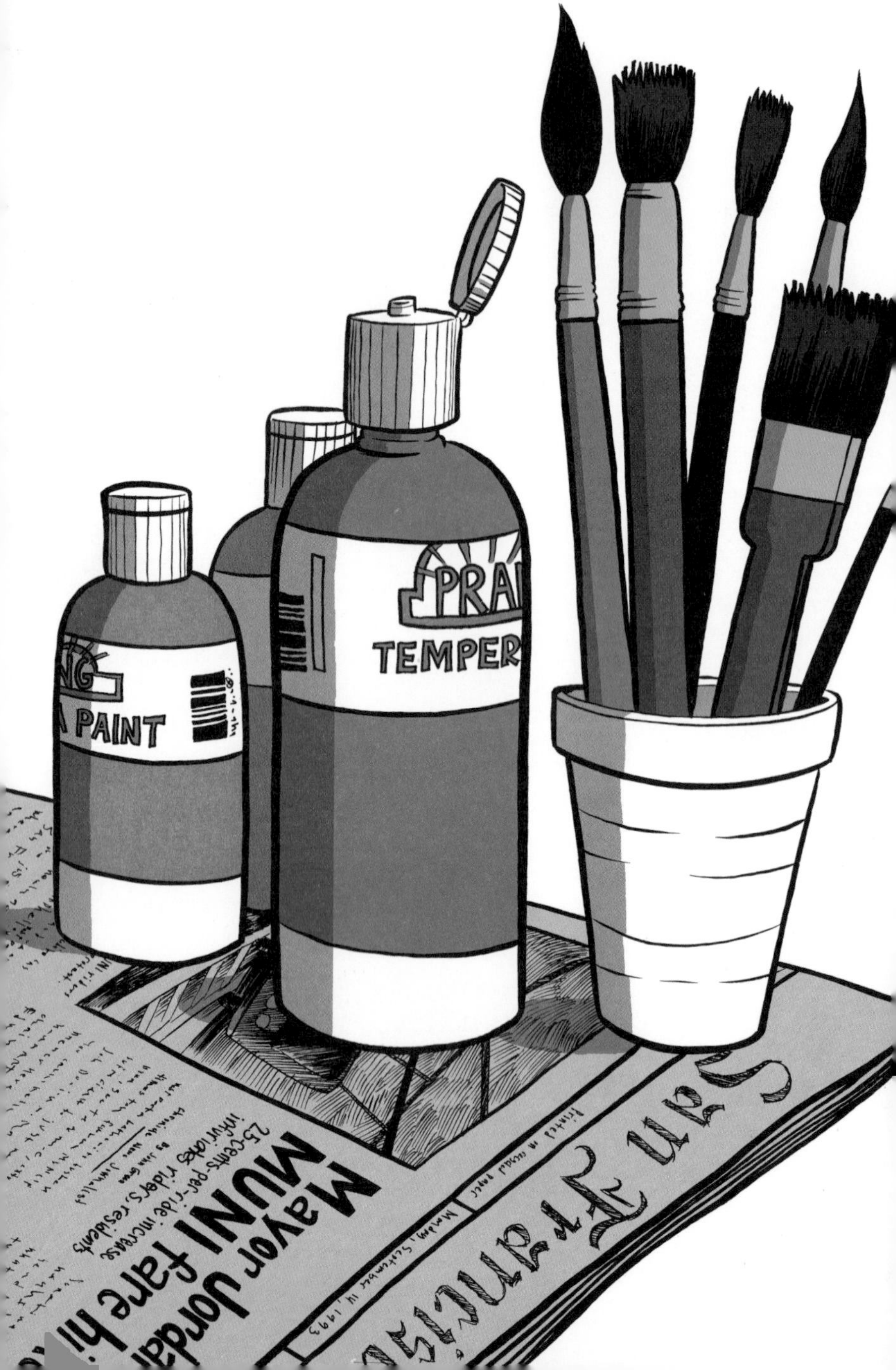
PRAN
TEMPER
PAINT
Mayor Jordan MUNI fare hi
25-cents-per-ride increase
infuriates riders, residents
San Francisc

CHAPTER EIGHT

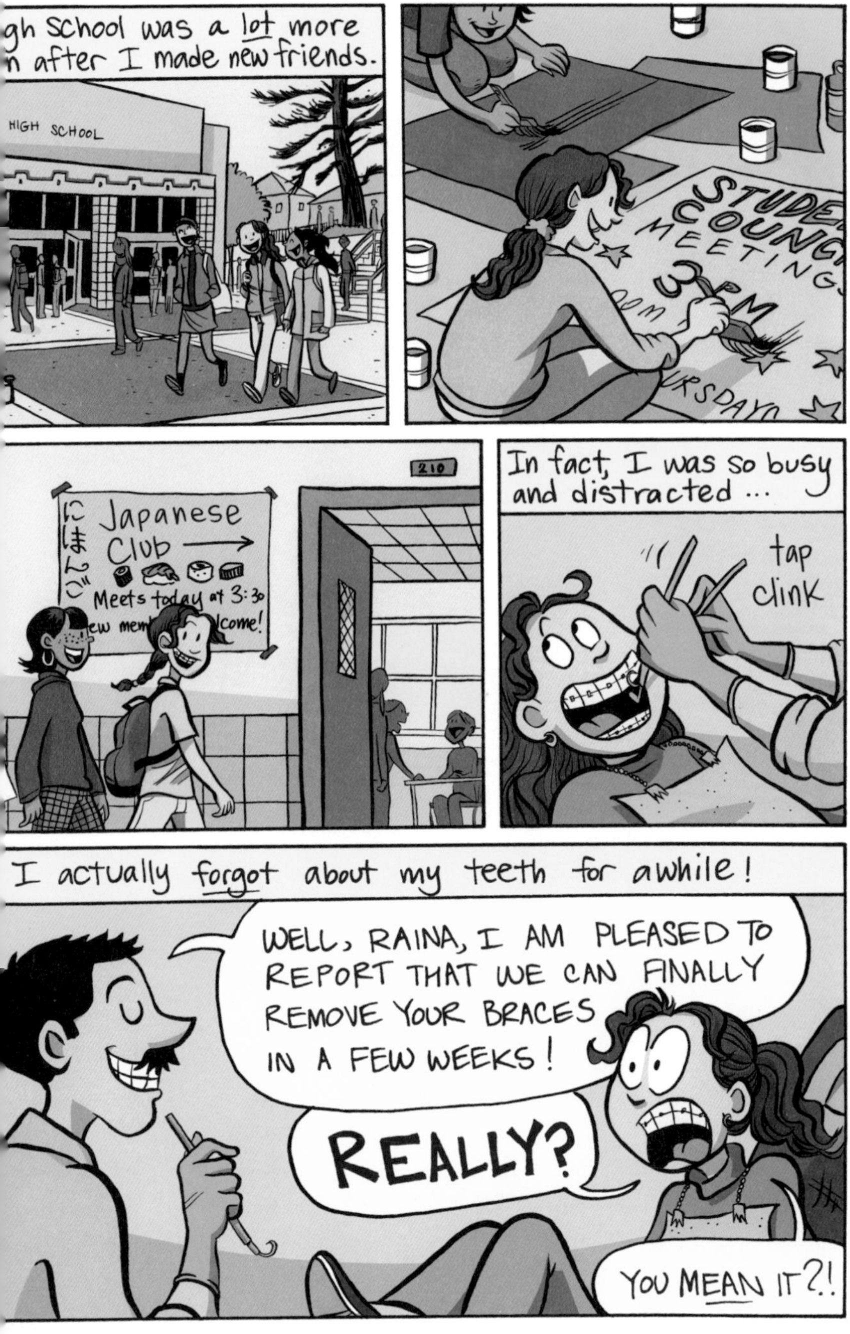

gh School was a lot more
n after I made new friends.
HIGH SCHOOL
STUDE
COUNC
MEETING
3PM
RSDAY
210
にほんご
Japanese
Club
Meets today at 3:30
ew mem lcome!
In fact, I was so busy and distracted ...
tap
clink
I actually forgot about my teeth for awhile!
WELL, RAINA, I AM PLEASED TO REPORT THAT WE CAN FINALLY REMOVE YOUR BRACES IN A FEW WEEKS!
REALLY?
YOU MEAN IT?!

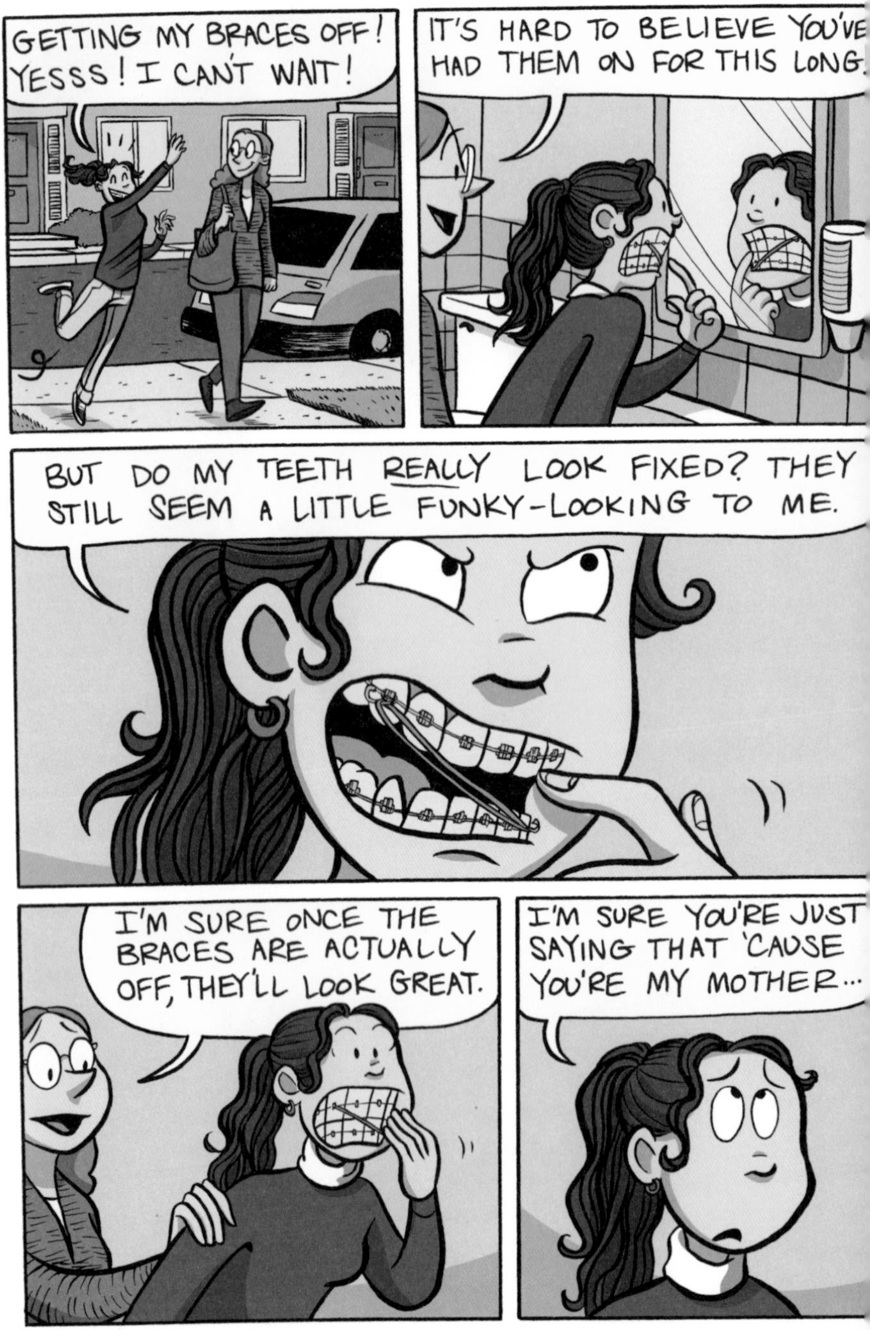
GETTING MY BRACES OFF! YESSS! I CAN'T WAIT!
IT'S HARD TO BELIEVE YOU'VE HAD THEM ON FOR THIS LONG.
BUT DO MY TEETH REALLY LOOK FIXED? THEY STILL SEEM A LITTLE FUNKY-LOOKING TO ME.
I'M SURE ONCE THE BRACES ARE ACTUALLY OFF, THEY'LL LOOK GREAT.
I'M SURE YOU'RE JUST SAYING THAT 'CAUSE YOU'RE MY MOTHER...

e big day finally arrived, a few eeks into my sophomore year.

GETTIN' MY BRACES OFF...

FIRST, WE'LL REMOVE ALL YOUR WIRES...

I'LL NEVER BE POKED AGAIN!

HEN WE PULL OFF ALL YOUR BRACKETS!

SCRRRRRRKK..!!

FINALLY, A QUICK POLISHING OF YOUR TEETH.

RRRRRRRR RRRRRRR RRR RRR

READY TO SEE YOUR BRAND-NEW SMILE?...

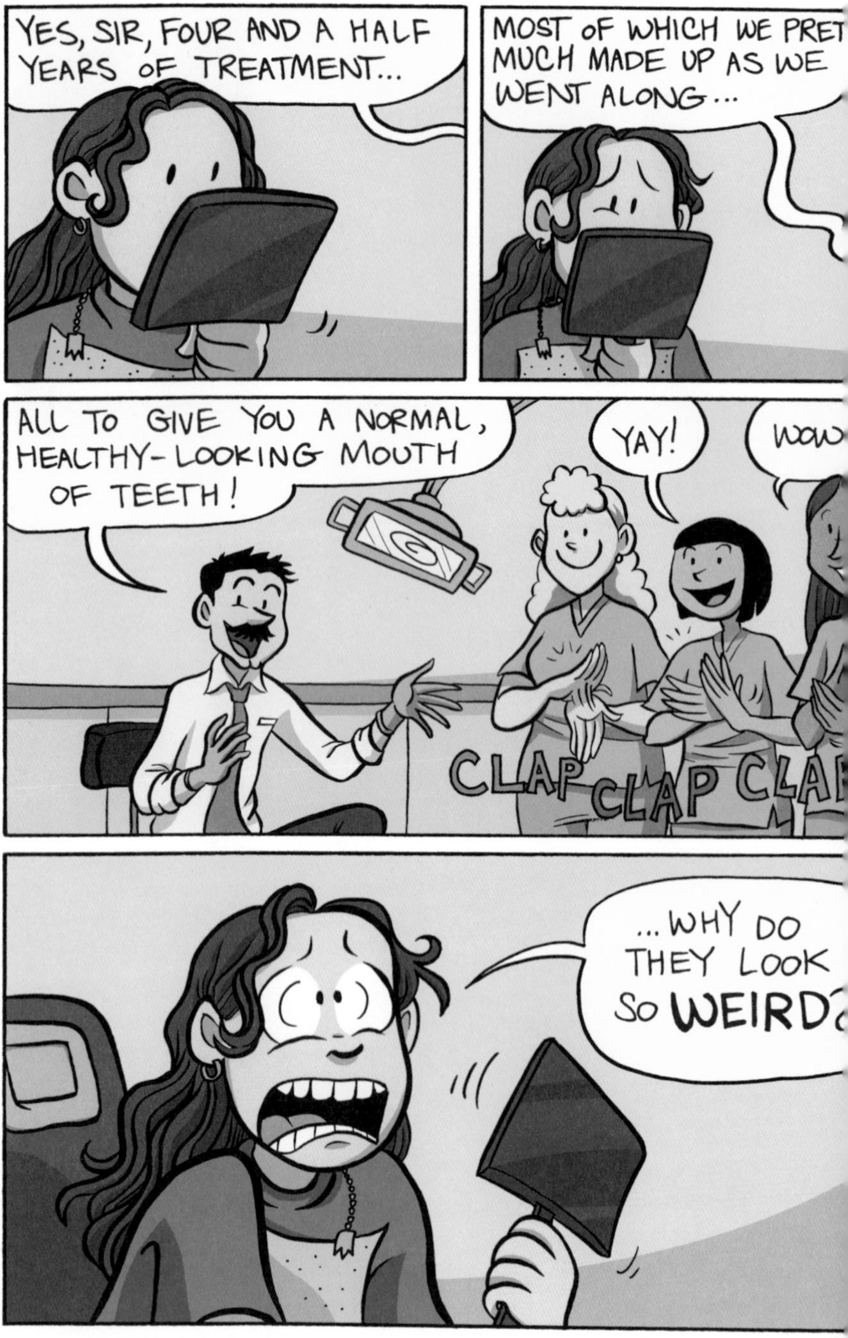
YES, SIR, FOUR AND A HALF YEARS OF TREATMENT...
MOST OF WHICH WE PRET
MUCH MADE UP AS WE WENT ALONG...
ALL TO GIVE YOU A NORMAL, HEALTHY-LOOKING MOUTH OF TEETH!
YAY!
CLAP CLAP
...WHY DO THEY LOOK SO WEIRD

EY DON'T LOOK <u>THAT</u> D! YOU'RE... JUST NOT ED TO THEM YET.

BUT THEY LOOK GREENISH! AND THEY'RE MISSHAPEN!

THAT STUPID RETAINER WITH THE <u>PLASTIC</u> TEETH ON IT WAS BETTER THAN **THIS**!!

E'VE DONE THE BEST WE OULD... CONSIDERING WE ASICALLY REARRANGED OUR WHOLE MOUTH...

ANYWAY, I HAVE SOMETHING THAT WILL CHEER YOU UP.

POPCOR

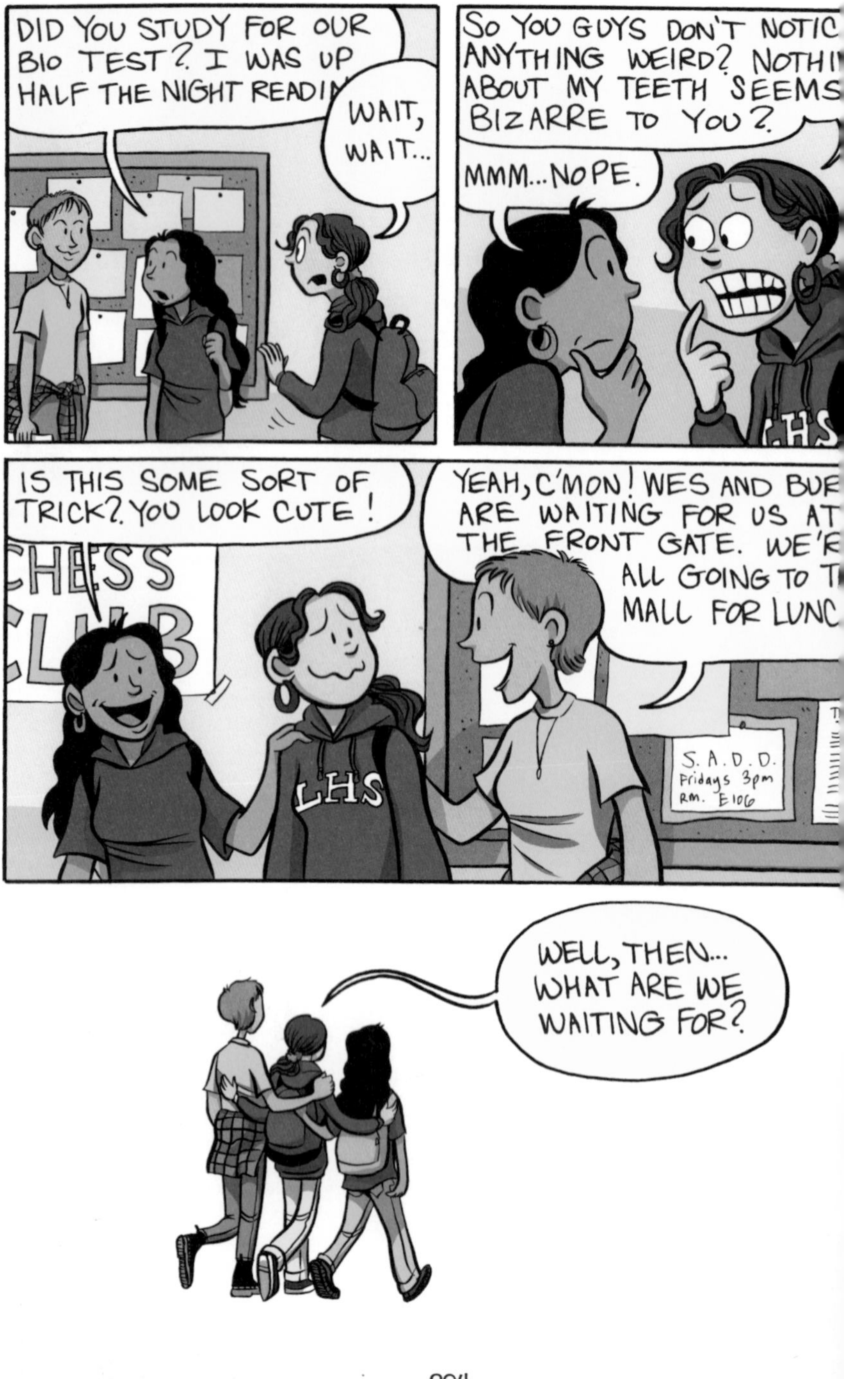
DID YOU STUDY FOR OUR BIO TEST? I WAS UP HALF THE NIGHT READI
WAIT, WAIT...
SO YOU GUYS DON'T NOTIC ANYTHING WEIRD? NOTHI ABOUT MY TEETH SEEMS BIZARRE TO YOU?
MMM...NOPE.
LHS
IS THIS SOME SORT OF TRICK? YOU LOOK CUTE!
CHESS CLUB
LHS
YEAH, C'MON! WES AND BU ARE WAITING FOR US AT THE FRONT GATE. WE'R ALL GOING TO T MALL FOR LUNC
S.A.D.D.
Fridays 3pm
Rm. E106
WELL, THEN... WHAT ARE WE WAITING FOR?

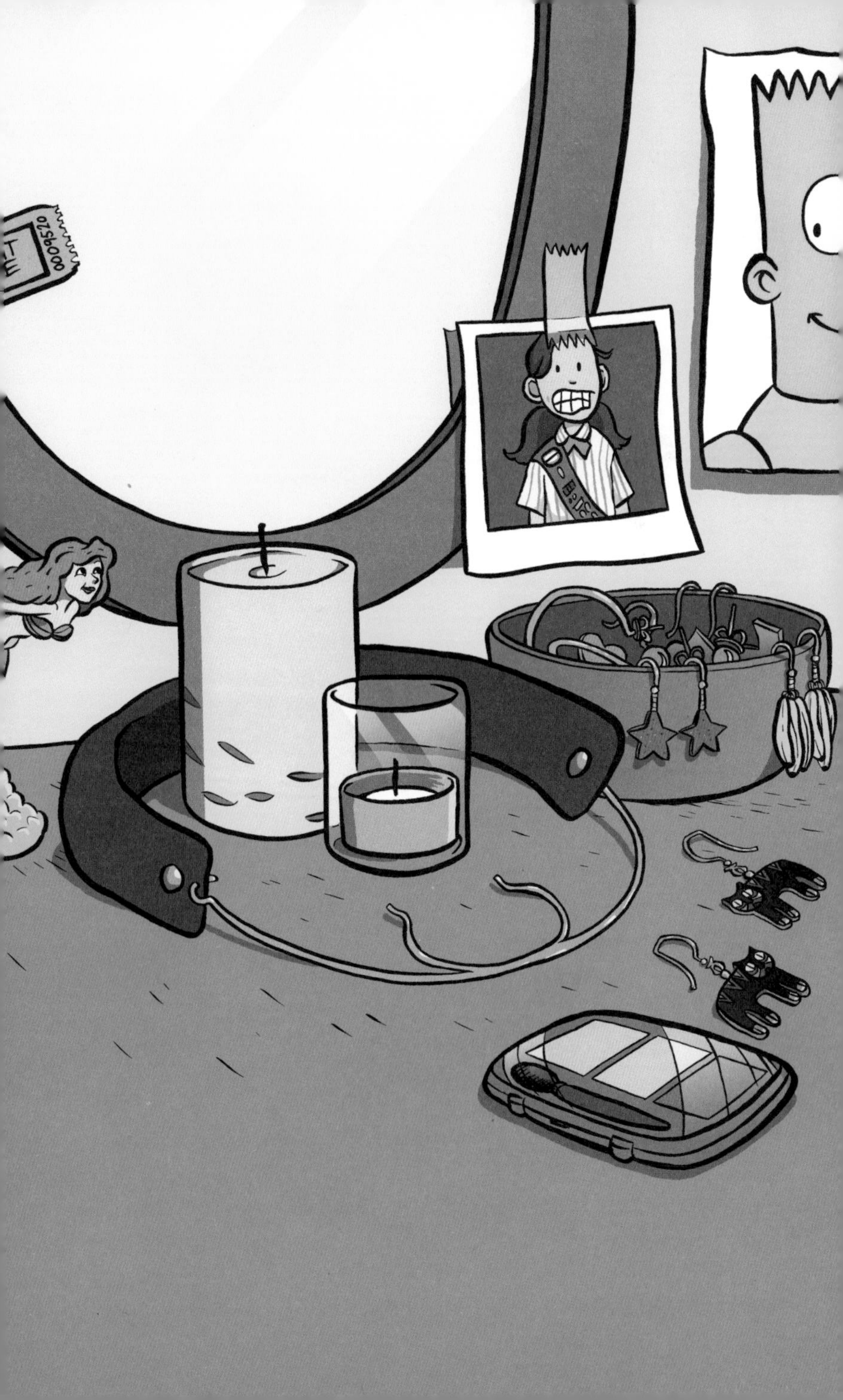
00095210

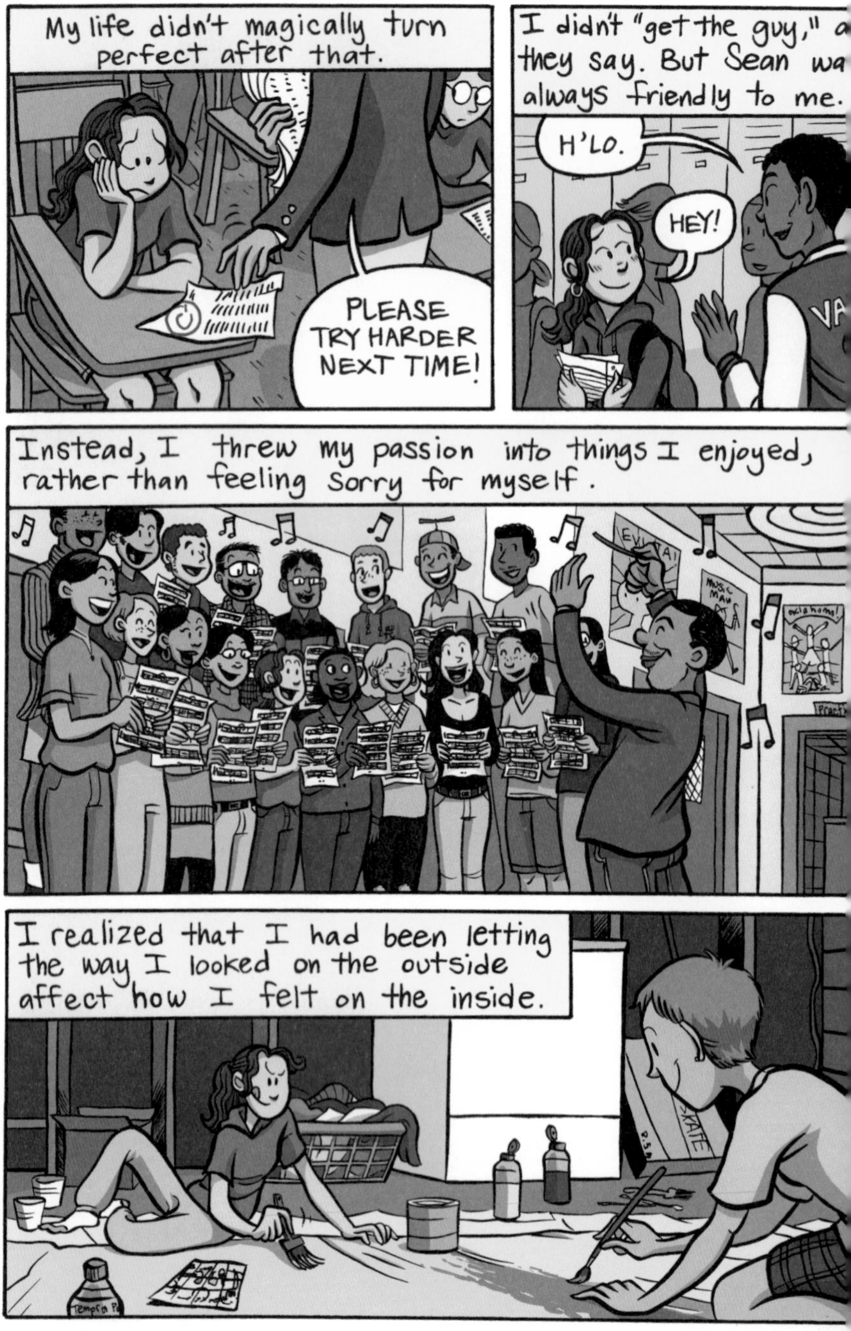
My life didn't magically turn perfect after that.
PLEASE TRY HARDER NEXT TIME!
I didn't "get the guy," a
they say. But Sean wa
always friendly to me.
H'LO.
HEY!
Instead, I threw my passion into things I enjoyed, rather than feeling sorry for myself.
I realized that I had been letting the way I looked on the outside affect how I felt on the inside.

But the more I focused on my interests, the more it brought out things I liked about myself.

And that affected the way other people saw me!

OH, RAINA... IT'S THE END OF AN ERA!

[NO] TIME FOR SENTIMENT, [M]OM! I DON'T WANT TO [B]E LATE FOR THE SCHOOL DANCE!!

...AND CALL ME IF YOU NEED A RIDE HOME. HAVE FUN, HONEY!

THANKS, MOM! BYE!

EXIT

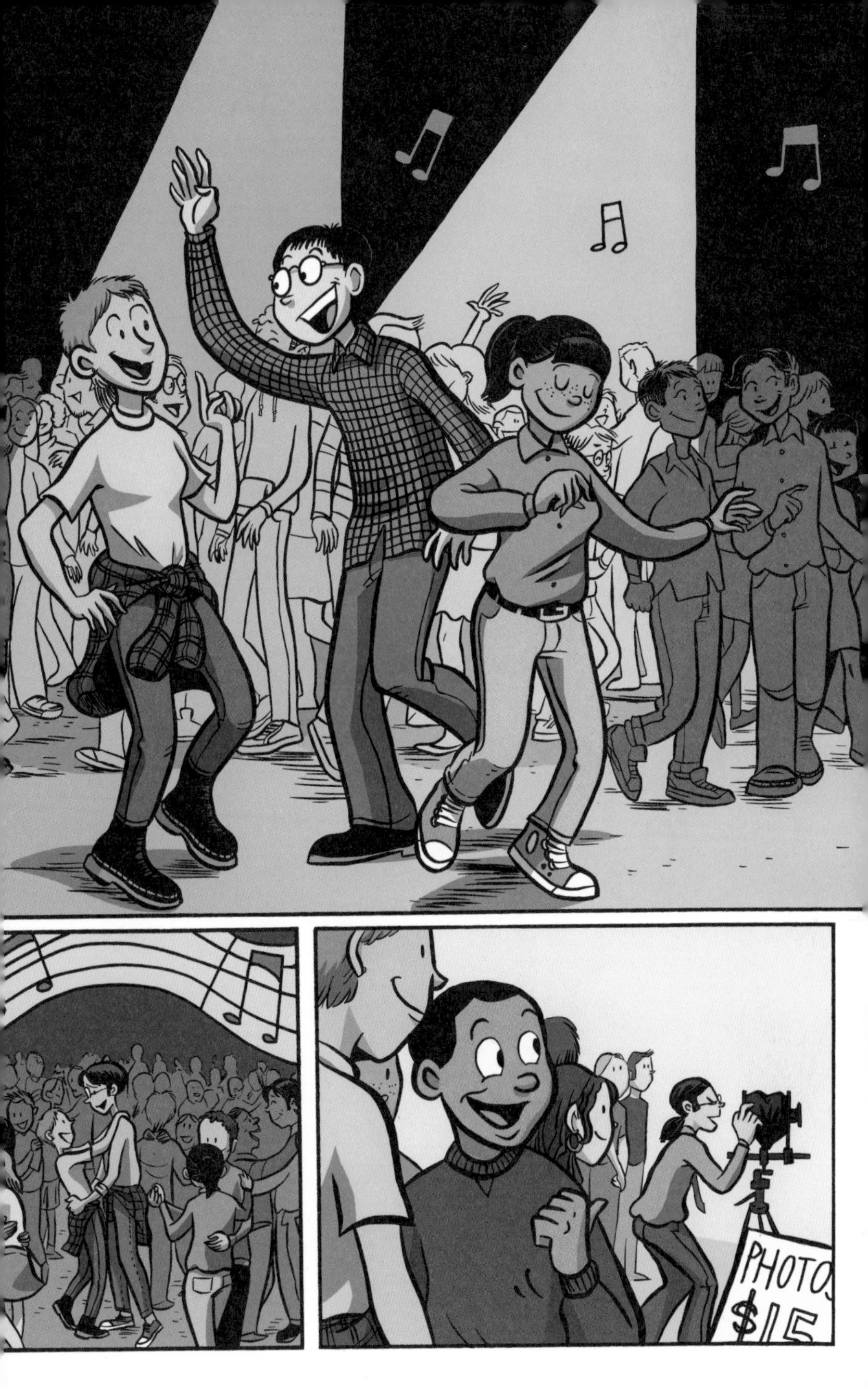
PHOTOS
$15

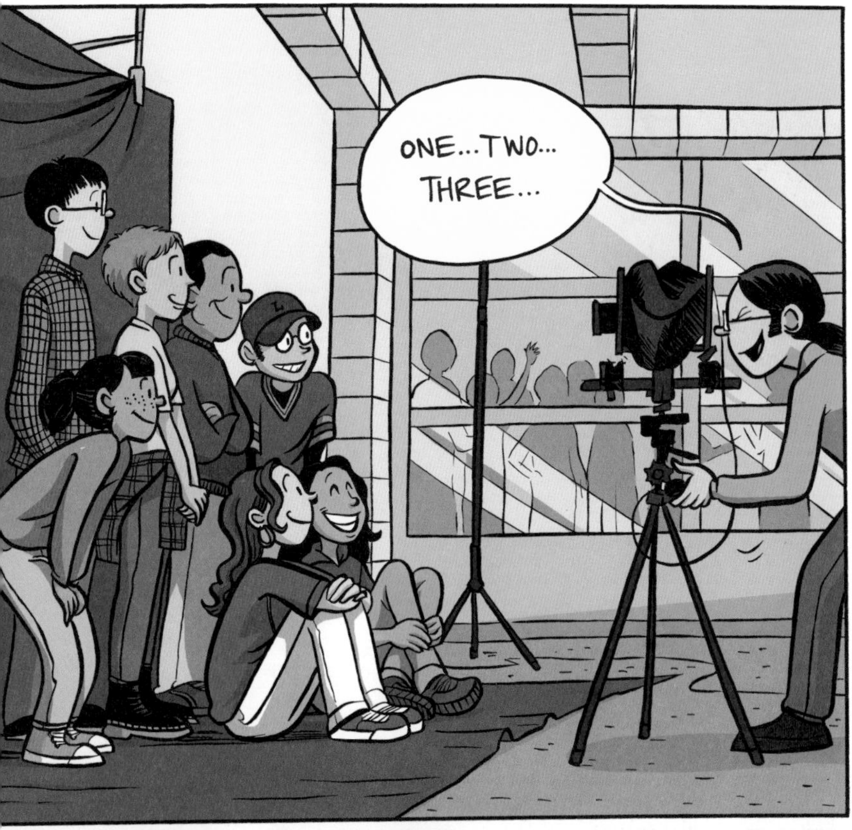
ONE...TWO...
THREE...

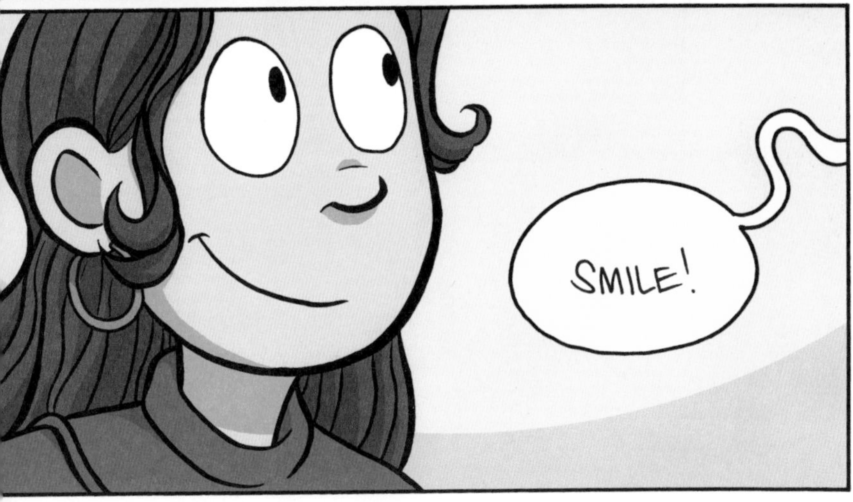
SMILE!

The End!

Thanks to ...

First and foremost, Dave Roman, who makes me smile every day.

Mom, Dad, Amara, Will, and Grandma, for being good sports and a great family.

Lea Ada Franco (Hernandez), Joey Manley, and everyone at Girlamatic.com, for giving a home to this project in its infancy. My friend and family dentist, Dr. Anne Spiegel, who evaluated the manuscript and gave me great encouragement along the way. David Saylor and Cassandra Pelham, for being a joy to work with. Phil Falco, John Green, and Stephanie Yue, for helping make my work beautiful. Judy Hansen, for being the best agent I could hope to have.

Alisa Harris, Braden Lamb, Carly Monardo, Craig Arndt, Dalton Webb, Hope Larson, Jordyn Bochon, Kean Soo, Matt Loux, Naseem Hrab, Rosemary Travale, Ryan Estrada, and Yuko Ota, for lending a helping hand during the final stages of production.

All of my friends who wrote me yearbook notes.

Everyone who has shared their own personal dental dramas with me.

The city of San Francisco, for giving me great backgrounds to draw!

Archwired.com, Janna Morishima, Heidi MacDonald, and Barbara Moon, for all their support and enthusiasm over the years.

Theresa Mendoza Pacheco, Marion Vitus, Steve Flack, Alison Wilgus, Zack Giallongo, Gina Gagliano, Bannister, Steve Hamaker, Seth Kushner, Neil Babra, and my extended family, wonderful friends, and readers, who have been invaluable.

Author's Note

I've been telling people about what happened to my teeth ever since I knocked them out in sixth grade. The story had plenty of strange twists and turns, and I found myself saying, "Wait, it gets worse!" a lot. Eventually, I realized I really needed to get it all down on paper.

I had been writing short-story comics for several years, and my tooth tale seemed like a good candidate for a longer narrative comic.

In 2004 I was invited to contribute to a comics-based Web site, Girlamatic.com, and decided to run *Smile* as a weekly Webcomic. This was at the same time I began working on The Baby-sitters Club graphic novels for Scholastic, so the two projects grew and evolved in tandem. By the time I completed the fourth BSC graphic novel, I had drawn, serialized, and posted over 120 pages of *Smile* on the Web!

As I wrote and drew the story, I was able to look back and actually laugh at some of my more painful experiences. What I went through with my teeth wasn't fun, but I lived to tell the tale and came out of it a stronger person. And once *Smile* started to receive reader feedback, I was amazed by how many people had dental stories similar to my own! The process of creating *Smile* has been therapeutic for me, and has also put me in touch with hundreds of kindred spirits. For this I am very grateful.

Even though my smile looks normal now, it's very possible I'll face more dental drama in the future. Amazingly, I'm not afraid of dentists, or dental work. I have a lot of faith and trust in dentistry, and how it can improve people's lives. And on the bright side of things, beyond the work I've had done on my front teeth, I haven't had a cavity since I was six!

Thanks so much for reading.

—Raina

Raina Telgemeier is the #1 *New York Times* bestselling, multiple Eisner Award-winning creator of *Smile* and *Sisters*, which are both graphic memoirs based on her childhood. She is also the creator of *Drama*, which was named a Stonewall Honor Book and was selected for YALSA's Top Ten Great Graphic Novels for Teens. Raina lives in the San Francisco Bay Area. To learn more, visit her online at www.goRaina.com.